The City and the Court

Science Research Associates, Inc., 259 East Erie Street, Chicago, Illinois 60611

A Subsidiary of IBM

Distributors

The City
and the Court

Five Seventeenth-Century
Comedies of London Life

Edited by

ROBIN CHAPMAN
and
ALLAN GRANT

CHANDLER PUBLISHING COMPANY
124 Spear Street, San Francisco, California 94105

*The cover includes portions of Vischer's
View of London, 1616.*

CONTENTS

FOREWORD

This book was first conceived as a collection of Jacobean Cockney* comedies; that is, comedies of the seventeenth century in which the action took place within the sound of Bow bells and at least the main characters were London born and bred. Further, in selecting five representative plays of the period we should make available to the interested but nonspecialist reader the work of authors otherwise difficult to obtain except in expensive collected editions, many of which are now out of print and available only in libraries. Finally, a third reason for republishing the plays was that they contained positive elements of dramatic entertainment that had been ignored or obscured by the majority of critics from the plays' own time to the present day.

Our view of both Elizabethan and Jacobean drama is coloured inevitably by the attitudes of the nineteenth century. We look through Freudian spectacles, as it were, at a drama which was constructed upon a different assessment of human behaviour. This is not to say that the motivations in man noted by Freud are necessarily untrue for the sixteenth and seventeenth centuries, but it is important to notice that the writers of the plays presented here did not consciously acknowledge them. From this thought springs another realisation: in the modern theatre, thanks to the work of Bertolt Brecht and Joan Littlewood, we have been able to observe a world primarily motivated by economics and class. "Grub first; then ethics," and Brecht might well have added that starvation or political oppression are motivations as basic in society as are personal emotions. Only the bourgeoisie have the leisure to indulge in introspection. In this area the plays of Jacobean London have a great deal to offer, indeed they leap into life. The characters in them are emblems of social urges and necessities, the plays' construction is more akin to parable than to psychological *realism*. Possibly, in a theatre now rejuvenated by this inevitable reaction against

---

* O.E.D. One born in the City of London (always contemptuous or bantering) 1600. "I scorn . . . To let a Bow-bell Cockney put me downe."

vii

realism, these plays will not seem so crude as they did to former critics. In publishing them we have the hope that they will be found worthy of performance. After all, a play, whenever it was written and whatever its reputation, whether it suffers from centuries of critical examination or from being ignored, is only a blueprint for performance, a script calling for the collaborative imagination of either present or future practioners within a living theatre. And however ill these plays may compare with Shakespeare, they are nevertheless superior to much that is performed today for the sake of novelty alone.

But to state the intentions of this collection is not to explain the theatre or the world it represents. To do this we must briefly examine the historical framework of the plays, the thought and feeling as well as the events affecting the theatre of the time.

The Elizabethan theatre, and so consequently, the Jacobean theatre, grew out of the religious drama of the Middle Ages. It is important that this truism be recalled because what we see in the Jacobean theatre is the complete secularisation of this world while the techniques of presentation remain at root the same, however sophisticated the stagecraft may have become. And it became extremely sophisticated with the roofing-in of the open theatres during the reign of James I. But the technique of play-making was still based on the *demonstration* of character in action while the climate of thought which enveloped the playwrights had changed and developed drastically. John Donne puts it thus:

> And new Philosophy calls all in doubt,
> The Element of fire is quite put out;

What was this new philosophy? What was the element of fire? Certainly Donne is referring to the break-up of an old order and to the equivocal nature of the new. He continues:

> The Sun is lost, and th' earth, and no man's wit
> Can well direct him where to look for it.
> And freely men confess that this world's spent,
> When in the Planets, and the Firmament
> They seeke so many new; . . .
> 'Tis all in peeces, all cohaerance gone;
> All just supply, and all Relation:
> Prince, Subject, Father, Sonne, are things forgot,

> For every man alone thinkes he hath got
> To be a Phoenix, . .

The old order was, crudely put, a hope of heaven and a fear of hell. Men were the heirs of God; society's structure was degree; kings were the earthly, secular representation of God's power and lesser men ranged in defined social degree below them. We remember Ulysses' warning to Agamemnon in Shakespeare's *Troilus and Cressida:*

> How could Communities,
> Degrees in Schooles, and Brother-hoods in Cities,
> Peaceful Commerce from dividable shores,
> The primogenitive, and due of Byrth,
> Prerogative of Age, Crownes, Scepters, Lawrels,
> (But by Degree) stand in Authentique place?
> Take but Degree away, un-tune that string,
> And hearke what Discord followes . . .

The plays collected here mirror this discord in the London of the time. And it is worth noticing that in 1605/6 Shakespeare caused Macbeth to kill Duncan; "Duncan is in his grave" becomes the epitaph for an era. No longer does divinity hedge in the king. A vital link in the great chain of being has been broken, only to be hastily repaired by Malcolm's perfunctory accession to the throne at the end of the play. But it is not the rightful heir restored that we remember from *Macbeth,* it is the new man pushed beyond his ability by his managerial wife. And from this moment the chain of being was to be broken again and again, and even the eighteenth century's rationalisation and glorification of it has a suspect hysteria behind it.

The emergence of scientific method, Donne's "new philosophy," together with Machiavelli's revelation of policy based on calculation rather than on moral principles, not to mention the discovery that the earth was no longer the fixed centre of the universe, all diminished Renaissance man in his own eyes. Now indeed "What a thing is Man?" became a question worth asking.

And alongside this reassessment of Man's nature and his place in the natural order came another more mundane but no less potent element: the inflation and price revolution that had reached England around 1525. F. W. Bateson in his *Guide to English Literature* remarks that no one has given a satisfactory explanation of this rise in the cost of living, although the influx of Spanish-American silver, which caused a similar inflation in Spain, had much to do with it. The result in England was that the old equation between work and money was no longer valid: the work of the day no longer sufficed the needs of the day. The Puritan solution was to work twice as hard. Alternatively there was the opportunism offered by the many Newfoundlands—the world was open to Renaissance enterprise; pirates became national heroes.

But commercial enterprise was not enough in itself. If a man was to succeed it was also necessary for him to secure some kind of protective patronage either of Church or State. And to achieve this he had to be presentable, hence the numerous books of rules that schooled the courtier or would-be courtier in compliment or etiquette, in "bravery" of dress and speech, the hat from Germany and the tag from Ovid. Here was an opportunity for ridicule and if Jonson was the first to realise its full potential, the playwrights that followed him were to mine this vein to its complete exhaustion. Yet it was not, ideally, a formal decorum. It had, to find favour, to be based on experience. Shakespeare's contempt for dull plodders reflected a general opinion and an attitude for satire; learning had to be coupled with a practical and sophisticated knowledge of the world to produce the desired brave gentility.

The chief result in Elizabethan drama was the Marlovian superman, a Tamburlane who risks everything for total conquest, or a Faustus whose intellectual appetite is voracious enough to devour damnation itself. Thus out of an economic inflation grew an inflation of appetite, of mind and of language. The language of the Elizabethan theatre acknowledges no limits; it risks sublimity and vulgarity equally. Its drive is emotional rather than intellectual; it is superbly of the theatre; and however much Ben Jonson, muscular intellectual and harbinger of the new local satire of the Jacobeans as he is, may condemn Shakespeare for being a natural, unthinking poet, the hard fact remains that the theatre is the enemy of intellect. No wonder Bernard Shaw, a latter-day Jonson, spluttered so much at the punyness of Shakespeare's mind. He, like Jonson, struggled to propel thought coupled with social comment naked into the theatre, but the theatre's function is to compress emotion into an action which provokes thought only after the emotions have been realised in the spectator. And to do this it is better for the playwright to be a poet than a philosopher.

In the Jacobean theatre the place of the Marlovian superman was taken by the Machiavellian aristocrat-criminal. The result was horror plays in which the main characters act only for the worst motives. Against these dramas must be read the social, satirical plays in which society saw itself realistically, if laughably, mirrored. The plays in this volume are of the second kind and the writers of them were influenced by the world I have described. It was a world in flux, a world remarkably like our own today, where man sought new values to cope with an apparently unstoppable economic expansion, in which the medieval notion of man as the helpless rope in a tug of war between God and the Devil had given way to the conception of man as the center of the world, as a reflection of God, as capable of choice between enormous good and enormous evil but where now even man himself was called into question. Although his behavior could be explained quasi-scientifically by means of the humours, other social phenomena were more complex.

The most important city in England, London, was growing. In it the Court still possessed great power (and over the theatres this power was crucial) but the City was near to equalling it, business was booming, and a nouveau riche capitalist class had emerged for the playwright to evaluate.

The accession of James I is a convenient dividing line between the old order and the new. One immediate change, a purely technical one, was to have persuasive influence over the kind of effects the drama aimed at, although it was intended merely to solve the dispute over the control of the theatres and to attempt to make them legitimate. The plague and the Puritan objection to the theatre—that it was a danger to the integrity of man to parcel himself out in playacting quite apart from the objectionable content of most plays—had often closed the playhouses and imperilled the actors. James I resolved the problem by annexing them to his own household. While this patronage improved the status and security of the players, it also made the theatre less open, more exclusive. The rift between Court and country had begun. The ordinary citizen stayed away from the theatre and plays became the exclusive entertainment of the upper class.

This more aristocratic audience had certain tastes that influenced the content of the plays. I have already referred to the "horror shows" of the Jacobean theatre, but there was another kind also—the tragi-comedy, artificial in plot and false in psychology, often with elaborate scenic display as the chief attraction. This kind of play had become possible only with the roofing-in of the theatres. Immediately artificial light became necessary, and with artificial light, however rudimentary, scenic illusion becomes possible. And the presence of scenery changed the text of the plays. It was no longer necessary to provide verbal scene-painting nor to convey richness of atmosphere in the verse. The drama as spectacle improved but its inner world was immeasureably impoverished. Many of the plays, whether horrific or sentimental, ended with grossly facile yet moralistic resolutions. The old heroic tragedy was quite dissipated and the sentimentalism introduced in its stead was to remain as an abiding and debilitating feature of English drama.

But meanwhile there was the Cockney comedy—the opposite in every way to the horrific and the sentimental, although, ironically, this new satirical drama was indebted to both. Everything, especially in the theatre, contains or posits its opposite. To understand how this kind of play could flourish in the increasingly vitiated air of the Jacobean and Cavalier theatre, four elements must be remembered. First, the new horror tragedy dealt in the politics of a corrupt society—usually wicked Venice or Florence—and although much was grossly exaggerated, the dubious machinations of the principle characters were clearly and boldly presented. Such motivations for believable characters in believable surroundings, such as London itself, could become comic. We remember that Jonson wrote two versions of *Every Man in his Humour*—the first set in Italy; the second, with the same characters renamed, in London. Secondly, the skill in manipulating situations induced by the comedies of intrigue and the tragedies of revenge had become a common fund for every writer to draw upon. Third, as we have seen, the time was apt for satire. The general decay in creative power, the interest in the surface appearance of men, the consciousness of civil abuses, the restricted audience and the generalised unconscious resentment that somehow man had become "sublunary" were, as they are now, factors conducive to satire. Finally, the genius of Ben Jonson, to whom all the playwrights in this collection are indebted, was more easily imitated and exploited than was that of Shakespeare.

Jonson's declared intentions were satiric and corrective. In his plays he promised the audience no sentimentalism, no bombast, but "deeds and language such as men do use"—a new realism that "would show an image of the times" and "sport with human follies." His "realism" can be questioned but his greatness lies in the creation of a world of greedy individualists fighting the class war to the death.

The plays here are a continuation and development of what Jonson began. In each one of them money and advancement are used as springs of the plot. The plays witness the establishment of the bourgeois mercantile class that triumphed with Puritanism and later, with the Restoration, wedded itself to the aristocracy.

Robin Chapman

NOTE ON THE STATE OF THE TEXTS

These texts have been edited from the principal editions listed in the bibliography and arranged in such a way as to provide the clearest possible modern reading consonant with the vitality and usages of the language of the early seventeenth century. Minor amendments, made in the interests of clarity and standardisation of the texts, have not been indicated and textual notes have been kept to a minimum.

Allan Grant

The City and the Court

Eastward Ho

(1604)

INTRODUCTION

At the turn of the sixteenth century the London theatres witnessed the rise of a vogue for plays depicting scenes and incidents from the life of the times. Plays on such themes had been written before 1599, but the fashion seems to have been initiated in that year by the production of Thomas Dekker's (1570?-1632) *The Shoemaker's Holiday* with its good-natured celebration of civic virtue and mercantile confidence. This was one of the most popular plays of its age and was followed, in 1602, by Thomas Heywood's (1574?-1641) *Fair Maid of the Exchange* and, two years later, by Middleton's (1580-1627) *Michaelmas Term* and *Westward Ho,* written by Dekker and John Webster (1580?-1625?). This last play was first performed by an acting company of the Children of St. Paul's and was immediately followed by *Eastward Ho,* which was written in answer to "that which is opposed to ours in title" by the three leading writers of the Blackfriars Theatre where, during these years, the Children of the Chapel were playing. Ben Jonson (1572-1637) had already written the successful *Everyman in his Humor* in 1598 for the Chamberlain's Men, to which company Shakespeare belonged. George Chapman (1560?-1634) was already known not only as a playwright but also as the translator of seven books of the *Iliad* and of the Latin poet Ovid, and as the completer of Christopher Marlowe's erotic narrative poem *Hero and Leander.* John Marston (1576-1634) had graduated from Brasenose College, Oxford, and spent some time as a member of the Inner Temple. He had written several plays and was known as the author of a number of verse satires.

It is beyond the scope of this brief preface to apportion the different contributions to *Eastward Ho:* collaboration of this kind was common practise in the theatre of the day. Jonson was considered eccentric and pretentious when he prepared for publication an edition of his *Opera* or *Works.* Philip Henslowe (d. 1616), who negotiated between writers and companies and who was managing the Blackfriars Theatre at this time, was a property speculator and a businessman, only interested in re-

3

sults. But *Eastward Ho* is more than a successful imitation, more than a parody of its own genre. The doggerel of Quicksilver's "Repentance" in the final prison scene and the predictably moral behavior of Golding and Mildred assure us that the story of the redeemed prodigal is not to be taken too seriously. The vitality of the play lies in its social and theatrical comedy. It abounds in satirical contemporary allusions, some of which were taken sufficiently seriously for Royal patronage to be withdrawn from the company and for two of its authors to find themselves in prison; Jonson for the second time in his career, having previously killed a fellow actor in a duel.

James I, whose accession to the English throne in 1603 had brought a host of Scottish knights down on his new capital, took offence at the references to them in Act Three. James was also guilty of indiscriminate bestowal of knighthoods—perhaps, it has been suggested, for the sake of the royal fees involved—and the newly dubbed, needy knight soon became a stock figure for theatrical ridicule.

But the play reaches further targets than those of the offending passages. These lines were omitted from editions subsequent to the first printing, without detracting from the play's continued popularity. In the action Court opposes City; gentleman and tradesman clash; speculation, encouraged by usury, is played off against honest mercantile thrift; and the individual is constantly exposed to the stark threats of the age—poverty (with its attendant civic charity), bankruptcy, and cuckoldry.

Eastward Ho and *The City Madam* cover, with different emphasis, much the same area of London life. The atmosphere of the earlier play is open, firmly secured to the bustling activity of the river Thames; the later is enclosed, much darker in tone and more bitter in feeling and attitude: the comparison is instructive.

The play was printed three times in 1605. The second version was merely a re-issue of the first quarto edition with the offending passages in Act Three omitted. The third version was a new edition.

CHARACTERS

TOUCHSTONE, a goldsmith

QUICKSILVER ⎱ apprentices to
GOLDING ⎰ Touchstone

SIR PETRONEL FLASH

SECURITY, an old usurer

BRAMBLE, a lawyer

SEAGULL, a sea captain

SCAPETHRIFT ⎱ adventurers
SPENDALL ⎰ bound for Virginia

SLITGUT, a butcher's apprentice

POLDAVY, a tailor

HOLDFAST ⎱ officers of the
WOLF ⎰ Counter

HAMLET, a footman

POTKIN, a tankard bearer

PAGE [to Sir Petronel Flash], A MESSENGER, A COACHMAN, A SCRIVENER, A DRAWER, [TWO GENTLEMEN], CONSTABLE, [OFFICERS], [TWO] PRISONERS, A FRIEND OF THE PRISONERS

MISTRESS TOUCHSTONE

GERTRUDE ⎱ her daughters
MILDRED ⎰

WINIFRED, wife of Security

SINDEFY, mistress to Quicksilver

BETTRICE, a waiting woman

MISTRESS FOND

MISTRESS GAZER

SCENE: London

PROLOGUE

Not out of envy, for there's no effect
Where there's no cause; nor out of imitation,
For we have evermore been imitated;
Nor out of our contention to do better
Than that which is opposed to ours in title,
For that was good; and better cannot be:
And for the title, if it seem affected,
We might as well have called it, "God you good even,"
Only that Eastward Westwards still exceeds—
Honour the sun's fair rising, not his setting.
Nor is our title utterly enforced,
As by the points we touch at you shall see.
Bear with our willing pains, if dull or witty;
We only dedicate it to the City.

ACT ONE

Scene One

[*Goldsmith's Row. Enter* MASTER TOUCHSTONE *and* QUICKSILVER
at several doors; QUICKSILVER *with his hat, pumps, short sword
and dagger, and a racket trussed up under his cloak. At the middle door, enter* GOLDING, *discovering a goldsmith's shop, and
walking short turns before it.*]

TOUCHSTONE And whither with you now? What loose action are
you bound for? Come, what comrades are you to meet withal?
Where's the supper? Where's the rendezvous?

QUICKSILVER Indeed, and in very good sober truth, sir—

TOUCHSTONE "Indeed, and in very good sober truth, sir"! Behind
my back thou wilt swear faster than a French footboy, and talk
more bawdily than a common midwife; and now "indeed and in
very good sober truth, sir"! But if a privy search should be made,
with what furniture are you rigged now? Sirrah, I tell thee, I am
thy master, William Touchstone, goldsmith, and thou my prentice, Francis Quicksilver; and I will see whither you are running.
Work upon that now!

QUICKSILVER Why, sir, I hope a man may use his recreation with
his master's profit.

TOUCHSTONE Prentices' recreations are seldom with their masters'
profit. Work upon that now! You shall give up your cloak,
though you be no alderman. Heyday, Ruffians' Hall! Sword,
pumps, here's a racket indeed!

[TOUCHSTONE *uncloaks* QUICKSILVER.]

QUICKSILVER Work upon that now!

TOUCHSTONE Thou shameless varlet, dost thou jest at thy lawful
master contrary to thy indentures?

QUICKSILVER Why, 's blood, sir, my mother's a gentlewoman, and
my father a Justice of Peace and of Quorum! And though I am a
younger brother and a prentice, yet I hope I am my father's son;
and by God's lid, 't is for your worship and for your commodity

---

Work upon that now: Several of these plays contain similar catch-
phrases, as does *The Shoemaker's Holiday,* from which they descend.
  of Quorum: One whose presence was necessary to the constitution of
the bench.

1   that I keep company. I am entertained among gallants, true! They
call me cousin Frank, right! I lend them moneys, good! They
spend it, well! But when they are spent, must not they strive to
get more, must not their land fly? And to whom? Shall not your
worship ha' the refusal? Well, I am a good member of the City, if
2   I were well considered. How would merchants thrive, if gentlemen would not be unthrifts? How could gentlemen be unthrifts, if
their humours were not fed? How should their humours be fed
but by white meat and cunning secondings? Well, the City might
consider us. I am going to an ordinary now; the gallants fall to
play; I carry light gold with me; the gallants call, "Cousin Frank,
3   some gold for silver!"; I change, gain by it; the gallants lose the
gold, and then call, "Cousin Frank, lend me some silver!" Why—

TOUCHSTONE   Why? I cannot tell. Seven score pound art thou out
in the cash; but look to it, I will not be gallanted out of my moneys. And as for my rising by other men's fall, God shield me!
4   Did I gain my wealth by ordinaries? No! By exchanging of gold?
No! By keeping of gallants' company? No! I hired me a little
shop, fought low, took small gain, kept no debt book, garnished
my shop, for want of plate, with good wholesome thrifty sentences, as "Touchstone, keep thy shop, and thy shop will keep
thee." "Light gains makes heavy purses." " 'T is good to be merry
5   and wise." And when I was wived, having something to stick to,
I had the horn of suretyship ever before my eyes. You all know
the device of the horn, where the young fellow slips in at the
butt end, and comes squeezed out at the buccal: and I grew up,
and, I praise Providence, I bear my brows now as high as the best
6   of my neighbours: but thou—well, look to the accounts; your father's bond lies for you; seven-score pound is yet in the rear.

QUICKSILVER   Why, 's lid, sir, I have as good, as proper gallants'
words for it as any are in London, gentlemen of good phrase, perfect language, passingly behaved, gallants that wear socks and
clean linen, and call me "kind cousin Frank," "good cousin
7   Frank," for they know my father: and, by God's lid, shall I not
trust 'em?—not trust?

[*Enter a* PAGE, *as inquiring for Touchstone's shop.*]

GOLDING   What do ye lack, sir? What is 't you'll buy, sir?

the horn of suretyship: A sixteenth century panel painting, entitled
"The Sea of Trouble," depicts a huge horn; an unfortunate wretch is
being thrust in at the wide end, while from the "buccal" or small end,
a head and arm appear. Nearby stands a previous victim in rags, wringing
his hands. An inscription reads "this horn emblem here doth show of
suretyship what harm doth grow" (Schelling).

TOUCHSTONE Ay, marry, sir; there's a youth of another piece. 1
There's thy fellow prentice, as good a gentleman born as thou art;
nay, and better meaned. But does he pump it, or racket it? Well,
if he thrive not, if he outlast not a hundred such crackling bavins
as though art, God and men neglect industry.

GOLDING [*to the* PAGE] It is his shop, and here my master walks. 2

TOUCHSTONE With me, boy?

PAGE My master, Sir Petronel Flash, recommends his love to you,
and will instantly visit you.

TOUCHSTONE To make up the match with my eldest daughter, my
wife's dilling, whom she longs to call madam. He shall find me 3
unwillingly ready, boy.

[*Exit* PAGE.]

There's another affliction, too. As I have two prentices, the one of
a boundless prodigality, the other of a most hopeful industry, so 4
have I only two daughters: the eldest of a proud ambition and
nice wantonness, the other of a modest humility and comely so-
berness. The one must be ladyfied, forsooth, and be attired just to
the court cut and long tail. So far is she ill natured to the place
and means of my preferment and fortune, that she throws all the 5
contempt and despite hatred itself can cast upon it. Well, a piece
of land she has, 't was her grandmother's gift, let her, and her Sir
Petronel, flash out that! But as for my substance, she that scorns
me as I am a citizen and tradesman, shall never pamper her pride
with my industry, shall never use me as men do foxes, keep themselves warm in the skin, and throw the body that bare it to the 6
dunghill. I must go entertain this Sir Petronel. Golding, my utmost care's for thee, and only trust in thee; look to the shop. As for
you, Master Quicksilver, think of husks, for thy course is running
directly to the Prodigal's hogs' trough: husks, sirrah! Work upon
that now! [*Exits*]
7
QUICKSILVER Marry faugh, goodman flatcap! 'S foot! though I am
a prentice, I can give arms; and my father's a Justice o' Peace by
descent, and 's blood—

GOLDING Fie, how you swear!

crackling bavins: Bundles of kindling wood, soon burned up.
court cut and long tail: Dogs of common people had their tails cut
short, hence "long tail" would be courtly fashion. Thus the word
"curtail."
flat cap: The flat hat of the citizen contrasts with the pointed hat
of the courtier.

1 QUICKSILVER 'S foot, man, I am a gentleman, and may swear by
my pedigree, God's my life! Sirrah Golding, wilt be ruled by a
fool? Turn good fellow, turn swaggering gallant, and let the welkin roar, and Erebus also. Look not westward to the fall of Dan
Phoebus, but to the East—Eastward Ho!

2   Where radiant beams of lusty Sol appear,
            And bright Eous makes the welkin clear.

We are both gentlemen, and therefore should be no coxcombs;
let's be no longer fools to this flatcap, Touchstone. Eastward,
bully! This satin belly and canvas-backed Touchstone—'s life,
man, his father was a malt man, and his mother sold gingerbread
3   in Christ Church!

GOLDING What would ye ha' me do?

QUICKSILVER Why, do nothing, be like a gentleman, be idle; the
curse of man is labour. Wipe thy bum with testons, and make
4   ducks and drakes with shillings. What, Eastward Ho! Wilt thou
cry, "What is 't ye lack?", stand with a bare pate and a dropping
nose under a wooden penthouse, and art a gentleman? Wilt thou
bear tankards, and may'st bear arms? Be ruled, turn gallant, Eastward Ho! Ta, lirra, lirra, ro! Who calls Jeronimo? Speak, here I
am. God's so, how like a sheep thou look'st! O' my conscience
5   some cowherd begot thee, thou Golding of Golding Hall! Ha,
boy?

GOLDING Go, ye are a prodigal coxcomb! I a cowherd's son, because I turn not a drunken whore-hunting rakehell like thyself!

6 QUICKSILVER Rakehell! Rakehell!

[*Offers to draw, and* GOLDING *trips up his heels and holds him.*]

GOLDING Pish, in soft terms ye are a cowardly bragging boy! I'll
ha' you whipped.

7 QUICKSILVER Whipped? That's good, i' faith! Untruss me!

GOLDING No, thou wilt undo thyself. Alas, I behold thee with pity,
not with anger, thou common shot-clog, gull of all companies;
methinks I see thee already walking in Moorfields without a
cloak, with half a hat, without a band, a doublet with three but-
8   tons, without a girdle, a hose with one point and no garter, with a
cudgel under thine arm, borrowing and begging threepence.

and let the welkin roar: Quicksilver misquotes rant from plays, here
Ancient Pistol of *Henry IV, Part II.*
teston: A Henry VII shilling, but here probably sixpence.
Jeronimo: From Kyd's *Spanish Tragedy.*

QUICKSILVER   Nay, 's life, take this and take all! As I am a gentle-   1
man born, I'll be drunk, grow valiant, and beat thee. [*Exits*]

GOLDING   Go, thou most madly vain, whom nothing can recover
but that which reclaims atheists, and makes great persons sometimes religious—calamity. As for my place and life, thus I have
read:—
                                                                              2

> Whate'er some vainer youth may term disgrace,
> The gain of honest pains is never base;
> From trades, from arts, from valour, honour springs;
> These three are founts of gentry, yea, of kings. [*Exits*]

                                                                              3

Scene Two

[*A room in Touchstone's house. Enter* GERTRUDE, MILDRED, BETT-
RICE, *and* POLDAVY, *a tailor;* POLDAVY *with a fair gown, Scotch*   4
farthingale, and French fall in his arms; GERTRUDE *in a French*
head attire and citizen's gown; MILDRED *sewing; and* BETTRICE
leading a monkey after her.]

GERTRUDE   For the passion of patience, look if Sir Petronel approach, that sweet, that fine, that delicate, that—for love's sake,
tell me if he come. O sister Mil, though my father be a low-   5
capped tradesman, yet I must be a lady; and, I praise God, my
mother must call me madam. Does he come? Off with this gown,
for shame's sake, off with this gown; let not my knight take me in
the city cut in any hand; tear 't, pax on 't—does he come?—tear 't
off. Thus whilst she sleeps, I sorrow for her sake, etc. [*Sings*]   6

MILDRED   Lord, sister, with what an immodest impatiency and dis-
graceful scorn do you put off your city tire; I am sorry to think
you imagine to right yourself in wronging that which hath made
both you and us.

GERTRUDE   I tell you I cannot endure it, I must be a lady: do you   7
wear your coif with a London licket, your stammel petticoat with
two guards, the buffin gown with the tuft-taffety cape, and the
velvet lace. I must be a lady, and I will be a lady. I like some
humours of the City dames well: to eat cherries only at an angel
a pound, good! To dye rich scarlet black, pretty! To line a gro-
gram gown clean through with velvet, tolerable! Their pure linen,   8
their smocks of three pounds a smock, are to be borne withal!
But your mincing niceries, taffeta pipkins, durance petticoats, and

---

"*Thus whilst she sleeps*": A song by John Dowland, "Sleep Wayward
Thoughts."

1 silver bodkins—God's my life, as I shall be a lady, I cannot endure it! Is he come yet? Lord, what a long knight 't is!—And ever she cried, Shoot home!—and yet I knew one longer. And ever she cried, Shoot home. Fa, la, ly, re, lo, la! [*Sings*]

MILDRED Well, sister, those that scorn their nest, oft fly with a sick
2 wing.

GERTRUDE Bow bell!

MILDRED Where titles presume to thrust before fit means to second them, wealth and respect often grow sullen, and will not follow. For sure in this I would for your sake I spake not truth: Where
3 ambition of place goes before fitness of birth, contempt and disgrace follow. I heard a scholar once say that Ulysses, when he counterfeited himself mad, yoked cats and foxes and dogs together to draw his plough, whilst he followed and sowed salt; but sure I judge them truly mad that yoke citizens and courtiers, tradesmen and soldiers, a goldsmith's daughter and a knight.
4 Well, sister, pray God my father sow not salt, too.

GERTRUDE Alas! poor Mil, when I am a lady, I'll pray for thee yet, i' faith; nay, and I'll vouchsafe to call thee Sister Mil still; for though thou art not like to be a lady as I am, yet sure thou art a creature of God's making, and mayest peradventure to be saved
5 as soon as I—does he come?—And ever and anon she doubled in her song. [*Sings*] Now, lady's my comfort, what a profane ape's here! Tailor, Poldavy, prithee, fit it, fit it: is this a right Scot? Does it clip close, and bear up round?

POLDAVY Fine and stiffly, i' faith! 'T will keep your thighs so cool and make your waist so small; here was a fault in your body, but
6 I have supplied the defect with the effect of my steel instrument, which, though it have but one eye, can see to rectify the imperfection of the proportion.

GERTRUDE Most edifying tailor! I protest you tailors are most sanctified members, and make many crooked thing go upright.
7 How must I bear my hands? Light, light?

POLDAVY O, ay, now you are in the lady fashion, you must do all things light. Tread light, light. Ay, and fall so: that's the Court amble.

GERTRUDE [*trips about the stage*] Has the Court ne'er a trot?
8 POLDAVY No, but a false gallop, lady.

GERTRUDE And if she will not go to bed—[*Sings*]

BETTRICE The knight's come, forsooth.

[*Enter* SIR PETRONEL, MASTER TOUCHSTONE, *and* MISTRESS
9 TOUCHSTONE.]

GERTRUDE Is my knight come? O the Lord, my band! Sister, do 1
my cheeks look well? Give me a little box o' the ear that I may
seem to blush; now, now! So, there, there, there! Here he is. O
my dearest delight! Lord, Lord, and how does my knight?

TOUCHSTONE Fie, with more modesty!

GERTRUDE Modesty! Why, I am no citizen now—modesty! Am I 2
not to be married? Y' are best to keep me modest, now I am to be
a lady.

SIR PETRONEL Boldness is good fashion and courtlike.

GERTRUDE Ay, in a country lady I hope it is, as I shall be. And
how chance ye came no sooner, knight? 3

SIR PETRONEL 'Faith, I was so entertained in the progress with one
Count Epernoum, a Welsh knight; we had a match at balloon,
too, with my Lord Whachum for four crowns.

GERTRUDE At baboon? Jesu! You and I will play at baboon in the
country, knight. 4

SIR PETRONEL O, sweet lady, 't is a strong play with the arm.

GERTRUDE With arm or leg or any other member, if it be a Court
sport. And when shall 's be married, my knight?

SIR PETRONEL I come now to consummate it, and your father may 5
call a poor knight son-in-law.

TOUCHSTONE Sir, ye are come. What is not mine to keep, I must
not be sorry to forego. A hundred pounds' land her grandmother
left her, 't is yours; herself (as her mother's gift) is yours. But if
you expect aught from me, know my hand and mine eyes open
together; I do not give blindly. Work upon that now! 6

SIR PETRONEL Sir, you mistrust not my means? I am a knight.

TOUCHSTONE Sir, sir, what I know not, you will give me leave to
say I am ignorant of.

MISTRESS TOUCHSTONE Yes, that he is, a knight; I know where he 7
had money to pay the gentlemen-ushers and heralds their fees.
Ay, that he is, a knight; and so might you have been, too, if you
had been ought else than an ass, as well as some of your neighbours. And I thought you would not ha' been knighted (as I am
an honest woman), I would ha' dubbed you myself. I praise God I
have wherewithal. But as for your daughter— 8

GERTRUDE Ay, mother, I must be a lady tomorrow; and by your
leave, mother (I speak it not without my duty, but only in the
right of my husband), I must take place of you, mother.

MISTRESS TOUCHSTONE That you shall, lady-daughter, and have a
coach as well as I, too. 9

1 GERTRUDE Yes, mother. But by your leave, mother (I speak it not without my duty, but only in my husband's right), my coach horses must take the wall of your coach horses.

2 TOUCHSTONE Come, come, the day grows low; 'tis suppertime; use my house; the wedding solemnity is at my wife's cost; thank me for nothing but my willing blessing, for, I cannot feign, my hopes are faint. And, sir, respect my daughter; she has refused for you wealthy and honest matches, known good men, well moneyed, better traded, best reputed.

3 GERTRUDE Body o' truth! Chittizens, chittizens! Sweet knight, as soon as ever we are married, take me to thy mercy out of this miserable chitty; presently carry me out of the scent of Newcastle coal, and the hearing of Bow bell; I beseech thee down with me, for God's sake!

4 TOUCHSTONE Well, daughter, I have read that old wit sings:
The greatest rivers flow from little springs.
Though thou art full, scorn not thy means at first;
He that's most drunk may soonest be a-thirst.

Work upon that now!

[*All but* TOUCHSTONE, MILDRED, *and* GOLDING *depart.*]

5 No, no! Yond' stand my hopes—Mildred, come hither, daughter! And how approve you your sister's fashion? How do you fancy her choice? What dost thou think?

MILDRED I hope, as a sister, well.

6 TOUCHSTONE Nay but, nay but, how dost thou like her behaviour and humour? Speak freely.

MILDRED I am loath to speak ill; and yet I am sorry of this, I cannot speak well.

7 TOUCHSTONE Well; very good, as I would wish, a modest answer! Golding, come hither, hither, Golding! How dost thou like the knight, Sir Flash? Does he not look big? How lik'st thou the elephant? He says he has a castle in the country.

GOLDING Pray heaven, the elephant carry not his castle on his back.

8 TOUCHSTONE 'Fore heaven, very well! But, seriously, how dost repute him?

GOLDING The best I can say of him is, I know him not.

TOUCHSTONE Ha, Golding! I commend thee, I approve thee and will make it appear my affection is strong to thee. My wife has

chittizen: An affected, Italianate pronunciation of citizen.

her humour, and I will ha' mine. Dost thou see my daughter ¹
here? She is not fair, well favoured or so, indifferent, which modest measure of beauty shall not make it thy only work to watch
her, nor sufficient mischance to suspect her. Thou art towardly,
she is modest; thou art provident, she is careful. She's now mine;
give me thy hand, she's now thine. Work upon that now!

GOLDING Sir, as your son, I honour you; and as your servant, obey ²
you.

TOUCHSTONE Sayest thou say? Come hither, Mildred. Do you see
yond' fellow? He is a gentleman, though my prentice, and has
somewhat to take, too; a youth of good hope, well friended, well
parted. Are you mine? You are his. Work you upon that now! ³

MILDRED Sir, I am all yours; your body gave me life; your care
and love, happiness of life; let your virtue still direct it, for to
your wisdom I wholly dispose myself.

TOUCHSTONE Say'st thou so? Be you two better acquainted. Lip ⁴
her, lip her, knave! So, shut up shop; in! We must make holiday.

[*Exeunt* GOLDING *and* MILDRED.]

> This match shall on, for I intend to prove
> Which thrives the best, the mean or lofty love.
> Whether fit wedlock vowed 'twixt like and like, ⁵
> Or prouder hopes, which daringly o'erstrike
> Their place and means. 'T is honest time's expense,
> When seeming lightness bears a moral sense.

Work upon that now! [*Exits*]

well parted: Of good parts.
'T is honest time's expense: It is a worthy expenditure of time when
apparent levity has a more serious purpose.

ACT TWO

Scene One

1   [*Goldsmith's Row*. TOUCHSTONE, GOLDING, *and* MILDRED, *sitting on either side of the stall*.]

TOUCHSTONE   Quicksilver! Master Francis Quicksilver! Master Quicksilver!

QUICKSILVER [*enters*]   Here, sir—Ump!

2   TOUCHSTONE   So, sir; nothing but flat Master Quicksilver (without any familiar addition) will fetch you! Will you truss my points, sir?

QUICKSILVER   Ay, forsooth—Ump!

3   TOUCHSTONE   How now, sir? The drunken hiccup so soon this morning?

QUICKSILVER   'T is but the coldness of my stomach, forsooth!

TOUCHSTONE   What, have you the cause natural for it? Y' are a very learned drunkard; I believe I shall miss some of my silver
4   spoons with your learning. The nuptial night will not moisten your throat sufficiently, but the morning likewise must rain her dews into your gluttonous weasand.

QUICKSILVER   An' 't please you, sir, we did but drink—Ump!—to the coming off of the knightly bridegroom.

5   TOUCHSTONE   To the coming off on him?

QUICKSILVER   Ay, forsooth! We drunk to his coming on—Ump! —when we went to bed; and now we are up, we must drink to his coming off; for that's the chief honour of a soldier, sir; and there-fore we must drink so much the more to it, forsooth—ump!

6   TOUCHSTONE   A very capital reason! So that you go to bed late, and rise early to commit drunkenness; you fulfil the scripture very sufficient wickedly, forsooth!

QUICKSILVER   The knight's men, forsooth, be still o' their knees at
7   it—Ump—and because 't is for your credit, sir, I would be loath to flinch.

TOUCHSTONE   I pray, sir, e'en to 'em again then; y' are one of the

truss my points: Hose were held up by laces (points) tied to the doublet.
fulfil the scripture: Isaiah, 5:2.

16

separated crew, one of my wife's faction, and my young lady's, with whom, and with their great match, I will have nothing to do. 1

QUICKSILVER So, sir, now I will go keep my—Ump!—credit with 'em, an' 't please you, sir!

TOUCHSTONE In any case, sir, lay one cup of sack more o' your cold stomach, I beseech you! 2

QUICKSILVER Yes, forsooth! [*Exits*]

TOUCHSTONE This is for my credit; servants ever maintain drunkenness in their master's house for their master's credit; a good idle servingman's reason. I thank Time the night is past; I ne'er waked to such cost; I think we have stowed more sorts of flesh in 3 our bellies than ever Noah's ark received; and for wine, why, my house turns giddy with it, and more noise in it than at a conduit. Ay me, even beasts condemn our gluttony! Well, 't is our city's fault, which, because we commit seldom, we commit the more sinfully; we lose no time in our sensuality, but we make amends 4 for it. O that we would do so in virtue and religious negligences! But see, here are all the sober parcels my house can show; I'll eavesdrop, hear what thoughts they utter this morning. [*Retires*]

[GOLDING *and* MILDRED *come forward.*]

GOLDING But is it possible that you, seeing your sister preferred to 5 the bed of a knight, should contain your affections in the arms of a prentice?

MILDRED I had rather make up the garment of my affections in some of the same piece, than, like a fool, wear gowns of two colours, or mix sackcloth with satin. 6

GOLDING And do the costly garments—the title and fame of a lady, the fashion, observation, and reverence proper to such preferment—no more inflame you than such convenience as my poor means and industry can offer to your virtues?

MILDRED I have observed that the bridle given to those violent flatteries of fortune is seldom recovered; they bear one headlong in 7 desire from one novelty to another, and where those ranging appetites reign, there is ever more passion than reason; no stay, and so no happiness. These hasty advancements are not natural. Nature hath given us legs to go to our objects, not wings to fly to 8 them.

GOLDING How dear an object you are to my desires I cannot express; whose fruition would my master's absolute consent and yours vouchsafe me, I should be absolutely happy. And though it were a grace so far beyond my merit that I should blush with un- 9

1 worthiness to receive it, yet thus far both my love and my means shall assure your requital: you shall want nothing fit for your birth and education; what increase of wealth and advancement the honest and orderly industry and skill of our trade will afford in any, I doubt not will be aspired by me; I will ever make your contentment the end of my endeavours; I will love you above all;

2 and only your grief shall be my misery, and your delight my felicity.

TOUCHSTONE   Work upon that now! By my hopes, he wooes honestly and orderly; he shall be anchor of my hopes! Look, see the ill-yoked monster, his fellow! [Aside]

3 QUICKSILVER   [enters unlaced, a towel about his neck, in his flatcap, drunk]   Eastward Ho! Holla, ye pampered jades of Asia!

TOUCHSTONE   Drunk now downright, o' my fidelity!

QUICKSILVER   Ump! Pull eo, pull eo! Showse, quoth the caliver.

4 GOLDING   Fie, fellow Quicksilver, what a pickle are you in!

QUICKSILVER   Pickle? Pickle in thy throat; zounds, pickle! Wa, ha, ho! Good morrow, Knight Petronel; morrow, Lady Goldsmith; come off, knight, with a counterbuff, for the honour of knighthood.

5 GOLDING   Why, how now, sir? Do ye know where you are?

QUICKSILVER   Where I am? Why, 's blood, you jolthead, where I am!

GOLDING   Go to, go to, for shame! Go to bed and sleep out this

6 immodesty; thou sham'st both my master and his house.

QUICKSILVER   Shame? What shame? I thought thou wouldst show thy bringing-up; and thou wert a gentleman as I am, thou wouldst think it no shame to be drunk. Lend me some money, save my credit; I must dine with the servingmen and their wives—and

7 their wives, sirrah!

GOLDING   E'en who you will; I'll not lend thee threepence.

QUICKSILVER   'S foot, lend me some money! Hast thou not Hiren here?

Eastward Ho, Westward Ho: Cries of the London watermen.
Holla, ye pampered jades of Asia: Tamberlaine's extravagant cry, from Part II of Marlowe's play.
Showse, quoth the caliver: "Bang went the gun" (Schelling). A caliver was a kind of arquebus.
Hast thou not Hiren here?: Pistol again from *Henry IV, Part II.*

TOUCHSTONE Why, how now, sirrah? What vein's this, ha? [*Comes* 1
forward]

QUICKSILVER Who cries on murther? Lady, was it you? How does
our master? Pray thee cry Eastward Ho!

TOUCHSTONE Sirrah, sirrah, y' are past your hiccup now; I see y'
are drunk— 2

QUICKSILVER 'T is for your credit, master.

TOUCHSTONE And hear you keep a whore in town—

QUICKSILVER 'T is for your credit, master.

TOUCHSTONE And what you are out in cash, I know. 3

QUICKSILVER So do I; my father's a gentleman. Work upon that
now! Eastward Ho!

TOUCHSTONE Sir, Eastward Ho will make you go Westward Ho.
I will no longer dishonest my house, nor endanger my stock with
your license. There, sir, there's your indenture; all your apparel 4
(that I must know) is on your back, and from this time my door
is shut to you; from me be free; but for other freedom, and the
moneys you have wasted, Eastward Ho shall not serve you.

QUICKSILVER Am I free o' my fetters? Rent, fly with a duck in thy
mouth, and now I tell thee, Touchstone— 5

TOUCHSTONE Good sir—

QUICKSILVER When this eternal substance of my soul—

TOUCHSTONE Well said; change your gold-ends for your play-ends.

QUICKSILVER Did live imprisoned in my wanton flesh—

TOUCHSTONE What then, sir? 6

QUICKSILVER I was a courtier in the Spanish Court,
And Don Andrea was my name.

TOUCHSTONE Good Master Don Andrea, will you march?

QUICKSILVER Sweet Touchstone, will you lend me two shillings? 7

TOUCHSTONE Not a penny!

QUICKSILVER Not a penny? I have friends, and I have
acquaintance; I will piss at thy shop post, and throw rotten eggs
at thy sign. Work upon that now! [*Exits staggering*]

Who cries on murther?: From *The Spanish Tragedy*.
Westward Ho: In this case, to Tyburn, to be hanged.
Rent, fly with a duck . . . : He will get no interest or profit.
When this eternal substance . . . : Again from *The Spanish Tragedy*;
here the opening lines.

1 TOUCHSTONE Now, sirrah you, hear you? You shall serve me no more neither—not an hour longer!

GOLDING What mean you, sir?

TOUCHSTONE I mean to give thee thy freedom, and with thy freedom my daughter, and with my daughter a father's love. And 2 with all these such a portion as shall make Knight Petronel himself envy thee! Y' are both agreed, are ye not?

BOTH With all submission, both of thanks and duty.

TOUCHSTONE Well then, the great Power of heaven bless and confirm you. And, Golding, that my love to thee may not show less 3 than my wife's love to my eldest daughter, thy marriage feast shall equal the knight's and hers.

GOLDING Let me beseech you, no, sir; the superfluity and cold meat left at their nuptials will with bounty furnish ours. The grossest prodigality is superfluous cost of the belly; nor would I wish 4 any invitement of states or friends, only your reverent presence and witness shall sufficiently grace and confirm us.

TOUCHSTONE Son to my own bosom, take her and my blessing. The nice fondling, my lady, sir-reverence, that I must not now presume to call daughter, is so ravished with desire to hansel her 5 new coach, and see her knight's Eastward Castle, that the next morning will sweat with her busy setting forth. Away will she and her mother, and while their preparation is making, ourselves, with some two or three other friends, will consummate the humble match we have in God's name concluded.

6   'T is to my wish; for I have often read
     Fit birth, fit age, keeps long a quiet bed.
     'T is to my wish; for tradesmen (well 't is known)
     Get with more ease than gentry keeps his own.

[*Exits with* GOLDING *and* MILDRED.]

7

Scene Two

[*A room in the house of Security.*]

8 SECURITY [*alone*] My privy guest, lusty Quicksilver, has drunk too deep of the bridebowl; but with a little sleep, he is much recovered; and, I think, is making himself ready to be drunk in a gallanter likeness. My house is, as 't were, the cave where the young outlaw hoards the stolen vails of his occupation; and here, when 9 he will revel it in his prodigal similitude, he retires to his trunks,

and (I may say softly) his punks: he dares trust me with the keeping of both; for I am Security itself; my name is Security, the famous usurer.

[*Enter* QUICKSILVER *in his prentice's coat and cap, his gallant breeches and stockings, gartering himself,* SECURITY *following.*]

QUICKSILVER Come, old Security, thou father of destruction! Th' indented sheepskin is burned wherein I was wrapped; and I am now loose to get more children of perdition into thy usurous bonds. Thou feed'st my lechery, and I thy covetousness; thou art pander to me for my wench, and I to thee for thy cozenages. Ka me, ka thee, runs through court and country.

SECURITY Well said, my subtle Quicksilver! These ka's ope the doors to all this world's felicity; the dullest forehead sees it. Let not master courtier think he carries all the knavery on his shoulders: I have known poor Hob in the country, that has worn hobnails on 's shoes, have as much villany in 's head as he that wears gold buttons in 's cap.

QUICKSILVER Why, man, 't is the London highway to thrift; if virtue be used, 't is but as a scrap to the net of villany. They that use it simply, thrive simply, I warrant. Weight and fashion makes goldsmiths cuckolds.

SINDEFY [*enters with* QUICKSILVER's *doublet, cloak, rapier, and dagger*] Here, sir, put off the other half of your prenticeship.

QUICKSILVER Well said, sweet Sin! Bring forth my bravery.
Now let my trunks shoot forth their silks concealed.
I now am free, and now will justify
My trunks and punks. Avaunt, dull flatcap, then!
Via the curtain that shadowed Borgia!
There lie, thou husk of my envassalled state,
I, Samson, now have burst the Philistines' bands,
And in thy lap, my lovely Dalila,
I'll lie, and snore out my enfranchised state. [*Sings*]

> When Samson was a tall young man,
> His power and strength increased than;
> He sold no more nor cup nor can;
> But did them all despise.
> Old Touchstone, now write to thy friends
> For one to sell thy base gold-ends;

These ka's: Pronounced kays (keys).
trunks: Here a pun, on "trousers" and "peashooter."
"When Samson" . . . The first two lines of the song are the opening of an old ballad.

1   Quicksilver now no more attends
         Thee, Touchstone.

But, dad, hast thou seen my running gelding dressed today?

SECURITY   That I have, Frank. The ostler o' th' Cock dressed him for a breakfast.

2   QUICKSILVER   What, did he eat him?

SECURITY   No, but he eat his breakfast for dressing him; and so dressed him for breakfast.

QUICKSILVER   O witty age, where age is young in wit,
And all youth's words have gray beards full of it!

3   SINDEFY   But alas, Frank, how will all this be maintained now? Your place maintained it before.

QUICKSILVER   Why, and I maintained my place. I'll to the Court, another manner of place for maintainance, I hope, than the silly City! I heard my father say, I heard my mother sing an old song
4   and a true: Thou art a she-fool, and know'st not what belongs to our male wisdom. I shall be a merchant, forsooth, trust my estate in a wooden trough as he does! What are these ships but tennis balls for the winds to play withal? Tossed from one wave to another; now under line, now over the house; sometimes brick-walled against a rock, so that the guts fly out again; sometimes
5   struck under the wide hazard, and farewell, master merchant!

SINDEFY   Well, Frank, well: the seas you say, are uncertain; but he that sails in your Court seas shall find 'em ten times fuller of hazard; wherein to see what is to be seen is torment more than a free spirit can endure; but when you come to suffer, how many inju-
6   ries swallow you! What care and devotion must you use to humour an imperious lord, proportion your looks to his looks, smiles to his smiles, fit your sails to the wind of his breath!

QUICKSILVER   Tush, he's no journeyman in his craft that cannot do that!

7   SINDEFY   But he's worse than a prentice that does it; not only humouring the lord, but every trencher bearer, every groom, that by indulgence and intelligence crept into his favour, and by panderism into his chamber; he rules the roast; and when my honourable lord says it shall be thus, my worshipful rascal, the groom of
8   his closestool, says it shall not be thus, claps the door after him, and who dares enter? A prentice, quoth you? 'T is but to learn to live; and does that disgrace a man? He that rises hardly stands firmly; but he that rises with ease, alas, falls as easily!

hazard: The serving court in tennis; here, of course, the sea, so completing the analogy.
rule the roast: Have the power, a common proverb.

QUICKSILVER   A pox on you! Who taught you this morality?   1

SECURITY   'T is long of this witty age, Master Francis. But, indeed, Mistress Sindefy, all trades complain of inconvenience, and therefore 't is best to have none. The merchant, he complains and says, "Traffic is subject to much uncertainty and loss." Let 'em keep their goods on dry land, with a vengeance, and not expose   2 other men's substances to the mercy of the winds, under protection of a wooden wall (as Master Francis says); and all for greedy desire to enrich themselves with unconscionable gain, two for one, or so; where I, and such other honest men as live by lending money, are content with moderate profit; thirty or forty i' th' hundred, so we may have it with quietness, and out of peril of   3 wind and weather, rather than run those dangerous courses of trading, as they do.

QUICKSILVER   Ay, dad, thou mayst well be called Security, for thou takest the safest course.

[*Exit* SINDEFY.]   4

SECURITY   Faith, the quieter, and the more contented, and, out of doubt, the more godly; for merchants, in their courses, are never pleased, but ever repining against heaven: one prays for a westerly wind to carry his ship forth; another for an easterly to bring   5 his ship home; and at every shaking of a leaf he falls into an agony to think what danger his ship is in on such a coast, and so forth. The farmer, he is ever at odds with the weather: sometimes the clouds have been too barren; sometimes the heavens forget themselves; their harvests answer not their hopes; sometimes the season falls out too fruitful, corn will bear no price, and so   6 forth. The artificer, he's all for a stirring world; if his trade be too full, and fall short of his expectation, then falls he out of joint. Where we that trade nothing but money are free from all this; we are pleased with all weathers, let it rain or hold up, be calm or windy; let the season be whatsoever, let trade go how it   7 will, we take all in good part, e'en what please the heavens to send us, so the sun stand not still, and the moon keep her usual returns, and make up days, months, and years.

QUICKSILVER   And you have good security!

SECURITY   Ay, marry Frank, that's the special point.   8

QUICKSILVER   And yet, forsooth, we must have trades to live withal; for we cannot stand without legs, nor fly without wings, and a number of such scurvy phrases. No, I say still, he that has wit, let him live by his wit; he that has none, let him be a tradesman.

SECURITY   Witty Master Francis, 't is pity any trade should dull   9 that quick brain of yours! Do but bring Knight Petronel into my

1　parchment toils once, and you shall never need to toil in any trade, o' my credit. You know his wife's land?

QUICKSILVER　Even to a foot, sir; I have been often there; a pretty fine seat, good land, all entire within itself.

SECURITY　Well wooded?

2

QUICKSILVER　Two hundred pounds' worth of wood ready to fell, and a fine sweet house, that stands just in the midst on 't, like a prick in the midst of a circle; would I were your farmer, for a hundred pound a year!

3　SECURITY　Excellent Master Francis, how I do long to do thee good! How I do hunger and thirst to have the honour to enrich thee! Ay, even to die that thou mightest inherit my living; even hunger and thirst! For o' my religion, Master Francis—and so tell Knight Petronel—I do it to do him a pleasure.

QUICKSILVER　Marry, dad, his horses are now coming up to bear
4　down his lady; wilt thou lend him thy stable to set 'em in?

SECURITY　Faith, Master Francis, I would be loath to lend my stable out of doors; in a greater matter I will pleasure him, but not in this.

5　QUICKSILVER　A pox of your hunger and thirst! Well, dad, let him have money; all he could any way get is bestowed on a ship now bound for Virginia; the frame of which voyage is so closely conveyed that his new lady nor any of her friends know it. Notwithstanding, as soon as his lady's hand is gotten to the sale of her inheritance, and you have furnished him with money, he will in-
6　stantly hoist sail and away.

SECURITY　Now, a frank gale of wind go with him, Master Frank! We have too few such knight adventurers. Who would not sell away competent certainties to purchase, with any danger, excellent uncertainties? Your true knight venturer ever does it. Let his
7　wife seal today; he shall have his money today.

QUICKSILVER　Tomorrow she shall, dad, before she goes into the country; to work her to which action with the more engines, I purpose presently to prefer my sweet Sin here to the place of her gentlewoman; whom you (for the more credit) shall present as
8　your friend's daughter, a gentlewoman of the country, new come up with a will for awhile to learn fashions, forsooth, and be toward some lady; and she shall buzz pretty devices into her lady's ear, feeding her humours so serviceable, as the manner of such as she is, you know—

9　SECURITY　True, good Master Francis!

[*Enter* SINDEFY.]   1

QUICKSILVER   That she shall keep her port open to anything she
commends to her.

SECURITY   O' my religion, a most fashionable project; as good she
spoil the lady, as the lady spoil her, for 't is three to one of one
side. Sweet Mistress Sin, how are you bound to Master Francis! I   2
do not doubt to see you shortly wed one of the head men of our
city.

SINDEFY   But, sweet Frank, when shall my father Security present
me?

QUICKSILVER   With all festination; I have broken the ice to it al-   3
ready; and will presently to the knight's house, whither, my good
old dad, let me pray thee with all formality to man her.

SECURITY   Command me, Master Francis, I do hunger and thirst to
do thee service. Come, sweet Mistress Sin, take leave of my Winifred, and we will instantly meet frank Master Francis at your   4
lady's.

WINIFRED [*enters above*]   Where is my Cu there? Cu?

SECURITY   Ay, Winnie!

WINIFRED   Wilt thou come in, sweet Cu?   5

SECURITY   Ay, Winnie, presently!

[*Exeunt* WINIFRED, SECURITY, *and* SINDEFY.]

QUICKSILVER   Ay, Winnie, quod he! That's all he can do, poor
man, he may well cut off her name at Winnie. O 't is an egregious   6
pander! What will not an usurous knave be, so he may be rich? O
't is a notable Jew's trump! I hope to live to see dogs' meat made
of the old usurer's flesh, dice of his bones, and indentures of his
skin; and yet his skin is too thick to make parchment, 't would
make good boots for a peterman to catch salmon in. Your only   7
smooth skin to make fine vellum is your Puritan's skin; they be
the smoothest and slickest knaves in a country. [*Exits*]

Scene Three   8

[*Before Sir Petronel's lodging. Enter* SIR PETRONEL *in boots, with a
riding wand, followed by* QUICKSILVER.]

SIR PETRONEL   I'll out of this wicked town as fast as my horse can
trot. Here's now no good action for a man to spend his time in.   9

1   Taverns grow dead; ordinaries are blown up; plays are at a stand; houses of hospitality at a fall; not a feather waving, nor a spur jingling anywhere. I'll away instantly.

QUICKSILVER   Y' 'ad best take some crowns in your purse, knight, or else your Eastward Castle will smoke but miserably.

2   SIR PETRONEL   O, Frank, my castle? Alas, all the castles I have are built with air, thou know'st!

QUICKSILVER   I know it, knight, and therefore wonder whither your lady is going.

3   SIR PETRONEL   Faith, to seek her fortune, I think. I said I had a castle and land eastward, and eastward she will, without contradiction; her coach and the coach of the sun must meet full butt. And the sun being outshined with her ladyship's glory, she fears he goes westward to hang himself.

4   QUICKSILVER   And I fear, when her enchanted castle becomes invisible, her ladyship will return and follow his example.

SIR PETRONEL   O that she would have the grace, for I shall never be able to pacify her, when she sees herself deceived so.

5   QUICKSILVER   As easily as can be. Tell her she mistook your directions, and that shortly yourself will down with her to approve it; and then clothe but her crupper in a new gown, and you may drive her any way you list. For these women, sir, are like Essex calves; you must wriggle 'em on by the tail still, or they will never drive orderly.

6   SIR PETRONEL   But alas, sweet Frank, thou know'st my hability will not furnish her blood with those costly humours.

QUICKSILVER   Cast that cost on me, sir. I have spoken to my old pander, Security, for money or commodity; and commodity (if you will) I know he will procure you.

7   SIR PETRONEL   Commodity! Alas, what commodity?

QUICKSILVER   Why, sir, what say you to figs and raisins?

SIR PETRONEL   A plague of figs and raisins, and all such frail commodities! We shall make nothing of 'em.

8   QUICKSILVER   Why then, sir, what say you to forty pound in roasted beef?

SIR PETRONEL   Out upon 't! I have less stomach to that than to the figs and raisins; I'll out of town, though I sojourn with a friend of

frail: The basket in which they were packed, and hence, uncertain.

mine; for stay here I must not; my creditors have laid to arrest 1
me, and I have no friend under heaven but my sword to bail me.

QUICKSILVER God's me, knight, put 'em in sufficient sureties,
rather than let your sword bail you! Let 'em take their choice,
either the King's Bench or the Fleet, or which of the two Counters they like best, for, by the Lord, I like none of 'em. 2

SIR PETRONEL Well, Frank, there is no jesting with my earnest necessity; thou know'st if I make not present money to further my
voyage begun, all's lost, and all I have laid out about it.

QUICKSILVER Why then, sir, in earnest, if you can get your wise
lady to set her hand to the sale of her inheritance, the blood- 3
hound, Security, will smell out ready money for you instantly.

SIR PETRONEL There spake an angel! To bring her to which conformity, I must feign myself extremely amorous; and alleging ur-
gent excuses for my stay behind, part with her as passionately as
she would from her foisting hound. 4

QUICKSILVER You have the sow by the right ear, sir. I warrant
there was never child longed more to ride a cockhorse or wear his
new coat, then she longs to ride in her new coach. She would
long for everything when she was a maid, and now she will run
mad for 'em. I lay my life, she will have every year four children; 5
and what charge and change of humour you must endure while
she is with child, and how she will tie you to your tackling till she
be with child, a dog would not endure. Nay, there is no turnspit
dog bound to his wheel more servilely than you shall be to her
wheel; for as that dog can never climb the top of his wheel but
when the top comes under him, so shall you never climb the top 6
of her contentment but when she is under you.

SIR PETRONEL 'S light, how thou terrifiest me!

QUICKSILVER Nay, hark you, sir; what nurses, what midwives,
what fools, what physicians, what cunning women must be sought
for (fearing sometimes she is bewitched, sometimes in a con- 7
sumption) to tell her tales, to talk bawdy to her, to make her
laugh, to give her glisters, to let her blood under the tongue and
betwixt the toes; how she will revile and kiss you, spit in your
face, and lick it off again; how she will vaunt you are her creature, she made you of nothing; how she could have had thou-
sand-mark jointures; she could have been made a lady by a 8
Scotch knight, and never ha' married him; she could have had
panadas in her bed every morning; how she set you up, and how
she will pull you down; you'll never be able to stand of your legs
to endure it.

SIR PETRONEL Out of my fortune, what a death is my life bound 9

1 face to face to! The best is, a large time-fitted conscience is bound
to nothing; marriage is but a form in the school of policy, to
which scholars sit fastened only with painted chains. Old Security's young wife is ne'er the further off with me.

QUICKSILVER Thereby lies a tale, sir. The old usurer will be here

2 instantly with my punk Sindefy, whom you know your lady has
promised me to entertain for her gentlewoman; and he (with a
purpose to feed on you) invites you most solemnly by me to supper.

SIR PETRONEL It falls out excellently fitly; I see desire of gain
makes jealousy venturous.

3

[*Enter* GERTRUDE.]

See, Frank, here comes my lady. Lord, how she views thee! She
knows thee not, I think, in this bravery.

4 GERTRUDE How now? Who be you, I pray?

QUICKSILVER One Master Francis Quicksilver, an' 't please your
ladyship.

GERTRUDE God's my dignity! As I am a lady, if he did not make
me blush so that mine eyes stood awater, would I were unmarried

5 again! Where's my woman, I pray?

[*Enter* SECURITY *and* SINDEFY.]

QUICKSILVER See, madam, she now comes to attend you.

6 SECURITY God save my honourable knight and his worshipful lady!

GERTRUDE Y' are very welcome; you must not put on your hat yet.

SECURITY No, madam; till I know your ladyship's further pleasure,
I will not presume.

GERTRUDE And is this a gentleman's daughter new come out of

7 the country?

SECURITY She is, madam; and one that her father hath a special
care to bestow in some honourable lady's service, to put her out
of her honest humours, forsooth; for she had a great desire to be
a nun, an' 't please you.

8 GERTRUDE A nun? What nun? A nun substantive, or a nun ad-
jective?

SECURITY A nun substantive, madam, I hope, if a nun be a noun.
But I mean, lady, a vowed maid of that order.

GERTRUDE I'll teach her to be a maid of the order, I warrant you!

9 And can you do any work belongs to a lady's chamber?

SINDEFY   What I cannot do, madam, I would be glad to learn.   1

GERTRUDE   Well said, hold up, then; hold up your head, I say!
Come hither a little.

SINDEFY   I thank your ladyship.

GERTRUDE   And hark you—good man, you may put on your hat
now; I do not look on you—I must have you of my faction now;   2
not of my knight's, maid!

SINDEFY   No, forsooth, madam, of yours.

GERTRUDE   And draw all my servants in my bow, and keep my
counsel, and tell me tales, and put me riddles, and read on a book   3
sometimes when I am busy, and laugh at country gentlewomen,
and command anything in the house for my retainers; and care
not what you spend, for it is all mine; and in any case be still a
maid, whatsoever you do, or whatsoever any man can do unto you.

SECURITY   I warrant your ladyship for that.   4

GERTRUDE   Very well; you shall ride in my coach with me into the
country tomorrow morning. Come, knight, I pray thee let's make
a short supper, and to bed presently.

SECURITY   Nay, good madam, this night I have a short supper at
home waits on his worship's acceptation.   5

GERTRUDE   By my faith, but he shall not go, sir; I shall swoun and
he sup from me.

SIR PETRONEL   Pray thee, forbear; shall he lose his provision?

GERTRUDE   Ay, by 'r lady, sir, rather than I lose my longing.   6
Come in, I say; as I am a lady, you shall not go.

QUICKSILVER [aside to SECURITY]   I told him what a burr he had
gotten.

SECURITY   If you will not sup from your knight, madam, let me entreat your ladyship to sup at my house with him.   7

GERTRUDE   No, by my faith, sir; then we cannot be abed soon
enough after supper.

SIR PETRONEL   What a med'cine is this! Well, Master Security, you
are new married as well as I; I hope you are bound as well. We   8
must honour our young wives, you know.

QUICKSILVER [aside to SECURITY]   In policy, dad, till tomorrow
she has sealed.

SECURITY   I hope in the morning, yet, your knighthood will breakfast with me?   9

1   Sir Petronel   As early as you will, sir.

Security   Thank your good worship; I do hunger and thirst to do you good, sir.

Gertrude   Come, sweet knight, come; I do hunger and thirst to be abed with thee.

2   *[Exeunt]*

ACT THREE

Scene One

[*A room in Security's house. Enter* SIR PETRONEL, QUICKSILVER, SECURITY, BRAMBLE, *and* WINIFRED.]   1

SIR PETRONEL   Thanks for our feastlike breakfast, good Master Security; I am sorry (by reason of my instant haste to so long a voyage as Virginia) I am without means by any kind amends to show how affectionately I take your kindness, and to confirm by   2 some worthy ceremony a perpetual league of friendship betwixt us.

SECURITY   Excellent knight, let this be a token betwixt us of inviolable friendship; I am new married to this fair gentlewoman, you know, and by my hope to make her fruitful, though I be something in years, I vow faithfully unto you to make you godfather   3 (though in your absence) to the first child I am blest withal; and henceforth call me gossip, I beseech you, if you please to accept it.

SIR PETRONEL   In the highest degree of gratitude, my most worthy gossip; for confirmation of which friendly title, let me entreat my   4 fair gossip, your wife here, to accept this diamond, and keep it as my gift to her first child, wheresoever my fortune, in event of my voyage, shall bestow me.

SECURITY   How now, my coy wedlock, make you strange of so noble a favour? Take it, I charge you, with all affection, and, by   5 way of taking your leave, present boldly your lips to our honourable gossip.

QUICKSILVER [*aside*]   How venturous he is to him, and how jealous to others!

SIR PETRONEL   Long may this kind touch of our lips print in our   6 hearts all the forms of affection. And now, my good gossip, if the writings be ready to which my wife should seal, let them be brought this morning before she takes coach into the country, and my kindness shall work her to dispatch it.

SECURITY   The writings are ready, sir. My learned counsel here,   7 Master Bramble the lawyer, hath perused them, and within this hour I will bring the scrivener with them to your worshipful lady.

SIR PETRONEL   Good Master Bramble, I will here take my leave of you then. God send you fortunate pleas, sir, and contentious clients!   8

31

1 BRAMBLE And you foreright winds, sir, and a fortunate voyage!
[*Exits*]

MESSENGER [*enters*] Sir Petronel, here are three or four gentlemen
desire to speak with you.

SIR PETRONEL What are they?

2 QUICKSILVER They are your followers in this voyage, knight, Captain Seagull and his associates; I met them this morning, and told
them you would be here.

SIR PETRONEL Let them enter, I pray you; I know they long to
be gone, for their stay is dangerous.

3 [*Enter* SEAGULL, SCAPETHRIFT, *and* SPENDALL.]

SEAGULL God save my honourable Colonel!

SIR PETRONEL Welcome, good Captain Seagull and worthy gentlemen. If you will meet my friend Frank here and me, at the Blue
4 Anchor Tavern by Billingsgate this evening, we will there drink to
our happy voyage, be merry, and take boat to our ship with all
expedition.

SPENDALL Defer it no longer, I beseech you, sir; but as your voyage is hitherto carried closely, and in another knight's name, so
5 for your own safety and ours, let it be continued, our meeting
and speedy purpose of departing known to as few as is possible,
lest your ship and goods be attached.

QUICKSILVER Well advised, Captain! Our colonel shall have
money this morning to dispatch all our departures; bring those
gentlemen at night to the place appointed, and with our skins full
6 of vintage we'll take occasion by the vantage, and away.

SPENDALL We will not fail but be there, sir.

SIR PETRONEL Good morrow, good Captain and my worthy associates. Health and all sovereignty to my beautiful gossip; for
you, sir, we shall see you presently with the writings.

7 SECURITY With writings and crowns to my honourable gossip. I do
hunger and thirst to do you good, sir!

[*Exeunt*]

8 ## Scene Two

[*An innyard.*]

COACHMAN [*enters in haste, in 's frock, feeding*] Here's a stir
9 when citizens ride out of town, indeed, as if all the house were

afire! 'S light, they will not give a man leave to eat 's breakfast
afore he rises!

HAMLET [*a footman, enters in haste*] What, coachman! My lady's
coach, for shame! Her ladyship's ready to come down.

POTKIN [*a tankard bearer, enters*] 'S foot, Hamlet, are you mad?
Whither run you now? You should brush up my old mistress!

[*Exit* HAMLET.]

SINDEFY [*enters*] What, Potkin? You must put off your tankard,
and put on your blue coat and wait upon Mistress Touchstone
into the country. [*Exits*]

POTKIN I will, forsooth, presently. [*Exits*]

[*Enter* MISTRESS FOND *and* MISTRESS GAZER.]

MISTRESS FOND Come, sweet Mistress Gazer, let's watch here, and
see my Lady Flash take coach.

MISTRESS GAZER O my word, here's a most fine place to stand
in. Did you see the new ship launched last day, Mistress Fond?

MISTRESS FOND O God, and we citizens should lose such a sight!

MISTRESS GAZER I warrant here will be double as many people
to see her take coach as there were to see it take water.

MISTRESS FOND O she's married to a most fine castle i' th' country, they say.

MISTRESS GAZER But there are no giants in the castle, are there?

MISTRESS FOND O no; they say her knight killed 'em all, and
therefore he was knighted.

MISTRESS GAZER Would to God her ladyship would come away!

[*Enter* GERTRUDE, MISTRESS TOUCHSTONE, SINDEFY, HAMLET,
POTKIN.]

MISTRESS FOND She comes, she comes, she comes!

MISTRESS GAZER ⎤
MISTRESS FOND ⎦ Pray heaven bless your ladyship!

GERTRUDE Thank you, good people! My coach, for the love of
heaven, my coach! In good truth I shall swoun else.

HAMLET Coach, coach, my lady's coach! [*Exits*]

Hamlet "My lady's coach!": The reference to the anachronism is
clear. Shakespeare's play is echoed several times in this scene.

1 GERTRUDE As I am a lady, I think I am with child already, I long for a coach so. May one be with child afore they are married, mother?

2 MISTRESS TOUCHSTONE Ay, by 'r lady, madam; a little thing does that; I have seen a little prick no bigger than a pin's head swell bigger and bigger till it has come to an income; and e'en so 't is in these cases.

HAMLET [*enters*] Your coach is coming, madam.

3 GERTRUDE That's well said. Now, heaven, methinks I am e'en up to the knees in preferment! [*Sings*]

> But a little higher, but a little higher,
> but a little higher,
> There, there, there lies Cupid's fire!

4 MISTRESS TOUCHSTONE But must this young man, an' 't please you, madam, run by your coach all the way a-foot?

GERTRUDE Ay, by my faith, I warrant him! He gives no other milk, as I have another servant does.

5 MISTRESS TOUCHSTONE Alas, 't is e'en pity, methinks! For God's sake, madam, buy him but a hobbyhorse; let the poor youth have something betwixt his legs to ease 'em. Alas, we must do as we would be done to!

GERTRUDE Go to, hold your peace, dame; you talk like an old fool, I tell you!

6 [*Enter* SIR PETRONEL *and* QUICKSILVER.]

SIR PETRONEL Wilt thou be gone, sweet honeysuckle, before I can go with thee?

7 GERTRUDE I pray thee, sweet knight, let me; I do so long to dress up thy castle afore thou com'st. But I marle how my modest sister occupies herself this morning, that she cannot wait on me to my coach, as well as her mother.

8 QUICKSILVER Marry, madam, she's married by this time to prentice Golding. Your father, and some one more, stole to church with 'em in all the haste, that the cold meat left at your wedding might serve to furnish their nuptial table.

GERTRUDE There's no base fellow, my father, now! But he's e'en fit to father such a daughter: he must call me daughter no more

"But a little higher . . .": A song from Thomas Campion's *Book of Airs* (1601).
gives no other milk: Serves no other purpose.

now; but "madam," and "please you, madam," and "please your 1
worship, madam," indeed. Out upon him, marry his daughter to a
base prentice!

MISTRESS TOUCHSTONE   What should one do? Is there no law for
one that marries a woman's daughter against her will? How shall
we punish him, madam?   2

GERTRUDE   As I am a lady, an' 't would snow, we'd so pebble 'em
with snowballs as they come from church; but, sirrah Frank
Quicksilver!

QUICKSILVER   Ay, madam.

GERTRUDE   Dost remember since thou and I clapped what-d'ye-   3
call-'ts in the garret?

QUICKSILVER   I know not what you mean, madam.

GERTRUDE [sings]

> His head as white as milk, all flaxen was his hair;   4
> But now he is dead, and laid in his bed,
> And never will come again.

God be at your labour!

[Enter TOUCHSTONE, GOLDING, MILDRED, with rosemary.]   5

SIR PETRONEL [aside]   Was there ever such a lady?

QUICKSILVER   See, madam, the bride and bridegroom!

GERTRUDE   God's my precious! God give you joy, Mistress What-
lack-you! Now out upon thee, baggage! My sister married in a   6
taffeta hat! Marry, hang you! Westward with a wanion t' ye! Nay,
I have done wi' ye, minion, then, i' faith; never look to have my
count'nance any more, nor anything I can do for thee. Thou ride
in my coach, or come down to my castle! Fie upon thee! I charge
thee in my ladyship's name, call me sister no more.
                                                                 7
TOUCHSTONE   An' 't please your worship, this is not your sister;
this is my daughter, and she calls me father, and so does not your
ladyship, an' 't please your worship, madam.

MISTRESS TOUCHSTONE   No, nor she must not call thee father by
heraldry, because thou mak'st thy prentice thy son as well as she. 8
Ah, thou misproud prentice, dar'st thou presume to marry a
lady's sister?

GOLDING   It pleased my master, forsooth, to embolden me with his
favour; and though I confess myself far unworthy so worthy a

a wanion t' ye: A plague upon you.

1 wife (being in part her servant, as I am your prentice) yet since (I may say it without boasting) I am born a gentleman, and by the trade I have learned of my master (which I trust taints not my blood) able with mine own industry and portion to maintain your daughter, my hope is heaven will so bless our humble begin-ning that in the end I shall be no disgrace to the grace with which

2 my master hath bound me his double prentice.

TOUCHSTONE Master me no more, son, if thou think'st me worthy to be thy father.

GERTRUDE Son? Now, good Lord, how he shines, and you mark

3 him! He's a gentleman!

GOLDING Ay, indeed, madam, a gentleman born.

SIR PETRONEL Never stand o' your gentry, Master Bridegroom; if your legs be no better than your arms, you'll be able to stand up-right on neither shortly.

4 TOUCHSTONE An' 't please your good worship, sir, there are two sorts of gentlemen.

SIR PETRONEL What mean you, sir?

TOUCHSTONE Bold to put off my hat to your worship—

5 SIR PETRONEL Nay, pray forbear, sir, and then forth with your two sorts of gentlemen.

TOUCHSTONE If your worship will have it so, I say there are two sorts of gentlemen. There is a gentleman artificial, and a gentle-man natural. Now though your worship be a gentleman natural

6 —work upon that now!

QUICKSILVER Well said, old Touchstone; I am proud to hear thee enter a set speech, i' faith! Forth, I beseech thee!

TOUCHSTONE Cry you mercy, sir, your worship's a gentleman I do not know. If you be one of my acquaintance, y' are very much

7 disguised, sir.

QUICKSILVER Go to, old quipper! Forth with thy speech, I say!

TOUCHSTONE What, sir, my speeches were ever in vain to your gracious worship; and therefore, till I speak to you—gallantry in-deed—I will save my breath for my broth anon. Come, my poor

8 son and daughter, let us hide ourselves in our poor humility, and live safe. Ambition consumes itself with the very show. Work upon that now!

[*Exeunt* TOUCHSTONE, GOLDING, *and* MILDRED.]

natural: Here with the implication of idiot.

GERTRUDE Let him go, let him go, for God's sake! Let him make 1
his prentice his son, for God's sake! Give away his daughter, for
God's sake; And when they come a-begging to us, for God's sake,
let's laugh at their good husbandry, for God's sake! Farewell,
sweet knight, pray thee make haste after.

SIR PETRONEL What shall I say? I would not have thee go. 2

QUICKSILVER
Now, O now, I must depart;
Parting though it absence move—

This ditty, knight, do I see in thy looks in capital letters.

What a grief 't is to depart, and leave the flower that has my 3
heart!
My sweet lady, and alack for woe, why should we part so?

Tell truth, knight, and shame all dissembling lovers; does not
your pain lie on that side?

SIR PETRONEL If it do, canst thou tell me how I may cure it? 4

QUICKSILVER Excellent easily! Divide yourself in two halves, just
by the girdlestead; send one half with your lady, and keep the t'
other yourself; or else do as all true lovers do—part with your
heart, and leave your body behind. I have seen 't done a hundred
times: 't is as easy a matter for a lover to part without a heart 5
from his sweetheart, and he ne'er the worse, as for a mouse to get
from a trap and leave her tail behind. See, here comes the writings.

[*Enter* SECURITY *with a* SCRIVENER.]
6

SECURITY Good morrow to my worshipful lady! I present your
ladyship with this writing, to which if you please to set your hand
with your knight's, a velvet gown shall attend your journey, o' my
credit.

GERTRUDE What writing is it, knight? 7

SIR PETRONEL The sale, sweetheart, of the poor tenement I told
thee of, only to make a little money to send thee down furniture
for my castle, to which my hand shall lead thee.

GERTRUDE Very well! Now give me your pen, I pray.

QUICKSILVER [*aside*] It goes down without chewing, i' faith! 8

SCRIVENER Your worships deliver this as your deed?

BOTH We do.

"*Now, O now* . . .": Misquoted from John Dowland's *First Book of Airs* (1597).

1 GERTRUDE So now, knight, farewell till I see thee!

SIR PETRONEL All farewell to my sweetheart!

MISTRESS TOUCHSTONE God-b' w' y', son knight!

SIR PETRONEL Farewell, my good mother!

2 GERTRUDE Farewell, Frank; I would fain take thee down if I could.

QUICKSILVER I thank your good ladyship; farewell, Mistress Sin-defy.

[*Exeunt* GERTRUDE *and her* PARTY.]

3 SIR PETRONEL O tedious voyage, whereof there is no end! What will they think of me?

QUICKSILVER Think what they list. They longed for a vagary into the country and now they are fitted. So a woman marry to ride in a coach, she cares not if she ride to her ruin. 'T is the great end
4 of many of their marriages. This is not the first time a lady has rid a false journey in her coach, I hope.

SIR PETRONEL Nay, 't is no matter, I care little what they think; he that weighs men's thoughts has his hands full of nothing. A man, in the course of this world, should be like a surgeon's in-
5 strument—work in the wounds of others, and feel nothing himself. The sharper and subtler, the better.

QUICKSILVER As it falls out now, knight, you shall not need to de-vise excuses, or endure her outcries, when she returns; we shall now be gone before, where they cannot reach us.

6 SIR PETRONEL Well, my kind compeer, you have now the assurance we both can make you; let me now entreat you, the money we agreed on may be brought to the Blue Anchor, near to Billings-gate, by six o'clock; where I and my chief friends, bound for this voyage, will with feasts attend you.

7 SECURITY The money, my most honourable compeer, shall without fail observe your appointed hour.

SIR PETRONEL Thanks, my dear gossip. I must now impart
To your approved love a loving secret,
As one on whom my life doth more rely
In friendly trust than any man alive.
8 Nor shall you be the chosen secretary
Of my affections for affection only:
For I protest (if God bless my return)
To make you partner in my actions' gain
As deeply as if you had ventured with me
9 Half my expenses. Know then, honest gossip,

I have enjoyed with such divine contentment 1
A gentlewoman's bed, whom you well know,
That I shall ne'er enjoy this tedious voyage,
Nor live the least part of the time it asketh,
Without her presence; so I thirst and hunger
To taste the dear feast of her company.
And if the hunger and the thirst you vow, 2
As my sworn gossip, to my wished good
Be (as I know it is) unfeigned and firm,
Do me an easy favour in your power.

SECURITY   Be sure, brave gossip, all that I can do,
To my best nerve, is wholly at your service: 3
Who is the woman, first, that is your friend?

SIR PETRONEL   The woman is your learned counsel's wife,
The lawyer, Master Bramble; whom would you
Bring out this even in honest neighbourhood,
To take his leave with you of me your gossip,
I, in the meantime, will send this my friend 4
Home to his house, to bring his wife disguised,
Before his face, into our company;
For love hath made her look for such a wile
To free her from his tyrannous jealousy.
And I would take this course before another, 5
In stealing her away to make us sport,
And gull his circumspection the more grossly.
And I am sure that no man like yourself
Hath credit with him to entice his jealousy
To so long stay abroad as may give time
To her enlargement in such safe disguise. 6

SECURITY   A pretty, pithy and most pleasant project!
Who would not strain a point of neighbourhood
For such a point-device, that, as the ship
Of famous Draco went about the world,
Will wind about the lawyer, compassing 7
The world himself; he hath it in his arms,
And that's enough for him without his wife.
A lawyer is ambitious, and his head
Cannot be praised nor raised too high,
With any fork of highest knavery.
I'll go fetch her straight. [*Exits*] 8

SIR PETRONEL   So, so. Now, Frank, go thou home to his house,

famous Draco: Sir Francis Drake, who returned from his circum-
navigation in 1581. His ship *The Golden Hind* was laid up in the
Thames at Deptford.

1   Stead of his lawyer's, and bring his wife hither,
     Who, just like to the lawyer's wife, is prisoned
     With his stern usurous jealousy, which could never
     Be overreached thus but with overreaching.

     SECURITY [*enters*]   And, Master Francis, watch you th' instant time
2   To enter with his exit: 't will be rare,
     Two fine horned beasts—a camel and a lawyer! [*Exits*]

     QUICKSILVER   How the old villain joys in villany!

     SECURITY [*enters*]   And hark you, gossip, when you have her here,
     Have your boat ready, ship her to your ship
3   With utmost haste, lest Master Bramble stay you.
     To o'erreach that head that outreacheth all heads,
     'T is a trick rampant! 'T is a very quiblin!
     I hope this harvest to pitch cart with lawyers,
     Their heads will be so forked. This sly touch
     Will get apes to invent a number such. [*Exits*]
4
     QUICKSILVER   Was ever rascal honeyed so with poison?
     He that delights in slavish avarice,
     Is apt to joy in every sort of vice.
     Well, I'll go fetch his wife, whilst he the lawyer's.

5   SIR PETRONEL   But stay, Frank, let's think how we may disguise
     her upon this sudden.

     QUICKSILVER   God's me, there's the mischief! But, hark you, here's
     an excellent device; 'fore God, a rare one! I will carry her a sail-
     or's gown and cap, and cover her, and a player's beard.

6   SIR PETRONEL   And what upon her head?

     QUICKSILVER   I tell you, a sailor's cap! 'S light, God forgive me,
     what kind of figent memory have you?

     SIR PETRONEL   Nay, then, what kind of figent wit hast thou?
     A sailor's cap? How shall she put it off
7   When thou present'st her to our company?

     QUICKSILVER   Tush, man, for that, makes her a saucy sailor.

     SIR PETRONEL   Tush, tush, 't is no fit sauce for such sweet mutton!
     I know not what t' advise.

8   SECURITY [*enters with his wife's gown*]   Knight, knight, a rare de-
     vice!

     SIR PETRONEL   'S wounds, yet again!

     QUICKSILVER   What stratagem have you now?

9   SECURITY   The best that ever! You talked of disguising?

SIR PETRONEL   Ay, marry, gossip, that's our present care.   1

SECURITY   Cast care away then; here's the best device
For plain security (for I am no better)
I think, that ever lived: here's my wife's gown,
Which you may put upon the lawyer's wife,
And which I brought you, sir, for two great reasons;   2
One is, that Master Bramble may take hold
Of some suspicion that it is my wife,
And gird me so, perhaps, with his law-wit;
The other (which is policy indeed)
Is that my wife may now be tied at home,
Having no more but her old gown abroad,   3
And not show me a quirk, while I firk others.
Is not this rare?

BOTH   The best that ever was.

SECURITY   Am I not born to furnish gentlemen?   4

SIR PETRONEL   O my dear gossip!

SECURITY   Well, hold, Master Francis! Watch when the lawyer's
out, and put it in. And now I will go fetch him. [*Does not go.*]

QUICKSILVER [*aside*]   O my dad! He goes, as 't were the devil, to   5
fetch the lawyer; and devil shall he be, if horns will make him.

SIR PETRONEL   Why, how now, gossip? Why stay you there mus-
ing?

SECURITY   A toy, a toy runs in my head, i' faith!   6

QUICKSILVER   A pox of that head! Is there more toys yet?

SIR PETRONEL   What is it, pray thee, gossip?

SECURITY   Why sir, what if you should slip away now with my
wife's best gown, I having no security for it?   7

QUICKSILVER   For that, I hope, dad, you will take our words.

SECURITY   Ay, by th' mass, your word! That's a proper staff
For wise Security to lean upon!
But 't is no matter, once I'll trust my name
On your cracked credits; let it take no shame.   8
Fetch the wench, Frank. [*Exits*]

QUICKSILVER   I'll wait upon you, sir,
And fetch you over, you were ne'er so fetched.
Go to the tavern, knight; your followers
Dare not be drunk, I think, before their captain. [*Exits*]   9

1   SIR PETRONEL   Would I might lead them to no hotter service
Till our Virginian gold were in our purses! [*Exits*]

Scene Three

2

[*Enter* SEAGULL, SPENDALL, *and* SCAPETHRIFT, *in the tavern, with a*
DRAWER.]

SEAGULL   Come, drawer, pierce your neatest hogsheads, and let's
have cheer, not fit for your Billingsgate tavern, but for our Vir-
3   ginian colonel; he will be here instantly.

DRAWER   You shall have all things fit, sir; please you have any
more wine?

SPENDALL   More wine, slave? Whether we drink it or no, spill it,
and draw more.

4

SCAPETHRIFT   Fill all the pots in your house with all sorts of liquor, and let 'em wait on us here like soldiers in their pewter
coats; and though we do not employ them now, yet we will maintain 'em till we do.

5   DRAWER   Said like an honourable captain; you shall have all you
can command, sir. [*Exits*]

SEAGULL   Come, boys, Virginia longs till we share the rest of her
maidenhead.

SPENDALL   Why, is she inhabited already with any English?

6   SEAGULL   A whole country of English is there, man, bred of those
that were left there in '79. They have married with the Indians,
and make 'em bring forth as beautiful faces as any we have in
England; and therefore the Indians are so in love with 'em, that
all the treasure they have they lay at their feet.

7   SCAPETHRIFT   But is there such treasure there, captain, as I have
heard?

SEAGULL   I tell thee, gold is more plentiful there than copper is
with us; and for as much red copper as I can bring, I'll have
thrice the weight in gold. Why, man, all their dripping pans and
8   their chamber pots are pure gold; and all the chains with which
they chain up their streets are massy gold; all the prisoners they

'79: In fact, the first colony was not established until 1585, planted
by Sir Richard Greville.
    all their dripping pans . . . : The passage echoes Sir Thomas More's
Utopia, English version 1551.

take are fettered in gold; and for rubies and diamonds, they go 1
forth on holidays and gather 'em by the seashore to hang on their
children's coats and stick in their caps, as commonly as our children wear saffron-gilt brooches and groats with holes in 'em.

SCAPETHRIFT   And is it a pleasant country withal?

SEAGULL   As ever the sun shined on; temperate and full of all sorts 2
of excellent viands; wild boar is as common there as our tamest
bacon is here; venison as mutton. And then you shall live freely
there, without sergeants, or courtiers, or lawyers, or intelligencers,
only a few industrious Scots, perhaps, who, indeed, are dispersed
over the face of the whole earth. But as for them, there are no 3
greater friends to Englishmen and England, when they are out on
't, in the world than they are. And for my own part, I would a
hundred thousand of 'em were there, for we are all one country-
men now, ye know, and we should find ten times more comfort
of them there than we do here. Then for your means to advancement there, it is simple, and not preposterously mixed. You may 4
be an alderman there, and never be a scavenger; you may be a
nobleman, and never be a slave. You may come to preferment
enough, and never be a pander; to riches and fortune enough, and
have never the more villany nor the less wit.

SPENDALL   God's me! And how far is it thither? 5

SEAGULL   Some six weeks' sail, no more, with any indifferent good
wind. And if I get to any part of the coast of Africa, I'll sail
thither with any wind; or when I come to Cape Finisterre, there's
a foreright wind continual wafts us till we come at Virginia. See,
our colonel's come. 6

[*Enter* SIR PETRONEL, *with his* FOLLOWERS.]

SIR PETRONEL   Well met, good Captain Seagull, and my noble gentlemen! Now the sweet hour of our freedom is at hand. Come,
drawer, fill us some carouses, and prepare us for the mirth that
will be occasioned presently. Here will be a pretty wench, gentle- 7
men, that will bear us company all our voyage.

SEAGULL   Whatsoever she be, here's to her health, noble Colonel,
both with cap and knee.

SIR PETRONEL   Thanks, kind Captain Seagull! She's one I love
dearly, and must not be known till we be free from all that know 8
us. And so, gentlemen, here's to her health!

ALL   Let it come, worthy Colonel. We do hunger and thirst for it.

with cap and knee: a health cup, drunk standing bareheaded and then
kneeling.

1   SIR PETRONEL   Afore heaven, you have hit the phrase of one that her presence will touch from the foot to the forehead, if ye knew it.

SPENDALL   Why, then, we will join his forehead with her health, sir; and, Captain Scapethrift, here's to 'em both!

2   [ALL *kneel and drink. Enter* SECURITY *and* BRAMBLE.]

SECURITY   See, see, Master Bramble, 'fore heaven, their voyage cannot but prosper! They are o' their knees for success to it.

BRAMBLE   And they pray to god Bacchus.

3   SECURITY   God save my brave colonel, with all his tall captains and corporals. See, sir, my worshipful learned counsel, Master Bramble, is come to take his leave of you.

SIR PETRONEL   Worshipful Master Bramble, how far do you draw
4   us into the sweetbrier of your kindness! Come, Captain Seagull, another health to this rare Bramble, that hath never a prick about him.

SEAGULL   I pledge his most smooth disposition, sir. Come, Master Security, bend your supporters, and pledge this notorious health here.

5   SECURITY   Bend you yours likewise, Master Bramble; for it is you shall pledge me.

SEAGULL   Not so, Master Security; he must not pledge his own health.

6   SECURITY   No, Master Captain?

[*Enter* QUICKSILVER, *with* WINNY *disguised*.]

Why, then, here's one is fitly come to do him that honour.

7   QUICKSILVER   Here's the gentlewoman your cousin, sir, whom, with much entreaty, I have brought to take her leave of you in a tavern; ashamed whereof, you must pardon her if she put not off her mask.

SIR PETRONEL   Pardon me, sweet cousin; my kind desire to see you
8   before I went, made me so importunate to entreat your presence here.

SECURITY   How now, Master Francis, have you honoured this presence with a fair gentlewoman?

QUICKSILVER   Pray, sir, take you no notice of her, for she will not
9   be known to you.

SECURITY But my learned counsel, Master Bramble here, I hope 1
may know her.

QUICKSILVER No more than you, sir, at this time; his learning
must pardon her.

SECURITY Well, God pardon her for my part, and I do, I'll be
sworn; and so, Master Francis, here's to all that are going east- 2
ward tonight towards Cuckold's Haven; and so to the health of
Master Bramble.

QUICKSILVER I pledge it, sir. [*Kneels*] Hath it gone round, Captains?

SEAGULL It has, sweet Frank; and the round closes with thee. 3

QUICKSILVER Well, sir, here's to all eastward and toward cuckolds,
and so to famous Cuckold's Haven, so fatally remembered.
[*Rises*]

SIR PETRONEL [*to* WINIFRED] Nay, pray thee, coz, weep not. Gos- 4
sip Security!

SECURITY Ay, my brave gossip!

SIR PETRONEL A word, I beseech you, sir! Our friend, Mistress
Bramble here, is so dissolved in tears that she drowns the whole
mirth of our meeting. Sweet gossip, take her aside and comfort 5
her.

SECURITY [*aside to* WINIFRED] Pity of all true love, Mistress
Bramble! What, weep you to enjoy your love? What's the cause,
lady? Is 't because your husband is so near, and your heart yearns
to have a little abused him? Alas, alas, the offence is too common 6
to be respected! So great a grace hath seldom chanced to so unthankful a woman, to be rid of an old jealous dotard, to enjoy the
arms of a loving young knight, that, when your prickless Bramble
is withered with grief of your loss, will make you flourish afresh
in the bed of a lady.

7

DRAWER [*enters*] Sir Petronel, here's one of your watermen come
to tell you it will be flood these three hours; and that 't will be
dangerous going against the tide, for the sky is overcast, and there
was a porpoise even now seen at London Bridge, which is always
the messenger of tempests, he says.

8

SIR PETRONEL A porpoise! What's that to th' purpose? Charge
him, if he love his life, to attend us; can we not reach Blackwall
(where my ship lies) against the tide, and in spite of tempests?
Captains and gentlemen, we'll begin a new ceremony at the beginning of our voyage, which I believe will be followed of all future
adventurers.

9

1 SEAGULL   What's that, good Colonel?

SIR PETRONEL   This, Captain Seagull. We'll have our provided supper brought aboard Sir Francis Drake's ship, that hath compassed
the world; where, with full cups and banquets, we will do sacrifice for a prosperous voyage. My mind gives me that some good
2 spirits of the waters should haunt the desert ribs of her, and be
auspicious to all that honour her memory, and will with like or-
gies enter their voyages.

SEAGULL   Rarely conceited! One health more to this motion, and
aboard to perform it. He that will not this night be drunk, may he
never be sober.
3

[*They compass in* WINIFRED, *dance the drunken round, and drink
carouses.*]

BRAMBLE   Sir Petronel and his honourable Captains, in these
4 young services we old servitors may be spared. We only came to
take our leaves, and with one health to you all, I'll be bold to do
so. Here, neighbour Security, to the health of Sir Petronel and all
his captains.

SECURITY   You must bend then, Master Bramble;

5 [*They kneel.*]

so, now I am for you. I have one corner of my brain, I hope, fit
to bear one carouse more. Here, lady, to you that are encom-
passed there, and are ashamed of our company. Ha, ha, ha! By
my troth, my learned counsel, Master Bramble, my mind runs so
6 of Cuckold's Haven tonight, that my head runs over with admiration.

BRAMBLE [*aside*]   But is not that your wife, neighbour?

SECURITY [*aside*]   No, by my troth, Master Bramble. Ha, ha, ha! A
pox of all Cuckold's Haven, I say!
7

BRAMBLE [*aside*]   O' my faith, her garments are exceeding like
your wife's.

SECURITY [*aside*]   *Cucullus non facit monachum,* my learned counsel; all are not cuckolds that seem so, nor all seem not that are so.
8 Give me your hand, my learned counsel; you and I will sup somewhere else than at Sir Francis Drake's ship tonight.—Adieu, my
noble gossip!

BRAMBLE   Good fortune, brave Captains; fair skies God send ye!

Cucullus non facit monachum: The hood does not make the monk;
a traditional Latin tag.

ALL Farewell, my hearts, farewell! 1

SIR PETRONEL Gossip, laugh no more at Cuckold's Haven, gossip.

SECURITY I have done, I have done, sir; will you lead, Master Bramble? Ha, ha, ha!

[*Exits with* BRAMBLE.] 2

SIR PETRONEL Captain Seagull, charge a boat!

ALL A boat, a boat, a boat! [*Exeunt*]

DRAWER Y' are in a proper taking, indeed, to take a boat, especially at this time of night, and against tide and tempest. They say 3 yet, "drunken men never take harm." This night will try the truth of that proverb. [*Exits*]

Scene Four 4

[*Outside Security's house.*]

SECURITY [*enters*] What, Winny! Wife, I say! Out of doors at this time! Where should I seek the gadfly? Billingsgate, Billingsgate, Billingsgate! She's gone with the knight, she's gone with the 5 knight! Woe be to thee, Billingsgate! A boat, a boat, a boat! A full hundred marks for a boat! [*Exits*]

ACT FOUR

Scene One

1 [*Enter* SLITGUT, *with a pair of ox horns, discovering Cuckold's Haven above.*]

SLITGUT All hail, fair haven of married men only, for there are none but married men cuckolds! For my part, I presume not to arrive here, but in my master's behalf (a poor butcher of East-

2 cheap) who sends me to set up (in honour of Saint Luke) these necessary ensigns of his homage. And up I got this morning, thus early, to get up to the top of this famous tree, that is all fruit and no leaves, to advance this crest of my master's occupation. Up then; heaven and Saint Luke bless me, that I be not blown into the

3 Thames as I climb, with this furious tempest. 'S light, I think the devil be abroad, in likeness of a storm, to rob me of my horns! Hark how he roars! Lord, what a coil the Thames keeps! She bears some unjust burthen, I believe, that she kicks and curvets thus to cast it. Heaven bless all honest passengers that are upon her back now; for the bit is out of her mouth, I see, and she will

4 run away with 'em! So, so, I think I have made it look the right way; it runs against London Bridge, as it were, even full butt. And now let me discover from this lofty prospect, what pranks the rude Thames plays in her desperate lunacy. O me, here's a boat has been cast away hard by! Alas, alas, see one of her pas-

5 sengers labouring for his life to land at this haven here! Pray heaven he may recover it! His next land is even just under me; hold out yet a little, whatsoever thou art; pray, and take a good heart to thee. 'T is a man; take a man's heart to thee; yet a little further, get up o' thy legs, man; now 't is shallow enough. So, so, so! Alas, he's down again! Hold thy wind, father; 't is a man in a

6 nightcap. So! Now he's got up again; now he's past the worst; yet, thanks be to heaven, he comes toward me pretty and strongly.

SECURITY [*enters without his hat, in a nightcap, wet band, etc.*] Heaven, I beseech thee, how have I offended thee! Where am I cast ashore now, that I may go a righter way home by land? Let me see. O, I am scarce able to look about me! Where is there

7 any seamark that I am acquainted withal?

SLITGUT Look up, father; are you acquainted with this mark?

in honour of St. Luke: On St. Luke's day a fair was held annually at Greenwich at which all manner of objects made of horn were sold, supposedly to commemorate an exploit of King John with a miller's wife.

48

SECURITY   What! Landed at Cuckold's Haven! Hell and damnation!   1
I will run back and drown myself. [*He falls down.*]

SLITGUT   Poor man, how weak he is! The weak water has washed
away his strength.

SECURITY   Landed at Cuckold's Haven! If it had not been to die
twenty times alive, I should never have scaped death! I will never   2
arise more; I will grovel here and eat dirt till I be choked; I will
make the gentle earth do that which the cruel water has denied
me!

SLITGUT   Alas, good father, be not so desperate! Rise, man; if you
will, I'll come presently and lead you home.   3

SECURITY   Home! Shall I make any know my home, that has
known me thus abroad? How low shall I crouch away, that no
eye may see me? I will creep on the earth while I live, and never
look heaven in the face more. [*Exits creeping.*]

SLITGUT   What young planet reigns now, trow, that old men are so   4
foolish? What desperate young swaggerer would have been
abroad such a weather as this upon the water? Ay me, see another remnant of this unfortunate shipwrack, or some other! A
woman, i' faith, a woman! Though it be almost at St. Katharine's,
I discern it to be a woman, for all her body is above the water,   5
and her clothes swim about her most handsomely. O, they bear
her up most bravely! Has not a woman reason to love the taking
up of her clothes the better while she lives, for this? Alas, how
busy the rude Thames is about her! A pox o' that wave! It will
drown her, i' faith, 't will drown her! Cry God mercy, she has
scaped it, I thank heaven she has scaped it! O how she swims like   6
a mermaid! Some vigilant body look out and save her. That's well
said; just where the priest fell in, there's one sets down a ladder,
and goes to take her up. God's blessing o' thy heart, boy! Now
take her up in thy arms and to bed with her. She's up, she's up!
She's a beautiful woman, I warrant her; the billows durst not devour her.   7

[*Enter the* DRAWER *from the tavern with* WINIFRED.]

DRAWER   How fare you now, lady?

WINIFRED   Much better, my good friend, than I wish; as one des-   8
perate of her fame, now my life is preserved.

DRAWER   Comfort yourself: that Power that preserved you from
death can likewise defend you from infamy, howsoever you deserve it. Were not you one that took boat late this night with a
knight and other gentlemen at Billingsgate?   9

1   WINIFRED   Unhappy that I am, I was.

    DRAWER   I am glad it was my good hap to come down thus far
    after you, to a house of my friend's here in St. Katherine's, since
    I am now happily made a mean to your rescue from the ruthless
    tempest, which (when you took boat) was so extreme, and the
2   gentleman that brought you forth so desperate and unsober, that I
    feared long ere this I should hear of your shipwrack, and there-
    fore (with little other reason) made thus far this way. And this I
    must tell you, since perhaps you may make use of it, there was
    left behind you at our tavern, brought by a porter (hired by the
    young gentleman that brought you), a gentlewoman's gown, hat,
3   stockings, and shoes; which, if they be yours, and you please to
    shift you, taking a hard bed here in this house of my friend, I will
    presently go fetch you.

    WINIFRED   Thanks, my good friend, for your more than good
    news. The gown with all things bound with it are mine; which if
    you please to fetch as you have promised, I will boldly receive the
4   kind favour you have offered till your return; entreating you, by
    all the good you have done in preserving me hitherto, to let none
    take knowledge of what favour you do me, or where such a one
    as I am bestowed, lest you incur me much more damage in my
    fame than you have done me pleasure in preserving my life.

5   DRAWER   Come in, lady, and shift yourself; resolve that nothing
    but your own pleasure shall be used in your discovery.

    WINIFRED   Thank you, good friend; the time may come, I shall re-
    quite you.

6   [Exeunt]

    SLITGUT   See, see, see! I hold my life, there's some other a-taking
    up at Wapping now! Look, what a sort of people cluster about
    the gallows there! In good troth it is so. O me, a fine young gen-
    tleman! What, and taken up at the gallows! Heaven grant he be
7   not one day taken down there! O' my life, it is ominous! Well, he
    is delivered for the time. I see the people have all left him; yet
    will I keep my prospect awhile, to see if any more have been
    shipwracked.

    QUICKSILVER [enters bareheaded]   Accursed that ever I was saved
        or born!
8   How fatal is my sad arrival here!
    As if the stars and Providence spake to me,
    And said, "The drift of all unlawful courses
    (Whatever end they dare propose themselves
    In frame of their licentious policies)
9   In the firm order of just Destiny

They are the ready highways to our ruins."   1
I know not what to do; my wicked hopes
Are, with this tempest, torn up by the roots.
O, which way shall I bend my desperate steps,
In which unsufferable shame and misery
Will not attend them? I will walk this bank,
And see if I can meet the other relics   2
Of our poor shipwracked crew, or hear of them.
The knight—alas!—was so far gone with wine,
And th' other three, that I refused their boat,
And took the hapless woman in another,
Who cannot but be sunk, whatever Fortune   3
Hath wrought upon the others' desperate lives. [*Exits*]

[*Enter* SIR PETRONEL, *and* SEAGULL, *bareheaded.*]

SIR PETRONEL   Zounds, Captain, I tell thee, we are cast up o' the coast of France! 'S foot, I am not drunk still, I hope! Dost remember where we were last night?   4

SEAGULL   No, by my troth, knight, not I; but methinks we have been a horrible while upon the water and in the water.

SIR PETRONEL   Ay me, we are undone for ever! Hast any money about thee?   5

SEAGULL   Not a penny, by heaven!

SIR PETRONEL   Not a penny betwixt us, and cast ashore in France!

SEAGULL   Faith, I cannot tell that; my brains nor mine eyes are not mine own yet.

     6

[*Enter* TWO GENTLEMEN.]

SIR PETRONEL   'S foot, wilt not believe me? I know 't by th' elevation of the pole, and by the altitude and latitude of the climate. See, here comes a couple of French gentlemen; I knew we were in France; dost thou think our Englishmen are so Frenchified that   7 a man knows not whether he be in France or in England, when he sees 'em? What shall we do? We must e'en to 'em, and entreat some relief of 'em. Life is sweet, and we have no other means to relieve our lives now but their charities.

SEAGULL   Pray you, do you beg on 'em then; you can speak   8 French.

SIR PETRONEL   Monsieur, plaist-il d'avoir pitié de nostre grande infortune. Je suis un povre chevalier d'Angleterre qui a souffri l'infortune de naufrage.

FIRST GENTLEMAN   Un povre chevalier d'Angleterre?   9

1   SIR PETRONEL   Oui, monsieur, il est trop vray; mais vous scavez
    bien nous sommes toutes subject à fortune.

    SECOND GENTLEMAN   A poor knight of England? A poor knight of
    Windsor, are you not? Why speak you this broken French, when
    y' are a whole Englishman? On what coast are you, think you?

2   SIR PETRONEL   On the coast of France, sir.

    FIRST GENTLEMAN   On the coast of Dogs, sir; y' are i' th' Isle o'
    Dogs, I tell you. I see y' 'ave been washed in the Thames here,
    and I believe ye were drowned in a tavern before, or else you
    would never have took boat in such a dawning as this was. Fare-
3   well, farewell; we will not know you for shaming you.—I ken the
    man weel; he's one of my thirty-pound knights.

    SECOND GENTLEMAN   No, no, this is he that stole his knighthood
    o' the grant day for four pound, giving to a page all the money in
    's purse, I wot well.

4   [*Exeunt* GENTLEMEN.]

    SEAGULL   Death, Colonel, I knew you were overshot!

    SIR PETRONEL   Sure I think now, indeed, Captain Seagull, we were
    something overshot.

5   [*Enter* QUICKSILVER.]

    What, my sweet Frank Quicksilver! Dost thou survive to rejoice
    me? But what! Nobody at thy heels, Frank? Ay me, what is be-
    come of poor Mistress Security?

6   QUICKSILVER   Faith, gone quite from her name, as she is from her
    fame, I think; I left her to the mercy of the water.

    SEAGULL   Let her go, let her go! Let us go to our ship at Blackwall,
    and shift us.

    SIR PETRONEL   Nay, by my troth, let our clothes rot upon us, and
7   let us rot in them; twenty to one our ship is attached by this time!
    If we set her not under sail this last tide, I never looked for any
    other. Woe, woe is me, what shall become of us? The last money
    we could make, the greedy Thames has devoured; and if our ship
    be attached, there is no hope can relieve us.

8   QUICKSILVER   'S foot, knight, what an unknightly faintness trans-

    A poor knight of Windsor: Retired officers, on pension, who lived in
    the Royal castle at Windsor and obviously poor since the term soon
    came to mean a beggar. See *The Lady of Pleasure,* Act V, Sc. i.
    I ken the man weel: Delivered in a Scots accent: a quip at the
    practise of James I.

ports thee! Let our ship sink, and all the world that's without us
be taken from us, I hope I have some tricks in this brain of mine
shall not let us perish.

SEAGULL   Well said, Frank, i' faith! O my nimble-spirited Quicksilver! 'Fore God, would thou hadst been our colonel!

SIR PETRONEL   I like his spirit rarely; but I see no means he has to
support that spirit.

QUICKSILVER   Go to, knight! I have more means than thou art
aware of. I have not lived amongst goldsmiths and goldmakers all
this while, but I have learned something worthy of my time with
'em. And not to let thee stink where thou stand'st, knight, I'll let
thee know some of my skill presently.

SEAGULL   Do, good Frank, I beseech thee!

QUICKSILVER   I will blanch copper so cunningly that it shall endure all proofs but the test; it shall endure malleation, it shall
have the ponderosity of Luna, and the tenacity of Luna, by no
means friable.

SIR PETRONEL   'S light, where learn'st thou these terms, trow?

QUICKSILVER   Tush, knight, the terms of this art every ignorant
quacksalver is perfect in! But I'll tell you how yourself shall
blanch copper thus cunningly. Take arsenic, otherwise called
realga (which, indeed, is plain ratsbane); sublime 'em three or
four times, then take the sublimate of this realga, and put 'em
into a glass, into chymia, and let 'em have a convenient decoction
natural, four and twenty hours, and he will become perfectly
fixed; then take this fixed powder, and project him upon well-purged copper, *et habebis magisterium.*

BOTH   Excellent Frank, let us hug thee!

QUICKSILVER   Nay, this I will do besides: I'll take you off twelvepence from every angel, with a kind of acqua-fortis, and never
deface any part of the image.

SIR PETRONEL   But then it will want weight?

QUICKSILVER   You shall restore that thus: take your sal achyme
prepared and your distilled urine, and let your angels lie in it but
four and twenty hours, and they shall have their perfect weight
again. Come on, now; I hope this is enough to put some spirit
into the livers of you; I'll infuse more another time. We have saluted the proud air long enough with our bare sconces. Now will

Luna: The alchemist's term for silver. This passage forcibly suggests
Jonson's hand. (See *The Alchemist.*)
et habebis magisterium: And you shall have the philosopher's stone.
(In fact you would have no more than false silver.)

I have you to a wench's house of mine at London, there make
shift to shift us, and after, take such fortunes as the stars shall
assign us.

BOTH   Notable Frank, we will ever adore thee!

[*Exeunt. Enter* DRAWER, *with* WINIFRED, *new-attired.*]

WINIFRED   Now, sweet friend, you have brought me near enough
your tavern, which I desired I might with some colour be seen
near, inquiring for my husband, who, I must tell you, stole thither
the last night with my wet gown we have left at your friends's,—
which, to continue your former honest kindness, let me pray you
to keep close from the knowledge of any; and so, with all vow of
your requital, let me now entreat you to leave me to my woman's
wit and fortune.

DRAWER   All shall be done you desire; and so all the fortune you
can wish for attend you. [*Exits*]

SECURITY [*enters*]   I will once more to this unhappy tavern before I
shift one rag of me more; that I may there know what is left behind, and what news of their passengers. I have bought me a hat
and band with the little money I had about me, and made the
streets a little leave staring at my nightcap.

WINIFRED   O my dear husband! Where have you been tonight? All
night abroad at taverns! Rob me of my garments, and fare as one
run away from me! Alas, is this seemly for a man of your credit,
of your age, and affection to your wife?

SECURITY   What should I say? How miraculously sorts this! Was
not I at home, and called thee last night?

WINIFRED   Yes, sir, the harmless sleep you broke; and my answer
to you would have witnessed it, if you had had the patience to
have stayed and answered me: but your so sudden retreat made
me imagine you were gone to Master Bramble's, and so rested patient and hopeful of your coming again, till this, your unbelieved
absence, brought me abroad with no less than wonder, to seek you
where the false knight had carried you.

SECURITY   Villain and monster that I was, how have I abused thee!
I was suddenly gone indeed; for my sudden jealousy transferred
me. I will say no more but this: dear wife, I suspected thee.

WINIFRED   Did you suspect me?

SECURITY   Talk not of it, I beseech thee; I am ashamed to imagine
it. I will home, I will home; and every morning on my knees ask
thee heartily forgiveness.

[*Exeunt*]

SLITGUT   Now will I descend my honourable prospect, the farthest   1
seeing seamark of the world; no marvel, then, if I could see two
miles about me. I hope the red tempest's anger be now over-
blown, which sure, I think, Heaven sent as a punishment for pro-
faning holy Saint Luke's memory with so ridiculous a custom.
Thou dishonest satire, farewell to honest married men; farewell to
all sorts and degrees of thee! Farewell, thou horn of hunger, that   2
call'st th' Inns o' Court to their manger! Farewell, thou horn of
abundance, that adornest the headsmen of the commonwealth!
Farewell, thou horn of direction, that is the city lanthorn! Farewell, thou horn of pleasure, the ensign of the huntsman! Farewell,
thou horn of destiny, th' ensign of the married man! Farewell,   3
thou horn tree, that bearest nothing but stone fruit! [*Exits*]

Scene Two

[*A room in Touchstone's house.*]   4

TOUCHSTONE [*enters*]   Ha, sirrah! Thinks my knight adventurer we
can no point of our compass? Do we not know north-north-east,
north-east-and-by-east, east-and-by-north, now plain eastward?
Ha! Have we never heard of Virginia? Nor the Cavallaria? Nor   5
the Colonaria? Can we discover no discoveries? Well, mine errant
Sir Flash, and my runagate Quicksilver, you may drink drunk,
crack cans, hurl away a brown dozen of Monmouth caps or so, in
sea ceremony to your bon voyage; but for reaching any coast,
save the coast of Kent or Essex, with this tide, or with this fleet,
I'll be your warrant for a Gravesend toast. There's that gone   6
afore will stay your admiral and vice admiral and rear admiral,
were they all (as they are) but one pinnace and under sail, as
well as a remora, doubt it not, and from this sconce, without either powder or shot. Work upon that now! Nay, and you'll show
tricks, we'll vie with you a little. My daughter, his lady, was sent
eastward by land, to a castle of his i' the air (in what region I   7
know not) and, as I hear, was glad to take up her lodging in her
coach, she and her two waiting women, her maid, and her
mother, like three snails in a shell, and the coachman a-top on
'em, I think. Since they have all found the way back again by   8

Farewell, thou horn . . . : Slitgut marshalls all the significances of
the horn, the dinner horn, cornucopia (and its association of cuckoldry),
the signpost (landhorn), the hunting horn, and again the cuckold's
horn. His last farewell is to the tree from which he has just climbed down.
   Cavallaria, Colonaria: Latin law terms; land tenure by a knight and
by a simple colonist.

1   Weeping Cross; but I'll not see 'em. And for two on 'em, madam and her malkin, they are like to bite o' the bridle for William, as the poor horses have done all this while that hurried 'em, or else go graze o' the common. So should my Dame Touchstone too; but she has been my cross these thirty years, and I'll now keep her to fright away sprites, i' faith. I wonder I hear no news of my

2   son Golding. He was sent for to the Guildhall this morning betimes, and I marvel at the matter; if I had not laid up comfort and hope in him, I should grow desperate of all. See he is come i' my thought! How now, son? What news at the Court of Aldermen?

3   GOLDING [*enters*]   Troth, sir, an accident somewhat strange, else it hath little in it worth the reporting.

TOUCHSTONE   What? It is not borrowing of money, then?

GOLDING   No, sir; it hath pleased the worshipful commoners of the city to take me one i' their number at presentation of the in-

4   quest—

TOUCHSTONE   Ha!

GOLDING   And the alderman of the ward wherein I dwell to appoint me his deputy—

5   TOUCHSTONE   How?

GOLDING   In which place I have had an oath ministered me, since I went.

TOUCHSTONE   Now, my dear and happy son, let me kiss thy new worship, and a little boast mine own happiness in thee. What a for-

6   tune was it (or rather my judgment, indeed) for me, first, to see that in his disposition which a whole city so conspires to second! Ta'en into the livery of his company the first day of his freedom! Now (not a week married) chosen commoner and alderman's deputy in a day! Note but the reward of a thrifty course. The wonder of his time! Well, I will honour Master Alderman for this

7   act (as becomes me) and shall think the better of the Common Council's wisdom and worship while I live, for thus meeting, or but coming after me, in the opinion of his desert. Forward, my sufficient son, and as this is the first, so esteem it the least step to that high and prime honour that expects thee.

8   GOLDING   Sir, as I was not ambitious of this, so I covet no higher place; it hath dignity enough, if it will but save me from contempt; and I had rather my bearing in this or any other office

bite o' the bridle: Champ the bit, probably proverbial.
inquest: Here, nominating committee.

should add worth to it, than the place give the least opinion to me. 1

TOUCHSTONE Excellently spoken! This modest answer of thine blushes, as if it said, I will wear scarlet shortly. Worshipful son! I cannot contain myself, I must tell thee; I hope to see thee one o' the monuments of our city, and reckoned among her worthies to 2 be remembered the same day with the Lady Ramsey and grave Gresham, when the famous fable of Whittington and his puss shall be forgotten, and thou and thy acts become the posies for hospitals; when thy name shall be written upon conduits, and thy deeds played i' thy lifetime by the best companies of actors, and be called their get-penny. This I divine; this I prophesy. 3

GOLDING Sir, engage not your expectation farther than my abilities will answer; I, that know mine own strengths, fear 'em; and there is so seldom a loss in promising the least, that commonly it brings with it a welcome deceit. I have other news for you, sir.

TOUCHSTONE None more welcome, I am sure! 4

GOLDING They have their degree of welcome, I dare affirm. The Colonel and all his company, this morning putting forth drunk from Billingsgate, had like to have been cast away o' this side Greenwich; and (as I have intelligence by a false brother) are come dropping to town like so many masterless men, i' their 5 doublets and hose, without hat, or cloak, or any other—

TOUCHSTONE A miracle! The justice of Heaven! Where are they? Let's go presently and lay for 'em.

GOLDING I have done that already, sir, both by constables and other officers, who shall take 'em at their old Anchor, and with 6 less tumult or suspicion than if yourself were seen in 't, under colour of a great press that is now abroad, and they shall here be brought afore me.

TOUCHSTONE Prudent and politic son! Disgrace 'em all that ever thou canst; their ship I have already arrested. How to my wish it 7 falls out, that thou hast the place of a justicer upon 'em! I am partly glad of the injury done to me, that thou mayst punish it. Be severe i' thy place, like a new officer o' the first quarter, unreflected. You hear how our lady is come back with her train from the invisible castle? 8

will wear scarlet: That is, wear the scarlet robes of an alderman.
Lady Ramsey: Wife of Sir Thomas Ramsey, Lord Mayor of London. 1577.
Gresham: See Glossary under EXCHANGE.
o' the first quarter: In his first term of office.

GOLDING   No; where is she?

TOUCHSTONE   Within; but I ha' not seen her yet, nor her mother, who now begins to wish her daughter undubbed, they say, and that she had walked a footpace with her sister. Here they come; stand back.

[*Enter* MISTRESS TOUCHSTONE, GERTRUDE, MILDRED, SINDEFY.]

God save your ladyship, save your good ladyship! Your ladyship is welcome from your enchanted castle, so are your beauteous retinue. I hear your knight errant is travelled on strange adventures. Surely, in my mind, your ladyship hath fished fair and caught a frog, as the saying is.

MISTRESS TOUCHSTONE   Speak to your father, madam, and kneel down.

GERTRUDE   Kneel? I hope I am not brought so low yet; though my knight be run away, and has sold my land, I am a lady still.

TOUCHSTONE   Your ladyship says true, madam; and it is fitter and a greater decorum, that I should curtesy to you that are a knight's wife, and a lady, than you be brought o' your knees to me, who am a poor cullion and your father.

GERTRUDE   Law! My father knows his duty.

MISTRESS TOUCHSTONE   O child!

TOUCHSTONE   And therefore I do desire your ladyship, my good Lady Flash, in all humility, to depart my obscure cottage, and return in quest of your bright and most transparent castle, however presently concealed to mortal eyes. And as for one poor woman of your train here, I will take that order, she shall no longer be a charge unto you, nor help to spend your ladyship; she shall stay at home with me, and not go abroad, not put you to the pawning of an odd coach horse or three wheels, but take part with the Touchstone. If we lack, we will not complain to your ladyship. And so, good madam, with your damosel here, please you to let us see your straight backs in equipage; for truly here is no roost for such chickens as you are, or birds o' your feather, if it like your ladyship.

GERTRUDE   Marry, fist o' your kindness! I thought as much. Come away, Sin, we shall as soon get a fart from a dead man, as a farthing of courtesy here.

MILDRED   O good sister!

GERTRUDE   Sister, sir reverence! Come away, I say, hunger drops out at his nose.

GOLDING   O madam, fair words never hurt the tongue.   1

GERTRUDE   How say you by that? You come out with your gold-
ends now!

MISTRESS TOUCHSTONE   Stay, lady daughter! Good husband!

TOUCHSTONE   Wife, no man loves his fetters, be they made of   2
gold. I list not ha' my head fastened under my child's girdle; as
she has brewed, so let her drink, o' God's name! She went witless
to wedding, now she may go wisely a-begging. It's but honey-
moon yet with her ladyship; she has coach horses, apparel, jewels
yet left; she needs care for no friends, nor take knowledge of father, mother, brother, sister, or anybody. When those are pawned   3
or spent, perhaps we shall return into the list of her acquaintance.

GERTRUDE   I scorn it, i' faith! Come, Sin.

MISTRESS TOUCHSTONE   O madam, why do you provoke your father thus?

                                                                        4

[*Exit* GERTRUDE *with* SINDEFY.]

TOUCHSTONE   Nay, nay; e'en let pride go afore, shame will follow
after, I warrant you. Come, why dost thou weep now? Thou art
not the first good cow hast had an ill calf, I trust.   5

[*Exit* MISTRESS TOUCHSTONE.]

What's the news with that fellow?

                                                                 *   6
[*Enter* CONSTABLE.]

GOLDING   Sir, the knight and your man Quicksilver are without;
will you ha' 'em brought in?

TOUCHSTONE   O by any means!
                                                                        7
[*Exit* CONSTABLE.]

And, son, here's a chair; appear terrible unto 'em on the first in-
terview. Let them behold the melancholy of a magistrate, and
taste the fury of a citizen in office.   8

GOLDING   Why, sir, I can do nothing to 'em, except you charge 'em
with somewhat.

my head fastened under my child's girdle: That is, under my daughter's
orders.

1   TOUCHSTONE   I will charge 'em and recharge 'em, rather than authority should want foil to set it off. [*Offers* GOLDING *a chair.*]

GOLDING   No, good sir, I will not.

TOUCHSTONE   Son, it is your place; by any means—

2   GOLDING   Believe it, I will not, sir.

[*Enter* SIR PETRONEL, QUICKSILVER, CONSTABLE, OFFICERS.]

SIR PETRONEL   How misfortune pursues us still in our misery!

QUICKSILVER   Would it had been my fortune to have been trussed
3   up at Wapping, rather than ever ha' come here!

SIR PETRONEL   Or mine to have famished in the island!

QUICKSILVER   Must Golding sit upon us?

CONSTABLE   You might carry an *M* under your girdle to Master
4   Deputy's worship.

GOLDING   What are those, Master Constable?

CONSTABLE   An' 't please your worship, a couple of masterless men
I pressed for the Low Countries, sir.

GOLDING   Why do you not carry 'em to Bridewell, according to
5   your order, they may be shipped away?

CONSTABLE   An' 't please your worship, one of 'em says he is a
knight; and we thought good to show him to your worship, for
our discharge.

GOLDING   Which is he?
6
CONSTABLE   This, sir!

GOLDING   And what's the other?

CONSTABLE   A knight's fellow, sir, an' 't please you.

GOLDING   What! A knight and his fellow thus accoutred? Where
7   are their hats and feathers, their rapiers and their cloaks?

QUICKSILVER   O they mock us!

CONSTABLE   Nay, truly, sir, they had cast both their feathers and
hats too, before we see 'em. Here's all their furniture, an' 't please
8   you, that we found. They say knights are now to be known without feathers, like cockerels by their spurs, sir.

foil: A goldsmith's metaphor. Foil was used in the setting to set off
the lights of a precious stone.
You might carry an M under your girdle: You might have the civility
to use the title "Master."

GOLDING What are their names, say they? 1

TOUCHSTONE [*aside*] Very well, this! He should not take knowledge of 'em in his place, indeed.

CONSTABLE This is Sir Petronel Flash.

TOUCHSTONE How! 2

CONSTABLE And this, Francis Quicksilver.

TOUCHSTONE Is 't possible? I thought your worship had been gone for Virginia, sir; you are welcome home, sir. Your worship has made a quick return, it seems, and no doubt a good voyage. Nay, pray you be covered, sir. How did your biscuit hold out, sir? 3 Methought I had seen this gentleman afore. Good Master Quicksilver, how a degree to the southward has changed you!

GOLDING Do you know 'em, father?—Forbear your offers a little, you shall be heard anon.

TOUCHSTONE Yes, Master Deputy; I had a small venture with 4 them in the voyage—a thing called a son-in-law, or so. Officers, you may let 'em stand alone, they will not run away; I'll give my word for them. A couple of very honest gentlemen. One of 'em was my prentice, Master Quicksilver here; and when he had two years to serve, kept his whore and his hunting nag, would play his hundred pound at gresco, or primero, as familiarly (and all o' my 5 purse) as any bright piece of crimson on 'em all; had his change-able trunks of apparel standing at livery, with his mare, his chest of perfumed linen, and his bathing tubs, which when I told him of, why he—he was a gentleman, and I a poor Cheapside groom! The remedy was, we must part. Since when, he hath had the gift of gathering up some small parcels of mine, to the value of five 6 hundred pound, dispersed among my customers, to furnish this his Virginian venture; wherein this knight was the chief, Sir Flash —one that married a daughter of mine, ladyfied her, turned two thousand pounds' worth of good land of hers into cash within the first week, bought her a new gown and a coach, sent her to seek 7 her fortune by land, whilst himself prepared for his fortune by sea; took in fresh flesh at Billingsgate, for his own diet, to serve him the whole voyage—the wife of a certain usurer called Secu-rity, who hath been the broker for 'em in all this business. Please, Master Deputy, work upon that now!

GOLDING If my worshipful father have ended. 8

TOUCHSTONE I have, it shall please Master Deputy.

GOLDING Well then, under correction—

TOUCHSTONE [*aside to* GOLDING] Now, son, come over 'em with some fine gird, as thus, "Knight, you shall be encountered, that is, 9

1 had to the Counter," or, "Quicksilver, I will put you into a crucible," or so.

2 GOLDING Sir Petronel Flash, I am sorry to see such flashes as these proceed from a gentleman of your quality and rank; for mine own part, I could wish I could say I could not see them; but such is the misery of magistrates and men in place, that they must not wink at offenders. Take him aside—I will hear you anon, sir.

TOUCHSTONE I like this well, yet; there's some grace i' the knight left—he cries.

3 GOLDING Francis Quicksilver, would God thou hadst turned quacksalver, rather than run into these dissolute and lewd courses! It is a great pity; thou art a proper young man, of an honest and clean face, somewhat near a good one; God hath done his part in thee; but thou hast made too much and been too proud of that face, with the rest of thy body; for maintenance of which in neat and garish attire (only to be looked upon by some

4 light housewives) thou hast prodigally consumed much of thy master's estate; and being by him gently admonished at several times, hast returned thyself haughty and rebellious in thine answers, thund'ring out uncivil comparisons, requiting all his kindness with a coarse and harsh behaviour, never returning thanks for any one benefit, but receiving all as if they had been debts to

5 thee, and no courtesies. I must tell thee, Francis, these are manifest signs of an ill nature; and God doth often punish such pride and outrecuidance with scorn and infamy, which is the worst of misfortune. My worshipful father, what do you please to charge them withal? From the press I will free 'em, Master Constable.

6 CONSTABLE Then I'll leave your worship, sir.

GOLDING No, you may stay; there will be other matters against 'em.

7 TOUCHSTONE Sir, I do charge this gallant, Master Quicksilver, on suspicion of felony; and the knight as being accessory in the receipt of my goods.

QUICKSILVER O God, sir!

8 TOUCHSTONE Hold thy peace, impudent varlet, hold thy peace! With what forehead or face dost thou offer to chop logic with me, having run such a race of riot as thou hast done? Does not the sight of this worshipful man's fortune and temper confound thee, that was thy younger fellow in household, and now come to have the place of a judge upon thee? Dost not observe this? Which of all thy gallants and gamesters, thy swearers and thy swaggerers, will come now to moan thy misfortune, or pity thy penury?

9 They'll look out at a window, as thou rid'st in triumph to Tyburn,

and cry, "Yonder goes honest Frank, mad Quicksilver!" "He was   1
a free boon companion, when he had money," says one; "Hang
him, fool!" says another, "he could not keep it when he had it!"
"A pox o' the cullion, his master," says a third, "he has brought
him to this"; when their pox of pleasure and their piles of perdition would have been better bestowed upon thee, that hast ven-   2
tured for 'em with the best, and by the clue of thy knavery
brought thyself weeping to the cart of calamity.

QUICKSILVER   Worshipful master!

TOUCHSTONE   Offer not to speak, crocodile; I will not hear a sound
come from thee. Thou hast learnt to whine at the play yonder.
Master Deputy, pray you commit 'em both to safe custody, till I   3
be able farther to charge 'em.

QUICKSILVER   O me, what an unfortunate thing am I!

SIR PETRONEL   Will you not take security, sir?

TOUCHSTONE   Yes, marry, will I, Sir Flash, if I can find him, and   4
charge him as deep as the best on you. He has been the plotter of
all this; he is your engineer, I hear. Master Deputy, you'll dispose
of these. In the meantime, I'll to my Lord Mayor, and get his
warrant to seize that serpent Security into my hands, and seal up
both house and goods to the King's use or my satisfaction.
                                                                     5
GOLDING   Officers, take 'em to the Counter.

SIR PETRONEL ⎫
QUICKSILVER   ⎬ O God!
              ⎭

TOUCHSTONE   Nay, on, on! You see the issue of your sloth. Of
sloth cometh pleasure, of pleasure cometh riot, of riot comes   6
whoring, of whoring comes spending, of spending comes want, of
want comes theft, of theft comes hanging; and there is my Quicksilver fixed.

[*Exeunt*]

ACT FIVE

Scene One

1   [*Gertrude's lodging.* GERTRUDE *and* SINDEFY.]

GERTRUDE   Ah, Sin, hast thou ever read i' the chronicle of any lady and her waiting woman driven to that extremity that we are, Sin?

2   SINDEFY   Not I, truly, madam; and if I had, it were but cold comfort should come out of books now.

GERTRUDE   Why, good faith, Sin, I could dine with a lamentable story now. O hone, hone, o no nera, etc.! Canst thou tell ne'er a one, Sin?

3   SINDEFY   None but mine own, madam, which is lamentable enough: first to be stolen from my friends, which were worshipful and of good accompt, by a prentice in the habit and disguise of a gentleman, and here brought up to London and promised marriage, and now likely to be forsaken, for he is in possibility to be hanged!

4   GERTRUDE   Nay, weep not, good Sin; my Petronel is in as good possibility as he. Thy miseries are nothing to mine, Sin: I was more than promised marriage, Sin; I had it, Sin, and was made a lady, and by a knight, Sin; which is now as good as no knight, Sin. And I was born in London, which is more than brought up,

5   Sin; and already forsaken, which is past likelihood, Sin; and instead of land i' the country, all my knight's living lies i' the Counter, Sin; there's his castle now!

SINDEFY   Which he cannot be forced out of, madam.

GERTRUDE   Yes, if he would live hungry a week or two. "Hunger,"
6   they say, "breaks stone walls." But he is e'en well enough served, Sin, that so soon as ever he had got my hand to the sale of my inheritance, run away from me, and I had been his punk, God bless us! Would the Knight o' the Sun, or Palmerin of England, have used their ladies so, Sin? Or Sir Lancelot, or Sir Tristram?

7   SINDEFY   I do not know, madam.

GERTRUDE   Then thou know'st nothing, Sin. Thou art a fool, Sin.

"O hone, hone . . .": The refrain of an Irish lament.
Knight o' the Sun, or Palmerin of England: Heroes of Spanish Romances.

64

The knighthood nowadays are nothing like the knighthood of old 1
time. They rid a-horseback; ours go a-foot. They were attended
by their squires; ours by their lackeys. They went buckled in their
armour; ours muffled in their cloaks. They travelled wildernesses
and deserts; ours dare scarce walk the streets. They were still
prest to engage their honour; ours still ready to pawn their
clothes. They would gallop on at sight of a monster; ours run 2
away at sight of a sergeant. They would help poor ladies; ours
make poor ladies.

SINDEFY   Ay, madam, they were knights of the Round Table at
Winchester, that sought adventures; but these of the Square Table
at ordinaries, that sit at hazard. 3

GERTRUDE   True, Sin, let him vanish. And tell me, what shall we
pawn next?

SINDEFY   Ay, marry, madam, a timely consideration; for our host-
ess (profane woman!) has sworn by bread and salt, she will not 4
trust us another meal.

GERTRUDE   Let it stink in her hand then. I'll not be beholding to
her. Let me see, my jewels be gone, and my gowns, and my red
velvet petticoat that I was married in, and my wedding silk stockings, and all thy best apparel, poor Sin! Good faith, rather than
thou shouldest pawn a rag more, I'd lay my ladyship in lavender 5
—if I knew where.

SINDEFY   Alas, madam, your ladyship?

GERTRUDE   Ay, why? You do not scorn my ladyship, though it is
in a waistcoat? God's my life, you are a peat indeed! Do I offer to 6
mortgage my ladyship for you and for your avail, and do you
turn the lip and the alas to my ladyship?

SINDEFY   No, madam; but I make question who will lend anything
upon it?

GERTRUDE   Who? Marry, enow, I warrant you, if you'll seek 'em 7
out. I'm sure I remember the time when I would ha' given one
thousand pounds (if I had had it) to have been a lady; and I
hope I was not bred and born with that appetite alone: some
other gentle-born o' the City have the same longing, I trust. And
for my part, I would afford 'em a penn'orth; my ladyship is little
the worse for the wearing, and yet I would bate a good deal of 8
the sum. I would lend it (let me see) for forty pound in hand,
Sin—that would apparel us—and ten pounds a year—that would
keep me and you, Sin (with our needles)—and we should never

lay . . . in lavender: That is, pawn.

1 need to be beholding to our scurvy parents. Good Lord, that
there are no fairies nowadays, Sin!

SINDEFY   Why, madam?

GERTRUDE   To do miracles, and bring ladies money. Sure, if we lay
in a cleanly house, they would haunt it, Sin. I'll try. I'll sweep the
2 chamber soon at night, and set a dish of water o' the hearth. A
fairy may come and bring a pearl or a diamond. We do not
know, Sin. Or, there may be a pot of gold hid o' the backside, if
we had tools to dig for 't? Why may not we two rise early 'i the
morning, Sin, afore anybody is up, and find a jewel i' the streets
worth a hundred pound? May not some great court lady, as she
3 comes from revels at midnight, look out of her coach as 't is running, and lose such a jewel, and we find it? Ha?

SINDEFY   They are pretty waking dreams, these.

GERTRUDE   Or may not some old usurer be drunk overnight, with
4 a bag of money, and leave it behind him on a stall? For God's
sake, Sin, let's rise tomorrow by break of day, and see. I protest,
law, if I had as much money as an alderman, I would scatter
some on 't i' th' streets for poor ladies to find, when their knights
were laid up. And, now I remember my song o' the Golden
Shower, why may not I have such a fortune? I'll sing it, and try
5 what luck I shall have after it.

> Fond fables tell of old
>   How Jove in Danäe's lap
> Fell in a shower of gold,
>   By which she caught a clap;
6   O had it been my hap
> (How ere the blow doth threaten)
>   So well I like the play,
>   That I could wish all day
> And night to be so beaten.

7 [*Enter* MISTRESS TOUCHSTONE.]

O here's my mother! Good luck, I hope. Ha' you brought any
money, mother? Pray you, mother, your blessing. Nay, sweet
mother, do not weep.

8 MISTRESS TOUCHSTONE   God bless you! I would I were in my
grave!

GERTRUDE   Nay, dear mother, can you steal no more money from
my father? Dry your eyes, and comfort me. Alas, it is my knight's
fault, and not mine, that I am in a waistcoat, and attired thus
9 simply.

MISTRESS TOUCHSTONE Simply? 'T is better than thou deserv'st. 1
Never whimper for the matter. Thou shouldst have looked before
thou hadst leaped. Thou wert afire to be a lady, and now your
ladyship and you may both blow at the coal, for ought I know.
Self do, self have. "The hasty person never wants woe," they say.

GERTRUDE Nay, then, mother, you should ha' looked to it. A body 2
would think you were the older; I did but my kind, I. He was a
knight, and I was fit to be a lady. 'T is not lack of liking, but lack
of living, that severs us. And you talk like yourself and a cittiner
in this, i' faith. You show what husband you come on, I wis. You
smell the Touchstone—he that will do more for his daughter that
he has married a scurvy gold-end man and his prentice, than he 3
will for his t' other daughter, that has wedded a knight and his
customer. By this light, I think he is not my legitimate father.

SINDEFY O good madam, do not take up your mother so!

MISTRESS TOUCHSTONE Nay, nay, let her e'en alone! Let her ladyship grieve me still, with her bitter taunts and terms. I have not 4
dole enough to see her in this miserable case, I, without her velvet
gown, without ribands, without jewels, without French wires, or
cheat-bread, or quails, or a little dog, or a gentleman-usher, or anything, indeed, that's fit for a lady—

SINDEFY [aside] Except her tongue. 5

MISTRESS TOUCHSTONE And I not able to relieve her, neither,
being kept so short by my husband. Well, God knows my heart. I
did little think that ever she should have had need of her sister
Golding.

GERTRUDE Why, mother, I ha' not yet. Alas, good mother, be not 6
intoxicate for me! I am well enough; I would not change husbands with my sister, I. The leg of a lark is better than the body
of a kite.

MISTRESS TOUCHSTONE I know that, but—

GERTRUDE What, sweet mother, what? 7

MISTRESS TOUCHSTONE It's but ill food when nothing's left but the
claw.

GERTRUDE That's true, mother. Ay me!

MISTRESS TOUCHSTONE Nay, sweet ladybird, sigh not. Child, 8
madam, why do you weep thus? Be of good cheer; I shall die, if
you cry and mar your complexion thus.

blow at the coal: Fend for oneself, proverbial.
A body would think . . . : . . . And therefore able to give advice.
French wires: Wire frames for ruffs.

1   GERTRUDE   Alas, mother, what should I do?

MISTRESS TOUCHSTONE   Go to thy sister's, child; she'll be proud thy ladyship will come under her roof. She'll win thy father to release thy knight, and redeem thy gowns and thy coach and thy horses, and set thee up again.

2   GERTRUDE   But will she get him to set my knight up too?

MISTRESS TOUCHSTONE   That she will, or anything else thou'lt ask her.

GERTRUDE   I will begin to love her if I thought she would do this.

3   MISTRESS TOUCHSTONE   Try her, good chuck, I warrant thee.

GERTRUDE   Dost thou think she'll do 't?

SINDEFY   Ay, madam, and be glad you will receive it.

MISTRESS TOUCHSTONE   That's a good maiden; she tells you true.
4   Come, I'll take order for your debts i' the alehouse.

GERTRUDE   Go, Sin, and pray for thy Frank, as I will for my Pet.

[*Exeunt*]

5

Scene Two

[*Goldsmith's Row. Enter* TOUCHSTONE, GOLDING, WOLF.]

6   TOUCHSTONE   I will receive no letters, Master Wolf; you shall pardon me.

GOLDING   Good father, let me entreat you.

TOUCHSTONE   Son Golding, I will not be tempted; I find mine own easy nature, and I know not what a well-penned subtle letter may
7   work upon it; there may be tricks, packing, do you see? Return with your packet, sir.

WOLF   Believe it, sir, you need fear no packing here; these are but letters of submission all.

TOUCHSTONE   Sir, I do look for no submission. I will bear myself
8   in this like blind Justice. Work upon that now! When the Sessions come, they shall hear from me.

GOLDING   From whom come your letters, Master Wolf?

WOLF   And 't please you, sir, one from Sir Petronel, another from
9   Francis Quicksilver, and a third from old Security, who is al-

most mad in prison. There are two to your worship, one from   1
Master Francis, sir, another from the knight.

TOUCHSTONE   I do wonder, Master Wolf, why you should travail
thus in a business so contrary to kind or the nature o' your place,
that you, being the keeper of a prison, should labour the release
of your prisoners! Whereas, methinks, it were far more natural   2
and kindly in you to be ranging about for more, and not let
these 'scape you have already under the tooth. But they say you
wolves, when you ha' sucked the blood once, that they are dry,
you ha' done.

WOLF   Sir, your worship may descant as you please o' my name;   3
but I protest I was never so mortified with any men's discourse or
behaviour in prison; yet I have had of all sorts of men i' the kingdom under my keys, and almost of all religions i' the land, as
Papist, Protestant, Puritan, Brownist, Anabaptist, Millenary, Family o' Love, Jew, Turk, Infidel, Atheist, Good Fellow, etc.
                                                                 4
GOLDING   And which of all these, thinks Master Wolf, was the best
religion?

WOLF   Troth, Master Deputy, they that pay fees best; we never examine their consciences farther.
                                                                 5
GOLDING   I believe you, Master Wolf. Good faith, sir, here's a
great deal of humility i' these letters.

WOLF   Humility, sir? Ay, were your worship an eyewitness of it,
you would say so. The knight will i' the Knight's Ward, do what
we can, sir; and Master Quicksilver would be i' the Hole, if we
would let him. I never knew or saw prisoners more penitent, or   6
more devout. They will sit you up all night singing of psalms and
edifying the whole prison; only Security sings a note too high
sometimes, because he lies i' the twopenny ward, far off, and cannot take his tune. The neighbours cannot rest for him, but come
every morning to ask what godly prisoners we have.   7

TOUCHSTONE   Which on 'em is 't is so devout—the knight or the
t' other?

WOLF   Both, sir; but the young man especially. I never heard his
like. He has cut his hair, too. He is so well given, and has such
                                                                 8

Brownist: A strict Puritan sect.
Family o' Love: A sect of mystics accused of teaching and practising
free love. Middleton attacked them in his comedy of the same name.
See also *The Lady of Pleasure*, Act I, Sc. i.
Knight's Ward: See Glossary under COUNTER.

1   good gifts. He can tell you almost all the stories of the Book of Martyrs, and speak you all "The Sick Man's Salve" without book.

TOUCHSTONE   Ay, if he had had grace—he was brought up where it grew, I wis. On, Master Wolf!

2   WOLF   And he has converted one Fangs, a sergeant, a fellow could neither write nor read, he was called the Bandog o' the Counter; and he has brought him already to pare his nails and say his prayers; and 't is hoped he will sell his place shortly, and become an intelligencer.

3   TOUCHSTONE   No more; I am coming already. If I should give any farther ear I were taken. Adieu, good Master Wolf! Son, I do feel mine own weaknesses; do not importune me. Pity is a rheum that I am subject to; but I will resist it. Master Wolf, fish is cast away that is cast in dry pools. Tell hypocrisy it will not do; I have touched and tried too often; I am yet proof, and I will remain so; when the Sessions come they shall hear from me. In the mean-

4   time, to all suits, to all entreaties, to all letters, to all tricks, I will be deaf as an adder, and blind as a beetle, lay mine ear to the ground, and lock mine eyes i' my hand against all temptations. [*Exits*]

GOLDING   You see, Master Wolf, how inexorable he is. There is no hope to recover him. Pray you commend me to my brother

5   knight, and to my fellow Francis; present 'em with this small token of my love;

[*Giving money*]

tell 'em, I wish I could do 'em any worthier office; but in this, 't is

6   desperate; yet I will not fail to try the uttermost of my power for 'em. And, sir, as far as I have any credit with you, pray you let 'em want nothing; though I am not ambitious they should know so much.

WOLF   Sir, both your actions and words speak you to be a true gentleman. They shall know only what is fit, and no more.

7   [*Exeunt*]

Scene Three

8   [*The Counter.* HOLDFAST, BRAMBLE; SECURITY *apart.*]

HOLDFAST   Who would you speak with, sir?

"The Sick Man's Salve": A popular Elizabethan book of devotions, often mentioned in the drama of the time.

BRAMBLE   I would speak with one Security, that is prisoner here.   1

HOLDFAST   You are welcome, sir! Stay there, I'll call him to you. Master Security!

SECURITY   Who calls?

HOLDFAST   Here's a gentleman would speak with you.   2

SECURITY   What is he? Is 't one that grafts my forehead now I am in prison, and comes to see how the horns shoot up and prosper?

HOLDFAST   You must pardon him, sir; the old man is a little crazed with his imprisonment.

SECURITY   What say you to me, sir? Look you here, my learned   3 counsel, Master Bramble! Cry you mercy, sir! When saw you my wife?

BRAMBLE   She is now at my house, sir; and desired me that I would come to visit you, and inquire of you your case, that we might work some means to get you forth.   4

SECURITY   My case, Master Bramble, is stone walls and iron grates; you see it, this is the weakest part on 't. And for getting me forth, no means but hang myself, and so to be carried forth, from which they have here bound me in intolerable bands.

BRAMBLE   Why, but what is 't you are in for, sir?   5

SECURITY   For my sins, for my sins, sir, whereof marriage is the greatest! O, had I never married, I had never known this purgatory, to which hell is a kind of cool bath in respect; my wife's confederacy, sir, with old Touchstone, that she might keep her jubilee, and the feast of her new moon. Do you understand me, sir?   6

QUICKSILVER [enters]   Good sir, go in and talk with him. The light does him harm, and his example will be hurtful to the weak prisoners. Fie, Father Security, that you'll be still so profane! Will nothing humble you?

[Exeunt SECURITY, BRAMBLE, HOLDFAST, and QUICKSILVER. Enter   7 TWO PRISONERS with a FRIEND.]

FRIEND   What's he?

FIRST PRISONER   O, he is a rare young man! Do you not know him?   8

FRIEND   Not I! I never saw him, I can remember.

SECOND PRISONER   Why, it is he that was the gallant prentice of London—Master Touchstone's man.

her new moon: Emblematic of the cuckold's horn.

1 FRIEND   Who? Quicksilver?

FIRST PRISONER   Ay, this is he.

FRIEND   Is this he? They say he has been a gallant indeed.

2 SECOND PRISONER   O, the royallest fellow that ever was bred up i'
the City! He would play you his thousand pound a-night at dice;
keep knights and lords company; go with them to bawdyhouses;
had his six men in a livery; kept a stable of hunting horses, and
his wench in her velvet gown and her cloth of silver. Here's one
knight with him here in prison.

FRIEND   And how miserably he is changed!

3 FIRST PRISONER   O, that's voluntary in him: he gave away all his
rich clothes as soon as ever he came in here among the prisoners;
and will eat o' the basket, for humility.

FRIEND   Why will he do so?

4 FIRST PRISONER   Alas, he has no hope of life! He mortifies himself.
He does but linger on till the Sessions.

5 SECOND PRISONER   O, he has penned the best thing, that he calls
his "Repentance" or his "Last Farewell," that ever you heard. He
is a pretty poet, and for prose—you would wonder how many
prisoners he has helped out, with penning petitions for 'em, and
not take a penny. Look! This is the knight, in the rug gown.
Stand by!

[*Enter* SIR PETRONEL, BRAMBLE, QUICKSILVER.]

6 BRAMBLE   Sir, for Security's case, I have told him. Say he should
be condemned to be carted or whipped for a bawd, or so, why,
I'll lay an execution on him o' two hundred pound; let him acknowledge a judgment, he shall do it in half an hour; they shall
not all fetch him out without paying the execution, o' my word.

7 SIR PETRONEL   But can we not be bailed, Master Bramble?

BRAMBLE   Hardly; there are none of the judges in town, else you
should remove yourself (in spite of him) with a habeas corpus.
But if you have a friend to deliver your tale sensibly to some justice o' the town, that he may have feeling of it (do you see) you
8 may be bailed; for as I understand the case, 't is only done *in
terrorem;* and you shall have an action of false imprisonment
against him when you come out, and perhaps a thousand pound
costs.

eat o' the basket: Refers to the sheriff's basket, the remains of food
sent to prisoners from the sheriff's table.

[*Enter* MASTER WOLF.]   1

QUICKSILVER   How now, Master Wolf? What news? What return?

WOLF   Faith, bad all! Yonder will be no letters received. He says
the Sessions shall determine it. Only Master Deputy Golding
commends him to you, and with this token wishes he could do   2
you other good. [*Giving money*.]

QUICKSILVER   I thank him. Good Master Bramble, trouble our
quiet no more; do not molest us in prison thus with your winding
devices; pray you depart. For my part, I commit my cause to
Him that can succour me; let God work His will. Master Wolf, I
pray you let this be distributed among the prisoners, and desire   3
'em to pray for us. [*Exits*]

WOLF   It shall be done, Master Francis.

FIRST PRISONER   An excellent temper!

SECOND PRISONER   Now God send him good luck!   4

[*Exeunt* BRAMBLE, TWO PRISONERS, *and* FRIEND.]

SIR PETRONEL   But what said my father-in-law, Master Wolf?

HOLDFAST [*enters*]   Here's one would speak with you, sir.
                                                                5
WOLF   I'll tell you anon, Sir Petronel. Who is 't?

HOLDFAST   A gentleman, sir, that will not be seen.

[*Enter* GOLDING.]

WOLF   Where is he? Master Deputy! Your worship is welcome—   6
GOLDING   Peace!

WOLF   Away, sirrah!

[*Exit* HOLDFAST *with* SIR PETRONEL.]

                                                                7
GOLDING   Good faith, Master Wolf, the estate of these gentlemen,
for whom you were so late and willing a suitor, doth much affect
me; and because I am desirous to do them some fair office, and
find there is no means to make my father relent so likely as to
bring him to be a spectator of their miseries, I have ventured on a
device, which is, to make myself your prisoner, entreating you   8
will presently go report it to my father, and (feigning an action at
suit of some third person) pray by this token

[*Giving a ring*]

that he will presently, and with all secrecy, come hither for my   9

1 bail; which train, if any, I know will bring him abroad; and then, having him here, I doubt not but we shall be all fortunate in the event.

WOLF   Sir, I will put on my best speed to effect it. Please you come in.

2 GOLDING   Yes; and let me rest concealed, I pray you. [*Exits*]

WOLF   See here a benefit truly done, when it is done timely, freely, and to no ambition. [*Exits*]

3   **Scene Four**

[*A room in Touchstone's house. Enter* TOUCHSTONE, WIFE, DAUGH-TERS, SINDEFY, WINIFRED.]

4 TOUCHSTONE   I will sail by you and not hear you, like the wise Ulysses.

MILDRED   Dear Father!

MISTRESS TOUCHSTONE   Husband!

GERTRUDE   Father!

5
WINIFRED *and* SINDEFY   Master Touchstone!

TOUCHSTONE   Away, sirens, I will immure myself against your cries, and lock myself up to your lamentations.

MISTRESS TOUCHSTONE   Gentle husband, hear me!

6 GERTRUDE   Father, it is I, Father, my Lady Flash. My sister and I am friends.

MILDRED   Good father!

WINIFRED   Be not hardened, good Master Touchstone!

7 SINDEFY   I pray you, sir, be merciful!

TOUCHSTONE   I am deaf, I do not hear you; I have stopped mine ears with shoemakers' wax, and drunk Lethe and mandragora to forget you. All you speak to me I commit to the air.

8 [*Enter* WOLF.]

MILDRED   How now, Master Wolf?

WOLF   Where's Master Touchstone? I must speak with him presently; I have lost my breath for haste.

9 MILDRED   What's the matter, sir? Pray all be well!

WOLF   Master Deputy Golding is arrested upon an execution, and   1
desires him presently to come to him, forthwith.

MILDRED   Ay me! Do you hear, father?

TOUCHSTONE   Tricks, tricks, confederacy, tricks! I have 'em in my
nose—I scent 'em!
                                                                   2
WOLF   Who's that? Master Touchstone?

MISTRESS TOUCHSTONE   Why, it is Master Wolf himself, husband.

MILDRED   Father!

TOUCHSTONE   I am deaf still, I say. I will neither yield to the song
of the siren, nor the voice of the hyena, the tears of the crocodile,   3
nor the howling o' the wolf. Avoid my habitation, monsters!

WOLF   Why, you are not mad, sir? I pray you look forth, and see
the token I have brought you, sir.

TOUCHSTONE   Ha! What token is it?

WOLF   Do you know it, sir?   4

TOUCHSTONE   My son Golding's ring! Are you in earnest, Master
Wolf?

WOLF   Ay, by my faith, sir! He is in prison, and required me to
use all speed and secrecy to you.
                                                                   5
TOUCHSTONE   My cloak, there—pray you be patient. I am plagued
for my austerity. My cloak! At whose suit, Master Wolf?

WOLF   I'll tell you as we go, sir.

[*Exeunt*]
                                                                   6

Scene Five

[*The Counter. Enter* FRIEND, TWO PRISONERS.]
                                                                   7
FRIEND   Why, but is his offence such as he cannot hope of life?

FIRST PRISONER   Troth, it should seem so; and 't is great pity, for
he is exceeding penitent.

FRIEND   They say he is charged but on suspicion of felony yet.

SECOND PRISONER   Ay, but his master is a shrewd fellow; he'll   8
prove great matter against him.

FRIEND   I'd as lief as anything I could see his "Farewell."

the voice of the hyena: According to Pliny, the hyena could imitate
a man's voice to lure him to destruction.

1 FIRST PRISONER   O 't is rarely written; why, Toby may get him to sing it to you; he's not curious to anybody.

SECOND PRISONER   O no! He would that all the world should take knowledge of his repentance, and thinks he merits in 't, the more shame he suffers.

2 FIRST PRISONER   Pray thee, try what thou canst do.

SECOND PRISONER   I warrant you he will not deny it, if he be not hoarse with the often repeating of it. [*Exits*]

FIRST PRISONER   You never saw a more courteous creature than he is, and the knight, too; the poorest prisoner of the house may
3 command 'em. You shall hear a thing admirably penned.

FRIEND   Is the knight any scholar, too?

FIRST PRISONER   No, but he will speak very well, and discourse admirably of running horses and White Friars, and against bawds, and of cocks; and talk as loud as a hunter, but is none.

4
[*Enter* WOLF *and* TOUCHSTONE.]

WOLF   Please you, stay here, sir; I'll call his worship down to you. [*Exits*]

5 [*Enter* SECOND PRISONER *with* QUICKSILVER, PETRONEL *and* SECURITY; GOLDING *with* WOLF, *who stand aside*.]

FIRST PRISONER   See, he has brought him, and the knight, too. Salute him, I pray. Sir, this gentleman, upon our report, is very desirous to hear some piece of your "Repentance."

6 QUICKSILVER   Sir, with all my heart; and, as I told Master Toby, I shall be glad to have any man a witness of it. And the more openly I profess it, I hope it will appear the heartier and the more unfeigned.

TOUCHSTONE [*aside*]   Who is this? My man Francis, and my son-
7 in-law?

QUICKSILVER   Sir, it is all the testimony I shall leave behind me to the world and my master that I have so offended.

FRIEND   Good sir!

QUICKSILVER   I writ it when my spirits were oppressed.

8 SIR PETRONEL   Ay, I'll be sworn for you, Francis!

QUICKSILVER   It is in imitation of Mannington's, he that was hanged at Cambridge, that cut off the horse's head at a blow.

Mannington's: A well-known ballad made by George Mannington before being hanged at Cambridge.

FRIEND   So, sir!   1

QUICKSILVER   To the tune of "I wail in woe, I plunge in pain."

SIR PETRONEL   An excellent ditty it is, and worthy of a new tune.

QUICKSILVER   In Cheapside, famous for gold and plate,
   Quicksilver, I did dwell of late;
   I had a master good and kind,   2
   That would have wrought me to his mind.
   He bade me still, Work upon that,
   But, alas, I wrought I knew not what!
   He was a Touchstone black, but true,
   And told me still what would ensue;   3
   Yet woe is me! I would not learn;
   I saw, alas, but could not discern!

FRIEND   Excellent, excellent well!

GOLDING [aside to WOLF]   O, let him alone; he is taken already.   4

QUICKSILVER   I cast my coat and cap away,
   I went in silks and satins gay;
   False metal of good manners I
   Did daily coin unlawfully.
   I scorned my master, being drunk;
   I kept my gelding and my punk;   5
   And with a knight, Sir Flash by name,
   Who now is sorry for the same—

SIR PETRONEL   I thank you, Francis.

QUICKSILVER   I thought by sea to run away,
   But Thames and tempest did me stay.   6

TOUCHSTONE [aside]   This cannot be feigned, sure. Heaven pardon my severity! The ragged colt may prove a good horse.

GOLDING [aside]   How he listens, and is transported! He has forgot me.

QUICKSILVER   Still Eastward Ho was all my word;   7
   But westward I had no regard,
   Nor never thought what would come after,
   As did, alas, his youngest daughter!
   At last the black ox trod o' my foot,
   And I saw then what longed unto 't;
   Now cry I, "Touchstone, touch me still,   8
   And make me current by thy skill."

the black ox: A symbol of trouble, or old age.
"Touchstone, touch me still": Gold was tested by rubbing on a touchstone.

1 TOUCHSTONE [*aside*]   And I will do it, Francis.

WOLF [*aside to* GOLDING]   Stay him, Master Deputy; now is the time; we shall lose the song else.

FRIEND   I protest it is the best that ever I heard.

2 QUICKSILVER   How like you it, gentlemen?

ALL   O admirable, sir!

QUICKSILVER   This stanza now following alludes to the story of Mannington, from whence I took my project for my invention.

3 FRIEND   Pray you go on, sir.

QUICKSILVER   O Mannington, thy stories show
            Thou cut'st a horse head off at a blow!
            But I confess, I have not the force
            For to cut off the head of a horse;
4   Yet I desire this grace to win,
            That I may cut off the horse head of Sin,
            And leave his body in the dust
            Of sin's highway and bogs of lust,
            Whereby I may take Virtue's purse,
            And live with her for better, for worse.

5 FRIEND   Admirable, sir, and excellently conceited!

QUICKSILVER   Alas, sir!

TOUCHSTONE [*coming to* GOLDING *and* WOLF]   Son Golding and Master Wolf, I thank you; the deceit is welcome, especially from thee, whose charitable soul in this hath shown a high point of
6 wisdom and honesty. Listen, I am ravished with his repentance, and could stand here a whole prenticeship to hear him.

FRIEND   Forth, good sir!

QUICKSILVER   This is the last, and the "Farewell."

7   Farewell, Cheapside, farewell, sweet trade
            Of Goldsmiths all, that never shall fade;
            Farewell, dear fellow prentices all,
            And be you warned by my fall:
            Shun usurers, bawds, and dice, and drabs;
            Avoid them as you would French scabs.
8   Seek not to go beyond your tether,
            But cut your thongs unto your leather;
            So shall you thrive by little and little,
            Scape Tyburn, Counters, and the Spital!

   Spital: Hospital.

TOUCHSTONE   And scape them shalt thou, my penitent and dear   1
Francis!

QUICKSILVER   Master!

SIR PETRONEL   Father!

TOUCHSTONE   I can no longer forbear to do your humility right.   2
Arise, and let me honour your repentance with the hearty and
joyful embraces of a father and friend's love. Quicksilver, thou
hast eat into my breast, Quicksilver, with the drops of thy sorrow,
and killed the desperate opinion I had of thy reclaim.

QUICKSILVER   O sir, I am not worthy to see your worshipful face!
   3
SIR PETRONEL   Forgive me, father!

TOUCHSTONE   Speak no more; all former passages are forgotten,
and here my word shall release you. Thank this worthy brother
and kind friend, Francis.—Master Wolf, I am their bail.

[*A shout in the prison.*]   4

SECURITY   Master Touchstone! Master Touchstone!

TOUCHSTONE   Who's that?

WOLF   Security, sir.
   5
SECURITY   Pray you, sir, if you'll be won with a song, hear my
lamentable tune too;

Song

O Master Touchstone,
  My heart is full of woe;   6
Alas, I am a cuckold!
  And why should it be so?
Because I was a usurer
  And bawd, as all you know,
For which, again I tell you,
  My heart is full of woe.   7

TOUCHSTONE   Bring him forth, Master Wolf, and release his bands.
This day shall be sacred to mercy, and the mirth of this encounter
in the Counter. See, we are encountered with more suitors!

[*Enter* MISTRESS TOUCHSTONE, GERTRUDE, MILDRED, SINDEFY,   8
WINIFRED.]
Save your breath, save your breath! All things have succeeded to
your wishes; and we are heartily satisfied in their events.

GERTRUDE   Ah, runaway, runaway! Have I caught you? And how
has my poor knight done all this while?
   9

1   SIR PETRONEL   Dear lady wife, forgive me!

GERTRUDE   As heartily as I would be forgiven, knight. Dear father, give me your blessing, and forgive me, too; I ha' been proud and lascivious, father, and a fool, father; and being raised to the state of a wanton coy thing, called a lady, father, have scorned you,
2   father, and my sister, and my sister's velvet cap, too; and would make a mouth at the City as I rid through it; and stop mine ears at Bow bell. I have said your beard was a base one, father; and that you looked like Twierpipe the taberer; and that my mother was but my midwife.

3   MISTRESS TOUCHSTONE   Now God forgi' you, child madam!

TOUCHSTONE   No more repetitions! What is else wanting to make our harmony full?

GOLDING   Only this, sir, that my fellow Francis make amends to Mistress Sindefy with marriage.

4   QUICKSILVER   With all my heart!

GOLDING   And Security give her a dower, which shall be all the restitution he shall make of that huge mass he hath so unlawfully gotten.

TOUCHSTONE   Excellently devised! A good motion! What says
5   Master Security?

SECURITY   I say anything, sir, what you'll ha' me say. Would I were no cuckold!

WINIFRED   Cuckold, husband? Why, I think this wearing of yellow has infected you.
6

TOUCHSTONE   Why, Master Security, that should rather be a comfort to you than a corsive. If you be a cuckold, it's an argument you have a beautiful woman to your wife; then you shall be much made of; you shall have store of friends, never want money; you shall be eased of much o' your wedlock pain, others will take it
7   for you. Besides, you being a usurer and likely to go to hell, the devils will never torment you, they'll take you for one o' their own race. Again, if you be a cuckold, and know it not, you are an innocent; if you know it, and endure it, a true martyr.

SECURITY   I am resolved, sir. Come hither, Winny!

8   TOUCHSTONE   Well, then, all are pleased, or shall be anon. Master Wolf, you look hungry, methinks; have you no apparel to lend Francis to shift him?

QUICKSILVER   No, sir, nor I desire none; but here make it my suit,

yellow: The colour of his prison garb, and associated with jealousy.

that I may go home through the streets in these, as a spectacle, or 1
rather an example, to the children of Cheapside.

TOUCHSTONE   Thou hast thy wish. Now, London, look about,
And in this moral see thy glass run out;
Behold the careful father, thrifty son,
The solemn deeds which each of us have done;
The usurer punished, and from fall so steep
The prodigal child reclaimed, and the lost sheep.

EPILOGUE

[QUICKSILVER]   Stay, sir, I perceive the multitude are gathered to-
gether to view our coming out at the Counter. See, if the streets
and the fronts of the houses be not stuck with people, and the
windows filled with ladies, as on the solemn day of the Pageant!
O may you find in this our pageant, here,
   The same contentment which you came to seek;
And as that show but draws you once a year,
   May this attract you hither once a week.

[*Exeunt*]

THE END

the Pageant: The Lord Mayor's Show.

A Trick
to Catch
the Old One

(*1608*)

INTRODUCTION

It has been established that Thomas Middleton was born in 1580 and went up to Queen's College, Oxford, in 1598, presumably as a poor London scholar since his father was a bricklayer. There is no record of his having taken a degree, although his early poems date from this period. He began writing plays for Philip Henslowe not later than 1602, but his success began with a series of comedies of London Life written during the next six years for companies of child actors. He collaborated with William Rowley (1585?-1642?) and with Thomas Dekker. With the latter he wrote *The Roaring Girl,* first produced in 1611, which is chiefly remembered, despite T. S. Eliot's special commendation of the heroine, for those scenes written in thieves' cant. After writing a number of shows and pageants for civic performance, Middleton was appointed City Chronologer in 1620, a post which he took seriously, unlike his successor. Jonson was appointed after Middleton's death in 1627 and felt himself under no compulsion to produce work for the authorities in return for his civic pension.

Despite their settings, the street life, the brothel and tavern scenes, and the wide social range from which his characters are drawn, Middleton's London comedies such as this one of 1608 or *A Chaste Maid in Cheapside* (first performed 1612), are inhabited exclusively by private individuals. The world beyond the sphere of action of the individual is taken for granted. Witgood, the impoverished gallant, plays the trick that catches the old ones, Lucre, his uncle, and Hoard, his uncle's adversary. Witgood's virtue is, as his name tells us, his quick intelligence which he skillfully employs against the older generation of moneygrubbers in the restoration of his fortune. Land is no longer merely good security as in *Eastward Ho,* but an attractive bait, the rumour of which is enough to gull the City financiers into the reckless pursuit of the rich widow. Character is sacrificed to action and Middleton appears to be the detached manipulator of a plot of vigorous intrigue. Philip Massinger borrowed heavily from this play for his best-known comedy, *A New Way to Pay Old Debts.*

Middleton has been called a cynical observer of contemporary life, but despite the perfunctory recantations at the end of the play where only the Courtesan behaves with any show of grace or human feeling, Middleton's characters are too generalised for us to have feelings for or against them. Notable, however, and largely irrelevant to the demands of the plot, is the savage attack on the law in Act IV, Scene v. The law is just another vast threat that hangs over the life of the individual. One is also struck by the number and variety of words in this play that surround the hierarchies of prostitution, perhaps a pointer to the central importance of the profession to the society of the age.

The play was first printed in 1608, but was written earlier. It was presented before the King on New Year's Night of that year and was re-issued in the same year.

CHARACTERS

[THEODORUS] WITGOOD

[PECUNIUS] LUCRE, his uncle

[WALKADINE] HOARD

ONESIPHORUS HOARD, his
  brother

LIMBER
KIX
LAMPREY } friends of Hoard
SPICHCOCK

HOST

[SAM] FREEDOM, son of Mistress
  Lucre [by a previous marriage]

MONEYLOVE

[HARRY] DAMPIT

GULF

GENTLEMEN

SIR LAUNCELOT

GEORGE [servant to Lucre]

[ARTHUR, servant to Hoard]

[THREE] CREDITORS, DRAWER,
BOY, [VINTNER], [SERGEANTS],
[TAILOR, BARBER, PERFUMER,
FALCONER, HUNTSMAN],
SCRIVENER

COURTESAN

MISTRESS LUCRE

JOYCE, niece to Hoard

AUDREY, servant to Dampit

LADY FOXSTONE

SCENE: A country town for the first two scenes; London thereafter.

ACT ONE

Scene One

[A street in a country town.]   1

WITGOOD *[enters]* All's gone! Still thou 'rt a gentleman, that's all;
but a poor one, that's nothing. What milk brings thy meadows
forth now? Where are thy goodly uplands, and thy down lands?
All sunk into that little pit, lechery. Why should a gallant pay but
two shillings for his ordinary that nourishes him, and twenty   2
times two for his brothel that consumes him? But where's Longacre? In my uncle's conscience, which is three years' voyage about:
he that sets out upon his conscience ne'er finds the way home
again; he is either swallowed in the quicksands of law-quillets, or
splits upon the piles of a praemunire; yet these old fox-brained
and ox-browed uncles have still defences for their avarice, and   3
apologies for their practises, and will thus greet our follies:

> He that doth his youth expose
>   To brothel, drink, and danger,
> Let him that is his nearest kin
>   Cheat him before a stranger: 4

and that's his uncle; 't is a principle in usury. I dare not visit the
city: there I should be too soon visited by that horrible plague,
my debts; and by that means I lose a virgin's love, her portion,
and her virtues. Well, how should a man live now that has no
living? hum,—why, are there not a million of men in the world   5
that only sojourn upon their brain, and make their wits their mer-
cers; and am I but one amongst that million, and cannot thrive
upon 't? Any trick, out of the compass of law, now would come
happily to me.

COURTESAN *[enters]* My love!   6

WITGOOD My loathing! Hast thou been the secret consumption of
my purse, and now comest to undo my last means, my wits? Wilt
leave no virtue in me, and yet thou ne'er the better?
Hence, courtesan, round-webbed tarantula,
That dry'st the roses in the cheeks of youth!   7

---

two shillings: The statutory price of a meal at an ordinary. See *The
Sparagus Garden* Act III, Sc. i.
   Longacre: Meaning his estate.
   quillets: Tricks or subtleties.
   praemunire: A sheriff's writ.

89

1 COURTESAN I've been true unto your pleasure; and all your lands
   Thrice racked was never worth the jewel which
   I prodigally gave you, my virginity:
   Land mortgaged may return, and more esteemed,
   But honesty once pawned, is ne'er redeemed.

2 WITGOOD Forgive: I do thee wrong
   To make thee sin, and then to chide thee for 't.

   COURTESAN I know I am your loathing now; farewell.

   WITGOOD Stay, best invention, stay.

   COURTESAN I that "have been the secret consumption of your
3 purse," shall I stay now "to undo your last means, your wits?
   hence, courtesan," away!

   WITGOOD I prithee, make me not mad at my own weapon: stay (a
   thing few women can do, I know that, and therefore they had
   need wear stays) be not contrary: dost love me? Fate has so cast
4 it that all my means I must derive from thee.

   COURTESAN From me? Be happy then;
   What lies within the power of my performance
   Shall be commanded of thee.

   WITGOOD Spoke like
   An honest drab, i' faith: it may prove something;
5 What trick is not an embryon at first,
   Until a perfect shape come over it?

   COURTESAN Come, I must help you: whereabouts left you?
   I'll proceed:
   Though you beget, 't is I must help to breed.
6 Speak, what is 't? I'd fain conceive it.

   WITGOOD So, so, so: thou shalt presently take the name and form
   upon thee of a rich country widow, four hundred a year valiant, in
   woods, in bullocks, in barns, and in rye stacks; we'll to London,
   and to my covetous uncle.

7 COURTESAN I begin to applaud thee; our states being both desperate, they are soon resolute; but how for horses?

   WITGOOD Mass, that's true; the jest will be of some continuance.
   Let me see; horses now, a bots on 'em! Stay, I have acquaintance
   with a mad host, never yet bawd to thee; I have rinsed the whore-
8 son's gums in mull sack many a time and often: put but a good
   tale into his ear now, so it come off cleanly, and there's horse and
   man for us, I dare warrant thee.

   COURTESAN Arm your wits then
   Speedily; there shall want nothing in me,
9 Either in behaviour, discourse, or fashion,

That shall discredit your intended purpose.   1
I will so artfully disguise my wants,
And set so good a courage on my state,
That I will be believed.

WITGOOD   Why, then, all's furnished. I shall go nigh to catch that
old fox mine uncle: though he make but some amends for my   2
undoing, yet there's some comfort in 't, he cannot otherwise
choose (though it be but in hope to cozen me again) but supply
any hasty want that I bring to town with me. The device well and
cunningly carried, the name of a rich widow, and four hundred
ayear in good earth, will so conjure up a kind of usurer's love in
him to me, that he will not only desire my presence,—which at   3
first shall scarce be granted him, I'll keep off a' purpose,—but I
shall find him so officious to deserve, so ready to supply! I know
the state of an old man's affection so well: if his nephew be poor
indeed, why, he lets God alone with him; but if he be once rich,
then he'll be the first man that helps him.

                                                                   4
COURTESAN   'T is right the world; for, in these days, an old man's
love to his kindred is like his kindness to his wife, 't is always
done before he comes at it.

WITGOOD   I owe thee for that jest. Begone: here's all my wealth;
prepare thyself, away. I'll to mine host with all possible haste; and
with the best art, and most profitable form, pour the sweet cir-   5
cumstance into his ear, which shall have the gift to turn all the
wax to honey.

[*Exit* COURTESAN.]

How now? O, the right worshipful seniors of our country!   6

[*Enter* ONESIPHORUS HOARD, LIMBER, *and* KIX.]

ONESIPHORUS HOARD   Who's that?

LIMBER   O, the common rioter; take no note of him.
                                                                   7
WITGOOD   You will not see me now; the comfort is,
      Ere it be long you will scarce see yourselves. [*Aside, and exits.*]

ONESIPHORUS HOARD   I wonder how he breathes; has consumed all
      Upon that courtesan.

LIMBER   We have heard so much.   8

ONESIPHORUS HOARD   You've heard all truth. His uncle and my
      brother
      Have been these three years mortal adversaries:
      Two old tough spirits, they seldom meet but fight,
      Or quarrel when 't is calmest: 9

1 I think their anger be the very fire
That keeps their age alive.

LIMBER   What was the quarrel, sir?

ONESIPHORUS HOARD   Faith, about a purchase, fetching over a
young heir. Master Hoard, my brother, having wasted much time
2 in beating the bargain, what did me old Lucre, but as his conscience moved him, knowing the poor gentleman, stept in between 'em and cozened him himself.

LIMBER   And was this all, sir?

ONESIPHORUS HOARD   This was e'en it, sir; yet for all this, I know
3 no reason but the match might go forward betwixt his wife's son
and my niece; what though there be a dissension between the two
old men, I see no reason it should put a difference between the
two younger; 't is as natural for old folks to fall out, as for young
to fall in. A scholar comes a-wooing to my neice; well, he's wise,
4 but he's poor: her son comes a-wooing to my neice; well, he's a
fool, but he's rich.

LIMBER   Ay, marry, sir.

ONESIPHORUS HOARD   Pray, now, is not a rich fool better than a
poor philosopher?

5 LIMBER   One would think so, i' faith.

ONESIPHORUS HOARD   She now remains at London with my
brother, her second uncle, to learn fashions, practise music; the
voice between her lips, and the viol between her legs, she'll be fit
for a consort very speedily: a thousand good pound is her por-
6 tion; if she marry, we'll ride up and be merry.

KIX   A match, if it be a match.

[*Exeunt*]

7 ## Scene Two

[*Another street in the same town. Enter* WITGOOD, *meeting* HOST.]

WITGOOD   Mine Host!

8 HOST   Young Master Witgood.

WITGOOD   I have been laying all the town for thee.

HOST   Why, what's the news, bully Had-land?

WITGOOD   What geldings are in the house, of thine own? Answer
9 me to that first.

HOST   Why, man, why?   1

WITGOOD   Mark me what I say: I'll tell thee such a tale in thine
ear, that thou shalt trust me spite of thy teeth, furnish me with
some money willy-nilly, and ride up with me thyself *contra voluntatem et professionem.*

HOST   How? Let me see this trick, and I'll say thou has more art   2
than a conjuror.

WITGOOD   Dost thou joy in my advancement?

HOST   Do I love sack and ginger?

WITGOOD   Comes my prosperity desiredly to thee?   3

HOST   Come forfeitures to a usurer, fees to an officer, punks to an
host, and pigs to a parson desiredly? Why, then, la.

WITGOOD   Will the report of a widow of four hundred ayear, boy,
make thee leap, and sing, and dance, and come to thy place
again?   4

HOST   Wilt thou command me now? I am thy spirit; conjure me
into any shape.

WITGOOD   I ha' brought her from her friends, turned back the
horses by a slight; not so much as one among her six men, goodly
large yeomanly fellows, will she trust with this her purpose: by   5
this light, all unmanned, regardless of her state, neglectful of
vain-glorious ceremony, all for my love. O, 't is a fine little volu-
ble tongue, mine host, that wins a widow!

HOST   No, 't is a tongue with a great T, my boy, that wins a
widow.   6

WITGOOD   Now, sir, the case stands thus: good mine host, if thou
lovest my happiness, assist me.

HOST   Command all my beasts i' th' house.

WITGOOD   Nay, that's not all neither: prithee take truce with thy
joy, and listen to me. Thou knowest I have a wealthy uncle i' th'   7
city, somewhat the wealthier by my follies: the report of this fortune, well and cunningly carried, might be a means to draw some
goodness from the usuring rascal; for I have put her in hope already of some estate that I have either in land or money: now, if
I be found true in neither, what may I expect but a sudden   8
breach of our love, utter dissolution of the match, and confusion
of my fortunes for ever?

HOST   Wilt thou but trust the managing of thy business with me?

contra voluntatem et professionem: Against will and judgment.

1 WITGOOD With thee? Why, will I desire to thrive in my purpose? Will I hug four hundred ayear, I that know the misery of nothing? Will that man wish a rich widow that has ne'er a hole to put his head in? With thee, mine host? Why, believe it, sooner with thee than with a covey of counsellors.

2 HOST Thank you for your good report, i' faith, sir; and if I stand you not in stead, why then let an host come off *hic et haec hostis,* a deadly enemy to dice, drink, and venery. Come, where's this widow?

WITGOOD Hard at Park End.

3 HOST I'll be her servingman for once.

WITGOOD Why, there we let off together: keep full time; my thoughts were striking then just the same number?

HOST I knew 't: shall we then see our merry days again?

4 WITGOOD Our merry nights—which ne'er shall be more seen. [*Aside*]

[*Exeunt*]

5 ## Scene Three

[*A street in London. Enter* LUCRE *and* HOARD *quarrelling:* LAMPREY, SPICHCOCK, FREEDOM, *and* MONEYLOVE, *coming between to pacify them.*]

6 LAMPREY Nay, good Master Lucre, and you, Master Hoard, anger is the wind which you're both too much troubled withal.

HOARD Shall my adversary thus daily affront me, ripping up the old wound of our malice, which three summers could not close
7 up, into which wound the very sight of him drops scalding lead instead of balsamum?

LUCRE Why, Hoard, Hoard, Hoard, Hoard, Hoard! May I not pass in the state of quietness to mine own house? Answer me to that, before witness, and why? I'll refer the cause to honest, even-minded gentlemen or require the mere indifferences of the
8 law to decide this matter. I got the purchase, true: was 't not any man's case? Yes: will a wise man stand as a bawd, whilst another wipes his nose of the bargain? No; I answer no in that case.

hic et haec hostis: An enemy of this and that.
wipes his nose: Cheats him.

LAMPREY   Nay, sweet Master Lucre.   1

HOARD   Was it the part of a friend—no, rather of a Jew;—mark
what I say—when I had beaten the bush to the last bird, or, as I
may term it, the price to a pound, then, like a cunning usurer, to
come in the evening of the bargain, and glean all my hopes in a
minute, to enter, as it were, at the back door of the purchase?   2
For thou ne'er camest the right way by it.

LUCRE   Hast thou the conscience to tell me so without any im-
peachment to thyself?.

HOARD   Thou that canst defeat thy own nephew, Lucre, lap his
lands into bonds, and take the extremity of thy kindred's forfeitures, because he's a rioter, a wastethrift, a brothel master, and so   3
forth; what may a stranger expect from thee but *vulnera dilacerata,* as the poet says dilacerate dealing?

LUCRE   Upbraidest thou me with a nephew? Is all imputation laid
upon me? What acquaintance have I with his follies? If he riot, 't   4
is he must want it; if he surfeit, 't is he must feel it; if he drab it,
't is he must lie by 't: what's this to me?

HOARD   What's all to thee? Nothing, nothing; such is the gulf of thy
desire and the wolf of thy conscience: but be assured, Old Pecu-
nius Lucre, if ever fortune so bless me, that I may be at leisure to
vex thee, or any means so favour me, that I may have opportu-   5
nity to mad thee, I will pursue it with that flame of hate, that
spirit of malice, unrepressed wrath, that I will blast thy comforts.

LUCRE   Ha, ha, ha!

LAMPREY   Nay, Master Hoard, you're a wise gentleman—   6

HOARD   I will so cross thee—

LUCRE   And I thee.

HOARD   So without mercy fret thee—

LUCRE   So monstrously oppose thee—   7

HOARD   Dost scoff at my just anger? O, that I had as much power
as usury has over thee!

LUCRE   Then thou wouldst have as much power as the devil has
over thee.

HOARD   Toad!   8

LUCRE   Aspic!

HOARD   Serpent!

   vulnera dilacerata: "Tearing wounds"—lacerations. Several Latin
writers use the phrase figuratively.

1 LUCRE Viper!

SPICHCOCK Nay, gentlemen, then we must divide you perforce.

LAMPREY When the fire grows too unreasonable hot, there's no better way than to take off the wood.

2 [*Exeunt* LAMPREY *and* SPICHCOCK, *drawing off* LUCRE *and* HOARD *different ways.*]

FREEDOM A word, good signior.

MONEYLOVE How now, what's the news?

3 FREEDOM 'T is given me to understand that you are a rival of mine in the love of Mistress Joyce, Master Hoard's niece: say me ay, say me no?

MONEYLOVE Yes, 't is so.

FREEDOM Then look to yourself, you cannot live long: I'm practis-
4 ing every morning; a month hence I'll challenge you.

MONEYLOVE Give me your hand upon 't; there's my pledge I'll meet you.

[*Strikes him, and exits.*]

5 FREEDOM O, O! what reason had you for that, sir, to strike before the month? You knew I was not ready for you, and that made you so crank: I am not such a coward to strike again, I warrant you. My ear has the law of her side, for it burns horribly. I will teach him to strike a naked face, the longest day of his life: 's lid,
6 it shall cost me some money but I'll bring this box into the chancery. [*Exits*]

Scene Four

7
[*Another street. Enter* WITGOOD *and* HOST.]

HOST Fear you nothing, sir; I have lodged her in a house of credit, I warrant you.

WITGOOD Hast thou the writings?
8
HOST Firm, sir.

WITGOOD Prithee, stay, and behold two the most prodigious rascals that ever slipt into the shape of men; Dampit, sirrah, and young Gulf his fellow caterpillar.

9 HOST Dampit? Sure I have heard of that Dampit?

WITGOOD   Heard of him? Why, man, he that has lost both his ears   1
may hear of him; a famous infamous trampler of time; his own
phrase. Note him well: that Dampit, sirrah, he in the uneven
beard and the serge cloak, is the most notorious, usuring, blasphemous, atheistical, brothel-vomiting rascal, that we have in these
latter times now extant; whose first beginning was the stealing of
a mastiff dog from a farmer's house.   2

HOST   He looked as if he would obey the commandments well,
when he began first with stealing.

WITGOOD   True: the next town he came at, he set the dogs together
by th' ears.   3

HOST   A sign he should follow the law, by my faith.

WITGOOD   So it followed, indeed; and being destitute of all fortunes, staked his mastiff against a noble, and by great fortune his
dog had the day; how he made it up ten shillings, I know not, but
his own boast is, that he came to town with but ten shillings in   4
his purse, and now is credibly worth ten thousand pound.

HOST   How the devil came he by it?

[*Enter* DAMPIT *and* GULF.]

WITGOOD   How the devil came he not by it? If you put in the devil   5
once, riches come with a vengeance: has been a trampler of the
law, sir; and the devil has a care of his footmen. The rogue has
spied me now; he nibbled me finely once, too: a pox search you!
[*Aside*]—O, Master Dampit!—the very loins of thee! [*Aside*]—
Cry you mercy, Master Gulf; you walk so low, I promise you I   6
saw you not, sir.

GULF   He that walks low walks safe, the poets tell us.

WITGOOD   And nigher hell by a foot and a half than the rest of his
fellows [*Aside*].—But, my old Harry!

DAMPIT   My sweet Theodorus!   7

WITGOOD   'T was a merry world when thou camest to town with ten
shillings in thy purse.

DAMPIT   And now worth ten thousand pound, my boy. Report it;
Harry Dampit, a trampler of time, say, he would be up in a
morning, and be here with his serge gown, dashed up to the hams   8
in a cause; have his feet stink about Westminster Hall, and come
home again; see the galleons, the galleasses, the great armadas of
the law; then there be hoys and petty vessels, oars and scullers of
the time; there be picklocks of time, too: then would I be here; I
would trample up and down like a mule: now to the judges,   9

1 "May it please your reverend honourable fatherhoods"; then to
my counsellor, "May it please your worshipful patience"; then to
the examiner's office, "May it please your mastership's gentleness"; then to one of the clerks, "May it please your worshipful
lousiness,"—for I find him scrubbing in his codpiece; then to the
hall again, then to the chamber again—

2 WITGOOD   And when to the cellar again?

DAMPIT   E'en when thou wilt again: tramplers of time, motions of
Fleet Street, and visions of Holborn; here I have fees of one,
there I have fees of another; my clients come about me, the fool-
3 iaminy and coxcombry of the country: I still trashed and trotted
for other men's causes; thus was poor Harry Dampit made rich
by others' laziness, who though they would not follow their own
suits, I made 'em follow me with their purses.

WITGOOD   Didst thou so, old Harry?

4 DAMPIT   Ay, and I soused 'em with bills of charges, i' faith; twenty
pound ayear have I brought in for boat hire, and I ne'er stept
into boat in my life.

WITGOOD   Tramplers of time!

DAMPIT   Ay, tramplers of time, rascals of time, bull beggars.

5 WITGOOD   Ah, thou 'rt a mad old Harry!—Kind Master Gulf, I am
bold to renew my acquaintance.

GULF   I embrace it, sir.

[*Exeunt*]

6

fooliaminy: Compare with "bawdriaminy" of Act III, Sc. iv, and
"babliaminy" Act IV, Sc. v.

ACT TWO

Scene One

[*A room in* LUCRE'S *house*.]   1

LUCRE [*enters*]   My adversary evermore twits me with my nephew,
forsooth, my nephew: why may not a virtuous uncle have a dissolute nephew? What though he be a brotheller, a wastethrift, a
common surfeiter, and, to conclude, a beggar, must sin in him
call up shame in me? Since we have no part in their follies, why   2
should we have part in their infamies? For my strict hand toward
his mortgage, that I deny not: I confess I had an uncle's pen'
worth; let me see, half in half, true: I saw neither hope of his
reclaiming, nor comfort in his being; and was it not then better
bestowed upon his uncle than upon one of his aunts?—I need not
say bawd, for every one knows what aunt stands for in the last   3
translation.

[*Enter* SERVANT.]

   Now, sir?   4

SERVANT   There's a country servingman, sir, attends to speak with
your worship.

LUCRE   I'm at best leisure now; send him in to me.

[*Exit* SERVANT.]

HOST [*enters, disgused as a servingman*]   Bless your venerable wor-   5
ship.

LUCRE   Welcome, good fellow.

HOST   He calls me thief at first sight, yet he little thinks I am an
host. [*Aside*]

LUCRE   What's thy business with me?   6

HOST   Faith, sir, I am sent from my mistress, to any sufficient gentleman indeed, to ask advice upon a doubtful point: 't is indifferent, sir, to whom I come, for I know none, nor did my mistress
direct me to any particular man, for she's as mere a stranger here
as myself; only I found your worship within, and 't is a thing I   7
ever loved, sir, to be despatched as soon as I can.

LUCRE   A good, blunt honesty; I like him well [*aside*].—What is
thy mistress?

   good fellow: At this time a cant term for thief. (Compare the name
Robin Goodfellow.)

1 HOST Faith, a country gentlewoman, and a widow, sir. Yesterday was the first flight of us; but now she intends to stay till a little term business be ended.

LUCRE Her name, I prithee?

HOST It runs there in the writings, sir, among her lands; Widow
2 Medler.

LUCRE Medler? Mass, have I ne'er heard of that widow?

HOST Yes, I warrant you, have you, sir; not the rich widow in Staffordshire?

3 LUCRE Cuds me, there 't is indeed; thou has put me into memory: there's a widow indeed; ah, that I were a bachelor again!

HOST No doubt your worship might do much then; but she's fairly promised to a bachelor already.

LUCRE Ah, what is he, I prithee?

4 HOST A country gentleman too; one of whom your worship knows not, I'm sure; has spent some few follies in his youth, but marriage, by my faith, begins to call him home: my mistress loves him, sir, and love covers faults, you know: one Master Witgood, if ever you have heard of the gentleman.

5 LUCRE Ha! Witgood, say'st thou?

HOST That's his name indeed, sir; my mistress is like to bring him to a goodly seat yonder; four hundred a year, by my faith.

LUCRE But, I pray, take me with you.

6 HOST Ay, sir.

LUCRE What countryman might this young Witgood be?

HOST A Leicestershire gentleman, sir.

LUCRE My nephew, by th' mass, my nephew? I'll fetch out more of this, i' faith: a simple country fellow, I'll work 't out of him
7 [aside].—And is that gentleman, say'st thou, presently to marry her?

HOST Faith, he brought her up to town, sir; has the best card in all the bunch for 't, her heart; and I know my mistress will be married ere she go down; nay, I'll swear that, for she's none of
8 those widows that will go down first, and be married after; she hates that, I can tell you, sir.

LUCRE By my faith, sir, she is like to have a proper gentleman, and a comely; I'll give her that gift.

take me with you: Let me understand you.

HOST Why, does your worship know him, sir? 1

LUCRE I know him? Does not all the world know him? Can a man of such exquisite qualities be hid under a bushel?

HOST Then your worship may save me a labour, for I had charge given me to inquire after him. 2

LUCRE Inquire of him? If I might counsel thee, thou shouldst ne'er trouble thyself further; inquire of him no more, but of me; I'll fit thee. I grant he has been youthful; but is he not now reclaimed? mark you that, sir: has not your mistress, think you, been wanton in her youth? If men be wags, are there not women wagtails?

HOST No doubt, sir. 3

LUCRE Does not he return wisest that comes home whipt with his own follies?

HOST Why, very true, sir.

LUCRE The worst report you can hear of him, I can tell you, is 4 that he has been a kind gentleman, a liberal, and a worthy; who but lusty Witgood, thrice-noble Witgood!

HOST Since your worship has so much knowledge in him, can you resolve me, sir, what his living might be? My duty binds me, sir, to have a care of my mistress' estate; she has been ever a good 5 mistress to me, though I say it: many wealthy suitors has she nonsuited for his sake; yet, though her love be so fixed, a man cannot tell whether his nonperformance may help to remove it, sir; he makes us believe he has lands and living.

LUCRE Who, young Master Witgood? Why, believe it, he has as 6 goodly a fine living out yonder,—what do you call the place.

HOST Nay, I know not, i' faith.

LUCRE Hum—see, like a beast, if I have not forgot the name— pooh! and out yonder again, goodly grown woods and fair meadows: pax on 't, I can ne'er hit of that place neither. He? Why, 7 he's Witgood of Witgood Hall; he an unknown thing!

HOST Is he so, sir? To see how rumour will alter! Trust me, sir, we heard once he had no lands, but all lay mortgaged to an uncle he has in town here.

LUCRE Pish, 't is a tale, 't is a tale. 8

HOST I can assure you, sir, 't was credibly reported to my mistress.

LUCRE Why, do you think, i' faith, he was ever so simple to mortgage his lands to his uncle? Or his uncle so unnatural to take the extremity of such a mortgage?

HOST That was my saying still, sir. 9

1 LUCRE Pooh, ne'er think it.

HOST Yet that report goes current.

LUCRE Nay, then you urge me: Cannot I tell that best that am his uncle?

2 HOST How, sir? What have I done!

LUCRE Why, how now! In a swoon, man?

HOST Is your worship his uncle, sir?

LUCRE Can that be any harm to you, sir?

3 HOST I do beseech you, sir, do me the favour to conceal it; what a beast was I to utter so much! Pray, sir, do me the kindness to keep it in; I shall have my coat pulled o'er my ears, an' 't should be known; for the truth is, an' 't please your worship, to prevent much rumour and many suitors, they intend to be married very suddenly and privately.

4 LUCRE And dost thou think it stands with my judgment to do them injury? Must I needs say the knowledge of this marriage comes from thee? Am I a fool at fifty-four? Do I lack subtlety now, that have got all my wealth by it? There's a leash of angels for thee: come, let me woo thee; speak, where lie they?

5 HOST So I might have no anger, sir—

LUCRE Passion of me, not a jot: prithee, come.

HOST I would not have it known, sir, it came by my means.

LUCRE Why, am I a man of wisdom?

6 HOST I dare trust your worship, sir; but I'm a stranger to your house; and to avoid all intelligencers, I desire your worship's ear.

LUCRE This fellow's worth a matter of trust [aside].—Come sir.

[HOST whispers to him.]

7 Why, now thou 'rt an honest lad.—Ah, sirrah, nephew!

HOST Please you, sir, now I have begun with your worship, when shall I attend for your advice upon that doubtful point? I must come warily now.

8 LUCRE Tut, fear thou nothing;
Tomorrow's evening shall resolve the doubt.

HOST The time shall cause my attendance.

LUCRE Fare thee well.

9 [Exit HOST.]

—There's more true honesty in such a country servingman than 1
in a hundred of our cloak companions: I may well call 'em companions, for since blue coats have been turned into cloaks, we can
scarce know the man from the master.—George!

GEORGE [*enters*]   Anon, sir.

LUCRE   List, hither: [*whispers*] keep the place secret: commend me 2
to my nephew; I know no cause, tell him, but he might see his
uncle.

GEORGE   I will, sir.

LUCRE   And, do you hear, sir?
Take heed to use him with respect and duty. 3

GEORGE   Here's a strange alteration; one day he must be turned
out like a beggar, and now he must be called in like a knight.
[*Aside and exits.*]

LUCRE   Ah, sirrah, that rich widow!—four hundred a year! beside I 4
hear she lays claim to a title of a hundred more. This falls un-
happily that he should bear a grudge to me now, being likely to
prove so rich: what is 't, trow, that he makes me a stranger for?
Hum,—I hope he has not so much wit to apprehend that I cozened him: he deceives me then. Good Heaven, who would have
thought it would ever have come to this pass! Yet he's a proper 5
gentleman, i' faith, give him his due,—marry, that's his mortgage;
but that I ne'er mean to give him: I'll make him rich enough in
words, if that be good: and if it come to a piece of money, I will
not greatly stick for 't; there may be hope some of the widow's
lands, too, may one day fall upon me, if things be carried wisely.
 6

[*Reenter* GEORGE.]

Now, sir, where is he?

GEORGE   He desires your worship to hold him excused; he has such
weighty business, it commands him wholly from all men. 7

LUCRE   Were those my nephew's words?

GEORGE   Yes, indeed, sir.

LUCRE   When men grow rich, they grow proud too, I perceive that;
he would not have sent me such an answer once within this twelve- 8
month: see what 't is when a man's come to his lands! [*Aside*]
—Return to him again, sir; tell him his uncle desires his company

cloak companion: A rogue.
blue coat: A servant's livery.

1   for an hour; I'll trouble him but an hour, say; 't is for his own good, tell him: and, do you hear, sir? put "worship" upon him: go to, do as I bid you; he's like to be a gentleman of worship very shortly.

GEORGE   This is good sport, i' faith. [*Aside, and exits.*]

2   LUCRE   Troth, he uses his uncle discourteously now: can he tell what I may do for him? Goodness may come from me in a minute, that comes not in seven year again: he knows my humour; I am not so usually good; 't is no small thing that draws kindness from me, he may know that an' he will. The chief cause that in-
3   vites me to do him most good is the sudden astonishing of old Hoard, my adversary: how pale his malice will look at my nephew's advancement! With what a dejected spirit he will behold his fortunes, whom but last day he proclaimed rioter, penurious makeshift, despised brothel master! Ha, ha! 'T will do me more secret joy than my last purchase, more precious comfort than all
4   these widow's revenues.

[*Reenter* GEORGE, *showing in* WITGOOD.]

Now, sir?

GEORGE   With much entreaty he's at length come, sir. [*Exits*]
5

LUCRE   O, nephew, let me salute you, sir! You're welcome, nephew.

WITGOOD   Uncle, I thank you.

LUCRE   You've a fault, nephew; you're a stranger here: Well,
6   Heaven give you joy!

WITGOOD   Of what, sir?

LUCRE   Hah, we can hear!
You might have known your uncle's house, i' faith,
You and your widow: go to, you were to blame;
7   If I may tell you so without offence.

WITGOOD   How could you hear of that, sir?

LUCRE   O, pardon me!
'T was your will to have kept it from me, I perceive now.

8   WITGOOD   Not for any defect of love, I protest, uncle.

LUCRE   Oh, 't was unkindness, nephew! Fie, fie, fie.

WITGOOD   I am sorry you take it in that sense, sir.

LUCRE   Pooh, you cannot colour it, i' faith, nephew.

9   WITGOOD   Will you but hear what I can say in my just excuse, sir.

LUCRE   Yes, faith, will I, and welcome.   1

WITGOOD   You that know my danger i' th' city, sir, so well, how great my debts are, and how extreme my creditors, could not out of your pure judgment, sir, have wished us hither.

LUCRE   Mass, a firm reason indeed.

WITGOOD   Else, my uncle's house! Why, 't had been the only   2
make-match.

LUCRE   Nay, and thy credit.

WITGOOD   My credit? Nay, my countenance: pish, nay, I know, uncle, you would have wrought it so by your wit, you would have   3
made her believe in time the whole house had been mine.

LUCRE   Ay, and most of the goods, too.

WITGOOD   La, you there! Well, let 'em all prate what they will, there's nothing like the bringing of a widow to one's uncle's house.   4

LUCRE   Nay, let nephews be ruled as they list, they shall find their uncle's house the most natural place when all's done.

WITGOOD   There they may be bold.

LUCRE   Life, they may do anything there, man, and fear neither   5
beadle nor summoner: an uncle's house! a very Cold Harbour. Sirrah, I'll touch thee near now: hast thou so much interest in thy widow, that by a token thou couldst presently send for her?

WITGOOD   Troth, I think I can, uncle.

LUCRE   Go to, let me see that.   6

WITGOOD   Pray, command one of your men hither, uncle.

LUCRE   George!

GEORGE [reenters]   Here, sir.

LUCRE   Attend my nephew.   7

[WITGOOD whispers to GEORGE, who then goes out.]

   I love a' life to prattle with a rich widow; 't is pretty, methinks, when our tongues go together: and then to promise much and perform little; I love that sport a' life, i' faith; yet I am in the   8
mood now to do my nephew some good, if he take me handsomely [aside].—What, have you despatched?

WITGOOD   I ha' sent, sir.

LUCRE   Yet I must condemn you of unkindness, nephew.

WITGOOD   Heaven forbid, uncle!   9

1 LUCRE   Yes, faith, must I. Say your debts be many, your creditors importunate, yet the kindness of a thing is all, nephew: you might have sent me close word on 't, without the least danger or prejudice to your fortunes.

2 WITGOOD   Troth, I confess it, uncle; I was to blame there; but, indeed, my intent was to have clapped it up suddenly, and so have broke forth like a joy to my friends, and a wonder to the world: beside, there's a trifle of a forty-pound matter toward the setting of me forth; my friends should ne'er have known on 't; I meant to make shift for that myself.

3 LUCRE   How, nephew? Let me not hear such a word again, I beseech you: shall I be beholden to you?

WITGOOD   To me? Alas, what do you mean, uncle?

LUCRE   I charge you, upon my love, you trouble nobody but myself.

4 WITGOOD   You've no reason for that, uncle.

LUCRE   Troth, I'll ne'er be friends with you while you live, an you do.

WITGOOD   Nay, an you say so, uncle, here's my hand; I will not do 't.

5 LUCRE   Why, well said! There's some hope in thee when thou wilt be ruled; I'll make it up fifty, faith, because I see thee so reclaimed. Peace; here comes my wife with Sam, her t' other husband's son.

[*Enter* MISTRESS LUCRE *and* FREEDOM.]

6 WITGOOD   Good aunt.

FREEDOM   Cousin Witgood, I rejoice in my salute; you're most welcome to this noble city, governed with the sword in the scabbard.

WITGOOD   And the wit in the pommel [*aside*].—Good Master Sam Freedom, I return the salute.

7 LUCRE   By the mass, she's coming, wife; let me see now how thou wilt entertain her.

MISTRESS LUCRE   I hope I am not to learn, sir, to entertain a widow; 't is not so long ago since I was one myself.

8 [*Enter* COURTESAN.]

WITGOOD   Uncle—

LUCRE   She's come indeed.

9 WITGOOD   My uncle was desirous to see you, widow, and I presumed to invite you.

COURTESAN The presumption was nothing, Master Witgood: is 1
this your uncle, sir?

LUCRE Marry am I, sweet widow; and his good uncle he shall find
me; ay, by this smack that I give thee

[*Kisses her*]
2
thou 'rt welcome.—Wife, bid the widow welcome the same way
again.

FREEDOM I am a gentleman now too by my father's occupation,
and I see no reason but I may kiss a widow by my father's copy:
truly, I think the charter is not against it; surely these are the
words, "The son once a gentleman may revel it, though his father 3
were a dauber"; 't is about the fifteenth page: I'll to her.

[*Aside, then offers to kiss the* COURTESAN, *who repulses him.*]

LUCRE You're not very busy now; a word with thee, sweet widow.
4
FREEDOM Coads-nigs! I was never so disgraced since the hour my
mother whipt me.

LUCRE Beside, I have no child of mine own to care for; she's my
second wife, old, past bearing; clap sure to him, widow; he's like
to be my heir, I can tell you.
5
COURTESAN Is he so, sir?

LUCRE He knows it already, and the knave's proud on 't; jolly rich
widows have been offered him here i' th' city, great merchants'
wives; and do you think he would once look upon 'em? Forsooth,
he'll none: you are beholding to him i' th' country, then, ere we 6
could be: nay, I'll hold a wager, widow, if he were once known
to be in town, he would be presently sought after; nay, and happy
were they that could catch him first.

COURTESAN I think so.

LUCRE O, there would be such running to and fro, widow! He 7
should not pass the streets for 'em: he'd be took up in one great
house or other presently: faugh! they know he has it, and must
have it. You see this house here, widow; this house and all comes
to him; goodly rooms, ready furnished, ceiled with plaster of
Paris, and all hung about with cloth of arras.—Nephew.
8
WITGOOD Sir.

LUCRE Show the widow your house; carry her into all the rooms,
and bid her welcome.—You shall see, widow.—Nephew, strike
all sure above an thou beest a good boy,—ah! [*Aside to* WIT-
GOOD]
9

1 WITGOOD Alas, sir, I know not how she would take it.

LUCRE The right way, I warrant t' ye: a pox, art an ass? Would I were in thy stead! Get you up, I am ashamed of you.

[*Exeunt* WITGOOD *and* COURTESAN.]

2 So: let 'em agree as they will now: many a match has been struck up in my house a' this fashion: let 'em try all manner of ways, still there's nothing like an uncle's house to strike the stroke in. I'll hold my wife in talk a little.—Now, Jenny, your son there goes a-wooing to a poor gentlewoman but of a thousand pound portion: see my nephew, a lad of less hope, strikes at four hun-
3 dred ayear in good rubbish.

MISTRESS LUCRE Well, we must do as we may, sir.

LUCRE I'll have his money ready told for him against he come down: let me see, too;—by th' mass, I must present the widow with some jewel, a good piece of plate, or such a device; 't will
4 hearten her on well: I have a very fair standing cup; and a good high standing cup will please a widow above all other pieces. [*Exits*]

MISTRESS LUCRE Do you mock us with your nephew?—I have a plot in my head, son;—i' faith, husband, to cross you.
5
FREEDOM Is it a tragedy plot, or a comedy plot, good mother?

MISTRESS LUCRE 'T is a plot shall vex him. I charge you, of my blessing, son Sam, that you presently withdraw the action of your love from Master Hoard's niece.

6 FREEDOM How, mother?

MISTRESS LUCRE Nay, I have a plot in my head, i' faith. Here, take this chain of gold, and this fair diamond: dog me the widow home to her lodging, and at thy best opportunity, fasten 'em both upon her. Nay, I have a reach: I can tell you thou art known
7 what thou art, son, among the right worshipful, all the twelve companies.

FREEDOM Truly, I thank 'em for it.

MISTRESS LUCRE He? He's a scab to thee: and so certify her thou has two hundred ayear of thyself, beside thy good parts—a
8 proper person and a lovely. If I were a widow, I could find in my heart to have thee myself, son; ay, from 'em all.

FREEDOM Thank you for your good will, mother; but, indeed, I had rather have a stranger: and if I woo her not in that violent fashion, that I will make her be glad to take these gifts ere I
9 leave her, let me never be called the heir of your body.

MISTRESS LUCRE Nay, I know there's enough in you, son, if you   1
    once come to put it forth.

FREEDOM I'll quickly make a bolt or a shaft on 't.

[*Exeunt*]

                                                                  2

Scene Two

[*A street. Enter* HOARD *and* MONEYLOVE.]

MONEYLOVE Faith, Master Hoard, I have bestowed many months   3
    in the suit of your niece, such was the dear love I ever bore to
    her virtues: but since she hath so extremely denied me, I am to
    lay out for my fortunes elsewhere.

HOARD Heaven forbid but you should, sir! I ever told you my
    niece stood otherwise affected.
                                                                  4
MONEYLOVE I must confess you did, sir; yet, in regard of my great
    loss of time, and the zeal with which I sought your niece, shall I
    desire one favour of your worship?

HOARD In regard of those two, 't is hard but you shall, sir.

MONEYLOVE I shall rest grateful: 't is not full three hours, sir,   5
    since the happy rumour of a rich country widow came to my
    hearing.

HOARD How? A rich country widow?

MONEYLOVE Four hundred a year landed.

HOARD Yea?   6

MONEYLOVE Most firm, sir; and I have learnt her lodging: here
    my suit begins, sir; if I might but entreat your worship to be a
    countenance for me, and speak a good word (for your words will
    pass), I nothing doubt but I might set fair for the widow; nor
    shall your labour, sir, end altogether in thanks; two hundred an-   7
    gels—

HOARD So, so: what suitors has she?

MONEYLOVE There lies the comfort, sir; the report of her is yet
    but a whisper; and only solicited by young riotous Witgood,
    nephew to your mortal adversary.   8

HOARD Ha! Art certain he's her suitor?

MONEYLOVE Most certain, sir; and his uncle very industrious to
    beguile the widow, and make up the match.

    make a bolt or a shaft: Take a risk; proverbial.

1 HOARD So: very good.

MONEYLOVE Now, sir, you know this young Witgood is a spend-thrift, dissolute fellow.

HOARD A very rascal.

2 MONEYLOVE A midnight surfeiter.

HOARD The spume of a brothel house.

MONEYLOVE True, sir; which being well told in your worship's phrase, may both heave him out of her mind, and drive a fair way for me to the widow's affections.

3 HOARD Attend me about five.

MONEYLOVE With my best care, sir. [*Exits*]

HOARD Fool, thou hast left thy treasure with a thief. To trust a widower with a suit in love! Happy revenge, I hug thee! I have not only the means laid before me, extremely to cross my ad-
4 versary, and confound the last hopes of his nephew, but thereby to enrich my estate, augment my revenues, and build mine own fortunes greater: ha, ha!
I'll mar your phrase, o'erturn your flatteries,
Undo your windings, policies, and plots,
5 Fall like a secret and despatchful plague
On your secured comforts. Why, I am able
To buy three of Lucre; thrice outbid him,
Let my out-moneys be reckoned and all.

[*Enter three of* WITGOOD'S CREDITORS.]

6 FIRST CREDITOR I am glad of this news.

SECOND CREDITOR So are we, by my faith.

THIRD CREDITOR Young Witgood will be a gallant again now.

HOARD Peace. [*Listening*]
7 FIRST CREDITOR I promise you, Master Cockpit, she's a mighty rich widow.

SECOND CREDITOR Why, have you ever heard of her?

FIRST CREDITOR Who? Widow Medler? She lies open to much ru-
8 mour.

THIRD CREDITOR Four hundred ayear, they say, in very good land.

FIRST CREDITOR Nay, tak' 't of my word, if you believe that, you believe the least.

9 SECOND CREDITOR And to see how close he keeps it!

FIRST CREDITOR   O, sir, there's policy in that, to prevent better sui- 1
tors.

THIRD CREDITOR   He owes me a hundred pound, and I protest I
ne'er looked for a penny.

FIRST CREDITOR   He little dreams of our coming; he'll wonder to
see his creditors upon him.   2

[*Exeunt* CREDITORS.]

HOARD   Good, his creditors: I'll follow. This makes for me:
   All know the widow's wealth; and 't is well known
   I can estate her fairly, ay, and will.   3
   In this one chance shines a twice happy fate;
   I both deject my foe and raise my state. [*Exits*]

ACT THREE

Scene One

1 [*Witgood's lodgings. Enter* WITGOOD *and* THREE CREDITORS.]

WITGOOD   Why, alas, my creditors, could you find no other time to undo me but now? Rather your malice appears in this than the justness of the debt.

2 FIRST CREDITOR   Master Witgood, I have forborne my money long.

WITGOOD   I pray, speak low, sir: what do you mean?

SECOND CREDITOR   We hear you are to be married suddenly to a rich country widow.

3 WITGOOD   What can be kept so close but you creditors hear on 't! Well, 't is a lamentable state, that our chiefest afflictors should first hear of our fortunes. Why, this is no good course, i' faith, sirs: if ever you have hope to be satisfied, why do you seek to confound the means that should work it? There's neither piety, no, nor policy in that. Shine favourably now: why, I may rise
4 and spread again, to your great comforts.

FIRST CREDITOR   He says true, i' faith.

WITGOOD   Remove me now, and I consume for ever.

SECOND CREDITOR   Sweet gentleman!

5 WITGOOD   How can it thrive which from the sun you sever?

THIRD CREDITOR   It cannot, indeed.

WITGOOD   O, then, show patience! I shall have enough
          To satisfy you all.

6 FIRST CREDITOR   Ay, if we could
          Be content, a shame take us!

WITGOOD   For, look you;
          I am but newly sure yet to the widow,
          And what a rend might this discredit make!
7   Within these three days will I bind you lands
          For your securities.

FIRST CREDITOR   No, good Master Witgood:
          Would 't were as much as we dare trust you with!

WITGOOD   I know you have been kind; however, now,
8   Either by wrong report or false incitement,

112

Your gentleness is injurèd: in such   1
A state as this a man cannot want foes.
If on the sudden he begin to rise,
No man that lives can count his enemies.
You had some intelligence, I warrant ye,
From an ill-willer.

SECOND CREDITOR   Faith, we heard you brought up a rich widow,   2
sir, and were suddenly to marry her.

WITGOOD   Ay, why there it was: I knew 't was so: but since you
are so well resolved of my faith toward you, let me be so much
favoured to you, I beseech you all—
                                                                         3
ALL   O, it shall not need, i' faith, sir!—

WITGOOD   —As to lie still awhile, and bury my debts in silence, till
I be fully possessed of the widow; for the truth is—I may tell you
as my friends—

ALL   O, O, O!—   4

WITGOOD   I am to raise a little money in the city, toward the setting forth of myself, for my own credit and your comfort; if my
former debts should be divulged, all hope of my proceedings were
quite extinguished.
                                                                         5
FIRST CREDITOR   Do you hear, sir? I may deserve your custom
hereafter; pray, let my money be accepted before a stranger's:
here's forty pound I received as I came to you; if that may
stand you in any stead, make use on 't.

[*Offers him money, which he at first declines.*]   6

   Nay, pray, sir; 't is at your service. [*Aside to* WITGOOD]

WITGOOD   You do so ravish me with kindness, that I am con-
strained to play the maid, and take it.

FIRST CREDITOR   Let none of them see it, I beseech you.   7

WITGOOD   Faugh!

FIRST CREDITOR   I hope I shall be first in your remembrance after
the marriage rites.

WITGOOD   Believe it firmly.   8

FIRST CREDITOR   So.—What, do you walk, sirs?

SECOND CREDITOR   I go.—Take no care, sir, for money to furnish
you; within this hour I send you sufficient [*aside to* WITGOOD].—
Come, Master Cockpit, we both stay for you.   9

1   THIRD CREDITOR   I ha' lost a ring, i' faith; I'll follow you presently

[*Exeunt* FIRST *and* SECOND CREDITORS.]

2   but you shall find it, sir; I know your youth and expenses have disfurnished you of all jewels: there's a ruby of twenty pound price, sir; bestow it upon your widow.

[*Offers him the ring, which he at first declines.*]

3   What, man! 't will call up her blood to you; beside, if I might so much work with you, I would not have you beholden to those bloodsuckers for any money.

WITGOOD   Not I, believe it.

THIRD CREDITOR   They're a brace of cutthroats.

WITGOOD   I know 'em.

4   THIRD CREDITOR   Send a note of all your wants to my shop, and I'll supply you instantly.

WITGOOD   Say you so? Why, here's my hand then, no man living shall do 't but thyself.

THIRD CREDITOR   Shall I carry it away from 'em both, then?

5   WITGOOD   I' faith, shalt thou.

THIRD CREDITOR   Troth, then, I thank you, sir.

WITGOOD   Welcome, good Master Cockpit.

6   [*Exit* THIRD CREDITOR.]

7   Ha, ha, ha! Why, is not this better now than lying abed? I perceive there's nothing conjures up wit sooner than poverty, and nothing lays it down sooner than wealth and lechery: this has some savour yet. O that I had the mortgage from mine uncle as sure in possession as these trifles! I would forswear brothel at noonday, and muscadine and eggs at midnight.

COURTESAN [*within*]   Master Witgood, where are you?

WITGOOD   Holla!

8   COURTESAN [*enters*]   Rich news?

WITGOOD   Would 't were all in plate!

COURTESAN   There's some in chains and jewels: I am so haunted with suitors, Master Witgood, I know not which to dispatch first.

9   WITGOOD   You have the better term, by my faith.

COURTESAN Among the number   1
One Master Hoard, an ancient gentleman.

WITGOOD Upon my life, my uncle's adversary.

COURTESAN It may well hold so, for he rails on you,
Speaks shamefully of him.
                                                                         2
WITGOOD As I could wish it.

COURTESAN I first denied him, but so cunningly,
It rather promised him assured hopes,
Than any loss of labour.

WITGOOD Excellent!   3

COURTESAN I expect him every hour with gentlemen,
With whom he labours to make good his words,
To approve you riotous, your state consumed.
Your uncle—
                                                                         4
WITGOOD Wench, make up thy own fortunes now; do thyself a
good turn once in thy days: he's rich in money, moveables,
and lands; marry him: he's an old doting fool, and that's worth
all; marry him: 't would be a great comfort to me to see thee do
well, i' faith; marry him: 't would ease my conscience well to see
thee well bestowed; I have a care of thee, i' faith.   5

COURTESAN Thanks, sweet Master Witgood.

WITGOOD I reach at farther happiness: first, I am sure it can be no
harm to thee, and there may happen goodness to me by it: prose-
cute it well; let's send up for our wits, now we require their best
and most pregnant assistance.   6

COURTESAN Step in, I think I hear 'em.

[*Exeunt. Enter* HOARD *and* GENTLEMEN, *with the* HOST *as Servant.*]

HOARD Art thou the widow's man? By my faith, sh' 'as a company   7
of proper men then.

HOST I am the worst of six, sir; good enough for blue coats.

HOARD Hark hither: I hear say thou art in most credit with her.

HOST Not so, sir.
                                                                         8
HOARD Come, come, thou 'rt modest: there's a brace of royals,
prithee, help me to th' speech of her.

[*Gives him money.*]

HOST I'll do what I may, sir, always saving myself harmless.   9

1   HOARD   Go to, do 't, I say; thou shalt hear better from me.

HOST   Is not this a better place than five mark ayear standing wages? Say a man had but three such clients in a day, methinks he might make a poor living on 't; beside, I was never brought up with so little honesty to refuse any man's money; never. What gulls

2   there are a' this side the world! now know I the widow's mind; none but my young master comes in her clutches: ha, ha, ha! [*Aside, and exits.*]

HOARD   Now, my dear gentlemen, stand firmly to me;
     You know his follies and my worth.

3   FIRST GENTLEMAN   We do, sir.

SECOND GENTLEMAN   But, Master Hoard, are you sure he is not
     I' th' house now?

HOARD   Upon my honesty, I chose this time
     A' purpose, fit: the spendthrift is abroad:
4   Assist me; here she comes.

[*Enter* COURTESAN]

                         Now, my sweet widow.

5   COURTESAN   You're welcome, Master Hoard.

HOARD   Despatch, sweet gentlemen, despatch.—
     I am come, widow, to prove those my words
     Neither of envy sprung nor of false tongues,
     But such as their deserts and actions
     Do merit and bring forth; all which these gentlemen,
6   Well known, and better reputed, will confess.

COURTESAN   I cannot tell
     How my affections may dispose of me;
     But surely if they find him so desertless,
     They'll have that reason to withdraw themselves:
7   And therefore, gentlemen, I do entreat you,
     As you are fair in reputation
     And in appearing form, so shine in truth:
     I am a widow, and, alas, you know,
     Soon overthrown! 'T is a very small thing
8   That we withstand, our weakness is so great:
     Be partial unto neither, but deliver,
     Without affection, your opinion.

HOARD   And that will drive it home.

COURTESAN   Nay, I beseech your silence, Master Hoard;
9   You are a party.

HOARD Widow, not a word.   1

FIRST GENTLEMAN The better first to work you to belief,
Know neither of us owe him flattery,
Nor t' other malice; but unbribèd censure,
So help us our best fortunes!

COURTESAN It suffices.   2

FIRST GENTLEMAN That Witgood is a riotous, undone man,
Imperfect both in fame and in estate,
His debts wealthier than he, and executions
In wait for his due body, we'll maintain
With our best credit and our dearest blood.   3

COURTESAN Nor land nor living, say you? Pray, take heed
You do not wrong the gentleman.

FIRST GENTLEMAN What we speak
Our lives and means are ready to make good.

COURTESAN Alas, how soon are we poor souls beguiled!   4

SECOND GENTLEMAN And for his uncle—

HOARD Let that come to me.
His uncle, a severe extortioner;
A tyrant at a forfeiture; greedy of others'
Miseries; one that would undo his brother,   5
Nay, swallow up his father, if he can,
Within the fathoms of his conscience.

FIRST GENTLEMAN Nay, believe it, widow,
You had not only matched yourself to wants,
But in an evil and unnatural stock.   6

HOARD Follow hard, gentlemen, follow hard. [*Aside to* GENTLE-
MEN]

COURTESAN Is my love so deceived? Before you all
I do renounce him; on my knees I vow [*kneeling*]
He ne'er shall marry me.   7

WITGOOD [*looking in*] Heaven knows he never meant it! [*Aside*]

HOARD There take her at the bound. [*Aside to* GENTLEMEN]

FIRST GENTLEMAN Then, with a new and pure affection,
Behold yon gentleman; grave, kind, and rich,   8
A match worthy yourself: esteeming him,
You do regard your state.

HOARD I'll make her a jointure, say. [*Aside to* GENTLEMEN]

FIRST GENTLEMAN He can join land to land, and will possess you
Of what you can desire.   9

1 SECOND GENTLEMAN   Come, widow, come.

COURTESAN   The world is so deceitful!

FIRST GENTLEMAN   There, 't is deceitful,
Where flattery, want, and imperfection lie;
But none of these in him: pish!

2 COURTESAN   Pray, sir—

FIRST GENTLEMAN   Come, you widows are ever most backward
when you should do yourselves most good; but were it to marry a
chin not worth a hair now, then you would be forward enough.
Come, clap hands, a match.

3 HOARD   With all my heart, widow.

[HOARD *and* COURTESAN *shake hands.*]

Thanks, gentlemen: I will deserve your labour, and [*to* COURTE-
4 SAN] thy love.

COURTESAN   Alas, you love not widows but for wealth! I promise
you I ha' nothing, sir.

HOARD   Well said, widow,
Well said; thy love is all I seek, before these gentlemen.

5 COURTESAN   Now I must hope the best.

HOARD   My joys are such they want to be expressed.

COURTESAN   But, Master Hoard, one thing I must remember you
of, before these gentlemen, your friends: how shall I suddenly
avoid the loathed soliciting of that perjured Witgood, and his te-
6 dious, dissembling uncle? who this very day hath appointed a
meeting for the same purpose, too; where, had not truth come
forth, I had been undone, utterly undone!

HOARD   What think you of that, gentlemen?

7 FIRST GENTLEMAN   'T was well devised.

HOARD   Hark thee, widow: train out young Witgood single; hasten
him thither with thee, somewhat before the hour; where, at the
place appointed, these gentlemen and myself will wait the opportunity, when, by some slight removing him from thee, we'll suddenly enter and surprise thee, carry thee away by boat to Cold
8 Harbour, have a priest ready, and there clap it up instantly. How
likest it, widow?

COURTESAN   In that it pleaseth you, it likes me well.

HOARD   I'll kiss thee for those words [*kisses her*].—Come gentle-
9 men,

Still must I live a suitor to your favours,   1
Still to your aid beholden.

FIRST GENTLEMAN   We're engaged, sir;
'T is for our credits now to see 't well ended.

HOARD   'T is for your honours, gentlemen; nay, look to 't,
Not only in joy, but I in wealth excell: 2
No more sweet widow, but sweet wife, farewell.

COURTESAN   Farewell, sir.

[*Exeunt* HOARD *and* GENTLEMEN. *Reenter* WITGOOD.]

WITGOOD   O for more scope! I could laugh eternally! Give you joy,   3
Mistress Hoard, I promise your fortune was good, forsooth;
you've fell upon wealth enough, and there's young gentlemen
enow can help you to the rest. Now it requires our wits: carry
thyself but heedfully now, and we are both—

HOST [*reenters*]   Master Witgood, your uncle.   4

WITGOOD   Cuds me! Remove thyself awhile; I'll serve for him.

[*Exeunt* COURTESAN *and* HOST.]

LUCRE [*enters*]   Nephew, good morning, nephew.   5

WITGOOD   The same to you, kind uncle.

LUCRE   How fares the widow? Does the meeting hold?

WITGOOD   O, no question of that, sir.

LUCRE   I'll strike the stroke, then, for thee; no more days.   6

WITGOOD   The sooner the better, uncle. O, she's mightily followed!

LUCRE   And yet so little rumoured!

WITGOOD   Mightily: here comes one old gentleman, and he'll make
her a jointure of three hundred a year, forsooth; another wealthy
suitor will estate his son in his lifetime, and make him weigh   7
down the widow; here a merchant's son will possess her with no
less than three goodly lordships at once, which were all pawns to
his father.

LUCRE   Peace, nephew, let me hear no more of 'em; it mads me.
Thou shalt prevent 'em all. No words to the widow of my coming   8
hither. Let me see—'t is now upon nine: before twelve, nephew,
we will have the bargain struck, we will, faith, boy.

WITGOOD   O, my precious uncle!

[*Exeunt*]   9

Scene Two

1 [*A room in Hoard's house. Enter* HOARD *and* JOYCE.]

HOARD Niece, sweet niece, prithee, have a care to my house; I
leave all to thy discretion. Be content to dream awhile; I'll have a
husband for thee shortly: put that care upon me, wench, for in
choosing wives and husbands I am only fortunate; I have that gift
2 given me. [*Exits*]

JOYCE But 't is not likely you should choose for me,
Since nephew to your chiefest enemy
Is he whom I affect: but, O, forgetful!
Why dost thou flatter thy affections so,
3 With name of him that for a widow's bed
Neglects thy purer love? Can it be so,
Or does report dissemble?

[*Enter* GEORGE.]

4   How now, sir?

GEORGE A letter, with which came a private charge.

JOYCE Therein I thank your care.

[*Exit* GEORGE.]

5
—I know this hand—
[*Reads*] "Dearer than sight, what the world reports of me, yet believe not; rumour will alter shortly: be thou constant; I am still
the same that I was in love, and I hope to be the same in fortunes. Theodorus Witgood."
6 I am resolved: no more shall fear or doubt
Raise their pale powers to keep affection out. [*Exits*]

Scene Three

7 [*A Tavern. Enter* HOARD, GENTLEMEN, *and* DRAWER.]

DRAWER You're very welcome, gentlemen.—Dick, show those
gentlemen the Pomegranate there.

HOARD Hist!

8 DRAWER Up those stairs, gentlemen.

Pomegranate: Hence probably a scarlet room.

HOARD   Hist! Drawer!   1

DRAWER   Anon, sir.

HOARD   Prithee, ask at the bar if a gentlewoman came not in lately.

DRAWER   William, at the bar, did you see any gentlewoman come in lately? Speak you ay, speak you no?   2

[*Within*]   No, none came in yet but one Mistress Florence. He says none came in yet, sir, but one Mistress Florence.

HOARD   What is that Florence? A widow?

DRAWER   Yes, a Dutch widow.

HOARD   How?   3

DRAWER   That's an English drab, sir: give your worship good morrow. [*Exits*]

HOARD   A merry knave, i' faith! I shall remember a Dutch widow the longest day of my life.   4

FIRST GENTLEMAN   Did not I use most art to win the widow?

SECOND GENTLEMAN   You shall pardon me for that, sir; Master Hoard knows I took her at best 'vantage.

HOARD   What's that, sweet gentlemen, what's that?   5

SECOND GENTLEMAN   He will needs bear me down, that his art only wrought with the widow most.

HOARD   O, you did both well, gentlemen, you did both well, I thank you.

FIRST GENTLEMAN   I was the first that moved her.   6

HOARD   You were, i' faith.

SECOND GENTLEMAN   But it was I that took her at the bound.

HOARD   Ay, that was you: faith, gentlemen, 't is right.

THIRD GENTLEMAN   I boasted least, but 't was I joined their hands.   7

HOARD   By th' mass, I think he did: you did all well, Gentlemen, you did all well; contend no more.

FIRST GENTLEMAN   Come, yon room's fittest.

HOARD   True, 't is next the door.   8

[*Exeunt. Enter* WITGOOD, COURTESAN, HOST, *and* DRAWER.]

DRAWER   You're very welcome: please you to walk up stairs; cloth's laid, sir.

Dutch widow: Cant term for a prostitute.

COURTESAN Up stairs? Troth, I am very weary, Master Witgood.

WITGOOD Rest yourself here awhile, widow; we'll have a cup of muscadine in this little room.

DRAWER A cup of muscadine? You shall have the best, sir.

WITGOOD But, do you hear, sirrah?

DRAWER Do you call? Anon, sir.

WITGOOD What is there provided for dinner?

DRAWER I cannot readily tell you, sir: if you please you may go into the kitchen and see yourself, sir; many gentlemen of worship do use to do it, I assure you, sir. [*Exits*]

HOST A pretty familiar, prigging rascal; he has his part without book.

WITGOOD Against you are ready to drink to me, widow, I'll be present to pledge you.

COURTESAN Nay, I commend your care, 't is done well of you.

[*Exit* WITGOOD.]

'Las, what have I forgot!

HOST What, mistress?

COURTESAN I slipt my wedding ring off when I washed, and left it at my lodging: prithee, run; I shall be sad without it.

[*Exit* HOST.]

So, he's gone. Boy!

BOY [*enters*] Anon, forsooth.

COURTESAN Come hither, sirrah: learn secretly if one Master Hoard, an ancient gentleman, be about house.

BOY I heard such a one named.

COURTESAN Commend me to him.

[*Reenter* HOARD *and* GENTLEMEN.]

HOARD Ay, boy, do thy commendations.

COURTESAN O, you come well: away, to boat, begone.

HOARD Thus wise men are revenged, give two for one.

[*Exeunt. Reenter* WITGOOD *and* VINTNER.]

WITGOOD   I must request   1
You, sir, to show extraordinary care:
My uncle comes with gentlemen, his friends,
And 't is upon a making.

VINTNER   Is it so?
I'll give a special charge, good Master Witgood.   2
May I be bold to see her?

WITGOOD   Who? The widow? With all my heart, i' faith, I'll bring
you to her.

VINTNER   If she be a Staffordshire gentlewoman, 't is much if I
know her not.
3
WITGOOD   How now? Boy! Drawer!

VINTNER   Hie!

BOY [*reenters*]   Do you call, sir?

WITGOOD   Went the gentlewoman up that was here?

BOY   Up, sir? She went out, sir.   4

WITGOOD   Out, sir?

BOY   Out, sir. One Master Hoard, with a guard of gentlemen, carried her out at back door, a pretty while since, sir.

WITGOOD   Hoard? Death and darkness? Hoard?
5
HOST [*reenters*]   The devil of ring I can find.

WITGOOD   How now? What news? Where's the widow?

HOST   My mistress? Is she not here, sir?

WITGOOD   More madness yet!
6
HOST   She sent me for a ring.

WITGOOD   A plot, a plot!—To boat! She's stole away.

HOST   What?

[*Enter* LUCRE *and* GENTLEMEN.]   7

WITGOOD   Follow! Inquire old Hoard, my uncle's adversary.

[*Exit* HOST.]

LUCRE   Nephew, what's that?
8
WITGOOD   Thrice-miserable wretch!

LUCRE   Why, what's the matter?

VINTNER   The widow's borne away, sir.

making: Matchmaking.

1 LUCRE   Ha? Passion of me!—A heavy welcome, gentlemen.

FIRST GENTLEMAN   The widow gone?

LUCRE   Who durst attempt it?

WITGOOD   Who but old Hoard, my uncle's adversary?

2 LUCRE   How?

WITGOOD   With his confederates.

LUCRE   Hoard, my deadly enemy?—Gentlemen, stand to me,
   I will not bear it; 't is in hate of me;
   That villain seeks my shame, nay, thirsts my blood;
3   He owes me mortal malice.
   I'll spend my wealth on this despiteful plot,
   Ere he shall cross me and my nephew thus.

WITGOOD   So maliciously!

4 [*Reenter* HOST.]

LUCRE   How now, you treacherous rascal?

HOST   That's none of my name, sir.

WITGOOD   Poor soul, he knew not on 't!

5 LUCRE   I'm sorry. I see then 't was a mere plot.

HOST   I traced 'em nearly—

LUCRE   Well?

HOST   And hear for certain
6   They have took Cold Harbour.

LUCRE   The devil's sanctuary!
   They shall not rest; I'll pluck her from his arms—
   Kind and dear gentlemen,
   If ever I had seat within your breasts—

7 FIRST GENTLEMAN   No more, good sir; it is a wrong to us
   To see you injured; in a cause so just
   We'll spend our lives but we will right our friends.

LUCRE   Honest and kind! Come we've delayed too long;
   Nephew, take comfort; a just cause is strong.

8 WITGOOD   That's all my comfort, uncle.

[*Exeunt all but* WITGOOD.]

   Ha, ha, ha!
9   Now may events fall luckily and well;
   He that ne'er strives, says wit, shall ne'er excel. [*Exits*]

Scene Four

[A room in Dampit's house.]   1

DAMPIT *[enters drunk]* When did I say my prayers? In anno 88, when the great armada was coming; and in anno 89, when the great thundering and lightning was, I prayed heartily then, i' faith, to overthrow Poovies' new buildings; I kneeled by my great iron chest, I remember.   2

AUDREY *[enters]* Master Dampit, one may hear you before they see you: you keep sweet hours, Master Dampit; we were all abed three hours ago.

DAMPIT Audrey?

AUDREY O, you're a fine gentleman!   3

DAMPIT So I am i' faith, and a fine scholar: do you use to go to bed so early, Audrey?

AUDREY Call you this early, Master Dampit?

DAMPIT Why, is 't not one of clock i' th' morning? Is not that   4
early enough? Fetch me a glass of fresh beer.

AUDREY Here, I have warmed your nightcap for you, Master Dampit.

DAMPIT Draw it on then, I am very weak truly: I have not eaten so much as the bulk of an egg these three days.   5

AUDREY You have drunk the more, Master Dampit.

DAMPIT What's that?

AUDREY You might, an you would, Master Dampit.

DAMPIT I answer you, I cannot: hold your prating; you prate too   6
much, and understand too little: are you answered? Give me a glass of beer.

AUDREY May I ask you how you do, Master Dampit?

DAMPIT How do I? I' faith, naught.   7

AUDREY I ne'er knew you do otherwise.

DAMPIT I eat not one penn'orth of bread these two years. Give me a glass of fresh beer. I am not sick, nor I am not well.

AUDREY Take this warm napkin about your neck, sir, whilst I help to make you unready.   8

make you unready: Undress you.

1   DAMPIT   How now, Audrey-prater, with your scurvy devices, what say you now?

     AUDREY   What say I, Master Dampit? I say nothing, but that you are very weak.

2   DAMPIT   Faith, thou hast more cony-catching devices than all London.

     AUDREY   Why, Master Dampit, I never deceived you in all my life.

     DAMPIT   Why was that? Because I never did trust thee.

     AUDREY   I care not what you say, Master Dampit.

3   DAMPIT   Hold thy prating: I answer thee, thou art a beggar, a quean, and a bawd: are you answered?

     AUDREY   Fie, Master Dampit! A gentleman, and have such words?

4   DAMPIT   Why, thou base drudge of infortunity, thou kitchen-stuff drab of beggary, roguery, and coxcombry, thou cavernesed quean of foolery, knavery, and bawdreaminy, I'll tell thee what, I will not give a louse for thy fortunes.

     AUDREY   No, Master Dampit? And there's a gentleman comes a-wooing to me, and he doubts nothing but that you will get me from him.

5   DAMPIT   I? If I would either have thee or lie with thee for two thousand pound, would I might be damned! Why, thou base, impudent quean of foolery, flattery, and coxcombry, are you answered?

     AUDREY   Come, will you rise and go to bed, sir?

6   DAMPIT   Rise, and go to bed too, Audrey? How does Mistress Proserpine?

     AUDREY   Fool!

7   DAMPIT   She's as fine a philosopher of a stinkard's wife, as any within the liberties. Faugh, faugh, Audrey!

     AUDREY   How now, Master Dampit?

     DAMPIT   Fie upon 't, what a choice of stinks here is! What hast thou done, Audrey? Fie upon 't, here's a choice of stinks indeed! Give me a glass of fresh beer, and then I will to bed.

8   AUDREY   It waits for you above, sir.

     DAMPIT   Foh! I think they burn horns in Barnard's Inn. If ever I smelt such an abominable stink, usury forsake me. [*Exits*]

9   AUDREY   They be the stinking nails of his trampling feet, and he talks of burning of horns. [*Exits*]

ACT FOUR

Scene One

[*An apartment at Cold Harbour. Enter* HOARD, COURTESAN, LAM- 1
PREY, SPICHCOCK, *and* GENTLEMEN.]

FIRST GENTLEMAN   Join hearts, join hands.
  In wedlock's bands,
  Never to part
  Till death cleave your heart.   2
  [*To* HOARD] You shall forsake all other women;
  [*To* COURTESAN] You, lords, knights, gentlemen, and yeomen.
  What my tongue slips
  Make up with your lips.

HOARD [*kisses her*]   Give you joy, Mistress Hoard; let the kiss come 3
about.

[*Knocking*]

  Who knocks? Convey my little pig-eater out.

LUCRE [*within*]   Hoard!   4

HOARD   Upon my life, my adversary, gentlemen!

LUCRE [*within*]   Hoard, open the door, or we will force it ope: give
us the widow.

HOARD   Gentlemen, keep 'em out.   5

LAMPREY   He comes upon his death that enters here.

LUCRE [*within*]   My friends, assist me!

HOARD   He has assistants, gentlemen.

LAMPREY   Tut, nor him nor them we in this action fear.   6

LUCRE [*within*]   Shall I, in peace, speak one word with the widow?

COURTESAN   Husband, and gentlemen, hear me but a word.

LAMPREY   Freely, sweet wife.

COURTESAN   Let him in peaceably;   7
  You know we're sure from any act of his.

HOARD   Most true.

COURTESAN   You may stand by and smile at his old weakness:
  Let me alone to answer him.   8

127

1 HOARD Content; 'T will be good mirth, i' faith. **How think you,**
   gentlemen?

LAMPREY Good gullery!

HOARD Upon calm conditions let him in.

2 LUCRE [*within*] All spite and malice!

LAMPREY Hear me, Master Lucre:
   So you will vow a peaceful entrance
   With those your friends, and only exercise
   Calm conference with the widow, without fury,
   The passage shall receive you.

3 LUCRE [*within*] I do vow it.

LAMPREY Then enter and talk freely: here she stands.

[*Enter* LUCRE, GENTLEMEN, *and* HOST.]

4 LUCRE O, Master Hoard, your spite has watched the hour!
   You're excellent at vengeance, Master Hoard.

HOARD Ha, ha, ha!

LUCRE I am the fool you laugh at:
5 You are wise, sir, and know the seasons well.—
   Come hither, widow: why is it thus?
   O, you have done me infinite disgrace,
   And your own credit no small injury!
   Suffer mine enemy so despitefully
   To bear you from my nephew? O, I had
6 Rather half my substance had been forfeit
   And begged by some starved rascal!

COURTESAN Why, what would you wish me do, sir?
   I must not overthrow my state for love:
   We have too many precedents for that;
7 From thousands of our wealthy undone widows
   One may derive some wit. I do confess
   I loved your nephew, nay, I did affect him
   Against the mind and liking of my friends;
   Believed his promises; lay here in hope
   Of flattered living, and the boast of lands:
8 Coming to touch his wealth and state, indeed,
   It appears dross; I find him not the man;
   Imperfect, mean, scarce furnished of his needs:
   In words, fair lordships; in performance, hovels
   Can any woman love the thing that is not?

9 LUCRE Broke you for this?

COURTESAN Was it not cause too much?   1
  Send to inquire his state: most part of it
  Lay two years mortgaged in his uncle's hands.

LUCRE Why, say it did, you might have known my mind:
  I could have soon restored it.

COURTESAN Ay, had I but seen any such thing performed,   2
  Why, 't would have tied my affection, and contained
  Me in my first desires: do you think, i' faith,
  That I could twine such a dry oak as this,
  Had promise in your nephew took effect?

LUCRE Why, and there's no time past; and rather than   3
  My adversary should thus thwart my hopes,
  I would—

COURTESAN Tut, you've been ever full of golden speech:
  If words were lands, your nephew would be rich.
                                                     4

LUCRE Widow, believe 't, I vow by my best bliss,
  Before these gentlemen, I will give in
  The mortgage to my nephew instantly,
  Before I sleep or eat.

FIRST GENTLEMAN [*friend to* LUCRE] We'll pawn our credits,   5
  Widow, what he speaks shall be performed
  In fulness.

LUCRE Nay, more; I will estate him
  In farther blessings; he shall be my heir;
  I have no son;   6
  I'll bind myself to that condition.

COURTESAN When I shall hear this done, I shall soon yield
  To reasonable terms.

LUCRE In the mean season,   7
  Will you protest, before these gentlemen,
  To keep yourself as you're now at this present?

COURTESAN I do protest, before these gentlemen,
  I will be as clear then as I am now.

LUCRE I do believe you. Here's your own honest servant,   8
  I'll take him along with me.

COURTESAN Ay, with all my heart.

LUCRE He shall see all performed, and bring you word.

COURTESAN That's all I wait for.   9

1 HOARD   What, have you finished, Master Lucre? Ha, ha, ha, ha!

LUCRE   So laugh, Hoard, laugh at your poor enemy, do;
      The wind may turn, you may be laughed at, too;
      Yes, marry, may you, sir.—Ha, ha, ha!

2 [*Exeunt* LUCRE, GENTLEMEN, *and* HOST.]

HOARD   Ha, ha, ha! If every man that swells in malice
      Could be revenged as happily as I,
      He would choose hate, and forswear amity.—
      What did he say, wife, prithee?

3 COURTESAN   Faith, spoke to ease his mind.

HOARD   O, O, O!

COURTESAN   You know how little to any purpose.

HOARD   True, true, true!

4 COURTESAN   He would do mountains now.

HOARD   Ay, ay, ay, ay.

LAMPREY   You've struck him dead, Master Hoard.

SPICHCOCK   And his nephew desperate.

5 HOARD   I know 't, sirs, I.
      Never did man so crush his enemy.

[*Exeunt*]

6 ## Scene Two

[*A room in Lucre's house. Enter* LUCRE, GENTLEMEN, *and* HOST,
  meeting FREEDOM.]

7 LUCRE   My son-in-law, Sam Freedom, where's my nephew?

FREEDOM   O man in lamentation, father.

LUCRE   How!

FREEDOM   He thumps his breast like a gallant dicer that has lost
      his doublet, and stands in 's shirt to do penance.

8 LUCRE   Alas, poor gentleman!

FREEDOM   I warrant you may hear him sigh in a still evening to
      your house at Highgate.

"*O man in desperation*": The name of a tune of the time.

LUCRE   I prithee send him in.   1

FREEDOM   Were it to do a greater matter, I will not stick with you,
sir, in regard you married my mother. [*Exits*]

LUCRE   Sweet gentlemen, cheer him up; I will but fetch the mortgage and return to you instantly.

FIRST GENTLEMAN   We'll do our best, sir.   2

[*Exit* LUCRE.]

See where he comes,

E'en joyless and regardless of all form.   3

[*Enter* WITGOOD.]

SECOND GENTLEMAN   Why, how now, Master Witgood? Fie! You
a firm scholar, and an understanding gentleman, and give your
best parts to passion?   4

FIRST GENTLEMAN   Come, fie fie!

WITGOOD   O, gentlemen—

FIRST GENTLEMAN   Sorrow of me, what a sigh was there, sir!
Nine such widows are not worth it.   5

WITGOOD   To be borne from me by that lecher Hoard!

FIRST GENTLEMAN   That vengeance is your uncle's; being done
More in despite to him than wrong to you:
But we bring comfort now.

WITGOOD   I beseech you, gentlemen—   6

SECOND GENTLEMAN   Cheer thyself, man; there's hope of her i'
faith.

WITGOOD   Too gladsome to be true.

LUCRE [*reenters*]   Nephew, what cheer?   7
Alas, poor gentleman, how art thou changed!
Call thy fresh blood into thy cheeks again:
She comes.

WITGOOD   Nothing afflicts me so much,
But that it is your adversary, uncle,
And merely plotted in despite of you.   8

LUCRE   Ay, that's it mads me, spites me! I'll spend my wealth ere
he shall carry her so, because I know 't is only to spite me. Ay,
this is it. Here, nephew

[*Giving a paper*]   9

1   before these kind gentlemen, I deliver in your mortgage, my promise to the widow. See, 't is done: be wise, you're once more master of your own. The widow shall perceive now you are not altogether such a beggar as the world reputes you; you can make shift to bring her to three hundred a year, sir.

2   FIRST GENTLEMAN   By'rlady, and that's no toy, sir.

LUCRE   A word, nephew.

FIRST GENTLEMAN [*to* HOST]   Now you may certify the widow.

LUCRE   You must conceive it aright, nephew, now;
To do you good I am content to do this.

3   WITGOOD   I know it, sir.

LUCRE   But your own conscience can tell I had it
Dearly enough of you.

WITGOOD   Ay, that's most certain.

4   LUCRE   Much money laid out, beside many a journey
To fetch the rent; I hope you'll think on 't, nephew.

WITGOOD   I were worse than a beast else, i' faith.

LUCRE   Although to blind the widow and the world,
I out of policy do 't, yet there's a conscience, nephew.

5   WITGOOD   Heaven forbid else!

LUCRE   When you are full possessed,
'T is nothing to return it.

WITGOOD   Alas, a thing quickly done, uncle!

6   LUCRE   Well said! You know I give it you but in trust.

WITGOOD   Pray, let me understand you rightly, uncle:
You give it me but in trust?

LUCRE   No.

7   WITGOOD   That is, you trust me with it?

LUCRE   True, true.

WITGOOD   But if ever I trust you with it again,
Would I might be trussed up for my labour! [*Aside*]

8   LUCRE   You can all witness, gentlemen; and you, sir yeoman?

HOST   My life for yours, sir, now, I know my mistress's mind so well toward your nephew, let things be in preparation, and I'll train her hither in most excellent fashion. [*Exits*]

9   LUCRE   A good old boy!—Wife! Jenny!

MISTRESS LUCRE [*enters*]   What's the news, sir?   1

LUCRE   The wedding day's at hand: prithee, sweet wife, express thy housewifery; thou 'rt a fine cook, I know 't; thy first husband married thee out of an alderman's kitchen; go to, he raised thee for raising of paste. What! Here's none but friends; most of our beginnings must be winked at.—Gentlemen, I invite you all to my nephew's wedding against Thursday morning.   2

FIRST GENTLEMAN   With all our hearts, and we shall joy to see Your enemy so mocked.

LUCRE   He laughed at me, gentlemen; ha, ha, ha!   3

[*Exeunt all but* WITGOOD.]

WITGOOD   He has no conscience, faith, would laugh at them:
They laugh at one another;
Who then can be so cruel? Troth, not I;
I rather pity now, than ought envy?   4
I do conceive such joy in mine own happiness,
I have no leisure yet to laugh at their follies.
Thou soul of my estate, I kiss thee! [*To the mortgage*]
I miss life's comfort when I miss thee
O, never will we part again,
Until I leave the sight of men!   5
We'll ne'er trust conscience of our kin,
Since cozenage brings that title in. [*Exits*]

Scene Three   6

[*A street. Enter* THREE CREDITORS.]

FIRST CREDITOR   I'll wait these seven hours but I'll see him caught.

SECOND CREDITOR   Faith, so will I.   7

THIRD CREDITOR   Hang him, prodigal! He's stript of the widow.

FIRST CREDITOR   A' my troth, she's the wiser; she has made the happier choice: and I wonder of what stuff those widows' hearts are made of, that will marry unfledged boys before comely thrum-chinned gentlemen.   8

BOY [*enters*]   News, news, news!

ought envy: Bear malice.
thrum-chinned: Rough-chinned. The thrum is the end of the warp in weaving.

1 FIRST CREDITOR   What, boy?

BOY   The rioter is caught.

FIRST CREDITOR   So, so, so, so! It warms me at the heart;
I love a' life to see dogs upon men.
O, here he comes.

2

[*Enter* SERGEANTS, *with* WITGOOD *in custody*.]

WITGOOD   My last joy was so great, it took away the sense of all
future afflictions. What a day is here o'ercast! How soon a black
tempest rises!

3

FIRST CREDITOR   O, we may speak with you now, sir! What's become of your rich widow? I think you may cast your cap at the
widow, may you not, sir?

SECOND CREDITOR   He a rich widow? Who, a prodigal, a daily
rioter, and a nightly vomiter? He a widow of account? He a hole
i' th' counter.

4

WITGOOD   You do well, my masters, to tyrannise over misery, to
afflict the afflicted; 't is a custom you have here amongst you; I
would wish you never leave it, and I hope you'll do as I bid you.

FIRST CREDITOR   Come, come, sir, what say you extempore now to
your bill of a hundred pound? A sweet debt for froating your
doublets.

5

SECOND CREDITOR   Here's mine of forty.

THIRD CREDITOR   Here's mine of fifty.

6 WITGOOD   Pray, sirs,—you'll give me breath?

FIRST CREDITOR   No, sir, we'll keep you out of breath still; then we
shall be sure you will not run away from us.

WITGOOD   Will you but hear me speak?

7

SECOND CREDITOR   You shall pardon us for that, sir; we know you
have too fair a tongue of your own; you overcame us too lately, a
shame take you! We are like to lose all that for want of witnesses: we dealt in policy then; always when we strive to be most
politic we prove most coxcombs: non plus ultra I perceive by us,
we're not ordained to thrive by wisdom, and therefore we must be

8

content to be tradesmen.

WITGOOD   Give me but reasonable time, and I protest I'll make you
ample satisfaction.

FIRST CREDITOR   Do you talk of reasonable time to us?

9

WITGOOD   'T is true, beasts know no reasonable time.

SECOND CREDITOR   We must have either money or carcass.   1

WITGOOD   Alas, what good will my carcass do you?

THIRD CREDITOR   O, 't is a secret delight we have amongst us! We that are used to keep birds in cages, have the heart to keep men in prison, I warrant you.   2

WITGOOD   I perceive I must crave a little more aid from my wits: do but make shift for me this once, and I'll forswear ever to trouble you in the like fashion hereafter; I'll have better employment for you, an I live [*aside*]—You'll give me leave, my masters, to make trial of my friends, and raise all means I can?

FIRST CREDITOR   That's our desire, sir.   3

HOST [*enters*]   Master Witgood.

WITGOOD   O, art thou come?

HOST   May I speak one word with you in private, sir?

WITGOOD   No, by my faith, canst thou; I am in hell here, and the devils will not let me come to thee.   4

FIRST CREDITOR   Do you call us devils? You shall find us Puritans. —Bear him away; let 'em talk as they go: we'll not stand to hear 'em—Ah, sir, am I a devil? I shall think the better of myself as long as I live: a devil, i' faith?   5

[*Exeunt*]

Scene Four   6

[*A room in Hoard's house.*]

HOARD [*enters*]   What a sweet blessing hast thou, Master Hoard, above a multitude! Wilt thou never be thankful? How dost thou think to be blest another time? Or dost thou count this the full measure of thy happiness? By my troth, I think thou dost: not only a wife large in possessions, but spacious in content; she's rich, she's young, she's fair, she's wise: when I wake, I think of her lands—that revives me; when I go to bed, I dream of her beauty—and that's enough for me: she's worth four hundred a year in her very smock, if a man knew how to use it. But the journey will be all, in troth, into the country; to ride to her lands in state and order following; my brother, and other worshipful gentlemen, whose companies I ha' sent down for already, to ride along with us in their goodly decorum beards, their broad velvet cassocks, and chains of gold twice or thrice double; against which   7   8   9

1 time I'll entertain some ten men of mine own into liveries, all of occupations or qualities; I will not keep an idle man about me: the sight of which will so vex my adversary Lucre—for we'll pass by his door of purpose, make a little stand for the nonce, and have our horses curvet before the window—certainly he will never endure it, but run up and hang himself presently.

2 [*Enter* SERVANT.]

How now, sirrah, what news? Any that offer their service to me yet?

3 SERVANT   Yes, sir, there are some i' th' hall that wait for your worship's liking, and desire to be entertained.

HOARD   Are they of occupation?

SERVANT   They are men fit for your worship, sir.

4 HOARD   Sayest so? Send 'em all in.

[*Exit* SERVANT.]

To see ten men ride after me in watchet liveries, with orange-tawny caps,—'t will cut his comb, i' faith.

5 [*Enter* TAILOR, BARBER, PERFUMER, FALCONER, *and* HUNTSMAN.]

How now? Of what occupation are you, sir?

TAILOR   A tailor, an' 't please your worship.

6 HOARD   A tailor? O, very good: you shall serve to make all the liveries.—What are you, sir?

BARBER   A barber, sir.

HOARD   A barber? Very needful. You shall shave all the house, and, if need require, stand for a reaper i' th' summer time.—You,

7 sir?

PERFUMER   A perfumer.

HOARD   I smelt you before: perfumers, of all men, had need carry themselves uprightly; for if they were once knaves, they would be smelt out quickly.—To you, sir?

8 FALCONER   A falconer, an' 't please your worship.

HOARD   Sa ho, sa ho, sa ho!—And you, sir?

HUNTSMAN   A huntsman, sir.

Sa ho; There, boy!: Hunting cries.

HOARD   There, boy, there, boy, there, boy! I am not so old but I
have pleasant days to come. I promise you, my masters, I take
such a good liking to you, that I entertain you all; I put you already into my countenance, and you shall be shortly in my livery;
but especially you two, my jolly falconer and my bonny huntsman; we shall have most need of you at my wife's manor houses
i' th' country; there's goodly parks and champaign grounds for
you; we shall have all our sports within ourselves; all the gentlemen a' th' country shall be beholden to us and our pastimes.

FALCONER   And we'll make your worship admire, sir.

HOARD   Sayest thou so? Do but make me admire, and thou shall
want for nothing.—My tailor.

TAILOR   Anon, sir.

HOARD   Go presently in hand with the liveries.

TAILOR   I will, sir.

HOARD   My barber.

BARBER   Here, sir.

HOARD   Make 'em all trim fellows, louse 'em well,—especially my
huntsman,—and cut all their beards of the Polonian fashion.—
My perfumer.

PERFUMER   Under your nose, sir.

HOARD   Cast a better savour upon the knaves, to take away the
scent of my tailor's feet, and my barber's lotium water.

PERFUMER   It shall be carefully performed, sir.

HOARD   But you, my falconer and huntsman, the welcomest men
alive, i' faith!

HUNTSMAN   And we'll show you that, sir, shall deserve your worship's favour.

HOARD   I prithee, show me that.—Go, you knaves all, and wash
your lungs i' th' buttery, go.

[*Exeunt* TAILOR, BARBER, PERFUMER, FALCONER, *and* HUNTSMAN.]

By th' mass, and well remembered! I'll ask my wife that question.—
Wife, Mistress Jane Hoard!

COURTESAN [*enters, altered in apparel*]   Sir, would you with me?

HOARD   I would but know, sweet wife, which might stand best to
thy liking, to have the wedding dinner kept here or i' th' country?

COURTESAN   Hum: —faith, sir, 't would like me better here; here
you were married, here let all rites be ended.

1 HOARD Could a marquesse give a better answer? Hoard, bear thy
head aloft, thou 'st a wife will advance it.

[*Enter* HOST *with a letter.*]

2 What haste comes here now? Yea, a letter? Some dreg of my adversary's malice. Come hither; what's the news?

HOST A thing that concerns my mistress, sir.

[*Giving letter to* COURTESAN.]

HOARD Why then it concerns me, knave.

3 HOST Ay, and you, knave, too (cry your worship mercy): you are
both like to come into trouble, I promise you, sir; a precontract.

HOARD How? a precontract, sayest thou?

4 HOST I fear they have too much proof on 't, sir: old Lucre, he
runs mad up and down, and will to law as fast as he can; young
Witgood laid hold on by his creditors, he exclaims upon you a' t'
other side, says you have wrought his undoing by the injurious
detaining of his contract.

HOARD Body a' me!

5 HOST He will have utmost satisfaction;
The law shall give him recompense, he says.

COURTESAN Alas, his creditors so merciless! My state being yet uncertain, I deem it not unconscionable to further him. [*Aside*]

HOST True, sir.

6 HOARD Wife, what says that letter? Let me construe it.

COURTESAN Cursed be my rash and unadvised words! [*Tears the
letter and stamps on it.*]
I'll set my foot upon my tongue
And tread my inconsiderate grant to dust.

7 HOARD Wife—

HOST A pretty shift, i' faith! I commend a woman when she can
make away a letter from her husband handsomely, and this was
cleanly done, by my troth. [*Aside*]

8 COURTESAN I did, sir;
Some foolish words I must confess did pass,
Which now litigiously he fastens on me.

HOARD Of what force? Let me examine 'em.

COURTESAN Too strong, I fear: would I were well freed of him!

9 HOARD Shall I compound?

COURTESAN No, sir, I'd have it done some nobler way

Of your side; I'd have you come off with honour;   1
Let baseness keep with them. Why, have you not
The means, sir? The occasion's offered you.

HOARD   Where? How, dear wife?

COURTESAN   He is now caught by his creditors; the slave's needy;
his debts petty; he'll rather bind himself to all inconveniences   2
than rot in prison; by this only means you may get a release from
him: 't is not yet come to his uncle's hearing; send speedily for
the creditors; by this time he's desperate; he'll set his hand to anything: take order for his debts, or discharge 'em quite: a pax on
him, let's be rid of a rascal!   3

HOARD   Excellent!
Thou dost astonish me.—Go, run, make haste;
Bring both the creditors and Witgood hither.

HOST   This will be some revenge yet. [*Aside, and exits.*]

HOARD   In the mean space I'll have a release drawn.—Within   4
there!

SERVANT [*enters*]   Sir?

HOARD   Sirrah, come take directions; go to my scrivener.

COURTESAN [*aside, while* HOARD *gives directions to the Servant*]   5
I'm yet like those whose riches lie in dreams,
If I be waked, they're false; such is my fate,
Who venture deeper than the desperate state.
Though I have sinned, yet could I become new,
For where I once vow, I am ever true.

HOARD   Away, despatch, on my displeasure quickly.   6

[*Exit* SERVANT]

Happy occasion! Pray Heaven he be in the right vein now to set
his hand to 't, that nothing alter him; grant that all his follies may
meet in him at once, to besot him enough! I pray for him, i' faith,   7
and here he comes.

[*Enter* WITGOOD *and* CREDITORS.]

WITGOOD   What would you with me now, my uncle's spiteful adversary?
                                                                    8
HOARD   Nay, I am friends.

WITGOOD   Ay, when your mischief's spent.

HOARD   I heard you were arrested.
                                                                    9
WITGOOD   Well, what then?
You will pay none of my debts, I am sure.

1 HOARD   A wise man cannot tell;
There may be those conditions 'greed upon
May move me to do much.

WITGOOD   Ay, when?—
'T is thou, perjured woman: (O, no name
2 Is vile enough to match thy treachery!)
That art the cause of my confusion.

COURTESAN   Out, you penurious slave!

HOARD   Nay, wife, you are too froward;
Let him alone; give losers leave to talk.

3 WITGOOD   Shall I remember thee of another promise
Far stronger than the first?

COURTESAN   I'd fain know that.

WITGOOD   'T would call shame to thy cheeks.

4 COURTESAN   Shame!

WITGOOD   Hark in your ear.

[*They converse apart.*]

Will he come off, think'st thou, and pay my debts roundly?

5 COURTESAN   Doubt nothing; there's a release a-drawing and all, to
which you must set your hand.

WITGOOD   Excellent!

COURTESAN   But methinks, i' faith, you might have made some
6 shift to discharge this yourself, having in the mortgage, and never
have burdened my conscience with it.

WITGOOD   A' my troth, I could not, for my creditors' cruelties extend to the present.

COURTESAN   No more.—
7 Why, do your worst for that, I defy you.

WITGOOD   You're impudent: I'll call up witnesses.

COURTESAN   Call up thy wits, for thou hast been devoted
To follies a long time.

HOARD   Wife, you're too bitter.—
8 Master Witgood, and you, my masters, you shall hear a mild
speech come from me now, and this it is: 't has been my fortune,
gentlemen, to have an extraordinary blessing poured upon me a'
late, and here she stands; I have wedded her, and bedded her, and
yet she is little the worse: some foolish words she hath passed to
9 you in the country, and some peevish debts you owe here in the

city; set the hare's head to the goose giblet; release you here of her   1
words, and I'll release you of your debts, sir.

WITGOOD   Would you so? I thank you for that, sir; I cannot blame
you, i' faith.

HOARD   Why, are not debts better than words, sir?

WITGOOD   Are not words promises, and are not promises debts, sir?   2

HOARD   He plays at back-racket with me. [*Aside*]

FIRST CREDITOR   Come hither, Master Witgood, come hither; be
ruled by fools once.

SECOND CREDITOR   We are citizens, and know what belongs to 't.   3

FIRST CREDITOR   Take hold of his offer: pax on her, let her go; if
your debts were once discharged, I would help you to a widow
myself worth ten of her.

THIRD CREDITOR   Mass, partner, and now you remember me on 't,
there's Master Mulligrub's sister newly fallen a widow.   4

FIRST CREDITOR   Cuds me, as pat as can be! there's a widow left for
you; ten thousand in money, beside plate, jewels, et cetera: I warrant it a match; we can do all in all with her; prithee, dispatch; we'll
carry thee to her presently.

WITGOOD   My uncle will ne'er endure me when he shall hear I set   5
my hand to a release.

SECOND CREDITOR   Hark, I'll tell thee a trick for that: I have spent
five hundred pound in suits in my time, I should be wise; thou 'rt
now a prisoner; make a release; take 't of my word, whatsoever a
man makes as long as he is in durance, 't is nothing in law, not   6
thus much. [*Snaps his fingers.*]

WITGOOD   Say you so, sir?

THIRD CREDITOR   I have paid for 't, I know 't.

WITGOOD   Proceed then; I consent.   7

THIRD CREDITOR   Why, well said.

HOARD   How now, my masters, what have you done with him?

FIRST CREDITOR   With much ado, sir, we have got him to consent.

HOARD   Ah-a-a! and what come his debts to now?   8

FIRST CREDITOR   Some eight-score odd pounds, sir.

HOARD   Naw, naw, naw, naw, naw! Tell me the second time; give

set the hare's head to the goose giblet: Probably proverbial; to meet
half way in a bargain.

1   me a lighter sum; they are but desperate debts, you know; ne'er
    called in but upon such an accident; a poor, needy knave, he
    would starve and rot in prison: come, come, you shall have ten
    shillings in the pound, and the sum down roundly.

FIRST CREDITOR   You must make it a mark, sir.

2   HOARD   Go to then, tell your money in the meantime; you shall
    find little less there.

[*Giving them money.*]

3   Come, Master Witgood, you are so unwilling to do yourself good
    now!

[*Enter* SCRIVENER]

Welcome, honest scrivener.—Now you shall hear the release read.

4   SCRIVENER [*reads*]   Be it known to all men, by these presents, that
    I, Theodorus Witgood, gentleman, sole nephew to Pecunius
    Lucre, having unjustly made title and claim to one Jane Medler,
    late widow of Anthony Medler, and now wife to Walkadine
    Hoard, in consideration of a competent sum of money to dis-
    charge my debts, do for ever hereafter disclaim any title, right,
5   estate, or interest in or to the said widow, late in the occupation
    of the said Anthony Medler, and now in the occupation of Wal-
    kadine Hoard; as also neither to lay claim by virtue of any for-
    mer contract, grant, promise, or demise, to any of her manors,
    manor houses, parks, groves, meadow grounds, arable lands,
    barns, stacks, stables, dove holes, and coney burrows; together
6   with all her cattle, money, plate, jewels, borders, chains, bracelets,
    furniture, hangings, moveables or immoveables. In witness
    whereof, I, the said Theodorus Witgood, have interchangeably set
    to my hand and seal before these presents, the day and date
    above written.

7   WITGOOD   What a precious fortune hast thou slipt here, like a beast
    as thou art!

HOARD   Come, unwilling heart, come.

WITGOOD   Well, Master Hoard, give me the pen; I see
    'T is vain to quarrel with our destiny. [*Signs the paper.*]
8
HOARD   O, as vain a thing as can be! you cannot commit a greater
    absurdity sir. So, so; give me that hand now; before all these pres-
    ents, I am friends for ever with thee.

WITGOOD   Troth, and it were pity of my heart now, if I should bear
9   you any grudge, i' faith.

HOARD   Content. I'll send for thy uncle against the wedding dinner;   1
we will be friends once again.

WITGOOD   I hope to bring it to pass myself, sir.

HOARD   How now? Is 't right, my masters?

FIRST CREDITOR   'T is something wanting, sir; yet it shall be suffi-   2
cient.

HOARD   Why, well said; a good conscience makes a fine show nowadays. Come, my masters, you shall all taste of my wine ere you
depart.

ALL THE CREDITORS   We follow you, sir.

3

[*Exeunt* HOARD *and* SCRIVENER.]

WITGOOD   I'll try these fellows now [*aside*].—A word, sir: what,
will you carry me to that widow now?

FIRST CREDITOR   Why, do you think we were in earnest, i' faith?
Carry you to a rich widow? We should get much credit by that: a   4
noted rioter! A contemptible prodigal! 'T was a trick we have
amongst us to get in our money: fare you well, sir.

[*Exeunt* CREDITORS.]

WITGOOD   Farewell, and be hanged, you short pig-haired, ram-   5
headed rascals! He that believes in you shall ne'er be saved, I
warrant him. By this new league I shall have some access unto my
love.

JOYCE [*appears above*]   Master Witgood!

WITGOOD   My life!   6

JOYCE   Meet me presently; that note directs you:

[*Throws him a letter.*]

I would not be suspected: our happiness attends us: farewell.

WITGOOD   A word's enough.   7

[*Exeunt severally.*]

Scene Five

8

[*Dampit's bedchamber.* DAMPIT *in bed;* AUDREY *spinning by his
side;* BOY.]

AUDREY [*singing*]

      Let the usurer cram him, in interest that excel,   9

1   There's pits enow to damn him, before he comes to hell;
    In Holborn some, in Fleet Street some,
    Where'er he come there's some, there's some.

DAMPIT   *Trahe, trahito,* draw the curtain; give me a sip of sack
more.

2   [*While he drinks, enter* LAMPREY *and* SPICHCOCK.]

LAMPREY   Look you; did not I tell you he lay like the devil in
chains, when he was bound for a thousand year?

SPICHCOCK   But I think the devil had no steel bedstaffs; he goes
3   beyond him for that.

LAMPREY   Nay, do but mark the conceit of his drinking; one must
wipe his mouth for him with a muckinder, do you see, sir?

SPICHCOCK   Is this the sick trampler? Why, he is only bedrid with
drinking.

4   LAMPREY   True, sir. He spies us.

DAMPIT   What, Sir Tristram? You come and see a weak man here,
a very weak man.

LAMPREY   If you be weak in body, you should be strong in prayer,
sir.

5   DAMPIT   O, I have prayed too much, poor man!

LAMPREY   There's a taste of his soul for you!

SPICHCOCK   Faugh, loathsome!

LAMPREY   I come to borrow a hundred pound of you, sir.

6   DAMPIT   Alas, you come at an ill time! I cannot spare it i' faith; I
ha' but two thousand i' th' house.

AUDREY   Ha, ha, ha!

DAMPIT   Out, you gernative quean, the mullipood of villainy, the
spinner of concupiscency!
7

[*Enter* SIR LAUNCELOT *and others.*]

SIR LAUNCELOT   Yea, gentlemen, are you here before us? How is
he now?

8   LAMPREY   Faith, the same man still: the tavern bitch has bit him i'
th' head.

SIR LAUNCELOT   We shall have the better sport with him: peace.
—And how cheers Master Dampit now?

DAMPIT   O, my bosom, Sir Launcelot, how cheer I! Thy presence
9   is restorative.

SIR LAUNCELOT   But I hear a great complaint of you, Master Dam-   1
pit, among gallants.

DAMPIT   I am glad of that, i' faith: prithee, what?

SIR LAUNCELOT   They say you are waxed proud a' late, and if a
friend visit you in the afternoon, you'll scarce know him.

DAMPIT   Fie, fie; proud? I cannot remember any such thing: sure I   2
was drunk then.

SIR LAUNCELOT   Think you so, sir?

DAMPIT   There 't was, i' faith; nothing but the pride of the sack;
and so certify 'em.—Fetch sack, sirrah.

BOY   A vengeance sack you once! [*Exit, and returns presently with*   3
sack.]

AUDREY   Why, Master Dampit, if you hold on as you begin, and
lie a little longer, you need not take care how to dispose your
wealth; you'll make the vintner your heir.

DAMPIT   Out, you babliaminy, you unfeathered, cremitoried quean,   4
you cullisance of scabiosity!

AUDREY   Good words, Master Dampit, to speak before a maid and
a virgin!

DAMPIT   Hang thy virginity upon the pole of carnality!   5

AUDREY   Sweet terms! My mistress shall know 'em.

LAMPREY   Note but the misery of this usuring slave: here he lies,
like a noisome dunghill, full of the poison of his drunken blasphe-
mies; and they to whom he bequeaths all, grudge him the very
meat that feeds him, the very pillow that eases him. Here may a   6
usurer behold his end: what profits it to be a slave in this world,
and a devil i' the next?

DAMPIT   Sir Launcelot, let me buss thee, Sir Launcelot; thou art
the only friend that I honour and respect.

SIR LAUNCELOT   I thank you for that, Master Dampit.   7

DAMPIT   Farewell, my bosom Sir Launcelot.

SIR LAUNCELOT   Gentlemen, an you love me, let me step behind
you, and one of you fall a-talking of me to him.

LAMPREY   Content.—Master Dampit—   8

DAMPIT   So, sir.

LAMPREY   Here came Sir Launcelot to see you e'en now.

DAMPIT   Hang him, rascal!

LAMPREY   Who? Sir Launcelot?   9

1 DAMPIT   Pythagorical rascal!

LAMPREY   Pythagorical?

DAMPIT   Ay, he changes his cloak when he meets a sergeant.

SIR LAUNCELOT   What a rogue's this!

2 LAMPREY   I wonder you can rail at him, sir; he comes in love to see you.

DAMPIT   A louse for his love! His father was a combmaker; I have no need of his crawling love: he comes to have longer day, the superlative rascal!

3 SIR LAUNCELOT   'S foot, I can no longer endure the rogue!—Master Dampit, I come to take my leave once again, sir.

DAMPIT   Who? My dear and kind Sir Launcelot, the only gentleman of England? Let me hug thee: "Farewell, and a thousand."

LAMPREY   Composed of wrongs and slavish flatteries!

4 SIR LAUNCELOT   Nay, gentlemen, he shall show you more tricks yet; I'll give you another taste of him.

LAMPREY   Is 't possible?

SIR LAUNCELOT   His memory is upon departing.

5 DAMPIT   Another cup of sack!

SIR LAUNCELOT   Mass, then 't will be quite gone! Before he drink that, tell him there's a country client come up, and here attends for his learned advice.

LAMPREY   Enough.

6 DAMPIT   One cup more, and then let the bell toll: I hope I shall be weak enough by that time.

LAMPREY   Master Dampit—

DAMPIT   Is the sack spouting?

7 LAMPREY   'T is coming forward, sir. Here's a countryman, a client of yours, waits for your deep and profound advice, sir.

DAMPIT   A coxcombry, where is he? Let him approach: set me up a peg higher.

LAMPREY [to SIR LAUNCELOT]   You must draw near, sir.

8 DAMPIT   Now good man fooliaminy, what say you to me now?

SIR LAUNCELOT   Please your good worship, I am a poor man, sir—

DAMPIT   What make you in my chamber then?

9 SIR LAUNCELOT   I would entreat your worship's device in a just and honest cause, sir.

DAMPIT I meddle with no such matters; I refer 'em to Master   1
No-man's office.

SIR LAUNCELOT I had but one house left me in all the world, sir,
which was my father's, my grandfather's, my great-grandfather's,
and now a villain has unjustly wrung me out, and took possession
on 't.   2

DAMPIT Has he such feats? Thy best course is to bring thy *ejec-*
tione firmae, and in seven year thou mayest shove him out by the
law.

SIR LAUNCELOT Alas, an' 't please your worship, I have small
friends and less money!   3

DAMPIT Hoyday! This gear will fadge well: hast no money? Why,
then, my advice is, thou must set fire a' th' house, and so get him
out.

LAMPREY That will break strife, indeed.

SIR LAUNCELOT I thank your worship for your hot counsel, sir.—   4
Altering but my voice a little, you see he knew me not: you may
observe by this, that a drunkard's memory holds longer in the
voice than in the person. But, gentlemen, shall I show you a
sight? Behold the little dive-dapper of damnation, Gulf the
usurer, for his time worse than t' other.   5

LAMPREY What's he comes with him?

SIR LAUNCELOT Why, Hoard, that married lately the Widow Medler.

LAMPREY O, I cry you mercy, sir.
     6
[*Enter* HOARD *and* GULF.]

HOARD Now, gentlemen, visitants, how does Master Dampit?

SIR LAUNCELOT Faith, here he lies, e'en drawing in, sir, good ca-
nary as fast as he can, sir; a very weak creature, truly, he is al-   7
most past memory.

HOARD Fie, Master Dampit! You lie lazing abed here, and I come
to invite you to my wedding dinner: up, up, up!

DAMPIT Who's this? Master Hoard? Who hast thou married, in
the name of foolery?   8

HOARD A rich widow.

DAMPIT A Dutch Widow?

ejectione firmae: "An action at law whereby a person ousted from an
estate for years may recover possession thereof" (O.E.D.).

1   HOARD   A rich widow; one Widow Medler.

     DAMPIT   Medler? She keeps open house.

     HOARD   She did, I can tell you, in her t' other husband's days; open house for all comers; horse and man was welcome, and room enough for 'em all.

2   DAMPIT   There's too much for thee, then; thou mayst let out some to thy neighbours.

     GULF   What, hung alive in chains? O spectacle! Bedstaffs of steel? *O monstrum horrendum, informe, ingens, cui lumen ademptum!* O Dampit, Dampit, here's a just judgment shown upon usury, ex-

3   tortion, and trampling villainy!

     SIR LAUNCELOT   This is excellent, thief rails upon the thief!

     GULF   Is this the end of cutthroat usury, brothel, and blasphemy? Now mayst thou see what race a usurer runs.

4   DAMPIT   Why, thou rogue of universality, do not I know thee? Thy sound is like the cuckoo, the Welch ambassador: thou cowardly slave, that offers to fight with a sick man when his weapon's down! Rail upon me in my naked bed? Why, thou great Lucifer's little vicar! I am not so weak but I know a knave at first sight: thou unconscionable rascal! Thou that goest upon Middlesex ju-

5   ries, and wilt make haste to give up thy verdict; because thou wilt not lose thy dinner! Are you answered?

     GULF   An' 't were not for shame— [*Draws his dagger.*]

     DAMPIT   Thou wouldst be hanged then.

6   LAMPREY   Nay, you must exercise patience, Master Gulf, always in a sick man's chamber.

     SIR LAUNCELOT   He'll quarrel with none, I warrant you, but those that are bedrid.

     DAMPIT   Let him come, gentlemen, I am armed: reach my close-

7   stool hither.

     SIR LAUNCELOT   Here will be a sweet fray anon: I'll leave you, gentlemen.

     LAMPREY   Nay, we'll go along with you.—Master Gulf—

8   GULF   Hang him, usuring rascal!

O monstrum horrendum . . . *:* "Oh, horrible monster, mis-shapen, vast, of sight deprived," the description of Polyphemus (Virgil, *Aeneid,* Bk. 3, 658).

Welch ambassador: So named because this bird supposedly migrated from the west.

SIR LAUNCELOT   Pish, set your strength to his, your wit to his!   1

AUDREY   Pray, gentlemen, depart; his hour's come upon him.—
Sleep in my bosom, sleep.

SIR LAUNCELOT   Nay, we have enough of him, i' faith; keep him
for the house.
Now make your best: 2
For thrice his wealth I would not have his breast.

GULF   A little thing would make me beat him now he's asleep.

SIR LAUNCELOT   Mass, then 't will be a pitiful day when he wakes:
I would be loth to see that day: come.
   3

GULF   You overrule me, gentlemen, i' faith.

[*Exeunt*]

ACT FIVE

Scene One

1 [*A room in Lucre's house. Enter* LUCRE *and* WITGOOD.]

WITGOOD Nay, uncle, let me prevail with you so much; i' faith, go, now he has invited you.

LUCRE I shall have great joy there when he has borne away the
2 widow!

WITGOOD Why, la, I thought where I should find you presently: uncle, a' ma troth, 't is nothing so.

LUCRE What's nothing so, sir? Is not he married to the widow?

WITGOOD No, by my troth, is he not, uncle.

3 LUCRE How?

WITGOOD Will you have the truth on 't? He is married to a whore, i' faith.

LUCRE I should laugh at that.

4 WITGOOD Uncle, let me perish in your favour if you find it not so; and that 't is I that have married the honest woman.

LUCRE Ha! I'd walk ten mile 'a foot to see that, i' faith.

WITGOOD And see 't you shall, or I'll ne'er see you again.

5 LUCRE A quean, i' faith? Ha, ha, ha!

[*Exeunt*]

6 ## Scene Two

[*A room in Hoard's house. Enter* HOARD, *tasting wine,* HOST *following in a livery cloak*.]

7 HOARD Pup, pup, pup, pup, I like not this wine: is there never a better tierce in the house?

HOST Yes, sir, there are as good tierces in the house as any are in England.

HOARD Desire your mistress, you knave, to taste 'em all over; she
8 has better skill.

150

HOST   Has she so? The better for her, and the worse for you. 1
  [*Aside and exits.*]

HOARD   Arthur!

[*Enter* ARTHUR.]

  Is the cupboard of plate set out? 2

ARTHUR   All's in order, sir. [*Exits*]

HOARD   I am in love with my liveries every time I think on 'em;
  they make a gallant show, by my troth. Niece!

JOYCE [*enters*]   Do you call, sir? 3

HOARD   Prithee, show a little diligence, and overlook the knaves a
  little; they'll filch and steal today, and send whole pasties home to
  their wives; an thou be'st a good niece, do not see me purloined.

JOYCE   Fear it not, sir—I have cause: though the feast be prepared for you, yet it serves fit for my wedding dinner, too. [*Aside* 4
  and exits.]

[*Enter* LAMPREY *and* SPICHCOCK.]

HOARD   Master Lamprey and Master Spichcock, two the most welcome gentlemen alive! Your fathers and mine were all free o' th' 5
  fishmongers.

LAMPREY   They were indeed, sir. You see bold guests, sir; soon entreated.

HOARD   And that's best, sir. 6

[*Enter* SERVANT.]

  How now, sirrah?

SERVANT   There's a coach come to th' door, sir. [*Exits*]
 7
HOARD   My Lady Foxstone, a' my life!—Mistress Jane Hoard! Wife!
  Mass, 't is her ladyship indeed!

[*Enter* LADY FOXSTONE.]

  Madam, you are welcome to an unfurnished house, dearth of 8
  cheer, scarcity of attendance.

LADY FOXSTONE   You are pleased to make the worst, sir.

HOARD   Wife!

[*Enter* COURTESAN.] 9

1 LADY FOXSTONE Is this your bride?

HOARD Yes, madam.—Salute my Lady Foxstone.

COURTESAN Please you, madam, awhile to taste the air in the garden?

2 LADY FOXSTONE 'T will please us well.

[*Exeunt* LADY FOXSTONE *and* COURTESAN.]

HOARD Who would not wed? the most delicious life!
No joys are like the comforts of a wife.

3 LAMPREY So we bachelors think, that are not troubled with them.

SERVANT [*reenters*] Your worship's brother, with other ancient gentlemen, are newly alighted, sir. [*Exits*]

HOARD Master Onesiphorus Hoard? Why, now our company begins to come in.

4

[*Enter* ONESIPHORUS HOARD, LIMBER, *and* KIX.]

My dear and kind brother, welcome, i' faith.

5 ONESIPHORUS HOARD You see we are men at an hour, brother.

HOARD Ay, I'll say that for you, brother; you keep as good an hour to come to a feast as any gentleman in the shire.—What, old Master Limber and Master Kix! Do we meet, i' faith, jolly gentlemen?

6 LIMBER We hope you lack guests, sir?

HOARD O, welcome, welcome! We lack still such guests as your worships.

ONESIPHORUS HOARD Ah, sirrah brother, have you catched up Widow Medler?

7 HOARD From 'em all, brother; and I may tell you I had mighty enemies, those that stuck sore; old Lucre is a sore fox, I can tell you, brother.

ONESIPHORUS HOARD Where is she? I'll go seek her out: I long to have a smack at her lips.

8 HOARD And most wishfully, brother, see where she comes.

[*Reenter* COURTESAN *and* LADY FOXSTONE.]

9 Give her a smack now we may hear it all the house over.

[COURTESAN *and* ONESIPHORUS HOARD *start and turn away*.]

COURTESAN O Heaven, I am betrayed! I know that face.

HOARD Ha, ha, ha! Why, how now? Are you both ashamed?—
Come, gentlemen, we'll look another way.

ONESIPHORUS HOARD Nay, brother, hark you: come, you're disposed to be merry.

HOARD Why do we meet else, man?

ONESIPHORUS HOARD That's another matter: I was ne'er so afraid
in my life but that you had been in earnest.

HOARD How mean you, brother?

ONESIPHORUS HOARD You said she was your wife.

HOARD Did I so? By my troth, and so she is.

ONESIPHORUS HOARD By your troth, brother?

HOARD What reason have I to dissemble with my friends, brother?
If marriage can make her mine, she is mine. Why—

ONESIPHORUS HOARD [about to retire] Troth, I am not well of a
sudden: I must crave pardon, brother; I came to see you, but I
cannot stay dinner, i' faith.

HOARD I hope you will not serve me so, brother?

LIMBER By your leave, Master Hoard—

HOARD What now? What now? Pray, gentlemen:—you were wont
to show yourselves wise men.

LIMBER But you have shown your folly too much here.

HOARD How?

KIX Fie, fie! A man of your repute and name!
You'll feast your friends, but cloy 'em first with shame.

HOARD This grows too deep; pray, let us reach the sense.

LIMBER In your old age dote on a courtesan!

HOARD Ha!

KIX Marry a strumpet!

HOARD Gentlemen!

ONESIPHORUS HOARD And Witgood's quean!

HOARD O! Nor lands nor living?

ONESIPHORUS HOARD Living!

HOARD [to Courtesan] Speak.

COURTESAN Alas, you know, at first, sir,
I told you I had nothing!

1 HOARD   Out, out! I am cheated; infinitely cozened!

LIMBER   Nay, Master Hoard—

[*Enter* LUCRE, WITGOOD, *and* JOYCE.]

2 HOARD   A Dutch widow! A Dutch widow! A Dutch widow!

LUCRE   Why, nephew, shall I trace thee still a liar?
Wilt make me mad? Is not yon thing the widow?

WITGOOD   Why, la, you are so hard a' belief, uncle! By my troth,
she's a whore.

3 LUCRE   Then thou 'rt a knave.

WITGOOD   *Negatur argumentum,* uncle.

LUCRE   *Probo tibi,* nephew; he that knows a woman to be a quean
must needs be a knave; thou sayest thou knowest her to be one;
ergo, if she be a quean, thou 'rt a knave.

4 WITGOOD   *Negatur sequela majoris,* uncle; he that knows a woman
to be a quean must needs be a knave; I deny that.

HOARD   Lucre and Witgood, you're both villains; get you out of my
house!

5 LUCRE   Why, didst not invite me to thy wedding dinner?

WITGOOD   And are not you and I sworn perpetual friends before
witness, sir, and were both drunk upon 't?

HOARD   Daintily abused! You've put a punk upon me!

LUCRE   Ha, ha, ha!

6 HOARD   A common strumpet!

WITGOOD   Nay, now
You wrong her, sir; if I were she, I'd have
The law on you for that; I durst depose for her
She ne'er had common use nor common thought.

7 COURTESAN   Despise me, publish me, I am your wife;
What shame can I have now but you'll have part?
If in disgrace you share, I sought not you;
You pursued, nay, forced me; had I friends would follow it,
Less than your action has been proved a rape.

8

Negatur argumentum: Your argument does not follow.
Probo tibi: Let me prove it to you.
Ergo: Therefore.
Negatur sequela majoris: I deny your major inference. In this parody
of a logical argument it is in fact Lucre's premise that Witgood denies.

ONESIPHORUS HOARD Brother!　　　　　　　　　　　　　　1

COURTESAN Nor did I ever boast of lands unto you,
　　Money, or goods; I took a plainer course,
　　And told you true, I'd nothing:
　　If error were committed, 't was by you;
　　Thank your own folly: nor has my sin been　　　　　2
　　So odious, but worse has been forgiven;
　　Nor am I so deformed, but I may challenge
　　The utmost power of any old man's love.
　　She that tastes not sin before twenty, twenty to one but she'll
　　taste it after: most of you old men are content to marry young
　　virgins, and take that which follows; where, marrying one of us,　3
　　you both save a sinner and are quit from a cuckold for ever:
　　And more, in brief, let this your best thoughts win,
　　She that knows sin, knows best how to hate sin.

HOARD Cursed be all malice! Black are the fruits of spite,
　　And poison first their owners. O, my friends,　　　　　4
　　I must embrace shame, to be rid of shame!
　　Concealed disgrace prevents a public name.
　　Ah, Witgood! Ah, Theodorus!

WITGOOD Alas, sir, I was pricked in conscience to see her well be-
　　stowed, and where could I bestow her better than upon your piti-　5
　　ful worship? Excepting but myself, I dare swear she's a virgin;
　　and now, by marrying your niece, I have banished myself for
　　ever from her: she's mine aunt now, by my faith, and there's no
　　meddling with mine aunt, you know: a sin against my nuncle.

COURTESAN Lo gentlemen, before you all　　　　　　　6
　　In true reclaimed form I fall. [Kneels]
　　Henceforth forever I defy
　　The glances of a sinful eye,
　　Waving of fans (which some suppose
　　Tricks of fancy), treading of toes,
　　Wringing of fingers, biting the lip,　　　　　　　　　7
　　The wanton gait, th' alluring trip;
　　All secret friends and private meetings,
　　Close-borne letters and bawds' greetings;
　　Feigning excuse to womens' labours
　　When we are sent for to th' next neighbour's;
　　Taking false physic, and ne'er start　　　　　　　　8
　　To be let blood though sign be at heart;
　　Removing chambers, shifting beds,

sign: Here, planetary sign. "According to the almanacs blood was
taken from particular parts under particular planets" (Dyce).

1 To welcome friends in husbands' steads,
Them to enjoy, and you to marry,
They first served, while you must tarry,
They to spend, and you to gather,
They to get, and you to father:
These, and thousand, thousand more,
2 New reclaimed, I now abhor.

LUCRE [*to* WITGOOD] Ah, here's a lesson, rioter, for you!

WITGOOD I must confess my follies; I'll down, too: [*Kneels*]
And here forever I disclaim
The cause of youth's undoing, game,
3 Chiefly dice, those true outlanders,
That shake out beggars, thieves, and panders;
Soul-wasting surfeits, sinful riots,
Queans' evils, doctors' diets,
'Pothecaries' drugs, surgeons' glisters;
4 Stabbing of arms for a common mistress;
Riband favours, ribald speeches;
Dear perfumed jackets, penniless breeches;
Dutch flapdragons, healths in urine;
Drabs that keep a man too sure in:
I do defy you all.
5 Lend me each honest hand, for here I rise
A reclaimed man, loathing the general vice.

HOARD So, so, all friends! The wedding dinner cools:
Who seem most crafty prove ofttimes most fools.

6 [*Exeunt*]

THE END

Dutch flapdragons: A flapdragon was a glass of liquor set alight and drunk off while it flamed. The Dutch are proverbially associated with drunkenness in Elizabethan and Jacobean literature.

The City Madam

(1624)

INTRODUCTION

Philip Massinger was born at Salisbury in 1583 and went up to St. Alban's Hall, Oxford, in 1602. He left without taking his degree and may have been an actor for some years until we find him employed as a writer by Philip Henslowe in or near the year 1613. After a period of collaboration with John Fletcher, Massinger assumed the older dramatist's place as regular writer to the King's company some time after Fletcher's death in 1625.

Massinger never achieved his predecessor's fame in his own lifetime but, since his death in 1640, his realistic comedy *A New Way to Pay Old Debts* (first published 1633, but written perhaps a decade earlier) has come to be recognized as one of the greatest dramatic compositions of the age. It shares with *The City Madam* a powerful evocation of social ambition spurred on by vast wealth. Two strands of serious preoccupation may be discerned in *The City Madam,* held together by the pivotal figure of Luke Frugal, the younger brother and disappointed scholar. The play contains the worlds of both *Eastward Ho,* with its apparatus of prodigal apprentices, needy knights, and ambitious citizens' wives, and of Jonson's own play *The Alchemist,* with its world of acquisitiveness. Luke, once he has been given control of his brother's fortune, becomes "a general scourge" to his socially pretentious sister-in-law and her selfish daughters. He humiliates them for the folly of their vain ambition to emulate the manners of the aristocracy. In turn his own "seeming" is tested and he is unmasked as the type of avaricious hypocrite. Despite the theatrical implausibilities that surround this strand of the double plot, there is no denying the vitality of Massinger's serious concern for his major theme: the threat to traditional standards of propriety and decorum represented by the accumulation of vast wealth, even when the law permits it. Luke is acting well within the law in pressing his debtors to the last scruple, but in this pursuit he must abandon conscience, humanity, and religious feeling. Although the playwright cannot be said to have broken new ground in this play, he is not a mere plagiarist. Luke's powerful speeches are worthy to stand beside those of

Jonson's and Marlowe's overreaching figures, from whom Luke ultimately derives.

The play was first licenced for performance in 1632 and first printed in 1658. It was probably written much earlier. Editors disagree over the actual date of composition, but it seems most likely that it was written between 1622 and 1624.

CHARACTERS

LORD LACY

SIR MAURICE LACY, son to Lord Lacy

SIR JOHN FRUGAL, a merchant

LUKE, brother to Sir John Frugal

MR. PLENTY, a country gentleman

OLD GOLDWIRE ⎱ two gentlemen
OLD TRADEWELL ⎰

YOUNG GOLDWIRE ⎱ their sons, apprentices
YOUNG TRADEWELL ⎰ to Sir John

STARGAZE, an astrologer

HOLDFAST, a steward

HOIST, a decayed gentleman

PENURY

SCENE: London

FORTUNE, a decayed merchant

RAMBLE ⎱ two hectors
SCUFFLE ⎰

DING'EM, a pimp

GETTALL, a boxkeeper

[PORTERS], PAGE to Sir Maurice Lacy, THREE SERVINGMEN, MUSICIANS, SHERIFF, MARSHALL, OFFICERS, [THREE] SERGEANTS, [YEOMAN], [SERVANTS], CERBERUS, CHARON, ORPHEUS, CHORUS

LADY FRUGAL, wife to Sir John

ANNE ⎱ her daughters
MARY ⎰

MILLICENT, her maid

SHAVE'EM, a wench

SECRET, a bawd

ACT ONE

Scene One

[*Enter* YOUNG GOLDWIRE *and* YOUNG TRADEWELL.]   1

YOUNG GOLDWIRE   The ship is safe in the Pool then?

YOUNG TRADEWELL   And makes good,
  In her rich fraught, the name she bears, the *Speedwell:*
  My master will find it, for on my certain knowledge
  For every hundred that he ventured in her   2
  She hath returned him five.

YOUNG GOLDWIRE   And it comes timely,
  For besides a payment on the nail for a manor
  Late purchased by my master, his young daughters
  Are ripe for marriage.   3

YOUNG TRADEWELL   Who? Nan and Mall?

YOUNG GOLDWIRE   Mistress Anne and Mary, and with some ad-
    dition,
  Or 't is more punishable in our house
  Than *scandalum magnatum.*   4

YOUNG TRADEWELL   'T is great pity
  Such a gentleman as my master (for that title
  His being a citizen cannot take from him)
  Hath no male heir to inherit his estate,
  And keep his name alive.   5

YOUNG GOLDWIRE   The want of one
  Swells my young mistresses, and their madam mother,
  With hopes above their birth and scale. Their dreams are
  Of being made countesses, and they take state
  As they were such already. When you went   6
  To the Indies, there was some shape and proportion
  Of a merchant's house in our family; but since
  My master, to gain precedency for my mistress
  Above some elder merchants' wives, was knighted,
  'T is grown a little court in bravery,
  Variety of fashions, and those rich ones: 7
  There are few great ladies going to a masque
  That do outshine ours in their everyday habits.

scandalum magnatum: Scandalous report against the peerage.

1 Young Tradewell 'T is strange my master in his wisdom can
Give the reins to such exorbitancy.

Young Goldwire   He must,
Or there's no peace nor rest for him at home;
I grant his state will bear it, yet he's censured
2 For his indulgence, and for Sir John Frugal,
By some styled Sir John Prodigal.

Young Tradewell   Is his brother,
Master Luke Frugal, living?

Young Goldwire   Yes, the more
3 His misery, poor man.

Young Tradewell   Still in the Counter?

Young Goldwire   In a worser place. He was redeemed from the
hole,
To live in our house in hell: since, his base usage
4 Considered, 't is no better. My proud lady
Admits him to her table; marry, ever
Beneath the salt, and there he sits the subject
Of her contempt and scorn; and dinner ended,
His courteous nieces find employment for him
5 Fitting an under-prentice, or a footman,
And not an uncle.

Young Tradewell   I wonder, being a scholar
Well read, and travelled, the world yielding means
For men of such desert, he should endure it.

6 Young Goldwire   He does, with a strange patience; and to us
The servants so familiar, nay humble.

[*Enter* Stargaze, Lady Frugal, Anne, Mary, Millicent, *in several
postures, with looking glasses at their girdles.*]

7 I'll tell you—but I am cut off. Look these
Like a citizen's wife and daughters?

Young Tradewell   In their habits
They appear other things; but what are the motives
Of this strange preparation?

8 Young Goldwire   The young wagtails
Expect their suitors: the first, the son and heir
Of the Lord Lacy, who needs my master's money,
As his daughter does his honour; the second, Master Plenty,

hole: See Glossary under Counter.
Beneath the salt: At the lower end of the table.

A roughhewn gentleman, and newly come
To a great estate; and so all aids of art
In them's excusable.

LADY FRUGAL   You have done your part here:
To your study, and be curious in the search
Of the nativities.

[*Exit* STARGAZE.]

YOUNG TRADEWELL   Methinks the mother,
As if she could renew her youth, in care,
Nay, curiosity to appear lovely,
Comes not behind her daughters.

YOUNG GOLDWIRE   Keeps the first place,
And though the church-book speak her fifty, they
That say she can write thirty, more offend her
Than if they taxed her honesty: t' other day
A tenant of hers, instructed in her humour,
But one she never saw, being brought before her,
For saying only, "Good young mistress, help me
To the speech of your lady mother," so far pleased her,
That he got his lease renewed for 't.

YOUNG TRADEWELL   How she bristles!
Prithee, observe her.

MILLICENT   As I hope to see
A country knight's son and heir walk bare before you
When you are a countess, as you may be one
When my master dies, or leaves trading; and I continuing
Your principal woman, take the upper hand
Of a squire's wife, though a justice, as I must
By the place you give me, you look now as young
As when you were married.

LADY FRUGAL   I think I bear my years well.

MILLICENT   Why should you talk of years? Time hath not ploughed
One furrow in your face; and were you not known
The mother of my young ladies, you might pass
For a virgin of fifteen.

YOUNG TRADEWELL   Here's no gross flattery:
Will she swallow this?

YOUNG GOLDWIRE   You see she does, and glibly.

walk bare: Go bareheaded, that is, as a page.

1 MILLICENT You never can be old; wear but a mask
Forty years hence, and you will still seem young
In your other parts. What a waist is here! O Venus!
That I had been born a King! and here a hand
To be kissed ever—pardon my boldness, madam—

2 Then, for a leg and foot, you will be courted
When a great-grandmother.

LADY FRUGAL   These indeed, wench, are not
So subject to decaying as the face;
Their comeliness lasts longer.

3 MILLICENT   Ever, ever!
Such a rare featured and proportion'd madam
London could never boast of.

LADY FRUGAL   Where are my shoes?

MILLICENT Those that your ladyship gave order should

4 Be made of the Spanish perfumed skins?

LADY FRUGAL   The same.

MILLICENT I sent the prison bird this morning for 'em,
But he neglects his duty.

5 ANNE   He is grown
Exceeding careless.

MARY   And begins to murmur
At our commands, and sometimes grumbles to us,
He is, forsooth, our uncle!

6 LADY FRUGAL   He is your slave,
And as such use him.

ANNE   Willingly, but he's grown
Rebellious, madam.

YOUNG GOLDWIRE Nay, like hen, like chicken.

7 LADY FRUGAL I'll humble him.

[*Enter* LUKE, *with shoes, garters, and roses.*]

YOUNG GOLDWIRE   Here he comes sweating all over;

8 He shows like a walking frippery.

LADY FRUGAL   Very good, sir:
Were you drunk last night, that you could rise no sooner
With humble diligence to do what my daughters
And woman did command you?

9 LUKE   Drunk, an 't please you?

LADY FRUGAL   Drunk, I said, sirrah! Dar'st thou in a look   1
  Repine, or grumble? Thou unthankful wretch,
  Did our charity redeem thee out of prison,
  (Thy patrimony spent), ragged and lousy,
  When the sheriff's basket, and his broken meat,
  Were your festival exceedings, and is this   2
  So soon forgotten?

LUKE   I confess I am
  Your creature, madam.

LADY FRUGAL   And good reason why
  You should continue so.   3

ANNE   Who did new clothe you?

MARY   Admitted you to the dining room?

MILLICENT   Allowed you
  A fresh bed in the garret?   4

LADY FRUGAL   Or from whom
  Received you spending money?

LUKE   I owe all this
  To your goodness, madam; for it you have my prayers,
  The beggar's satisfaction; all my studies   5
  (Forgetting what I was, but with all duty
  Rememb'ring what I am) are how to please you.
  And if in my long stay I have offended,
  I ask your pardon. Though you may consider,
  Being forced to fetch these from the Old Exchange,
  These from the Tower, and these from Westminster,   6
  I could not come much sooner.*

YOUNG GOLDWIRE   Here was a walk
  To breathe a footman!

ANNE   'T is a curious fan.   7

MARY   These roses will show rare; would 't were in fashion
  That the garters might be seen, too.

MILLICENT   Many ladies
  That know they have good legs, wish the same with you:
  Men that way have th' advantage.   8

  sheriff's basket: the remains of food sent were sent to prisoners from
  the sheriff's table.
  festival exceedings: "College slang for extra commons allowed on
  festival occasions" (Kirk).
  * Luke must have walked at least six miles.

1 LUKE [*aside to* YOUNG GOLDWIRE]   I was with
The lady, and delivered her the satin
For her gown, and velvet for her petticoat;
This night she vows she'll pay you.

YOUNG GOLDWIRE   How I am bound
2 To your favour, Master Luke!

MILLICENT   As I live, you will
Perfume all rooms you walk in.

LADY FRUGAL   Get your fur,
You shall pull 'em on within.

3 YOUNG GOLDWIRE   That servile office
Her pride imposes on him.

[*Exit* LUKE.]

4 SIR JOHN [*within*]   Goldwire! Tradewell!

YOUNG TRADEWELL   My master calls.—We come, sir.

[*Exeunt* YOUNG GOLDWIRE, YOUNG TRADEWELL. *Enter* HOLDFAST
with PORTERS.]

5
LADY FRUGAL   What have you brought there?

HOLDFAST   The cream of the market, provision enough
To serve a garrison. I weep to think on 't.
When my master got his wealth, his family fed
6 On roots and livers, and necks of beef on Sundays.
But now I fear it will be spent in poultry.
Butcher's meat will not go down.

LADY FRUGAL   Why, you rascal, is it
At your expense? What cooks have you provided?

7 HOLDFAST   The best of the city. They have wrought at my Lord
Mayor's.

ANNE   Fie on 'em! They smell of Fleet Lane and Pie Corner.

MARY   And think the happiness of man's life consists
In a mighty shoulder of mutton.
8
LADY FRUGAL   I'll have none
Shall touch what I shall eat, you grumbling cur,
But Frenchmen and Italians; they wear satin,
And dish no meat but in silver.

HOLDFAST You may want, though, 1
A dish or two when the service ends.

LADY FRUGAL Leave prating,
I'll have my will; do you as I command you.

[*Exeunt*] 2

Scene Two

[*Enter* SIR MAURICE LACY *and* PAGE.]

SIR MAURICE You were with Plenty? 3

PAGE Yes, sir.

SIR MAURICE And what answer
Returned the clown?

PAGE Clown, sir! He is transformed, 4
And grown a gallant of the last edition;
More rich than gaudy in his habit; yet
The freedom and the bluntness of his language
Continues with him. When I told him that
You gave him caution, as he loved the peace
And safety of his life, he should forbear
To pass the merchant's threshold, until you,
Of his two daughters, had made choice of her
Whom you designed to honour as your wife,
He smiled in scorn.

SIR MAURICE In scorn? 6

PAGE His words confirmed it.
They were few, but to this purpose: "Tell your master,
Though his lordship in reversion were now his,
It cannot awe me, I was born a freeman,
And will not yield in the way of affection 7
Precedence to him. I will visit 'em,
Though he sat porter to deny my entrance.
When I meet him next I'll say more to his face.
Deliver thou this"—then gave me a piece
To help my memory, and so we parted. 8

SIR MAURICE Where got he this spirit?

grown a gallant: See the education of Hoyden in *The Sparagus Garden;* compare also that of Kastril in *The Alchemist* by **Ben** Jonson.

1 PAGE   At the academy of valour,
    Newly erected for the institution
    Of elder brothers, where they're taught the ways,
    Though they refuse to seal for a duellist,
    How to decline a challenge. He himself
2   Can best resolve you.

[*Enter* PLENTY *and* THREE SERVINGMEN.]

SIR MAURICE   You, sir!

PLENTY   What with me, sir?
3   How big you look! I will not loose a hat
    To a hair's breadth. Move your beaver, I'll move mine,
    Or if you desire to prove your sword, mine hangs
    As near my right hand, and will as soon out,
    Though I keep not a fencer to breathe me.
    Walk into Moorfields—I dare look on your Toledo.
4   Do not show a foolish valour in the streets,
    To make work for shopkeepers and their clubs;
    'T is scurvy, and the women will laugh at us.

SIR MAURICE   You presume on the protection of your hinds.

5 PLENTY   I scorn it:
    Though I keep men, I fight not with their fingers,
    Nor make it my religion to follow
    The gallant's fashion, to have my family
    Consisting in a footman and a page,
    And those two sometimes hungry. I can feed these,
6   And clothe 'em too, my gay sir.

SIR MAURICE   What a fine man
    Hath your tailor made you!

PLENTY   'T is quite contrary,
    I have made my tailor, for my clothes are paid for
7   As soon as put on, a sin your man of title
    Is seldom guilty of, but heaven forgive it.
    I have other faults, too, very incident
    To a plain gentleman. I eat my venison
    With my neighbours in the country, and present not
    My pheasants, partridges, and grouse to the usurer,
8   Nor ever yet paid brokage to his scrivener.

clubs: On a cry of "Clubs!" shopkeepers and their apprentices would be called out to break up street fights.

hinds: That is, the servingmen who wait on Plenty; literally "farm-hands."

I flatter not my mercer's wife, nor feast her   1
With the first cherries, or peascods, to prepare me
Credit with her husband, when I come to London.
The wool of my sheep, or a score or two of fat oxen
In Smithfield, give me money for my expenses.
I can make my wife a jointure of such lands, too,   2
As are not encumbered, no annuity
Or statute lying on 'em. This I can do,
And it please your future honour, and why therefore
You should forbid my being a suitor with you
My dullness apprehends not.

PAGE   This is bitter.   3

SIR MAURICE   I have heard you, sir, and in my patience shown
   Too much of the stoic's. But to parley further,
   Or answer your gross jeers, would write me coward.
   This only: thy great-grandfather was a butcher,
   And his son a grazier; thy sire, constable   4
   Of the hundred, and thou the first of your dunghill
   Created gentleman. Now you may come on, sir,
   You, and your thrashers.

PLENTY [*to his* SERVINGMEN]   Stir not on your lives.—
   This for the grazier, this for the butcher.   5

[*They fight.*]

SIR MAURICE   So, sir!

PAGE   I'll not stand idle. [*To the* SERVINGMEN] Draw! My little
   rapier   6
   Against your bumb blades. I'll one by one despatch you,
   Then house this instrument of death and horror.

[*Enter* SIR JOHN, LUKE, YOUNG GOLDWIRE, YOUNG TRADEWELL.]

SIR JOHN   Beat down their weapons. My gate Ruffians' Hall!   7
   What insolence is this?

LUKE   Noble Sir Maurice,
   Worshipful Master Plenty—

SIR JOHN   I blush for you.   8
   Men of your quality expose your fame
   To every vulgar censure! This at midnight
   After a drunken supper in a tavern,
   (No civil man abroad to censure it)
   Had shown poor in you, but in the day, and view
   Of all that pass by, monstrous!   9

1 PLENTY   Very well, sir;
   You Looked for this defence.

   SIR MAURICE   'T is thy protection,
   But it will deceive thee.

   SIR JOHN   Hold! If you proceed thus
2 I must make use of the next justice's power,
   And leave persuasion, and in plain terms tell you

   [*Enter* LADY FRUGAL, ANNE, MARY, *and* MILLICENT.]

   Neither your birth, Sir Maurice, nor [*to* PLENTY] your wealth,
3 Shall privilege this riot. See whom you have drawn
   To be spectators of it! Can you imagine
   It can stand with the credit of my daughters,
   To be the argument of your swords? I' th' street too?
   Nay, ere you do salute, or I give way
   To any private conference, shake hands
4 In sign of peace. He that draws back, parts with
   My good opinion.

   [*They shake hands.*]

                          This is as it should be.
5 Make your approaches, and if their affection
   Can sympathize with yours, they shall not come,
   On my credit, beggars to you. I will hear
   What you reply within.

   SIR MAURICE [*to* ANNE]   May I have the honour
6 To support you, lady?

   PLENTY [*to* MARY]   I know not what's supporting,
   But by this fair hand, glove and all, I love you.

   [*Exeunt all except* LUKE. *To him enter* HOIST, PENURY, FORTUNE.]

7
   LUKE   You are come with all advantage. I will help you
   To the speech of my brother.

   FORTUNE   Have you moved him for us?

   LUKE   With the best of my endeavours, and I hope
   You'll find him tractable.
8
   PENURY   Heaven grant he prove so.

   HOIST   Howe'er, I'll speak my mind.

   [*Enter* LORD LACY.]

   with all advantage: At the best time.

LUKE   Do so, Master Hoist.   1
   Go in. I'll pay my duty to this lord,
   And then I am wholly yours.

[*Exeunt* HOIST, PENURY, FORTUNE.]

                      —Heaven bless your honour.   2

LORD LACY   Your hand, Master Luke. The world's much changed
     with you
   Within these few months; then you were the gallant:
   No meeting at the horse race, cocking, hunting,
   Shooting, or bowling, at which Master Luke   3
   Was not a principal gamester, and companion
   For the nobility.

LUKE   I have paid dear
   For those follies, my good lord; and 't is but justice
   That such as soar above their pitch, and will not
   Be warned by my example, should like me   4
   Share in the miseries that wait upon 't.
   Your honour in your charity may do well
   Not to upbraid me with those weaknesses
   Too late repented.

LORD LACY   I nor do, nor will;   5
   And you shall find I'll lend a helping hand
   To raise your fortunes. How deals your brother with you?

LUKE   Beyond my merit, I thank his goodness for 't.
   I am a freeman, all my debts discharged,
   Nor does one creditor undone by me   6
   Curse my loose riots. I have meat and clothes,
   Time to ask heaven remission for what's past;
   Cares of the world by me are laid aside,
   My present poverty's a blessing to me;
   And though I have been long, I dare not say   7
   I ever lived till now.

LORD LACY   You bear it well;
   Yet as you wish I should receive for truth
   What you deliver, with that truth acquaint me
   With your brother's inclination. I have heard
   In the acquisition of his wealth, he weighs not   8
   Whose ruins he builds upon.

LUKE   In that, report
   Wrongs him, my lord. He is a citizen,
   And would increase his heap, and will not lose   9
   What the law gives him. Such as are wordly wise

1 Pursue that track, or they will ne'er wear scarlet.
But if your honour please to know his temper,
You are come opportunely. I can bring you
Where you unseen shall see and hear his carriage
Towards some poor men, whose making or undoing
Depend upon his pleasure.

2 LORD LACY   To my wish:
I know no object that could more content me.

[*Exeunt*]

3
Scene Three

[*Enter* SIR JOHN, HOIST, FORTUNE, PENURY, YOUNG GOLDWIRE.]

SIR JOHN   What would you have me do? Reach me a chair.
4 When I lent my moneys I appeared an angel;
But now I would call in mine own, a devil.

HOIST   Were you the devil's dam, you must stay till I have it,
For as I am a gentleman—

5 [*Enter* LUKE, *placing the* LORD LACY.]

LUKE   There you may hear all.

HOIST   I pawned you my land for the tenth part of the value.
Now, 'cause I am a gamester, and keep ordinaries,
And a livery punk or so, and trade not with
6 The money-mongers' wives, not one will be bound for me.
'T is a hard case; you must give me longer day
Or I shall grow very angry.

SIR JOHN   Fret, and spare not.
I know no obligation lies upon me
7 With my honey to feed drones. But to the purpose:
How much owes Penury?

YOUNG GOLDWIRE   Two hundred pounds:
His bond three times since forfeited.

SIR JOHN   Is it sued?
8
YOUNG GOLDWIRE   Yes, sir, and execution out against him.

wear scarlet: Become civic officials.
trade: Here, meant sexually.
longer day: More time to pay.
Is it sued?: Has a judgment been sought?

SIR JOHN For body and goods?   1

YOUNG GOLDWIRE   For both, sir.

SIR JOHN   See it served.

PENURY I am undone; my wife and family
  Must starve for want of bread.   2

SIR JOHN   More infidel thou,
  In not providing better to support 'em.
  What's Fortune's debt?

YOUNG GOLDWIRE   A thousand, sir.

SIR JOHN   An estate   3
  For a good man! You were the glorious trader,
  Embraced all bargains; the main venturer
  In every ship that launched forth; kept your wife
  As a lady; she had her coach, her choice
  Of summer houses, built with other men's moneys
  Took up at interest, the certain road   4
  To Ludgate in a citizen. Pray you acquaint me,
  How were my thousand pounds employed?

FORTUNE   Insult not
  On my calamity, though being a debtor,
  And a slave to him that lends, I must endure it. 5
  You hear me speak thus much in my defence;
  Losses at sea, and those, sir, great and many,
  By storms and tempests, not domestical riots
  In soothing my wife's humour, or mine own,
  Have brought me to this low ebb.   6

SIR JOHN   Suppose this true,
  What is 't to me? I must and will have my money,
  Or I'll protest you first, and that done have
  The statute made for bankrupts served upon you.

FORTUNE 'T is in your power, but not in mine to shun it. 7

LUKE [*comes forward*] Not as a brother, sir, but with such duty
  As I should use unto my father, since
  Your charity is my parent, give me leave
  To speak my thoughts.

SIR JOHN   What would you say?   8

LUKE   No word, sir,
  I hope shall give offence; nor let it relish
  Of flattery, though I proclaim aloud
  I glory in the bravery of your mind,
  To which your wealth's a servant. Not that riches 9

1 Is or should be contemned, it being a blessing
Derived from heaven, and by your industry
Pulled down upon you; but in this, dear sir,
You have many equals: such a man's possessions
Extend as far as yours, a second hath
His bags as full; a third in credit flies
2 As high in the popular voice: but the distinction
And noble difference by which you are
Divided from 'em, is that you are styled
Gentle in your abundance, good in plenty,
And that you feel compassion in your bowels
3 Of others' miseries (I have found it, sir,
Heaven keep me thankful for 't), while they are cursed
As rigid and inexorable.

SIR JOHN   I delight not
To hear this spoke to my face.

4 LUKE   That shall not grieve you.
Your affability and mildness, clothed
In the garments of your debtors' breath,
Shall everywhere, though you strive to conceal it,
Be seen and wondered at, and in the act
With a prodigal hand rewarded. Whereas such
5 As are born only for themselves, and live so,
Though prosperous in worldly understandings,
Are but like beasts of rapine, that by odds
Of strength, usurp and tyrannize o'er others
Brought under their subjection.

6 LORD LACY   A rare fellow!
I am strangely taken with him.

LUKE   Can you think, sir,
In your unquestioned wisdom, I beseech you,
The goods of this poor man sold at an outcry,
7 His wife turned out of doors, his children forced
To beg their bread: this gentleman's estate,
By wrong extorted, can advantage you?

HOIST If it thrive with him, hang me, as it will damn him
If he be not converted.

8 LUKE   You are too violent.—
Or that the ruin of this once brave merchant
(For such he was esteemed, though now decayed)
Will raise your reputation with good men?
But you may urge—pray you pardon me, my zeal
9 Makes me thus bold and vehement—in this

You satisfy your anger and revenge 1
For being defeated. Suppose this, it will not
Repair your loss, and there was never yet
But shame and scandal in a victory
When the rebels unto reason, passions, fought it.
Then for revenge, by great souls it was ever
Contemned, though offered; entertained by none 2
But cowards, base and abject spirits, strangers
To moral honesty, and never yet
Acquainted with religion.

LORD LACY   Our divines
Cannot speak more effectually. 3

SIR JOHN   Shall I be
Talked out of my money?

LUKE   No, sir, but entreated
To do yourself a benefit, and preserve 4
What you possess entire.

SIR JOHN   How, my good brother?

LUKE   By making these your beadsmen. When they eat,
Their thanks, next heaven, will be paid to your mercy;
When your ships are at sea, their prayers will swell 5
The sails with prosperous winds, and guard 'em from
Tempests and pirates: keep your warehouses
From fire, or quench 'em with their tears—

SIR JOHN   No more.
6
LUKE   —Write you a good man in the people's hearts,
Follow you everywhere.

SIR JOHN   If this could be—

LUKE   It must, or our devotions are but words.
I see a gentle promise in your eye, 7
Make it a blessed act, and poor me rich
In being the instrument.

SIR JOHN   You shall prevail.
Give 'em longer day. But do you hear, no talk of 't.
Should this arrive at twelve on the Exchange, 8
I shall be laughed at for my foolish pity,
Which money men hate deadly. Take your own time,
But see you break not. Carry 'em to the cellar,
Drink a health, and thank your orator.

PENURY   On our knees, sir. 9

1 FORTUNE Honest Master Luke!

HOIST   I bless the Counter where
You learned this rhetoric.

LUKE   No more of that, friends.

2 [*Exeunt* LUKE, HOIST, FORTUNE, PENURY. LORD LACY *comes forward.*]

SIR JOHN My honourable lord.

LORD LACY   I have seen and heard all—
3 Excuse my manners—and wish heartily
You were all of a piece. Your charity to your debtors,
I do commend, but where you should express
Your piety to the height, I must boldly tell you
You show yourself an atheist.

4 SIR JOHN   Make me know
My error, and for what I am thus censured,
And I will purge myself, or else confess
A guilty cause.

LORD LACY   It is your harsh demeanour
5 To your poor brother.

SIR JOHN   Is that all?

LORD LACY   'T is more
Than can admit defence. You keep him as
A parasite to your table, subject to
6 The scorn of your proud wife, an underling
To his own nieces. And can I with mine honour
Mix my blood with his, that is not sensible
Of his brother's miseries?

SIR JOHN   Pray you, take me with you,
7 And let me yield my reasons why I am
No opener handed to him. I was born
His elder brother, yet my father's fondness
To him, the younger, robbed me of my birthright:
He had a fair estate, which his loose riots
8 Soon brought to nothing. Wants grew heavy on him,
And when laid up for debt, of all forsaken,
And in his own hopes lost, I did redeem him.

LORD LACY You could not do less.

take me with you: Hear me out.

SIR JOHN   Was I bound to it, my lord?   1
   What I possess, I may with justice call
   The harvest of my industry. Would you have me,
   Neglecting mine own family, to give up
   My estate to his disposure?

LORD LACY   I would have you,   2
   What's passed forgot, to use him as a brother—
   A brother of fair parts, of a clear soul,
   Religious, good, and honest.

SIR JOHN   Outward gloss
   Often deceives; may it not prove so in him!   3
   And yet my long acquaintance with his nature
   Renders me doubtful; but that shall not make
   A breach between us. Let us in to dinner,
   And what trust, or employment you think fit
   Shall be conferred upon him. If he prove
   True gold in the touch, I'll be no mourner for it.   4

LORD LACY   If counterfeit, I'll never trust my judgment.

[*Exeunt*]

  in the touch: Gold was tested by rubbing it on a touchstone.

ACT TWO

Scene One

1 [*Enter* LUKE, HOLDFAST, YOUNG GOLDWIRE, YOUNG TRADEWELL.]

HOLDFAST   The like was never seen.

LUKE   Why in this rage, man?

HOLDFAST   Men may talk of country Christmases, and court glut-
2   tony,
    Their thirty-pound buttered eggs, their pies of carps' tongues,
    Their pheasants drenched with ambergris, the carcases
    Of three fat wethers bruised for gravy to
    Make sauce for a single peacock, yet their feasts
    Were fasts compared with the City's.
3

YOUNG TRADEWELL   What dear dainty
    Was it thou murmur'st at?

HOLDFAST   Did you not observe it?
    There were three sucking pigs served up in a dish,
    Took from the sow as soon as farrowed,
4   A fortnight fed with dates and muscadine,
    That stood my master in twenty marks apiece,
    Besides the puddings in their bellies made
    Of I know not what. I dare swear the cook that dressed it
    Was the devil disguised like a Dutchman.

5 YOUNG GOLDWIRE   Yet all this
    Will not make you fat, fellow Holdfast.

HOLDFAST   I am rather
    Starved to look on 't. But here's the mischief—though
    The dishes were raised one upon another
6   As woodmongers do billets, for the first,
    The second, and third course, and most of the shops
    Of the best confectioners in London ransacked
    To furnish out a banquet, yet my lady
    Called me penurious rascal, and cried out,
    There was nothing worth the eating.
7

YOUNG GOLDWIRE   You must have patience,
    This is not done often.

HOLDFAST   'T is not fit it should;
    Three such dinners more would break an alderman,
8   And make him give up his cloak. I am resolved

180

To have no hand in 't. I'll make up my accompts,   1
And since my master longs to be undone,
The great fiend be his steward; I will pray
And bless my self from him. [*Exits*]

YOUNG GOLDWIRE   The wretch shows in this
An honest care.   2

LUKE   Out on him! With the fortune
Of a slave, he has the mind of one. However
She bears me hard, I like my lady's humour,
And my brother's suffrage to it. They are now
Busy on all hands; one side eager for   3
Large portions, the other arguing strictly
For jointures and security; but this
Being above our scale, no way concerns us.
How dull you look! In the meantime how intend you
To spend the hours?
                                                                     4

YOUNG GOLDWIRE   We well know how we would,
But dare not serve our wills.

YOUNG TRADEWELL   Being prentices,
We are bound to attendance.
                                                                     5
LUKE   Have you almost served out
The term of your indentures, yet make conscience
By starts to use your liberty? [*To* YOUNG TRADEWELL] Hast
    thou traded
In the other world, exposed unto all dangers,
To make thy master rich, yet dar'st not take   6
Some portion of the profit for thy pleasure?
[*To* YOUNG GOLDWIRE] Or wilt thou, being keeper of the cash,
Like an ass that carries dainties, feed on thistles?
Are you gentlemen born, yet have no gallant tincture
Of gentry in you? You are no mechanics,   7
Nor serve some needy shopkeeper, who surveys
His everyday takings. You have in your keeping
A mass of wealth, from which you may take boldly,
And no way be discovered. He's no rich man
That knows all he possesses, and leaves nothing
For his servants to make prey of. I blush for you,   8
Blush at your poverty of spirit, you,
The brave sparks of the city!

YOUNG GOLDWIRE   Master Luke,
I wonder you should urge this, having felt
What misery follows riot.   9

1   YOUNG TRADEWELL   And the penance
You endured for 't in the Counter.

    LUKE   You are fools,
The case is not the same. I spent mine own money,
And my stock being small, no marvel 't was soon wasted.

2   But you without the least doubt or suspicion,
If cautelous, may make bold with your master's.
As for example: when his ships come home,
And you take your receipts, as 't is the fashion,
For fifty bales of silk you may write forty;
Or for so many pieces of cloth of bodkin,

3   Tissue, gold, silver, velvets, satins, taffetas,
A piece of each deducted from the gross
Will never be missed; a dash of a pen will do it.

    YOUNG TRADEWELL   Aye, but our fathers' bonds that lie in pawn
For our honesties must pay for 't.

4   LUKE   A mere bugbear
Invented to fright children! As I live,
Were I the master of my brother's fortunes,
I should glory in such servants. Did'st thou know
What ravishing lechery it is to enter

5   An ordinary, cap-a-pie, trimmed like a gallant,
(For which in trunks concealed be ever furnished),
The reverence, respect, the crouches, cringes,
The musical chime of gold in your crammed pockets
Commands from the attendants, and poor porters—

6   YOUNG TRADEWELL   O rare!

    LUKE   Then sitting at the table with
The braveries of the kingdom, you shall hear
Occurrents from all corners of the world,
The plots, the counsels, the designs of princes,
And freely censure 'em; the City wits

7   Cried up, or decried, as their passions lead 'em;
Judgment having nought to do there.

    YOUNG TRADEWELL   Admirable!

    LUKE   My lord no sooner shall rise out of his chair,
8   The gaming lord I mean, but you may boldly
By the privilege of a gamester fill his room,
For in play you are all fellows; have your knife
As soon in the pheasant; drink your health as freely;

lechery: Here, pleasure.
room: Here, place.

And striking in a lucky hand or two,
        1
Buy out your time.

YOUNG TRADEWELL This may be: but suppose
We should be known.

LUKE   Have money and good clothes,
And you may pass invisible. Or if
        2
You love a madam-punk, and your wide nostril
Be taken with the scent of cambric smocks,
Wrought and perfumed—

YOUNG GOLDWIRE   There, there, Master Luke,
There lies my road of happiness.
        3

LUKE   Enjoy it,
And pleasures stol'n being sweetest, apprehend
The raptures of being hurried in a coach
To Brentford, Staines, or Barnet.

YOUNG GOLDWIRE   'T is enchanting,
        4
I have proved it.

LUKE   Hast thou?

YOUNG GOLDWIRE   Yes, in all these places
I have had my several pagans billeted
        5
For my own tooth, and after ten-pound suppers,
The curtain drawn, my fiddlers playing all night
"The Shaking of the Sheets," which I have danced
Again and again with my cockatrice. Master Luke,
You shall be of my counsel, and we two sworn brothers,
And therefore I'll be open, I am out now
        6
Six hundred in the cash, yet if on a sudden
I should be called to account, I have a trick
How to evade it, and make up the sum.

YOUNG TRADEWELL Is 't possible?

LUKE   You can instruct your tutor. 7
How, how, good Tom?

YOUNG GOLDWIRE   Why, look you. We cashkeepers
Hold correspondence, supply one another
On all occasions. I can borrow for a week
Two hundred pounds of one, as much of a second,
        8
A third lays down the rest, and when they want,
As my master's moneys come in, I do repay it:
Ka me, ka thee.

LUKE   An excellent knot! 'T is pity
It e'er should be unloosed; for me it shall not.
        9

1   You are shown the way, friend Tradewell, you may make use
on 't,
Or freeze in the warehouse, and keep company
With the cater Holdfast.

YOUNG TRADEWELL   No, I am converted.
2   A Barbican broker will furnish me with outside,
And then a crash at the ordinary!

YOUNG GOLDWIRE   I am for
The lady you saw this morning, who indeed is
My proper recreation.

3 LUKE   Go to, Tom,
What did you make me?

YOUNG GOLDWIRE   I'll do as much for you,
Employ me when you please.

LUKE   If you are inquired for,
4   I will excuse you both.

YOUNG TRADEWELL   Kind Master Luke!

YOUNG GOLDWIRE   We'll break my master to make you. You
know—

5 LUKE   I cannot love money. Go, boys!

[*Exeunt* YOUNG GOLDWIRE *and* YOUNG TRADEWELL.]

                           When times serves
It shall appear, I have another end in 't. [*Exits*]
6

Scene Two

[*Enter* SIR JOHN, LORD LACY, SIR MAURICE LACY, PLENTY, LADY
FRUGAL, ANNE, MARY, MILLICENT.]
7

SIR JOHN   Ten thousand pounds apiece I'll make their portions,
And after my decease it shall be double,
Provided you assure them for their jointures
Eight hundred pounds per annum, and entail
8   A thousand more upon the heirs male
Begotten on their bodies.

LORD LACY   Sir, you bind us
To very strict conditions.

PLENTY   You, my lord,
9

May do as you please: but to me it seems strange,   1
We should conclude of portions, and of jointures,
Before our hearts are settled.

LADY FRUGAL   You say right.
There are counsels of more moment and importance
On the making up of marriages to be
Considered duly, than the portion, or the jointures,   2
In which a mother's care must be exacted,
And I by special privilege may challenge
A casting voice.

LORD LACY   How's this?

LADY FRUGAL   Even so, my lord;   3
In these affairs I govern.

LORD LACY   Give you way to 't?

SIR JOHN   I must, my lord.

LADY FRUGAL   'T is fit he should, and shall.   4
You may consult of something else, this province
Is wholly mine.

SIR MAURICE   By the city custom, madam?

LADY FRUGAL   Yes, my young sir, and both must look my daugh-   5
ters
Will hold it by my copy.

PLENTY   Brave, i' faith!

SIR JOHN   Give her leave to talk, we have the power to do;
And now touching the business we last talked of,   6
In private if you please.

LORD LACY   'T is well remembered;
You shall take your own way, madam.

[*Exeunt* LORD LACY *and* SIR JOHN.]   7

SIR MAURICE   What strange lecture
Will she read unto us?

LADY FRUGAL   Such as wisdom warrants
From the superior bodies. Is Stargaze ready   8
With his several schemes?

MILLICENT   Yes, madam, and attends

Your pleasure. [*Exits*]

1 SIR MAURICE   Stargaze, Lady? What is he?

LADY FRUGAL   Call him in. You first shall know him, then admire
him
For a man of many parts, and those parts rare ones.
He's every thing, indeed; parcel physician,
2 And as such prescribes my diet, and foretells
My dreams when I eat potatoes; parcel poet,
And sings encomiums to my virtues sweetly;
My antecedent, or my gentleman usher;
And as the stars move, with that due proportion
He walks before me; but an absolute master
3 In the calculation of nativities,
Guided by that ne'er-erring science called
Judicial astrology.

PLENTY   Stargaze! Sure
I have a penny almanac about me
4 Inscribed to you, as to his patroness,
In his name published.

LADY FRUGAL   Keep it as a jewel.
Some statesmen that I will not name are wholly
Governed by his predictions, for they serve
For any latitude in Christendom,
5 As well as our own climate.

[*Enter* MILLICENT *and* STARGAZE, *with two schemes.*]

SIR MAURICE   I believe so.
6
PLENTY   Must we couple by the almanac?

LADY FRUGAL   Be silent,
And e'er we do articulate, much more
Grow to a full conclusion, instruct us
Whether this day and hour, by the planets, promise
7 Happy success in marriage.

STARGAZE   *In omni*
Parte, et toto.

PLENTY   Good learned sir, in English;
8 And since it is resolved we must be coxcombs;
Make us so in our own language.

STARGAZE   You are pleasant:
Thus in our vulgar tongue then.

In omni parte, et toto: In each part and in the whole.

LADY FRUGAL   Pray you observe him.   1

STARGAZE Venus in the west angle, the house of marriage the
seventh house, in trine of Mars, in conjunction of Luna, and
Mars almuten, or lord of the horoscope.

PLENTY Hoy-day!   2

LADY FRUGAL The angels' language! I am ravished! Forward.

STARGAZE Mars, as I said, lord of the horoscope, or geniture, in
mutual reception of each other, she in her exaltation, and he in
his triplicity, trine, and face, assure a fortunate combination to
Hymen, excellent prosperous and happy.   3

LADY FRUGAL Kneel, and give thanks.

[*The women kneel.*]

SIR MAURICE   For what we understand not? 4

PLENTY And have as little faith in 't?

LADY FRUGAL   Be incredulous;
To me, 't is oracle.

STARGAZE Now for the sovereignty of my future ladies, your   5
daughters, after they are married.—

PLENTY Wearing the breeches, you mean?

LADY FRUGAL   Touch that point home,
It is a principal one, and with London ladies
Of main consideration.   6

STARGAZE This is infallible: Saturn out of all dignities in his
detriment and fall, combust: and Venus in the south angle
elevated above him, lady of both their nativities, in her essential
and accidental dignities; occidental from the sun, oriental from
the angle of the east, in cazimi of the sun, in her joy, and free   7
from the malevolent beams of infortunes; in a sign commanding,
and Mars in a constellation obeying; she fortunate, and he dejected: the disposers of marriage in the radix of the native in
feminine figures, argue, foretell, and declare rule, preeminence,
and absolute sovereignty in women.

                                                                       8
SIR MAURICE Is 't possible!

STARGAZE 'T is drawn, I assure you, from the aphorisms of the
old Chaldeans, Zoroastes the first and greatest magician, Mercu-
rius Trismegistus, the later Ptolemy, and the everlasting prognos-
ticator, old Erra Pater.   9

1   LADY FRUGAL   Are you yet satisfied?

PLENTY   In what?

LADY FRUGAL   That you
  Are bound to obey your wives, it being so
  Determined by the stars, against whose influence
2   There is no opposition.

PLENTY   Since I must
  Be married by the almanac, as I may be,
  'T were requisite the services and duties
  Which, as you say, I must pay to my wife,
3   Were set down in the calendar.

SIR MAURICE   With the date
  Of my apprenticeship.

LADY FRUGAL   Make your demands;
  I'll sit as moderatrix, if they press you
4   With over-hard conditions.

SIR MAURICE   Mine hath the van;
  I stand your charge, sweet.

STARGAZE   Silence.

5   ANNE   I require first
  (And that since 't is in fashion with kind husbands,
  In civil manners you must grant) my will
  In all things whatsoever, and that will
  To be obeyed, not argued.

6   LADY FRUGAL   And good reason.

PLENTY   A gentle *imprimis!*

SIR MAURICE   This in gross contains all;
  But your special items, lady.

ANNE   When I am one
7   (And you are honoured to be styled my husband)
  To urge my having my page, my gentleman usher,
  My woman sworn to my secrets, my caroch
  Drawn by six Flanders mares, my coachmen, grooms,
  Postillion, and footmen.

8   SIR MAURICE   Is there ought else
  To be demanded?

ANNE   Yes, sir, mine own doctor;
  French and Italian cooks; musicians, songsters,
  And a chaplain that must preach to please my fancy;
9   A friend at court to place me at a masque;

The private box took up at a new play   1
For me, and my retinue; a fresh habit,
Of a fashion never seen before, to draw
The gallants' eyes that sit on the stage upon me;
Some decayed lady for my parasite,
To flatter me, and rail at other madams;   2
And there ends my ambition.

SIR MAURICE   Your desires
Are modest, I confess.

ANNE   These toys subscribed to,
And you continuing an obedient husband   3
Upon all fit occasions, you shall find me
A most indulgent wife.

LADY FRUGAL   You have said; give place
And hear your younger sister.

PLENTY   If she speak   4
Her language, may the great fiend, booted and spurred,
With a scythe at his girdle, as the Scotchman says,
Ride headlong down her throat.

SIR MAURICE   Curse not the judge
Before you hear the sentence.   5

MARY   In some part
My sister hath spoke well for the city pleasures,
But I am for the country's, and must say,
Under correction, in her demands she was
Too modest.   6

SIR MAURICE How like you this exordium?

PLENTY   Too modest, with a mischief!

MARY   Yes, too modest:
I know my value, and prize it to the worth,
My youth, my beauty—   7

PLENTY   How your glass deceives you!

MARY   —The greatness of the portion I bring with me,
And the sea of happiness that from me flows to you.

SIR MAURICE   She bears up close.
                                                                         8
MARY   And can you in your wisdom,
Or rustical simplicity, imagine
You have met some innocent country girl, that never
Looked further than her father's farm, nor knew more

may the great fiend . . . : A proverbial saying.

1   Than the price of corn in the market; or at what rate
Beef went a stone? that would survey your dairy,
And bring in mutton out of cheese and butter?
That could give directions at what time of the moon
To cut her cocks, for capons against Christmas,
Or when to raise up goslings?

2 PLENTY   These are arts
Would not misbecome you, though you should put in
Obedience and duty.

  MARY   Yes, and patience,
To sit like a fool at home, and eye your threshers;
3   Then make provision for your slavering hounds,
When you come drunk from an alehouse after hunting,
With your clowns and comrades as if all were yours,
You the lord paramount, and I the drudge;
The case, sir, must be otherwise.

4 PLENTY   How, I beseech you?

  MARY   Marry, thus: I will not like my sister challenge
What's useful or superfluous from my husband,
That's base all o'er. Mine shall receive from me,
What I think fit. I'll have the state conveyed
5   Into my hands, and he put to his pension,
Which the wise viragos of our climate practise;
I will receive your rents—

  PLENTY   You shall be hanged first.

  MARY   —Make sale, or purchase. Nay, I'll have my neighbours
6   Instructed, when a passenger shall ask,
"Whose house is this?" though you stand by, to answer,
"The Lady Plenty's." Or, "Who owes this manor?"
"The Lady Plenty." "Whose sheep are these? Whose
    oxen?"
7   "The Lady Plenty's."

  PLENTY   A plentiful pox upon you!

  MARY   And when I have children, if it be inquired
By a stranger whose they are, they still shall echo,
"My Lady Plenty's," the husband never thought on.

8 PLENTY   In their begetting, I think so.

  MARY   Since you'll marry
In the city for our wealth, in justice we
Must have the country's sovereignty.

9 PLENTY   And we nothing.

MARY   A nag of forty shillings, a couple of spaniels,   1
   With a sparhawk, is sufficient, and these too,
   As you shall behave yourself, during my pleasure,
   I will not greatly stand on. I have said, sir,
   Now if you like me, so.

LADY FRUGAL   At my entreaty,   2
   The articles shall be easier.

PLENTY   Shall they, i' faith?
   Like bitch, like whelps.

SIR MAURICE   Use fair words.

PLENTY   I cannot;   3
   I have read of a house of pride, and now I have found one;
   A whirlwind overturn it!

SIR MAURICE   On these terms,
   Will your minxship be a lady?

PLENTY   A lady in a morris;   4
   I'll wed a pedlar's punk first—

SIR MAURICE   Tinker's trull,
   A beggar without a smock.

PLENTY   Let Monsieur Almanac,   5
   Since he is so cunning with his Jacob's staff,
   Find you out a husband in a bowling alley.

SIR MAURICE   The general pimp to a brothel.

PLENTY   Though that now
   All the loose desires of man were raked up in me,   6
   And no means but thy maidenhead left to quench 'em,
   I would turn cinders, or the next sowgelder,
   On my life, should lib me, rather than embrace thee.

ANNE   Wooing do you call this?

MARY   A bearbaiting rather.   7

PLENTY   Were you worried, you deserve it, and I hope
   I shall live to see it.

SIR MAURICE   I'll not rail, nor curse you,
   Only this: you are pretty peats, and your great portions
   Add much unto your handsomeness, but as   8
   You would command your husbands you are beggars,
   Deformed and ugly.

   Jacob's staff: An instrument to take the sun's position, but here also
an innuendo.

1 LADY FRUGAL   Hear me.
  PLENTY   Not a word more.

[*Exeunt* SIR MAURICE LACY *and* PLENTY. *Both Daughters speak, weeping.*]

2 ANNE I ever thought 't would come to this.
  MARY   We may
    Lead apes in hell for husbands, if you bind us
    T' articulate thus with our suitors.
  STARGAZE   Now the cloud breaks,
3   And the storm will fall on me.
  LADY FRUGAL   You rascal! Juggler!

[*She breaks his head, and beats him.*]

4 STARGAZE Dear madam.
  LADY FRUGAL   Hold you intelligence with the stars,
    And thus deceive me!
  STARGAZE   My art cannot err;
    If it does, I'll burn my astrolabe. In mine own star
5   I did foresee this broken head, and beating;
    And now your ladyship sees, as I do feel it,
    It could not be avoided.
  LADY FRUGAL   Did you?
  STARGAZE   Madam,
6   Have patience but a week, and if you find not
    All my predictions true touching your daughters,
    And a change of fortune to yourself, a rare one,
    Turn me out of doors. These are not the men the planets
    Appointed for their husbands; there will come
    Gallants of another metal.
7 MILLICENT   Once more trust him.
  ANNE, MARY Do, lady mother.
  LADY FRUGAL   I am vexed, look to it;
    Turn o'er your books; if once again you fool me,
8   You shall graze elsewhere: come girls.

[*Exeunt* LADY FRUGAL, ANNE, MARY, MILLICENT.]

STARGAZE I am glad I scaped thus. [*Exits*]

lead apes in hell: A proverbial fate for old maids.

Scene Three

[Enter LORD LACY *and* SIR JOHN FRUGAL.] 1

LORD LACY   The plot shows very likely.

SIR JOHN   I repose
My principal trust in your lordship; 't will prepare
The physic I intend to minister
To my wife and daughters. 2

LORD LACY   I will do my part
To set it off to the life.

[Enter SIR MAURICE LACY *and* PLENTY.]

3

SIR JOHN   It may produce
A scene of no vulgar mirth. Here come the suitors;
When we understand how they relish my wife's humours,
The rest is feasible.

LORD LACY   Their looks are cloudy. 4

SIR JOHN   How sits the wind? Are you ready to launch forth
Into this sea of marriage?

PLENTY   Call it rather
A whirlpool of afflictions.

SIR MAURICE   If you please 5
To enjoin me to it, I will undertake
To find the north passage to the Indies sooner
Than plough with your proud heifer.

PLENTY   I will make
A voyage to hell first.— 6

SIR JOHN   How, sir?

PLENTY   —And court Proserpine
In the sight of Pluto, his three-headed porter
Cerberus standing by, and all the furies
With their whips to scourge me for 't, than say, "I Jeffrey 7
Take you Mary for my wife."

LORD LACY   Why, what's the matter?

SIR MAURICE   The matter is, the mother (with your pardon,
I cannot but speak so much) is a most insufferable,
Proud, insolent lady. 8

PLENTY   And the daughters worse.
The dam in years had th' advantage to be wicked,
But they were so in her belly.

1   SIR MAURICE   I must tell you,
      With reverence to your wealth, I do begin
      To think you of the same leaven.

      PLENTY   Take my counsel;
      'T is safer for your credit to profess
2   Yourself a cuckold, and upon record,
      Than say they are your daughters.

      SIR JOHN   You go too far, sir.

      SIR MAURICE   They have so articled with us—

      PLENTY   And will not take us
3   For their husbands, but their slaves, and so aforehand
      They do profess they'll use us.

      SIR JOHN   Leave this heat:
      Though they are mine, I must tell you, the perverseness
      Of their manners (which they did not take from me,
4   But from their mother) qualified, they deserve
      Your equals.

      SIR MAURICE   True, but what's bred in the bone
      Admits no hope of cure.

      PLENTY   Though saints and angels
5   Were their physicians.

      SIR JOHN   You conclude too fast.

      PLENTY   God be wi' you! I'll travel three years, but I'll bury
      This shame that lives upon me.

6   SIR MAURICE   With your licence,
      I'll keep him company.

      LORD LACY   Who shall furnish you
      For your expenses?

      PLENTY   He shall not need your help,
7   My purse is his; we were rivals, but now friends,
      And will live and die so.

      SIR MAURICE   Ere we go, I'll pay
      My duty as a son.

8   PLENTY   And till then leave you.

[*Exeunt* SIR MAURICE LACY *and* PLENTY.]

LORD LACY   They are strangely moved.

    upon record: Before witnesses.

SIR JOHN   What's wealth, accompanied   1
  With disobedience in a wife and children?
  My heart will break.

LORD LACY   Be comforted, and hope better;
  We'll ride abroad; the fresh air and discourse
  May yield us new inventions.   2

SIR JOHN   You are noble,
  And shall in all things, as you please, command me.

[*Exeunt*]

ACT THREE

Scene One

1   [*Enter* SHAVE'EM *and* SECRET.]

SECRET   Dead doings, daughter.

SHAVE'EM   Doings! sufferings, mother:
  For poor men have forgot what doing is,
  And such as have to pay for what they do,
2   Are impotent, or eunuchs.

SECRET   You have a friend yet,
  And a striker too, I take it.

SHAVE'EM   Goldwire is so, and comes
3   To me by stealth, and as he can steal, maintains me
  In clothes, I grant; but alas, dame, what's one friend?
  I would have a hundred; for every hour, and use,
  And change of humour I am in, a fresh one.
  'T is a flock of sheep that makes a lean wolf fat,
  And not a single lambkin. I am starved,
4   Starved in my pleasures. I know not what a coach is,
  To hurry me to the Burse, or Old Exchange.
  The Neathouse for muskmelons, and the gardens
  Where we traffic for asparagus, are to me
  In the other world.

5 SECRET   There are other places, lady,
  Where you might find customers.

SHAVE'EM   You would have me foot it
  To the dancing of the ropes, sit a whole afternoon there
  In expectation of nuts and pippins;
6   Gape round about me, and yet not find a chapman
  That in courtesy will bid a chop of mutton,
  Or a pint of drum wine for me.

SECRET   You are so impatient!
  But I can tell you news will comfort you,
7   And the whole sisterhood.

doings: This word often implies the sexual act as a second meaning.
Compare with "foot it."
Burse: See Glossary.
Neathouse: See Glossary, and compare the action of *The Sparagus
Garden.*
To the dancing of the ropes: A popular act at fairs or in theatres.

SHAVE'EM   What's that? 1

SECRET   I am told
Two ambassadors are come over: A French monsieur,
And a Venetian, one of the clarissimi,
A hot-reined marmoset. Their followers,
For their countries' honour, after a long vacation, 2
Will make a full term with us.

SHAVE'EM   They indeed are
Our certain and best customers:

[*Knock within*] 3
                      Who knocks there?

RAMBLE [*within*]   Open the door.

SECRET   What are you?

RAMBLE [*within*]   Ramble.
4
SCUFFLE [*within*]   Scuffle.

RAMBLE [*within*]   Your constant visitants.

SHAVE'EM   Let 'em not in.
I know 'em—swaggering, suburbian roarers,
Sixpenny truckers. 5

RAMBLE [*within*]   Down go all your windows
And your neighbours, too, shall suffer.

SCUFFLE [*within*]   Force the doors.

SECRET   They are outlaws, Mistress Shave'em, and there is 6
No remedy against 'em. What should you fear?
They are but men; lying at your close ward,
You have foiled their betters.

SHAVE'EM   Out, you bawd! You care not
Upon what desperate service you employ me, 7
Nor with whom, so you have your fee.

SECRET   Sweet ladybird,
Sing in a milder key.

[*Enter* RAMBLE *and* SCUFFLE.]
8
SCUFFLE   Are you grown proud?

RAMBLE   I knew you a waistcoateer in the garden alleys,
And would come to a sailor's whistle.

SECRET   Good Sir Ramble,

A hot-reined marmoset: A lustful monkey.

Use her not roughly. She is very tender.

RAMBLE   Rank and rotten, is she not?

SHAVE'EM [*draws her knife*]   Your spittle rogueships

[RAMBLE *draws his sword.*]

Shall not make me so.

SECRET   As you are a man, Squire Scuffle,
Step in between 'em. A weapon of that length
Was ne'er drawn in my house.

SHAVE'EM   Let him come on,
I'll scour it in your guts, you dog.

RAMBLE   You brach,
Are you turned mankind? You forgot I gave you,
When we last joined issue, twenty pound.

SHAVE'EM   O'er night and kicked it out of me in the morning.
I was then a novice, but I know to make
My game now. Fetch the constable.

[*Enter* YOUNG GOLDWIRE *like a Justice of Peace,* DING'EM *like a
Constable, the* MUSICIANS *like Watchmen.*]

SECRET   Ah me!
Here's one unsent for, and a justice of peace, too.

SHAVE'EM   I'll hang you both, you rascals—I can but ride—
You for the purse you cut in Paul's at a sermon.
I have smoked you! And you for the bacon you took on the
highway
From the poor market woman as she rode from Romford.

RAMBLE   Mistress Shave'em.

SCUFFLE   Mistress Secret, on our knees
We beg your pardon.

RAMBLE   Set a ransom on us.

SECRET   We cannot stand trifling. If you mean to save them,
Shut them out at the back door.

SHAVE'EM   First, for punishment,
They shall leave their cloaks behind 'em, and in sign
I am their sovereign, and they my vassals,
For homage kiss my shoe-sole, rogues, and vanish.

[*Exeunt* RAMBLE *and* SCUFFLE.]

YOUNG GOLDWIRE My brave virago! The coast's clear. Strike up. 1

[YOUNG GOLDWIRE, *and the rest discovered*.]

SHAVE'EM My Goldwire made a justice!

SECRET   And your scout   2
Turned constable, and the musicians watchmen!

YOUNG GOLDWIRE We come not to fright you, but to make you
merry.
A light lavolta!

[*They dance*.]   3

SHAVE'EM   I am tired. No more.
This was your device?

DING'EM   Wholly his own. He is
No pig-sconce, mistress.   4

SECRET   He has an excellent headpiece.

YOUNG GOLDWIRE Fie, no, not I! Your jeering gallants say
We citizens have no wit.

DING'EM   He dies that says so.
This was a masterpiece.   5

YOUNG GOLDWIRE   A trifling stratagem,
Not worth the talking of.

SHAVE'EM   I must kiss thee for it
Again, and again.   6

DING'EM   Make much of her. Did you know
What suitors she had since she saw you—

YOUNG GOLDWIRE   I' the way of marriage?

DING'EM Yes, sir; for marriage, and the other thing, too;
The commodity is the same. An Irish lord offered her   7
Five pound a week.

SECRET   And a cashiered captain, half
Of his entertainment.

DING'EM   And a new-made courtier,
The next suit he could beg.   8

YOUNG GOLDWIRE   And did my sweet one
Refuse all this for me?

SHAVE'EM   Weep not for joy,
'T is true. Let others talk of lords, and commanders,   9

And country heirs for their servants; but give me
My gallant prentice. He parts with his money
So civilly, and demurely; keeps no account
Of his expenses, and comes ever furnished.
I know thou hast brought money to make up
My gown and petticoat, with th' appurtenances.

YOUNG GOLDWIRE   I have it here, duck; thou shalt want for
nothing.

SHAVE'EM   Let the chamber be perfumed, [to DING'EM] and get
you, sirrah,
His cap and pantables ready.

YOUNG GOLDWIRE   There's for thee,
And thee: that for a banquet.

SECRET   And a caudle
Against you rise.

YOUNG GOLDWIRE   There.

SHAVE'EM   Usher us up in state.

YOUNG GOLDWIRE   You will be constant?

SHAVE'EM   Thou art the whole world to me.

[*Exeunt, wanton music played before 'em.*]

Scene Two

[*Enter* LUKE.]

ANNE [*within*]   Where is this uncle?

LADY FRUGAL [*within*]   Call this beadsman-brother:
He hath forgot attendance.

MARY [*within*]   Seek him out:
Idleness spoils him.

LUKE   I deserve much more
Than their scorn can load me with, and 't is but justice
That I should live the family's drudge, designed
To all the sordid offices their pride
Imposes on me; since if now I sat
A judge in mine own cause, I should conclude
I am not worth their pity. Such as want
Discourse, and judgment, and through weakness fall,
May merit man's compassion; but I,

That knew profuseness of expense the parent
Of wretched poverty, her fatal daughter,
To riot out mine own, to live upon
The alms of others, steering on a rock
I might have shunned! O heaven! 'T is not fit
I should look upward, much less hope for mercy.

[*Enter* LADY FRUGAL, ANNE, MARY, STARGAZE, *and* MILLICENT.]

LADY FRUGAL   What are you devising, sir?

ANNE   My uncle is much given
To his devotion.

MARY   And takes time to mumble
A paternoster to himself.

LADY FRUGAL   Know you where
Your brother is? It better would become you
(Your means of life depending wholly on him)
To give your attendance.

LUKE   In my will I do:
But since he rode forth yesterday with Lord Lacy,
I have not seen him.

LADY FRUGAL   And why went not you
By his stirrup? How do you look! Were his eyes closed,
You'd be glad of such employment.

LUKE   'T was his pleasure
I should wait your commands, and those I am ever
Most ready to receive.

LADY FRUGAL   I know you can speak well,
But say and do.

[*Enter* LORD LACY *with a will.*]

LUKE   Here comes my lord.

LADY FRUGAL   Further off:
You are no companion for him, and his business
Aims not at you, as I take it.

LUKE [*aside*]   Can I live
In this base condition?

LADY FRUGAL   I hoped, my lord,
You had brought Master Frugal with you, for I must ask
An account of him from you.

1   LORD LACY   I can give it, lady;
But with the best discretion of a woman
And a strong fortified patience, I desire you
To give it hearing.

LUKE   My heart beats.

2

LADY FRUGAL   My lord, you much amaze me.

LORD LACY   I shall astonish you. The noble merchant,
Who living was for his integrity
And upright dealing (a rare miracle
In a rich citizen) London's best honour;

3

Is—I am loath to speak it.

LUKE   Wondrous strange!

LADY FRUGAL   I do suppose the worst, not dead I hope?

4   LORD LACY   Your supposition's true, your hopes are false.
He's dead.

LADY FRUGAL   Ay me!

ANNE   My father!

5   MARY   My kind father!

LUKE   Now they insult not.

LORD LACY   Pray hear me out.
He's dead. Dead to the world, and you. And now

6

Lives only to himself.

LUKE   What riddle's this?

LADY FRUGAL   Act not the torturer in my afflictions;
But make me understand the sum of all
That I must undergo.

7

LORD LACY   ·   In few words take it:
He is retired into a monastery
Where he resolves to end his days.

LUKE   More strange.

8   LORD LACY   I saw him take post for Dover, and the wind
Sitting so fair, by this he's safe at Calais,
And ere long will be at Louvain.

LADY FRUGAL   Could I guess
What were the motives that induced him to it,

9

'T were some allay to my sorrows.

LORD LACY　　　　　　　　　　I'll instruct you,　　　　　　　1
And chide you into that knowledge. 'T was your pride
Above your rank, and stubborn disobedience
Of these your daughters, in their milk sucked from you:
At home the harshness of his entertainment,
You wilfully forgetting that your all　　　　　　　　　　　2
Was borrowed from him; and to hear abroad
The imputations dispersed upon you,
And justly too, I fear, that drew him to
This strict retirement; and thus much said for him,
I am myself to accuse you.

LADY FRUGAL　　　　　　　I confess　　　　　　　　　　　3
A guilty cause to him, but in a thought,
My lord, I ne'er wronged you.

LORD LACY　　　　　　　　　　In fact you have;
The insolent disgrace you put upon
My only son, and Master Plenty; (men, that loved　　　　4
Your daughters in a noble way) to wash off
The scandal, put a resolution in 'em
For three years' travel.

LADY FRUGAL　　　　　　I am much grieved for it.

LORD LACY　One thing I had forgot; your rigour to　　　　5
His decayed brother, in which your flatteries,
Or sorceries, made him a co-agent with you,
Wrought not the least impression.

LUKE　　　　　　　　　　　　Humph! this sounds well.
　　　　　　　　　　　　　　　　　　　　　　　　　　　　6
LADY FRUGAL　'T is now past help: after these storms, my lord,
A little calm, if you please.

LORD LACY　　　　　　　　　If what I have told you
Showed like a storm, what now I must deliver
Will prove a raging tempest. His whole estate　　　　　　7
In lands and leases, debts and present moneys,
With all the moveables he stood possessed of,
With the best advice which he could get for gold
From his learned counsel, by this formal will
Is passed o'er to his brother. With it take
The key of his countinghouse. Not a groat left you,　　　8
Which you can call your own.

LADY FRUGAL　　　　　　Undone forever!

ANNE, MARY　What will become of us?

LUKE　　　　　　　　　　　　Humph!　　　　　　　9

1 [LADY FRUGAL, ANNE, *and* MARY *kneel to* LORD LACY.]

LORD LACY   The scene's changed,
And he that was your slave, by fate appointed
Your governor. You kneel to me in vain,
I cannot help you, I discharge the trust
2 Imposed upon me. This humility
From him may gain remission, and perhaps
Forgetfulness of your barbarous usage to him.

LADY FRUGAL   Am I come to this?

LORD LACY   Enjoy your own, good sir,
3 But use it with due reverence. I once heard you
Speak most divinely in the opposition
Of a revengeful humour; to these show it,
And such who then depended on the mercy
Of your brother, wholly now at your devotion,
And make good the opinion I held of you,
4 Of which I am most confident.

LUKE [*to* LADY FRUGAL, ANNE, MARY]   Pray you rise,
And rise with this assurance, I am still,
As I was of late, your creature; and if raised
In any thing, 't is in my power to serve you,
5 My will is still the same.—[*to* LORD LACY] O my lord!
This heap of wealth which you possess me of,
Which to a worldly man had been a blessing,
And to the messenger might with justice challenge
A kind of adoration, is to me
6 A curse I cannot thank you for; and much less
Rejoice in that tranquility of mind
My brother's vows must purchase. I have made
A dear exchange with him. He now enjoys
My peace and poverty, the trouble of
His wealth conferred on me, and that a burden
7 Too heavy for my weak shoulders.

LORD LACY   Honest soul,
With what feeling he receives it.

LADY FRUGAL   You shall have
My best assistance, if you please to use it,
8 To help you to support it.

LUKE   By no means!
The weight shall rather sink me, than you part
With one short minute from those lawful pleasures
Which you were born to, in your care to aid me.
9 You shall have all abundance. In my nature

I was ever liberal—my lord you know it—   1
Kind, affable. And now methinks I see
Before my face the jubilee of joy,
When it is assured my brother lives in me,
His debtors in full cups crowned to my health,
With paeans to my praise will celebrate.   2
For they well know 't is far from me to take
The forfeiture of a bond. Nay, I shall blush,
The interest never paid after three years,
When I demand my principal. And his servants,
Who from a slavish fear paid their obedience
By him exacted, now when they are mine   3
Will grow familiar friends, and as such use me,
Being certain of the mildness of my temper,
Which my change of fortune, frequent in most men,
Hath not the power to alter.

LORD LACY   Yet take heed, sir,   4
You ruin not with too much lenity,
What his fit severity raised.

LADY FRUGAL   And we fall from
That height we have maintained.

LUKE   I'll build it higher,   5
To admiration higher. With disdain
I look upon these habits, no way suiting
The wife and daughters of a knighted citizen
Blessed with abundance.

LORD LACY   There, sir, I join with you;   6
A fit decorum must be kept, the Court
Distinguished from the City.

LUKE   With your favour,
I know what you would say, but give me leave
In this to be your advocate. You are wide,   7
Wide the whole region in what I purpose.
Since all the titles, honours, long descents
Borrow their gloss from wealth, the rich with reason
May challenge their prerogatives. And it shall be
My glory, nay a triumph to revive
In the pomp that these shall shine, the memory   8
Of the Roman matrons, who kept captive queens
To be their handmaids. And when you appear
Like Juno in full majesty, and my nieces
Like Iris, Hebe, or what deities else
Old poets fancy (your crammed wardrobes richer   9

1   Than various nature's), and draw down the envy
     Of our western world upon you, only hold me
     Your viligant Hermes with aerial wings,
     My caduceus my strong zeal to serve you,
     Pressed to fetch in all rarities may delight you,
     And I am made immortal.
2
LORD LACY   A strange frenzy!

LUKE Off with these rags, and then to bed. There dream
     Of future greatness, which when you awake
     I'll make a certain truth: but I must be
3   A doer, not a promiser. The performance
     Requiring haste, I kiss your hands, and leave you. [*Exits*]

LORD LACY Are we all turned statues? Have his strange words
        charmed us?
     What muse you on, lady?

4 LADY FRUGAL   Do not trouble me.

LORD LACY Sleep you too, young ones?

ANNE   Swift-winged time till now
     Was never tedious to me. Would 't were night.

5 MARY Nay, morning rather.

LORD LACY   Can you ground your faith
     On such impossibilities? Have you so soon
     Forgot your good husband?

LADY FRUGAL   He was a vanity
6   I must no more remember.

LORD LACY   Excellent!
     You, your kind father?

ANNE   Such an uncle never
     Was read of in story!

7 LORD LACY   Not one word in answer
     Of my demands?

MARY   You are but a lord; and know,
     My thoughts soar higher.

8 LORD LACY   Admirable! I will leave you
     To your castles in the air. [*Aside*] When I relate this,
     It will exceed belief, but he must know it. [*Exits*]

STARGAZE Now I may boldly speak. May it please you, madam,
     To look upon your vassal; I foresaw this,
9   The stars assured it.

LADY FRUGAL .   I begin to feel   1
  Myself another woman.

STARGAZE   Now you shall find
  All my predictions true, and nobler matches
  Prepared for my young ladies.

MILLICENT   Princely husbands.   2

ANNE I'll go no less.

MARY   Not a word more;
  Provide my night rail.

MILLICENT   What shall we be tomorrow!   3

[*Exeunt*]

Scene Three

                                                                                4
LUKE [*enters with a key*]
  'T was no fantastic object, but a truth,
  A real truth; nor dream: I did not slumber,
  And could wake ever with a brooding eye
  To gaze upon 't! It did endure the touch;
  I saw, and felt it. Yet what I beheld   5
  And handled oft, did so transcend belief
  (My wonder and astonishment passed o'er)
  I faintly could give credit to my senses.—
  [*Addressing the key*] Thou dumb magician, that without a charm
  Did'st make my entrance easy, to possess   6
  What wise men wish and toil for. Hermes' moly,
  Sibylla's golden bough, the great elixir,
  Imagined only by the alchemist,
  Compared with thee are shadows, thou the substance
  And guardian of felicity. No marvel,
  My brother made thy place of rest his bosom,   7
  Thou being the keeper of his heart, a mistress
  To be hugged ever. In by-corners of
  This sacred room, silver in bags heaped up
  Like billets sawed, and ready for the fire,
  Unworthy to hold fellowship with bright gold
  That flowed about the room, concealed itself.   8
  There needs no artificial light; the splendour
  Makes a perpetual day there, night and darkness
  By that still-burning lamp forever banished.
  But when, guided by that, my eyes had made
  Discovery of the caskets, and they opened,   9

1 Each sparkling diamond from itself shot forth .
   A pyramid of flames, and in the roof
   Fixed it a glorious star, and made the place
   Heaven's abstract, or epitome: rubies, sapphires,
   And ropes of orient pearl, these seen, I could not
2 But look on with contempt. And yet I found,
   What weak credulity could have no faith in,
   A treasure far exceeding these. Here lay
   A manor bound fast in a skin of parchment,
   The wax continuing hard, the acres melting.
   Here a sure deed of gift for a market town,
3 If not redeemed this day, which is not in
   The unthrift's power: there being scarce one shire
   In Wales or England, where my moneys are not
   Lent out at usury, the certain hook
   To draw in more. I am sublimed! Gross earth
   Supports me not. I walk on air!—Who's there?
4 Thieves! Raise the street! Thieves!

[*Enter* LORD LACY *with* SIR JOHN FRUGAL, SIR MAURICE LACY, *and*
PLENTY, *as Indians.*]

5 LORD LACY   What strange passion's this?
   Have you your eyes? Do you know me?

   LUKE   You, my lord,
   I do: but this retinue, in these shapes, too,
   May well excuse my fears. When 't is your pleasure
6 That I should wait upon you, give me leave
   To do it at your own house, for I must tell you,
   Things as they now are with me, well considered,
   I do not like such visitants.

   LORD LACY   Yesterday
7 When you had nothing, praise your poverty for 't,
   You could have sung secure before a thief;
   But now you are grown rich, doubts and suspicions,
   And needless fears possess you. Thank a good brother,
   But let not this exalt you.

8 LUKE   A good brother!
   Good in his conscience, I confess, and wise
   In giving o'er the world. But his estate,
   Which your lordship may conceive great, no way answers
   The general opinion. Alas,
9 With a great charge, I am left a poor man by him.

LORD LACY   A poor man, say you?   1

LUKE   Poor, compared with what
'T is thought I do possess. Some little land,
Fair household furniture, a few good debts,
But empty bags, I find: yet I will be
A faithful steward to his wife and daughters,   2
And to the utmost of my power obey
His will in all things.

LORD LACY   I'll not argue with you
Of his estate, but bind you to performance
Of his last request, which is, for testimony   3
Of his religious charity, that you would
Receive these Indians, lately sent him from
Virginia, into your house; and labour
At any rate with the best of your endeavours,
Assisted by the aids of our divines,   4
To make 'em Christians.

LUKE   Call you this, my lord,
Religious charity? To send infidels,
Like hungry locusts, to devour the bread
Should feel his family? I neither can,
Nor will consent to 't.   5

LORD LACY   Do not slight it; 't is
With him a business of such consequence,
That should he only hear 't is not embraced,
And cheerfully, in this his conscience aiming
At the saving of three souls, 't will draw him o'er   6
To see it himself accomplished.

LUKE   Heaven forbid
I should divert him from his holy purpose
To worldly cares again! I rather will
Sustain the burden, and with the converted   7
Feast the converters, who I know will prove
The greatest feeders.

SIR JOHN   Oh, ha, enewah Chrish bully leika.

PLENTY   Enaula.
                                                           8
SIR MAURICE   Harrico botikia bonnery.

LUKE   Ha! in this heathen language,
How is it possible our doctors should
Hold conference with 'em, or I use the means
For their conversion?   9

1 LORD LACY   That shall be no hindrance
To your good purposes. They have lived long
In the English colony, and speak our language
As their own dialect; the business does concern you:
Mine own designs command me hence. Continue,
2 As in your poverty you were, a pious
And honest man. [*Exits*]

LUKE   That is, interpreted,
A slave and beggar.

SIR JOHN   You conceive it right,
3 There being no religion, nor virtue
But in abundance, and no vice but want.
All deities serve Plutus.

LUKE   Oracle!

SIR JOHN Temples raised to ourselves in the increase
4 Of wealth and reputation, speak a wise man;
But sacrifice to an imagined power,
Of which we have no sense but in belief,
A superstitious fool.

LUKE   True worldly wisdom!

5 SIR JOHN All knowledge else is folly.

SIR MAURICE   Now we are yours,
Be confident your better angel is
Entered your house.

PLENTY   There being nothing in
6 The compass of your wishes, but shall end
In their fruition to the full.

SIR JOHN   As yet,
You do not know us, but when you understand
The wonders we can do, and what the ends were
7 That brought us hither, you will entertain us
With more respect.

LUKE [*aside*]   There's something whispers to me,
These are no common men.—My house is yours,
Enjoy it freely: only grant me this,
Not to be seen abroad till I have heard
8 More of your sacred principles. Pray enter.
You are learn'd Europeans, and we worse
Than ignorant Americans.

SIR JOHN   You shall find it.

9 [*Exeunt*]

ACT FOUR

Scene One

[*Enter* DING'EM, GETTALL, AND HOLDFAST.]

1

DING'EM   Not speak with him! With fear survey me better,
Thou figure of famine.

GETTALL   Coming, as we do,
From his quondam patrons, his dear ingles now,
The brave spark Tradewell—

2

DING'EM   And the man of men
In the service of a woman, gallant Goldwire!

[*Enter* LUKE.]

3

HOLDFAST   I know 'em for his prentices without
These flourishes.—[*To* LUKE] Here are rude fellows, sir.

DING'EM   Not yours, you rascal!

HOLDFAST   No, don pimp; you may seek 'em
In Bridewell, or the hole; here are none of your comrogues.

4

LUKE   One of 'em looks as he would cut my throat:
Your business, friends?

HOLDFAST   I'll fetch a constable;
Let him answer him in the stocks.

5

DING'EM   Stir and thou dar'st.
Fright me with Bridewell and the stocks! They are fleabitings
I am familiar with. [*Draws*]

LUKE   Pray you put up—
[*To* HOLDFAST] And sirrah, hold your peace.

6

DING'EM   Thy word's a law,
And I obey. Live, scrape-shoe, and be thankful.
Thou man of muck and money, for as such
I now salute thee, the suburbian gamesters
Have heard thy fortunes, and I am in person
Sent to congratulate.

7

GETTALL   The news hath reached
The ordinaries, and all the gamesters are
Ambitious to shake the golden golls
Of worshipful Master Luke. I come from Tradewell,
Your fine facetious factor.

8

1 DING'EM   I from Goldwire;
He and his Helen have prepared a banquet,
With the appurtenances, to entertain thee,
For I must whisper in thine ear, thou art
To be her Paris; but bring money with thee
To quit old scores.

2
GETTALL   Blind chance hath frowned upon
Brave Tradewell. He's blown up, but not without
Hope of recovery, so you supply him
With a good round sum. In my house, I can assure you,
There's half a million stirring.

3
LUKE   What hath he lost?

GETTALL   Three hundred.

LUKE   A trifle.

GETTALL   Make it up a thousand,
4 And I will fit him with such tools as shall
Bring in a myriad.

LUKE   They know me well,
Nor need you use such circumstances for 'em.
What's mine is theirs. They are my friends, not servants,
5 But in their care to enrich me, and these courses
The speeding means. Your name, I pray you?

GETTALL   Gettall;
I have been many years an ordinarykeeper,
My box my poor revenue.

6 LUKE   Your name suits well
With your profession. Bid him bear up; he shall not
Sit long on penniless-bench.

GETTALL   There spake an angel.

7 LUKE   You know Mistress Shave'em?

GETTALL   The pontifical punk?

LUKE   The same. Let him meet me there some two hours hence,
And tell Tom Goldwire I will then be with him,
Furnished beyond his hopes; and let your mistress
8 Appear in her best trim.

DING'EM   She will make thee young,
Old Aeson. She is ever furnished with
Medea's drugs, restoratives. I fly

My box: A winning gamester paid a gratuity to the boxkeeper.

To keep 'em sober till thy worship come;   1
They will be drunk with joy else.

GETTALL   I'll run with you.

[*Exeunt* DING'EM *and* GETTALL.]

HOLDFAST   You will not do as you say, I hope.   2

LUKE   Inquire not;
I shall do what becomes me—To the door.

[*Knocking within.*]

                                                                      3
New visitants: what are they?

HOLDFAST   A whole batch, sir,
Almost of the same leaven: your needy debtors,
Penury, Fortune, Hoist.

LUKE   They come to gratulate   4
The fortune fall'n upon me.

HOLDFAST   Rather, sir,
Like the others, to prey on you.

LUKE   I am simple;
They know my good nature. But let 'em in however.   5

HOLDFAST   All will come to ruin! I see beggary
Already knocking at the door.—You may enter;
But use a conscience, and do not work upon
A tenderhearted gentleman too much;
'T will show like charity in you.   6

[*Enter* FORTUNE, PENURY, *and* HOIST.]

LUKE   Welcome, friends;
I know your hearts and wishes; you are glad
You have changed your creditor.   7

PENURY   I weep for joy
To look upon his worship's face.

FORTUNE   His worship's!
I see lord mayor written on his forehead;
The cap of maintenance, and city sword   8
Borne up in state before him.

HOIST   Hospitals,
And a third Burse erected by his honour.

Burse: See Glossary.

1 PENURY   The city poet on the pageant day
    Preferring him before Gresham.

HOIST   All the conduits
    Spouting canary sack.

2 FORTUNE   Not a prisoner left,
    Under ten pounds.

PENURY   We his poor beadsmen feasting
    Our neighbours on his bounty.

LUKE   May I make good
3   Your prophecies, gentle friends, as I'll endeavour
    To the utmost of my power.

HOLDFAST   Yes, for one year,
    And break the next.

LUKE   You are ever prating, sirrah.
4   Your present business, friends?

FORTUNE   Were your brother present,
    Mine had been of some consequence; but now
    The power lies in your worship's hand, 't is little,
    And will I know, as soon as asked, be granted.

5 LUKE 'T is very probable.

FORTUNE   The kind forbearance
    Of my great debt, by your means, heav'n be praised for 't,
    Hath raised my sunk estate. I have two ships,
    Which I long since gave lost, above my hopes
6   Returned from Barbary, and richly freighted.

LUKE   Where are they?

FORTUNE   Near Gravesend.

LUKE   I am truly glad of 't.
7
FORTUNE   I find your worship's charity, and dare swear so.
    Now may I have your licence, as I know
    With willingness I shall, to make the best
    Of the commodities—though you have execution,
    And after judgment against all that's mine,
8   As my poor body—I shall be enabled
    To make payment of my debts to all the world,
    And leave myself a competence.

Gresham: See Glossary under EXCHANGE.

LUKE   You much wrong me,   1
  If you only doubt it. Yours, Master Hoist?

HOIST   'T is the surrend'ring back the mortgage of
  My lands, and on good terms, but three days' patience;
  By an uncle's death I have means left to redeem it,
  And cancel all the forfeited bonds I sealed to   2
  In my riots to the merchant, for I am
  Resolved to leave off play, and turn good husband.

LUKE   A good intent, and to be cherished in you.
  Yours, Penury?

PENURY   My state stands as it did, sir: 3
  What I owed I owe, but can pay nothing to you.
  Yet if you please to trust me with ten pounds more,
  I can buy a commodity of a sailor
  Will make me a freeman. There, sir, is his name;
  And the parcels I am to deal for.   4

[Gives him a paper.]

LUKE   You are all so reasonable
  In your demands, that I must freely grant 'em.   5
  Some three hours hence meet me on the Exchange,
  You shall be amply satisfied.

PENURY   Heaven preserve you.

FORTUNE   Happy were London if within her walls
  She had many such rich men.   6

LUKE   No more, now leave me;

[Exeunt FORTUNE, HOIST, *and* PENURY.]

  I am full of various thoughts. Be careful, Holdfast,   7
  I have much to do.

HOLDFAST   And I something to say,
  Would you give me hearing.

LUKE   At my better leisure.   8
  Till my return, look well unto the Indians.
  In the meantime, do you as this directs you.

[Gives him a paper. Exeunt]

Scene Two

1 [*Enter* YOUNG GOLDWIRE, YOUNG TRADEWELL, SHAVE'EM, SECRET, GETTALL, *and* DING'EM.]

YOUNG GOLDWIRE "All that is mine is theirs." Those were his words?

2 DING'EM   I am authentical.

YOUNG TRADEWELL   And that I should not
Sit long on penniless-bench?

GETTALL   But suddenly start up
A gamester at the height, and cry "At all!"

3 SHAVE'EM   And did he seem to have an inclination
To toy with me?

DING'EM   He wished you would put on
Your best habiliments, for he resolved
To make a jovial day on 't.

4 YOUNG GOLDWIRE   Hug him close, wench,
And thou may'st eat gold and amber, I well know him
For a most insatiate drabber. He hath given,
Before he spent his own estate, which was
Nothing to the huge mass he's now possessed of,
5 A hundred pound a leap.

SHAVE'EM   Hell take my doctor!
He should have brought me some fresh oil of talc;
These ceruses are common.

SECRET   'Troth, sweet lady,
6 The colours are well laid on.

YOUNG GOLDWIRE   And thick enough;
I find that on my lips.

SHAVE'EM   Do you so, Jack Sauce!
I'll keep 'em further off.

7 YOUNG GOLDWIRE   But be assured first
Of a new maintainer e'er you cashier the old one.
But bind him fast by thy sorceries, and thou shalt
Be my revenue; the whole college study
The reparation of thy ruined face;
8 Thou shalt have thy proper and baldheaded coachman;

cry "At all!": So the dicecaster cries when he wishes to bet against all comers.

Thy tailor and embroiderer shall kneel   1
To thee, their idol. Cheapside and the Exchange
Shall court thy custom, and thou shalt forget
There ever was a St. Martin's. Thy procurer
Shall be sheathed in velvet, and a reverend veil
Pass her for a grave matron. Have an eye to the door,
And let loud music when this monarch enters   2
Proclaim his entertainment.

DING'EM   That's my office.

[*Cornets flourish.*]

The consort's ready.   3

[*Enter* LUKE.]

YOUNG TRADEWELL   And the god of pleasure,
Master Luke our Comus, enters.

YOUNG GOLDWIRE   Set your face in order,   4
I will prepare him.—Live I to see this day,
And to acknowledge you my royal master?

YOUNG TRADEWELL   Let the iron chests fly open, and the gold,
Rusty for want of use, appear again!

GETTALL   Make my ordinary flourish!   5

SHAVE'EM   Welcome, sir,
To your own palace.

[*Music*]

YOUNG GOLDWIRE   Kiss your Cleopatra,   6
And show yourself in your magnificent bounties
A second Anthony!

DING'EM   All the Nine Worthies!

SECRET   Variety of pleasures wait on you,
And a strong back!   7

LUKE   Give me leave to breathe, I pray you.
I am astonished! All this preparation
For me? And this choice modest beauty wrought
To feed my appetite?
                                                                                        8
ALL   We are all your creatures.

LUKE   A house well furnished!

YOUNG GOLDWIRE   At your own cost, sir,
Glad I the instrument. I prophesied
You should possess what now you do, and therefore   9

1 Prepared it for your pleasure. There's no rag
This Venus wears, but on my knowledge was
Derived from your brother's cash. The lease of the house
And furniture, cost near a thousand, sir.

SHAVE'EM   But now you are master both of it and me,
2 I hope you'll build elsewhere.

LUKE   And see you placed,
Fair one, to your desert. As I live, friend Tradewell,
I hardly knew you, your clothes so well become you.
What is your loss? Speak truth.

3 YOUNG TRADEWELL   Three hundred, sir.

GETTALL   But on a new supply he shall recover
The sum told twenty times o'er.

SHAVE'EM   There is a banquet,
And after that a soft couch that attends you.

4
LUKE   I couple not in the daylight. Expectation
Heightens the pleasure of the night, my sweet one.
Your music's harsh, discharge it. I have provided
A better consort, and you shall frolic it
In another place.

5
[*Cease music*]

YOUNG GOLDWIRE But have you brought gold, and store, sir?

YOUNG TRADEWELL   I long to "Ware the caster!"

6 YOUNG GOLDWIRE   I to appear
In a fresh habit.

SHAVE'EM   My mercer and my silkman
Waited me two hours since.

LUKE   I am no porter,
7 To carry so much gold as will supply
Your vast desires, but I have ta'en order for you;

[*Enter* SHERIFF, MARSHALL, *and* OFFICERS.]

8 You shall have what is fitting, and they come here
Will see it performed.—Do your offices: you have
My lord chief justice's warrant for 't.

SHERIFF   Seize 'em all.

"Ware the caster!": Another gaming call.

SHAVE'EM   The city marshall!   1

YOUNG GOLDWIRE   And the sheriff! I know him.

SECRET   We are betrayed.

DING'EM   Undone.

GETTALL   Dear Master Luke.   2

YOUNG GOLDWIRE   You cannot be so cruel. Your persuasion
  Chid us into these courses, oft repeating,
  "Show yourselves city sparks, and hang up money."

LUKE   True, when it was my brother's I contemned it,
  But now it is mine own, the case is altered.   3

YOUNG TRADEWELL   Will you prove yourself a devil? Tempt us
    to mischief,
  And then discover it?

LUKE   Argue that hereafter.   4
  In the meantime, Master Goldwire, you that made
  Your ten-pound suppers; kept your punks at livery
  In Brentford, Staines, and Barnet, and this in London;
  Held correspondence with your fellow cashiers,
  Ka me, ka thee; and knew in your accompts
  To cheat my brother—if you can, evade me.   5
  If there be law in London your fathers' bonds
  Shall answer for what you are out.

YOUNG GOLDWIRE   You often told us
  It was a bugbear.

LUKE   Such a one as shall fright 'em   6
  Out of their estates to make me satisfaction
  To the utmost scruple. And for you, madam,
  My Cleopatra, by your own confession
  Your house, and all your moveables, are mine;
  Nor shall you nor your matron need to trouble   7
  Your mercer, or your silkman; a blue gown,
  And a whip to boot, as I will handle it,
  Will serve the turn in Bridewell; and these soft hands,
  When they are inured to beating hemp, be scoured
  In your penitent tears, and quite forget
  Powders and bitter almonds.   8

SHAVE'EM, SECRET, DING'EM   Will you show no mercy?

LUKE   I am inexorable.

  blue gown: the Bridewell uniform. See Glossary.

GETTALL   I'll make bold
To take my leave; the gamesters stay my coming.

LUKE   We must not part so, gentle Master Gettall.
Your box, your certain income, must pay back
Three hundred, as I take it, or you lie by it.
There's half a million stirring in your house,
This a poor trifle.—Master Sheriff and Master Marshall,
On your perils do your offices.

YOUNG GOLDWIRE [*to* YOUNG TRADEWELL] Dost thou cry now
Like a maudlin gamester after loss? I'll suffer
Like a Roman, and now in my misery, [*to* LUKE]
In scorn of all thy wealth, to thy teeth tell thee
Thou wert my pander.

LUKE   Shall I hear this from
My prentice?

MARSHALL   Stop his mouth.

SHERIFF   Away with 'em.

[*Exeunt* SHERIFF, MARSHALL, *and the rest.*]

LUKE   A prosperous omen in my entrance to
My altered nature! These house thieves removed,
And what was lost, beyond my hopes recovered,
Will add unto my heap. Increase of wealth
Is the rich man's ambition, and mine
Shall know no bounds. The valiant Macedon,
Having in his conceit subdued one world,
Lamented that there were no more to conquer:
In my way he shall be my great example.
And when my private house in crammed abundance
Shall prove the chamber of the city poor,
And Genoese bankers shall look pale with envy
When I am mentioned, I shall grieve there is
No more to be exhausted in one kingdom.
Religion, conscience, charity, farewell!
To me you are words only, and no more;
All human happiness consists in store.

Scene Three

[*Enter three* SERGEANTS, YEOMAN, FORTUNE, HOIST, PENURY.]

FORTUNE   At Master Luke's suit? The action twenty thousand?

or you lie by it: Or you go to prison.

FIRST SERGEANT With two or three executions, which shall grind 1
    you
  To powder when we have you in the Counter.

FORTUNE Thou dost belie him, varlet. He, good gentleman,
  Will weep when he hears how we are used.

FIRST SERGEANT   Yes, millstones. 2

PENURY He promised to lend me ten pound for a bargain;
  He will not do it this way.

SECOND SERGEANT   I have warrant
  For what I have done. You are a poor fellow,
  And there being little to be got by you, 3
  In charity, as I am an officer,
  I would not have seen you, but upon compulsion,
  And for mine own security.

THIRD SERGEANT   You are a gallant,
  And I do you a courtesy; provided 4
  That you have money. For a piece an hour
  I'll keep you in the house, till you send for bail.

SECOND SERGEANT In the meantime, yeoman, run to the other
    Counter,
  And search if there be ought else out against him. 5

THIRD SERGEANT That done, haste to his creditors. He's a prize,
  And as we are city pirates by our oaths,
  We must make the best on 't.

[*Exit* YEOMAN.]
         6

HOIST   Do your worst, I care not.
  I'll be removed to the Fleet, and drink and drab there
  In spite of your teeth. I now repent I ever
  Intended to be honest.

[*Enter* LUKE.] 7

THIRD SERGEANT   Here he comes
  You had best tell so.

FORTUNE   Worshipful sir,
  You come in time to free us from these bandogs.
  I know you gave no way to 't. 8

PENURY   Or if you did,
  'T was but to try our patience.

HOIST   I must tell you
  I do not like such trials. 9

1 LUKE   Are you sergeants
Acquainted with the danger of a rescue,
Yet stand here prating in the street? The Counter
Is a safer place to parley in.

FORTUNE   Are you in earnest?

2 LUKE Yes, faith, I will be satisfied to a token,
Or build upon 't, you rot there.

FORTUNE   Can a gentleman
Of your soft and silken temper, speak such language?

PENURY So honest, so religious?

3

HOIST   That preached
So much of charity for us to your brother?

LUKE Yes, when I was in poverty it showed well;
But I inherit with his state, his mind,
And rougher nature. I grant, then I talked

4 For some ends to myself concealed, of pity,
The poor man's orisons; and such like nothing.
But what I thought, you all shall feel, and with rigour.
Kind Master Luke says it.—[*To the* SERGEANTS] Who pays for
   your attendance?

5 Do you wait gratis?

FORTUNE   Hear us speak.

LUKE   While I,
Like the adder, stop mine ears. Or did I listen,
Though you spake with the tongues of angels to me,

6 I am not to be altered.

FORTUNE   Let me make the best
Of my ships, and their freight.

PENURY Lend me the ten pounds you promised.

7 HOIST A day or two's patience to redeem my mortgage,
And you shall be satisfied.

FORTUNE   To the utmost farthing.

LUKE I'll show some mercy; which is, that I will not
Torture you with false hopes, but make you know
What you shall trust to.—[*To* FORTUNE] Your ships to my use

8 Are seized on.—[*To* PENURY] I have got into my hands

Like the adder, stop mine ears: Compare this speech with Psalm 58:
3-5.

Tongues of angels: See I Corinthians, 13:1. Luke's duplicity is blasphemous.

Your bargains from the sailor, 't was a good one   1
For such a petty sum.—[*To* Hoist] I will likewise take
The extremity of your mortgage, and the forfeit
Of your several bonds; the use and principal
Shall not serve.—Think of the basket, wretches,
And a coal sack for a winding sheet.
                                                          2
FORTUNE   Broker!

HOIST   Jew!

FORTUNE   Imposter!

HOIST   Cutthroat!
                                                          3
FORTUNE   Hypocrite!

LUKE   Do, rail on.
Move mountains with your breath, it shakes not me.

PENURY   On my knees I beg compassion. My wife and children
Shall hourly pray for your worship.   4

FORTUNE   Mine betake thee
To the devil thy tutor.

PENURY   Look upon my tears.

HOIST   My rage.
                                                          5
FORTUNE   My wrongs.

LUKE   They are all alike to me:
Entreaties, curses, prayers, or imprecations.
Do your duties, sergeants, I am elsewhere looked for. [*Exits*]

THIRD SERGEANT   This your kind creditor?   6

SECOND SERGEANT   A vast villain, rather.

PENURY   See, see, the sergeants pity us. Yet he's marble.

HOIST   Buried alive!

FORTUNE   There's no means to avoid it.   7

[*Exeunt*]

Scene Four
                                                          8
[*Enter* HOLDFAST, STARGAZE, *and* MILLICENT.]

STARGAZE   Not wait upon my lady?

HOLDFAST   Nor come at her;
You find it not in your almanac.   9

1 MILLICENT   Nor I have licence
To bring her breakfast.

HOLDFAST   My new master hath
Decreed this for a fasting day. She hath feasted long,
And after a carnival, Lent ever follows.

2 MILLICENT Give me the key of her wardrobe. You'll repent this:
I must know what gown she'll wear.

HOLDFAST   You are mistaken,
Dame president of the sweetmeats. She and her daughters
Are turned philosophers, and must carry all
3 Their wealth about 'em. They have clothes laid in their chamber,
If they please to put 'em on, and without help, too,
Or they may walk naked. You look, Master Stargaze,
As you had seen a strange comet, and had now foretold
The end of the world, and on what day. And you,
As the wasps had broke into the gallipots,
4 And eaten up your apricots.

LADY FRUGAL [*within*]   Stargazer! Millicent!

MILLICENT My lady's voice.

HOLDFAST   Stir not, you are confined here—
5 Your ladyship may approach them if you please,
But they are bound in this circle.

LADY FRUGAL [*within*]   Mine own bees
Rebel against me! When my kind brother knows this
I will be so revenged—

6 HOLDFAST   The world's well altered.
He's your kind brother now, but yesterday
Your slave and jesting-stock.

[*Enter* LADY FRUGAL, ANNE, MARY, *in coarse habit, weeping.*]

7 MILLICENT   What witch hath transformed you?

STARGAZE Is this the glorious shape your cheating brother
Promised you should appear in?

MILLICENT   My young ladies
8 In buffin gowns, and green aprons! Tear 'em off,
Rather show all than be seen thus.

HOLDFAST   'T is more comely,
Iwis, than their other whim-whams.

MILLICENT   A French hood, too;
9 Now 't is out of fashion, a fool's cap would show better.

LADY FRUGAL   We are fooled indeed! By whose command are we   1
    used thus?

[*Enter* LUKE.]

HOLDFAST   Here he comes that can best resolve you.
                                         2

LADY FRUGAL   O good brother!
    Do you thus preserve your protestation to me?
    Can queens envy this habit? or did Juno
    E'er feast in such a shape?

ANNE   You talked of Hebe,   3
    Of Iris, and I know not what; but were they
    Dressed as we are, they were sure some chandler's daughters
    Bleaching linen in Moorfields.

MARY   Or Exchange wenches,
    Coming from eating pudding-pies on a Sunday   4
    At Pimlico, or Islington.

LUKE   Save you, sister.
    I now dare style you so: you were before
    Too glorious to be looked on; now you appear
    Like a city matron, and my pretty nieces
    Such things as were born and bred there. Why should you ape   5
    The fashions of court ladies, whose high titles,
    And pedigrees of long descent, give warrant
    For their superfluous bravery? 'T was monstrous:
    Till now you ne'er looked lovely.

LADY FRUGAL   Is this spoken   6
    In scorn?

LUKE   Fie, no! with judgment. I make good
    My promise, and now show you like yourselves,
    In your own natural shapes, and stand resolved
    You shall continue so.   7

LADY FRUGAL   It is confessed, sir.

LUKE   Sir? Sirrah. Use your old phrase, I can bear it.

LADY FRUGAL   That, if you please, forgotten. We acknowledge
    We have deserved ill from you, yet despair not;   8
    Though we are at your disposure, you'll maintain us
    Like your brother's wife and daughters.

LUKE   'T is my purpose.

LADY FRUGAL   And not make us ridiculous.   9

1 LUKE   Admired rather,
  As fair examples for our proud city dames,
  And their proud brood to imitate. Do not frown;
  If you do, I laugh, and glory that I have
  The power, in you, to scourge a general vice,
  And rise up a new satirist. But hear gently,
2 And in a gentle phrase I'll reprehend
  Your late disguised deformity, and cry up
  This decency and neatness, with th' advantage
  You shall receive by 't.

  LADY FRUGAL   We are bound to hear you.

3 LUKE With a soul inclined to learn. Your father was
  An honest country farmer, Goodman Humble,
  By his neighbours ne'er called Master. Did your pride
  Descend from him? But let that pass. Your fortune,
  Or rather your husband's industry, advanced you
  To the rank of a merchant's wife. He made a knight,
4 And your sweet mistress-ship ladyfied, you wore
  Satin on solemn days, a chain of gold,
  A velvet hood, rich borders, and sometimes
  A dainty miniver cap, a silver pin
  Headed with a pearl worth threepence, and thus far
5 You were privileged, and no man envied it;
  It being for the city's honour, that
  There should be a distinction between
  The wife of a patrician, and plebeian.

  MILLICENT Pray you, leave preaching, or choose some other text;
  Your rhetoric is too moving, for it makes
6 Your auditory weep.

  LUKE   Peace, chattering magpie,
  I'll treat of you anon.—But when the height
  And dignity of London's blessings grew
  Contemptible, and the name lady mayoress
7 Became a byword, and you scorned the means
  By which you were raised, my brother's fond indulgence
  Giving the reins to 't; and no object pleased you
  But the glittering pomp and bravery of the court:
  What a strange, nay monstrous metamorphosis followed!
8 No English workman then could please your fancy;
  The French and Tuscan dress your whole discourse;
  This bawd to prodigality entertained
  To buzz into your ears what shape this countess
  Appeared in the last masque, and how it drew
  The young lords' eyes upon her; and this usher
9 Succeeded in the eldest prentice's place
  To walk before you.

LADY FRUGAL   Pray you, end.   1

HOLDFAST   Proceed, sir;
I could fast almost a prenticeship to hear you,
You touch 'em so to the quick.

LUKE   Then as I said,
The reverend hood cast off, your borrowed hair   2
Powdered and curled, was by your dresser's art
Formed like a coronet, hanged with diamonds,
And the richest orient pearl; your carcanets
That did adorn your neck of equal value;
Your Hungerland bands, and Spanish quellio ruffs;
Great lords and ladies feasted to survey   3
Embroidered petticoats; and sickness feigned
That your night rails of forty pounds apiece
Might be seen with envy of the visitants;
Rich pantables in ostentation shown,
And roses worth a family; you were served in plate;   4
Stirred not a foot without your coach. And going
To church not for devotion, but to show
Your pomp, you were tickled when the beggars cried,
"Heaven save your honour!" This idolatry
Paid to a painted room.
                                                          5
HOLDFAST   Nay, you have reason
To blubber, all of you.

LUKE   And when you lay
In childbed, at the christ'ning of this minx,
I well remember it, as you had been
An absolute princess, since they have no more,   6
Three several chambers hung. The first with arras,
And that for waiters; the second crimson satin,
For the meaner sort of guests; the third of scarlet,
Of the rich Tyrian dye; a canopy
To cover the brat's cradle; you in state   7
Like Pompey's Julia.

LADY FRUGAL   No more, I pray you.

LUKE   Of this be sure you shall not. I'll cut off
Whatever is exorbitant in you,
Or in your daughters, and reduce you to   8
Your natural forms and habits; not in revenge
Of your base usage of me, but to fright
Others by your example. 'T is decreed
You shall serve one another, for I will
Allow no waiter to you. Out of doors   9
With these useless drones!

1 **HOLDFAST**   Will you pack?

MILLICENT   Not till I have
My trunks along with me.

LUKE   Not a rag! you came
Hither without a box.

2 **STARGAZE**   You'll show to me,
I hope, sir, more compassion.

HOLDFAST   Troth I'll be
Thus far a suitor for him. He hath printed
An almanac for this year at his own charge;
3 Let him have th' impression with him to set up with.

LUKE For once I'll be entreated. Let it be
Thrown to him out of the window.

STARGAZE   O cursed stars
That reigned at my nativity! How have you cheated
4 Your poor observer.

ANNE   Must we part in tears?

MARY Farewell, good Millicent.

LADY FRUGAL   I am sick, and meet with
5 A rough physician. O my pride and scorn!
How justly am I punished!

MARY   Now we suffer
For our stubbornness and disobedience
To our good father.

6 **ANNE**   And the base conditions
We imposed upon our suitors.

LUKE   Get you in,
And caterwaul in a corner.

7 **LADY FRUGAL**   There's no contending.

[LADY FRUGAL, ANNE, MARY, *go off at one door;* STARGAZE *and*
MILLICENT *at the other.*]

LUKE How lik'st thou my carriage, Holdfast?

8 **HOLDFAST**   Well in some part,
But it relishes I know not how, a little
Of too much tyranny.

LUKE   Thou art a fool;
He's cruel to himself, that dares not be
9 Severe to those that used him cruelly.

ACT FIVE

Scene One

[*Enter* LUKE *with* SIR JOHN FRUGAL, SIR MAURICE LACY, *and*   1
PLENTY *in their Indian disguise.*]

LUKE   You care not then, as it seems, to be converted
To our religion.

SIR JOHN   We know no such word,   2
Nor power but the devil, and him we serve for fear,
Not love.

LUKE   I am glad that charge is saved.

SIR JOHN   We put
That trick upon your brother, to have means   3
To come to the city. Now to you we'll discover
The close design that brought us, with assurance
If you lend your aids to furnish us with that
Which in the colony was not to be purchased,
No merchant ever made such a return
For his most precious venture, as you shall   4
Receive from us; far, far above your hopes,
Or fancy to imagine.

LUKE   It must be
Some strange commodity, and of a dear value,
(Such an opinion is planted in me   5
You will deal fairly) that I would not hazard.
Give me the name of 't.

SIR MAURICE   I fear you will make
Some scruple in your conscience to grant it.

LUKE   Conscience! No, no; so it may be done with safety,   6
And without danger of the law.

PLENTY   For that
You shall sleep securely. Nor shall it diminish,
But add unto your heap such an increase,
As what you now possess shall appear an atom   7
To the mountain it brings with it.

LUKE   Do not rack me
With expectation.

SIR JOHN   Thus then in a word:
The devil—Why start you at his name? If you   8

229

1 Desire to wallow in wealth and wordly honours,
You must make haste to be familiar with him.
This devil, whose priest I am, and by him made
A deep magician (for I can do wonders),
Appeared to me in Virginia, and commanded
With many stripes (for that's his cruel custom)
2 I should provide on pain of his fierce wrath
Against the next great sacrifice, at which
We, grovelling on our faces, fall before him,
Two Christian virgins, that with their pure blood
Might dye his horrid altars, and a third
3 (In his hate to such embraces as are lawful)
Married, and with your ceremonious rites,
As an oblation unto Hecate,
And wanton Lust, her favourite.

LUKE   A devilish custom:
And yet why should it startle me? There are
4 Enough of the sex fit for this use; but virgins,
And such a matron as you speak of, hardly
To be wrought to it.

PLENTY   A mine of gold for a fee
Waits him that undertakes it, and performs it.

5 SIR MAURICE   Know you no distressed widow, or poor maids,
Whose want of dower, though well born, makes 'em weary
Of their own country?

SIR JOHN   Such as had rather be
Miserable in another world, than where
6 They have surfeited in felicity?

LUKE   Give me leave.—
[*Aside*] I would not lose this purchase. A grave matron!
And two pure virgins. Umph! I think my sister,
Though proud, was ever honest; and my nieces
Untainted yet. Why should not they be shipped
7 For this employment? They are burdensome to me,
And eat too much. And if they stay in London,
They will find friends that to my loss will force me
To composition. 'T were a masterpiece
If this could be effected. They were ever
8 Ambitious of title. Should I urge,
Matching with these, they shall live Indian queens,
I may do much. But what shall I feel here,
Knowing to what they are designed? They absent,
The thought of them will leave me. It shall be so.
—I'll furnish you, and to endear the service,
9 In mine own family, and my blood, too.

SIR JOHN   Make this good, and your house shall not contain   1
The gold we'll send you.

LUKE   You have seen my sister,
And my two nieces?

SIR JOHN   Yes, sir.

LUKE   These persuaded   2
How happily they shall live, and in what pomp
When they are in your kingdoms, for you must
Work 'em a belief that you are kings—

PLENTY   We are so.

LUKE   I'll put it in practise instantly. Study you   3
For moving language.—Sister! Nieces!

[*Enter* LADY FRUGAL, ANNE, MARY.]

                                        How!   4
Still mourning? Dry your eyes, and clear these clouds
That do obscure your beauties. Did you believe
My personated reprehension, though
It showed like a rough anger, could be serious?
Forget the fright I put you in. My end
In humbling you was to set off the height   5
Of honour, principal honour, which my studies
When you least expect it shall confer upon you.
Still you seem doubtful: be not wanting to
Yourselves, nor let the strangeness of the means,
With the shadow of some danger, render you
Incredulous.   6

LADY FRUGAL   Our usage hath been such,
As we can faintly hope that your intents
And language are the same.

LUKE   I'll change those hopes   7
To certainties.

SIR JOHN [*aside*]   With what art he winds about them!

LUKE   What will you say, or what thanks shall I look for,
If now I raise you to such eminence as
The wife and daughters of a citizen   8
Never arrived at? Many for their wealth, I grant,
Have written ladies of honour, and some few
Have higher titles, and that's the farthest rise
You can in England hope for. What think you
If I should mark you out a way to live
Queens in another climate?   9

1 ANNE   We desire
A competence.

MARY   And prefer our country's smoke
Before outlandish fire.

2 LADY FRUGAL   But should we listen
To such impossibilities, 't is not in
The power of man to make it good.

LUKE   I'll do 't;
Nor is this seat of majesty far removed.
It is but to Virginia.

3 LADY FRUGAL   How! Virginia!
High heaven forbid! Remember, sir, I beseech you,
What creatures are shipped thither.

4 ANNE   Condemned wretches,
Forfeited to the law.

MARY   Strumpets and bawds,
For the abomination of their life,
Spewed out of their own country.

5 LUKE   Your false fears
Abuse my noble purpose. Such indeed
Are sent as slaves to labour there, but you
To absolute sovereignty. Observe these men,
With reverence observe them. They are kings,
Kings of such spacious territories and dominions,
6 As our great Britain measured will appear
A garden to 't.

SIR MAURICE   You shall be adored there
As goddesses.

SIR JOHN   Your litters made of gold
Supported by your vassals, proud to bear
7 The burden on their shoulders.

PLENTY   Pomp and ease,
With delicates that Europe never knew,
Like pages shall wait on you.

8 LUKE   If you have minds
To entertain the greatness offered to you,
With outstretched arms and willing hands embrace it.
But this refused, imagine what can make you
Most miserable here, and rest assured,
In storms it falls upon you. Take 'em in,
9

And use your best persuasion. If that fail,   1
I'll send 'em aboard in a dry vat.

[*Exeunt* SIR MAURICE LACY, PLENTY, LADY FRUGAL, ANNE, MARY.]

SIR JOHN   Be not moved, sir;
We'll work 'em to your will. Yet e'er we part,   2
Your worldly cares deferred, a little mirth
Would not misbecome us.

LUKE   You say well. And now
It comes into my memory, this is my birthday,
Which with solemnity I would observe,   3
But that it would ask cost.

SIR JOHN   That shall not grieve you.
By my art I will prepare you such a feast,
As Persia in her height of pomp and riot
Did never equal; and ravishing music   4
As the Italian princes seldom heard
At their greatest entertainments. Name your guests.

LUKE   I must have none.

SIR JOHN   Not the city senate?

LUKE   No;   5
Nor yet poor neighbours. The first would argue me
Of foolish ostentation; the latter
Of too much hospitality, a virtue
Grown obsolete and useless. I will sit
Alone, and surfeit in my store, while others   6
With envy pine at it: my genius pampered
With the thought of what I am, and what they suffer
I have marked out to misery.

SIR JOHN   You shall;
And something I will add, you yet conceive not,
Nor will I be slow paced.   7

LUKE   I have one business,
And that dispatched I am free.

SIR JOHN   About it, sir,
Leave the rest to me.   8

LUKE   Till now I ne'er loved magic.

[*Exeunt*]

---

dry vat: Vat for storing dry goods, and so not watertight.

Scene Two

1 [*Enter* LORD LACY, OLD GOLDWIRE, *and* OLD TRADEWELL.]

LORD LACY   Believe me, gentlemen! I never was
So cozened in a fellow. He disguised
Hypocrisy in such a cunning shape
Of real goodness, that I would have sworn
2 This devil a saint. Master Goldwire, and Master Tradewell,
What do you mean to do? Put on.

OLD GOLDWIRE   With your lordship's favour.

LORD LACY   I'll have it so.

3 OLD TRADEWELL   Your will, my lord, excuses
The rudeness of our manners.

LORD LACY   You have received
Penitent letters from your sons, I doubt not?

OLD TRADEWELL   They are our only sons.

4 OLD GOLDWIRE   And as we are fathers,
Rememb'ring the errors of our youth,
We would pardon slips in them.

OLD TRADEWELL   And pay for 'em
In a moderate way.

5 OLD GOLDWIRE   In which we hope your lordship
Will be our mediator.

LORD LACY   All my power

[*Enter* LUKE, *richly dressed.*]

6
You freely shall command. 'T is he! You are well met,
And to my wish—and wondrous brave! Your habit
Speaks you a merchant royal.

LUKE   What I wear,
7 I take not upon trust.

LORD LACY   Your betters may,
And blush not for 't.

LUKE   If you have nought else
With me but to argue that, I will make bold
8 To leave you.

put on: Put your hats on again.
upon trust: On credit.

LORD LACY   You are very peremptory;   1
Pray you stay. I once held you an upright
Honest man.

LUKE   I am honester now
By a hundred thousand pound, I thank my stars for 't,
Upon the Exchange; and if your late opinion   2
Be altered, who can help it? Good my lord,
To the point. I have other business than to talk
Of honesty and opinions.

LORD LACY   Yet you may
Do well, if you please, to show the one, and merit
The other from good men, in a case that now   3
Is offered to you.

LUKE   What is 't? I am troubled.

LORD LACY   Here are two gentlemen, the fathers of
Your brother's prentices.

LUKE   Mine, my lord, I take it.   4

LORD LACY   Master Goldwire, and Master Tradewell.

LUKE   They are welcome,
If they come prepared to satisfy the damage
I have sustained by their sons.   5

OLD GOLDWIRE   We are, so you please
To use a conscience.

OLD TRADEWELL   Which we hope you will do,
For your own worship's sake.
      6
LUKE   Conscience, my friends,
And wealth, are not always neighbours. Should I part
With what the law gives me, I should suffer mainly
In my reputation. For it would convince me
Of indiscretion. Nor will you, I hope, move me   7
To do myself such prejudice.

LORD LACY   No moderation?

LUKE   They cannot look for 't and preserve in me
A thriving citizen's credit. Your bonds lie
For your sons' truth, and they shall answer all
They have run out. The masters never prospered   8
Since gentlemen's sons grew prentices. When we look
To have our business done at home, they are
Abroad in the tennis court, or in Partridge Alley,
In Lambeth Marsh, or a cheating ordinary
Where I found your sons. I have your bonds, look to 't.   9

1   A thousand pounds apiece, and that will hardly
Repair my losses.

LORD LACY   Thou dar'st not show thyself
Such a devil!

LUKE   Good words.

2

LORD LACY   Such a cutthroat! I have heard
Of the usage of your brother's wife and daughters.
You shall find you are not lawless, and that your moneys
Cannot justify your villainies.

LUKE   I endure this.

3   And, good my lord, now you talk in time of moneys,
Pay in what you owe me. And give me leave to wonder
Your wisdom should have leisure to consider
The business of these gentlemen, or my carriage
To my sister, or my nieces, being yourself

4   So much in my danger.

LORD LACY   In thy danger?

LUKE   Mine.
I find in my countinghouse a manor pawned,
Pawned, my good lord, Lacy Manor, and that manor

5   From which you have the title of a lord,
And it please your good lordship. You are a noble man,
Pray you pay in my moneys. The interest
Will eat faster in 't, than aqua fortis in iron.
Now though you bear me hard, I love your lordship.
I grant your person to be privileged

6   From all arrests. Yet there lives a foolish creature
Called an undersheriff, who being well paid, will serve
An extent on lords' or lowns' land. Pay it in;
I would be loath your name should sink, or that
Your hopeful son, when he returns from travel,

7   Should find you, my lord, without land. You are angry
For my good counsel. Look you to your bonds; had I known
Of your coming, believe it I would have had sergeants ready.
Lord how you fret! But that a tavern's near
You should taste a cup of muscadine in my house,
To wash down sorrow, but there it will do better;

8   I know you'll drink a health to me. [*Exits*]

LORD LACY   To thy damnation.
Was there ever such a villain! Heaven forgive me
For speaking so unchristianly, though he deserves it.

lawless: Above the law.

OLD GOLDWIRE   We are undone.

OLD TRADEWELL   Our families quite ruined.

LORD LACY   Take courage, gentlemen. Comfort may appear,
And punishment overtake him, when he least expects it.

[*Exeunt*]

Scene Three

[*Enter* SIR JOHN FRUGAL, *and* HOLDFAST.]

SIR JOHN   Be silent on your life.

HOLDFAST   I am o'erjoyed.

SIR JOHN   Are the pictures placed as I directed?

HOLDFAST   Yes, sir.

SIR JOHN   And the musicians ready?

HOLDFAST   All is done.
As you commanded.

SIR JOHN   Make haste, and be careful;
[*At the door*] You know your cue, and postures?

PLENTY [*within*]   We are perfect.

SIR JOHN   'T is well. The rest are come too?

HOLDFAST   And disposed of
To your own wish.

SIR JOHN   Set forth the table. So.

[*Enter* SERVANTS *with a rich banquet.*]

A perfect banquet. At the upper end,
His chair in state, he shall feast like a prince.

HOLDFAST   And rise like a Dutch hangman.

[*Enter* LUKE.]

SIR JOHN   •   Not a word more.—
How like you the preparation? Fill your room,
And taste the cates; then in your thought consider
A rich man, that lives wisely to himself,
In his full height of glory.

1 LUKE   I can brook
No rival in this happiness. How sweetly
These dainties, when unpaid for, please my palate!
Some wine. Jove's nectar! Brightness to the star
That governed at my birth. Shoot down thy influence,
And with a perpetuity of being
2 Continue this felicity, not gained
By vows to saints above, and much less purchased
By thriving industry; nor fall'n upon me
As a reward to piety and religion,
Or service for my country. I owe all this
To my dissimulation, and the shape
3 I wore of goodness. Let my brother number
His beads devoutly, and believe his alms
To beggars, his compassion to his debtors,
Will wing his better part, disrobed of flesh,
To soar above the firmament. I am well,
4 And so I surfeit here in all abundance,
Though styled a cormorant, a cutthroat, Jew,
And prosecuted with the fatal curses
Of widows, undone orphans, and what else
Such as malign my state can load me with,
I will not envy it. You promised music?

5 SIR JOHN   And you shall hear the strength and power
Of it, the spirit of Orpheus raised to make it good,
And in those ravishing strains with which he moved
Charon and Cerberus to give him way
To fetch from hell his lost Eurydice.
6 —Appear swifter than thought.

[*Music. Enter at one door* CERBERUS, *at the other* CHARON, OR-
PHEUS, CHORUS.]

LUKE   'T is wondrous strange.

7 [*They mime the story of Orpheus.*]

SIR JOHN   Does not the object and the accent take you?

LUKE   A pretty fable.

[*Exeunt* ORPHEUS *and the rest.*]
8   But that music should
Alter in fiends their nature, is to me

cormorant: Compare with the character of Sir Giles Overreach in
A New Way to Pay Old Debts.

Impossible; since in myself I find
What I have once decreed shall know no change.

SIR JOHN   You are constant to your purposes, yet I think
That I could stagger you.

LUKE   How?

SIR JOHN   Should I present
Your servants, debtors, and the rest that suffer
By your fit severity, I presume the sight
Would move you to compassion.

LUKE   Not a mote.
The music that your Orpheus made was harsh,
To the delight I should receive in hearing
Their cries and groans. If it be in your power,
I would now see 'em.

SIR JOHN   Spirits in their shapes
Shall show them as they are. But if it should move you?

LUKE   If it do, may I ne'er find pity.

SIR JOHN   Be your own judge.—Appear as I commanded.

[*Sad music. Enter* YOUNG GOLDWIRE *and* YOUNG TRADEWELL, *as
from prison;* FORTUNE, HOIST, PENURY *following after them;*
SHAVE'EM *in a blue gown;* SECRET, DING'EM, OLD TRADEWELL,
and OLD GOLDWIRE *with* SERGEANTS. *As directed, they all kneel
to* LUKE, *heaving up their hands for mercy;* STARGAZE *with a
pack of almanacs,* MILLICENT.]

LUKE   Ha, ha, ha!
This move me to compassion, or raise
One sign of seeming pity in my face?
You are deceived. It rather renders me
More flinty, and obdurate. A south wind
Shall sooner soften marble, and the rain
That slides down gently from his flaggy wings
O'erflow the Alps, than knees or tears or groans
Shall wrest compunction from me. 'T is my glory
That they are wretched, and by me made so;
It sets my happiness off. I could not triumph
If these were not my captives. Ha! my terriers
As it appears have seized on these old foxes,
As I gave order. New addition to
My scene of mirth. Ha! ha! They now grow tedious;
Let 'em be removed. Some other object, if
Your art can show it.

1 [*Exeunt* YOUNG GOLDWIRE *and the rest*.]

SIR JOHN   You shall perceive 't is boundless.
Yet one thing real, if you please?

LUKE   What is it?

2 SIR JOHN Your nieces, e'er they put to sea, crave humbly,
Though absent in their bodies, they may take leave
Of their late suitors' statues.

[*Enter* LADY FRUGAL, ANNE, *and* MARY.]

3 LUKE   There they hang;
In things indifferent, I am tractable.

SIR JOHN There pay your vows; you have liberty.

ANNE   O sweet figure
Of my abused Lacy! When removed
4 Into another world, I'll daily pay
A sacrifice of sighs to thy remembrance;
And with a shower of tears strive to wash off
The stain of that contempt my foolish pride
And insolence threw upon thee.

5 MARY   I had been
Too happy if I had enjoyed the substance,
But far unworthy of it, now I fall
Thus prostrate to thy statue.

LADY FRUGAL   My kind husband,
Blessed in my misery, from the monastery
6 To which my disobedience confined thee,
With thy soul's eye, which distance cannot hinder,
Look on my penitence. O, that I could
Call back time past! Thy holy vow dispensed,
With what humility would I observe
7 My long-neglected duty.

SIR JOHN   Does this not move you?

LUKE Yes, as they do the statues, and her sorrow
My absent brother. If by your magic art
You can give life to these, or bring him hither
8 To witness her repentance, I may have
Perchance some feeling of it.

SIR JOHN   For your sport
You shall see a masterpiece. Here's nothing but
A superficies—colours, and no substance.
9 Sit still, and to your wonder and amazement

I'll give these organs. This the sacrifice   1
To make the great work perfect.

[*Burns incense, and makes mystical gesticulations.* SIR MAURICE
LACY *and* PLENTY *give signs of animation.*]

LUKE   Prodigious!   2
SIR JOHN   Nay, they have life and motion. Descend.

[SIR MAURICE LACY *and* PLENTY *descend and come forward.*]

And for your absent brother—This washed off,
Against your will you shall know him. [*Discovers himself*]   3

[*Enter* LORD LACY *and the rest.*]

LUKE   I am lost.
Guilt strikes me dumb.

SIR JOHN   You have seen, my lord, the pageant?   4

LORD LACY   I have, and am ravished with it.

SIR JOHN   What think you now
Of this clear soul? this honest, pious man?
Have I stripped him bare? Or will your lordship have
A farther trial of him? 'T is not in   5
A wolf to change his nature.

LORD LACY   I long since
Confessed my error.

SIR JOHN   Look up, I forgive you,
And seal your pardons thus.   6

[*Raises and embraces* LADY FRUGAL, ANNE, *and* MARY.]

LADY FRUGAL   I am too full
Of joy to speak it.
                                                                              7
ANNE   I am another creature,
Not what I was.

MARY   I vow to show myself,
When I am married, an humble wife,
Not a commanding mistress.
                                                                              8
PLENTY   On those terms,
I gladly thus embrace you.

SIR MAURICE [*to* ANNE]   Welcome to
My bosom. As the one half of myself,
I'll love you, and cherish you.   9

1 YOUNG GOLDWIRE   Mercy!

YOUNG TRADEWELL AND THE REST   Good sir, mercy!

SIR JOHN This day is sacred to it. All shall find me,
As far as lawful pity can give way to 't,
Indulgent to your wishes, though with loss
2   Unto myself. My kind and honest brother,
Looking into yourself, have you seen the Gorgon?
What a golden dream you have had in the possession
Of my estate!—but here's a revocation
That wakes you out of it. Monster in nature!
3   Revengeful, avaricious atheist,
Transcending all example! But I shall be
A sharer in thy crimes, should I repeat 'em.
What wilt thou do? Turn hypocrite again,
With hope dissimulation can aid thee?
Or that one eye will shed a tear in sign
4   Of sorrow for thee? I have warrant to
Make bold with mine own, pray you uncase. This key, too,
I must make bold with. Hide thyself in some desert,
Where good men ne'er may find thee: or in justice
Pack to Virginia, and repent; not for
5   Those horrid ends to which thou did'st design these.

LUKE I care not where I go; what's done with words
Cannot be undone. [Exits]

LADY FRUGAL   Yet, sir, show some mercy;
Because his cruelty to me, and mine,
6   Did good upon us.

SIR JOHN   Of that at better leisure,
As his penitency shall work me. Make you good
Your promised reformation, and instruct
Our city dames, whom wealth makes proud, to move
7   In their own spheres, and willingly to confess
In their habits, manners, and their highest port,
A distance 'twixt the City and the Court.

[Exeunt omnes]

THE END

The Sparagus Garden

(1635)

INTRODUCTION

The first mention of the name of Richard Brome appears in the Induction to Ben Jonson's *Bartholomew Fair* (1614). The date of his birth is unknown, but 1590 seems likely. The connection with Jonson is reaffirmed in a sonnet written by the older poet for Brome's *The Northern Lass* when it was printed in 1632.

> I had you for a servant, once, Dick Brome;
> And you perform'd a servant's faithful parts,
> Now you are got into a nearer room,
> Of fellowship, professing my old arts.
> And you do them well, with good applause,
> Which you have justly gained from the stage
> By observation of those comic laws
> Which I, your master, first did teach the age. . . .

It has never been confirmed that Brome was Jonson's man-servant; however, that the relationship was more than that of the professional and his apprentice seems clear from the above. Thomas Dekker also wrote flattering verses to this play, dedicated to "My Son Broom and his Lass."

Brome was known as a "son of Ben" in the theatrical world but his *Sparagus Garden* appears to be equally indebted to the work of Dekker. Brome's play *A Jovial Crew or the Merry Beggars* was the last to be performed before the closing of the theatres by order of Cromwell's government in 1642. It is not known when Brome died, but it must have been in 1652 or 1653.

A number of plays with the names of popular resorts for titles appeared on the London stage in the early 1630's. The first of these, *Holland's Leaguer* by Shakerley Marmion (1603-1639), appeared in 1631 at the very time when a notorious brothel by that name was under seige by the City authorities. In the following year Brome's *Covent Garden Weeded* was performed, and James Shirley wrote *Hyde Park,* presumably to celebrate its opening to the public. (When Samuel Pepys saw this play, horses were led across the stage during the races in the fourth act, causing much excitement.) In 1635 *The Sparagus Garden* was first acted. If the contemporary accounts are to be believed, this play was one of the biggest financial successes of its time.

As in the other plays of its kind, the scenes of topical interest are an irrelevant interlude with only the most tenuous connection with the plot. The apologetic tone of the prologue to the play forewarns us of this, and the epilogue disarms criticism on this score. The main plot is an intrigue drama dependent for its success on information available at the beginning being withheld from the audience until the last possible moment, and on the unearthing, again in the last scene, of a thirty-year-old secret. All other dramatic effects are sacrificed to achieve this theatrical surprise; the characters are drawn from the common stock of repertory and only the "stale bachelor and ridiculous lover of women" echoes the spirit of Jonson's comedy of humours from which the characterisation derives.

The subplot is livelier and more engaging, full of references to contemporary manners and events. The stock figure of the penniless knight joins with the trading classes to gull the would-be gentleman up from the country in search of an identity and an inheritance. The scenes of the bumpkin's education are not only full of a spendid theatrical vitality, but also of the author's robust satire on the hypocrisy of courtly behaviour.

The play was first printed in 1640. The present text is edited from the reprint of 1873, and has attempted to reduce spelling and punctuation to a consistency consonant with the practise of the time and a clear reading. The west country dialect spoken by a few minor characters owes more to theatrical convention than to phonetic reproduction. (Brome used this device in *The Northern Lass* for the heroine, a north country girl.) No attempt has been made to render it less outlandish than it must sound, although in this text it has been given an internal coherence which the original lacks.

CHARACTERS

GILBERT [GOLDWIRE]
WALTER [CHAMLET] } young gentlemen and friends

[SAMSON] TOUCHWOOD
[WILL] STRIKER } old adversaries and Justices

SAMUEL, son of Touchwood

SIR HUGH MONEYLACKS, a needy knight

BRITTLEWARE
SPRING } confederates of Moneylacks

TIMOTHY HOYDEN, the new-made gentleman

COULTER, Hoyden's servant

THOMAS HOYDEN, Hoyden's brother

SIR ARNOLD CAUTIOUS, a stale bachelor and ridiculous lover of women

GARDENER

CURATE, [Mr. Pankridge]

TRAMPLER, a lawyer

[GENTLEMAN], [TWO] SERVING BOYS, THREE COURTIERS, [SERVANT to GARDENER], [LITTERMAN], SERVINGMEN

ANNABEL, daughter to Moneylacks and grandchild to Striker

FRISWOOD, her nurse and housekeeper to Striker

REBECCA, wife to Brittleware

MARTHA, the Gardener's wife

[GENTLEWOMAN], THREE LADIES, [CITY WIFE]

SCENE: London

PROLOGUE

He that his wonted modesty retains,
And never set a price upon his brains
Above your judgments; nor did ever strive
By arrogance or ambition to achieve
More praise unto himself, or more applause
Unto his scenes than such as know the laws
Of comedy do give; he only those
Now prays may scan his verse and weigh his prose.
Yet thus far he thinks meet to let you know
Before you see 't, the subject is so low
That to expect high language or much cost
Were a sure way now to make all be lost.
Pray look for none: he'll promise such hereafter
To take your graver judgments; now your laughter
Is all he aims to move. I had more to say.
The title too may prejudice the play.
It says *The Sparagus Garden;* if you look
To feast on that, the title spoils the book.
We have yet a taste of it, which he doth lay
I' th' midst o' th' journey, like a bait by th' way.
Now see with candour: as our poet's free,
Pray let be so your ingenuity.

ACT ONE

Scene One

[*Before Touchwood's house. Enter* WALTER, GILBERT, *and* TOUCHWOOD.]

WALTER I fear we shall do no good upon him.

GILBERT We shall nevertheless discharge the office of friends in our endeavour. I mean to put it home to him.

WALTER And so will I.

GILBERT But be sure you lie at a close ward the while, for he is a most subtle and dangerous fencer to deal withal.

WALTER I understand you.

GILBERT He has not his name for nothing; old *Touchwood!* He is all fire if he be incensed, but so soft and gentle that you may wind him about your finger, or carry him in your bosom if you handle him rightly; but still be wary, for the least spark kindles him. He comes.

TOUCHWOOD With me, gentlemen?

GILBERT Only a few neighbourly and friendly words, sir.

TOUCHWOOD Oh you are most friendly welcome, good Master Gilbert Goldwire and Master Walter Chamlet, I take you to be.

BOTH The same, sir, at your service.

TOUCHWOOD Your fathers both were my good neighbours indeed; worthy and well-reputed members of the City while they lived; but that may be read upon the Hospital walls, and gates; it is enough for me to say they loved me—Samson Touchwood! And I were a wretch if I should not honour their memory in their happy succession. Again, gentlemen, you are welcome.

GILBERT Yet you may be pleased, sir, to remember, though our fathers were both loving friends to you, yet they were sometimes at odds one with another.

TOUCHWOOD True, true, ever at odds: they were the common talk of the town for a pair of wranglers; still at strife for one trifle or other: they were at law loggerheads together, in one match that held 'em tugging t' one the t' other by the purse strings, a matter of nine years, and all for a matter of nothing. They coursed one another from court to court, and through every court temporal and spiritual; and held one another play till they lost a thousand

249

1 pound a man to the lawyers, and till it was very sufficiently adjudged that your father was one fool [*to* GILBERT], and your father was another fool [*to* WALTER]. And so again, gentlemen, you are welcome. Now, your business.

2 WALTER You may now be pleased, sir, to remember that our fathers grew friends at last.

TOUCHWOOD Heaven forbid else.

3 GILBERT And note the cause, the ground of their reconciliation, which was upon the love betwixt me and this gentleman's sister. My father's son married his father's daughter, and our two fathers grew friends, and wise men again.

TOUCHWOOD To the point, good gentlemen, yet you are welcome.

GILBERT Troth, sir, the point is this: you know (and the town had ta'en sufficient notice of it) that there has been a long contention betwixt you and old Master Striker your neighbour—

4 TOUCHWOOD Ha?

GILBERT —And the cause or ground of your quarrel (for ought any body knows but yourselves) may be as trivial as that which was derided in our fathers.

TOUCHWOOD Are you there with me?

5 GILBERT And great hopes there are, and wagers laid by your friends on both sides, that you two will be friends.

TOUCHWOOD I'll hold you an hundred pounds o' that.

6 GILBERT Nay, more, that Master Striker will be willing to give his grandchild to your son, so you'll give your consent.

TOUCHWOOD And your coming is to persuade that, is it not? If it be so, speak; deal plainly with me, gentlemen, whilst you are yet welcome.

7 WALTER In sooth it is so; we come to negotiate the match for your son, and your friendship with old Master Striker.

TOUCHWOOD You are not welcome.

8 GILBERT But when you weigh the reasons, and consider the perfect love of the young pair, and how the world will praise your reconciliation, and bless the providence that made their loves the means to work their parents' charity.

TOUCHWOOD Again, you are not welcome.

GILBERT Yourself but now commended the atonement
Of our two fathers, wrought by the same means:
I mean my marriage with his sister here
9 Against as great an opposition.

WALTER   But our fathers loved their children.   1

TOUCHWOOD   Your fathers were a couple of doting fools, and you a pair of saucy knaves; now you are not welcome: and more than so, get you out of my doors.

GILBERT   Will you, sir, by your wilfulness, cast away your son?

TOUCHWOOD   My son? No son of mine, I have cast him off already   2
for casting an eye upon the daughter of mine enemy: let him go, let him pack; let him perish: he comes not within these doors, and you, that are his fine-spoken spokesmen, get you off o' my ground I charge you.

WALTER   We are gone, sir, only but wishing you, Master Touch-   3
wood, to remember that your son's your son.

TOUCHWOOD   Indefinitely not, sir, until he does not only renounce all interest in the love of that baggage, but do some extraordinary mischief in that family to right me for the trespass he has done, and so win my good opinion, till which be done, a daily curse of   4
mine he shall not miss. And so you may inform him. [*Exits*]

GILBERT   What an uncharitable wretch is this?

WALTER   The touchiest piece of touchwood that e'er I met withal.

GILBERT   I feared we should inflame him.   5

WALTER   All the comfort is, his son may yet outlive him.

Scene Two

6

GILBERT   But the danger is, his father may disinherit him.

WALTER   He cannot be so devilish; here comes his son, a gentle-man of so sweet a disposition, and so contrary to his crabbed sire, that a man who never heard of his mother's virtue might wonder who got him for him.   7

GILBERT   Not at all, I assure you. Sam is his father's known son: for the old man, you see, is gentle enough till he be incensed; and the son being moved, is as fiery as the father.

WALTER   But he is very seldom and slowly moved; his father often and o' the sudden.   8

[*Enter* SAMUEL *to them.*]

GILBERT   I prithee, would'st thou have green wood take fire as soon as that which is old and sere?

WALTER   He is deep in thought.   9

1   GILBERT   Over head and ears in his mistress' contemplation.

    SAMUEL   To disobey a father, is a crime
    In any son unpardonable. Is this rule
    So general that it can bear no exception?
    Or is a father's power so illimitable,
2   As to command his son's affections?
    And so control the conquerer of all men,
    Even Love himself? No, he that enterprises
    So great a work, forgets he is a man;
    And must in that forget he is a father,
    And so, if he forego his nature, I
3   By the same law may leave my piety.
    But stay, I would not lose myself in following
    This wild conceit.

    GILBERT   How now, Sam, whither away?

4   SAMUEL   I was but casting how to find the way
    Unto myself. Can you direct me, gentlemen?

    WALTER   Yes, yes; your father has told us the way.

    SAMUEL   Ha' you had conference with him? Ha' ye? Speak.

5   GILBERT   Marry sir, ha' we, and I think to purpose.

    SAMUEL   Ha' you won ought upon him to my advantage?

    WALTER   As much as may restore you to acquaintance
    With him again, can you but make good use on 't.

6   SAMUEL   Pray do not trifle with me; tell me briefly.

    GILBERT   Briefly he says you must not dare to see him;
    Nor hope to receive blessing to the value
    Of a new threepence, till you disclaim your love
    In your fair Annabel; and not only so,
7   But you must do some villainous, mischievous act
    To vex his adversary, her grandfather;
    Or walk beneath his curse in banishment.

    SAMUEL   A most uncharitable and unnatural sentence.

8   WALTER   But think withal, it is your father that
    Makes this decree; obey him in th' execution:
    He has a great estate, you are his only son:
    Do not lose him, your fortune, and yourself
    For a frail piece of beauty: shake her off;
    And do some notable thing against her house
9   To please your father.

SAMUEL   The Devil speaks it in thee,   1
And with this spell I must conjure him out. [*He draws.*]

GILBERT   Oh, friend, you are too violent.

SAMUEL   He's too desperate,
To urge me to an act of such injustice.   2
Can her fair love, to whom my faith is given,
Be answered with so loud an injury?
Or can my faith, so broken, yield a sound
Less terrible than thunder, to affright
All love and constancy out of the breast
Of every virgin that shall hear the breach   3
Of my firm faith?

GILBERT   Be not so passionate.

SAMUEL   I have no further power to do an outrage
Against that family to whom my heart   4
Is linked, than to rip out this troubled heart,
The only ominous cause, indeed, of all
My over-passionate father's cruelty; and that
(If I must needs do an injurious office)
Alone shall be my act to calm his fury.

                                                                 5
GILBERT   Prithee, blow o'er this passion; thou wert wont
To affect wit, and canst not be a lover
Truly without it. Love is wit itself,
And through a thousand lets will find a way
To his desired end.

                                                                 6
SAMUEL   The ballad taught you that.

GILBERT   Well said, "Love will find out the way":
I see thou art coming to thyself again,
Can there no shift, no witty sleight be found
(That have been common in all times and ages)   7
To blind the eyes of a weak-sighted father,
And reconcile these dangerous differences,
But by bloodshedding, or outrageous deeds,
To make the feud the greater? Recollect
Thyself, good Sam; my house, my purse, my counsel
Shall all be thine, and Wat shall be thy friend.   8

WALTER   Let me entreat your friendship.

SAMUEL   And me your pardon.

GILBERT   So, so, all friends; let's home and there consult   9

1   To lay the tempest of thy father's fury,
     Which cannot long be dangerous; 't is but like
     A storm in April, spent in swift extremes,
     When straight the sun shoots forth his cheerful beams.

     [*Exeunt*]

2

Scene Three

[*A room in Striker's house. Enter* STRIKER *and* MONEYLACKS.]

3

STRIKER   You will not assault me in mine own house? I hope you
     will not; nor urge me beyond my patience with your borrowing
     attempts! Good sir Hugh Moneylacks, I hope you will not.

MONEYLACKS   I hope I moved you not but in fair language, sir;
4   Nor spoke a syllable that might offend you.
     I have not used the word of "loan," or "borrowing";
     Only some private conference I requested.

STRIKER   Private conference! A new-coined word for borrowing of
     money. I tell you, your very face, your countenance (though it be
5   glossed with knighthood) looks so borrowingly, that the best
     words you give me are as dreadful as "Stand and deliver," and
     there I think I was wi' ye. I am plain w' ye sir, old Will Striker, I.

MONEYLACKS   My father Striker, I am bold to call you.

STRIKER   Your father! No, I desire no such near acquaintance with
6   you, good sir Hugh Moneylacks. You are a knight and a noble
     gentleman, I am but an esquire and out of debt; and there I think
     I was w' ye again.

MONEYLACKS   I shall be with you anon, when you have talked
     yourself out of breath. [*Aside*]

7   STRIKER   'T is true I had the honour to be your worship's father-in-
     law when time was that your knighthood married and ladyfied a
     poor daughter of mine: but yet she had five thousand pounds in
     her purse, if you please to remember it; and, as I remember, you
     had then fourteen hundred ayear: but where is it now? and
     where is my daughter now? poor abused innocent; your riotous-
8   ness abroad, and her long night watches at home shortened her
     days, and cast her into her grave—And 't was not long, before all

     "*Stand and deliver*": The cry of the highwayman to his intended
     victim.
     I was wi' ye: I got the better of you. *To be with* also means to be
     revenged. Catchphrases are common in these plays: see *Eastward Ho.*

your estate was buried too; and there I was w' ye again, I take it: 1
but that could not fetch her again.

MONEYLACKS   No, sir, I with my life might have excused
Hers, far more precious: never had a man
A juster cause to mourn.

STRIKER   Nor mourned more justly, it is your only wearing; you 2
have just none other: nor have had means to purchase better any
time these seven years as I take it. By which means you have got
the name of the mourning Knight; and there I am sure I was w'
ye.

MONEYLACKS   Sir, if you will not be pleased to hear my desires to 3
you, let me depart without your derision.

STRIKER   Even when you please, and whither you please, good Sir
Hugh Moneylacks: my house shall be no enchanted castle to detain your knight-errantship from your adventures. I hope your errand hither was but for your dinner; and so far forth (and espe- 4
cially at your going forth) you are welcome. Your daughter I do
keep, and will, for her poor mother's sake (that was my daughter), peace be with her—she shall be no more a trouble to you;
nor be your child any longer: I have made her mine; I will adopt
her into mine own name, and make her a Striker; she shall be no
more a Moneylacks, and if she please me well in matching with a 5
husband, I know what I will do for her.

MONEYLACKS   I thank you, sir.

STRIKER   Do you thank me, sir? I assure you you need not; for I
mean so to order her estate, and bind it up in that trust that you
shall never finger a farthing on 't. Am I w' ye, sir? 6

MONEYLACKS   I cannot choose but thank you, though, in behalf of
my child.

STRIKER   Call her your child again, or let me but hear that you
suffer her to ask you a bare blessing, I'll send her after you upon
adventures, Sir Knight: and who shall give a portion with her 7
then? Or what can she hope from a father that groans under the
weight of a knighthood for want of means to support it?

MONEYLACKS   I shall find means to live without your trouble hereafter. 8

STRIKER   You may, you may; you have a wit, Sir Hugh, and a pro-
jective one; what, have you some new project afoot now, to outgo
that of the handbarrows? what call you 'em—the Sedams? Oh,
cry you mercy, cry you mercy; I heard you had put in for a share

Sedams: Sedan chairs were a great novelty at this time.

1   at the Asparagus Garden: or that at least you have a pension thence; to be their gather-guest and bring 'em custom, and that you play the fly of the new inn there; and sip with all companies: am I w' ye there, sir?

MONEYLACKS   You may be when you please, sir, I can command the best entertainment there for your money.

2

STRIKER   In good time, sir.

MONEYLACKS   In the meantime, sir, I had no mind to beg nor borrow of you, and though you will not give me leave to call you father, nor my daughter my daughter, yet I thought it might be-
3   come my care to advertise you (that have taken the care of her from me) of a danger that will much afflict you, if it be not carefully prevented.

STRIKER   How's this?

MONEYLACKS   You have an adversary—

4   STRIKER   But one that I know, the rascal my neighbour Touch-wood.

MONEYLACKS   There I am w' ye, sir, I am informed that his only son is an earnest suitor to your daughter: (I must not call her mine).

5

STRIKER   How's that?

MONEYLACKS   That there is a deep, secret love betwixt 'em; and that they have had many private meetings: and a stol'n match very likely to be made if you prevent it not.

6   STRIKER   Can this be true?

MONEYLACKS   Give me but a piece from you, and if by due examination you find it not so, I'll never see your face again till you send for me.

STRIKER   To be rid of you, take it. [*Gives him money*]

7

MONEYLACKS   I am gone, sir, and yet I think I'm w' ye. [*Exits*]

STRIKER   Is the devil become a matchbroker? What? Who within there? What? Annabel? What? Friswood?

8

Scene Four

FRISWOOD [*enters*]   Here, sir, I am here, forsooth.

STRIKER   Are you so, forsooth? But where's your mistress, for-
9   sooth?

FRISWOOD List'ning is good sometimes; I heard their talk, and am   1
glad on 't. [*Aside*]

STRIKER Where is your mistress I say.

FRISWOOD My mistress, Annabel, forsooth, my young mistress?

STRIKER What other mistress hast thou but the Devil's dam her-   2
self, your old mistress? And her I ask not for; good mistress Flibber de Jib with the French flyflap o' your coxcomb.

FRISWOOD Is the old man mad, trow?

STRIKER I ask for Annabel.

FRISWOOD Bless me! How do you look?   3

STRIKER Where's Annabel I say! Fetch her me quickly, lest I bast
her out of your old whit-leather hide.

FRISWOOD How youthful you are grown! She is not far to fetch,
sir; you know you commanded her to her chamber, and not to
appear in sight, till her debauched father was gone out o' the   4
house.

STRIKER And is he not gone now, forsooth? Why call you her not?

FRISWOOD I warrant he has told you some tale on her. That lewd
knight, now he has undone himself by his unthrifty practises, be-   5
gins to practise the undoing of his daughter, too! Is it not so forsooth? Has he not put some wickedness into your head to set you
against her?

STRIKER I never knew thee a witch till now.

FRISWOOD Ha, ha, ha; I warrant he told you that your adversary   6
Touchwood's son, and my mistress Annabel are in love league together.

STRIKER Marry did he; and I will know the truth.

FRISWOOD Ha, ha, ha.

STRIKER Dar'st thou laugh at me?   7

FRISWOOD No, no; but I laugh at the poor knight's officiousness, in
hope of some great reward for the gullery that I put upon him:
ha, ha, ha. Good sir, a little patience, and I will tell you. Ha, ha,
ha—'t was I that devised it for a lie, and told it him in hope that   8
his telling it to you, would provoke you to beat him out o' the
house; for reporting a thing that had no probability or resemblance of truth in it.

STRIKER Is it but so?

FRISWOOD Sir, I have been your creature this thirty years, down-   9

1   lying and uprising (as you know); and you should believe me, you had me in my old mistress' days—

STRIKER   Ay, thou wast a handsome young wench then; now thou art old.

FRISWOOD   Yet not so wondrous old as to be sung in a ballad for 't,
2   or to have been able ere Adam wore beard to have crept into Eve's bed, as I did into my mistress's. (Heaven pardon you, as I do with all my heart.) [*She weeps.*]

STRIKER   What, in thy fooleries now?

FRISWOOD   Nor so old neither but you are content to make a sorry
3   shift with me still; as your abilities will serve you— [*She weeps still.*]

STRIKER   Come, come; thou art not old.

FRISWOOD   Nay, that's not what troubles me; but that I, that served
    you before your daughter was born (I mean your daughter that
4   was mother to this daughter which now you have made your daughter); that I that saw the birth, the marriage, and the death of your daughter; and have had the governance of this her daughter ever since, till now she is marriageable; and have all this while been as pliant as a twig about you, and as true as the sheath
5   to your steel as we say, that I should now be mistrusted to connive at an ill match for her, for whom my chiefest care has been from the cradle? There's the unkindness. [*She weeps again.*]

STRIKER   Enough, enough; Fid, I believe there is no such matter.

FRISWOOD   I thought you had known me— [*She weeps.*]

6 STRIKER   I do, I do; I prithee, good Fid, be quiet; it was a witty trick of thee to mock the poor knight withal: but a pox on him, he cost me a piece for his news; there's another for thee;

[*Giving her money*]

7   but the best is he hath tied himself by it, never to trouble me more; I have that into my bargain.

FRISWOOD   And you would tie me so, too, would you?

STRIKER   Not so, Fid, not so: but look to my girl, and thus far mark me. If ever I find that young Touchwood, the son of that
8   miscreant, whose hatred I would not lose for all the good neighbourhood in the parish; if ever, I say, he and your charge do but look upon one another, I'll turn her and you both out o' doors; there I will be w' ye. Look to 't.

FRISWOOD   Agreed, sir; agreed.

9 STRIKER   Look to 't I say. I must abroad, my anger is not over yet:

I would I could meet my adversary to scold it out; I shall be sick   1
else. [*Exits*]

FRISWOOD 'T was well I overheard 'em, my young lovers had been
spoiled else: had not I crossed the old angry man's purpose before he had met with the young timorous virgin, she had confessed all; and all had been dashed now.   2

Scene Five

[*Enter* ANNABEL *to* FRISWOOD.]   3

ANNABEL How now, Fris, is my grandfather gone out of door?

FRISWOOD If he were as safe out o' the world, it were well for you.

ANNABEL Nay, say not so, good Fris.

FRISWOOD Your unlucky father has destroyed all your hopes in   4
Master Sam Touchwood; in discovering your loves (what devil
soever gave him the intelligence) and you must resolve never to
see your sweet Sam again.

ANNABEL I must resolve to die first: oh! [*She sinks down.*]
                                                                   5
FRISWOOD Odds pity! How now! Why mistress, why Annabel, why
Mistress Annabel; look up, look up I say, and you shall have him
spite of your grandfather and all his works. What do you think I
am, an infidel, to take Master Samuel's forty pieces? And a ronlet
of old muscadine for nothing? Come, be well, and indeed you
shall have him.   6

ANNABEL Oh Sam, sweet Sam—

FRISWOOD These lovesick maids seldom call upon other saints than
their sweethearts; look up I say, your sweet Sam is coming.

ANNABEL Ha, where? Where is he? Why do you abuse me?   7

[*Enter* SAMUEL TOUCHWOOD.]

FRISWOOD I say he will come presently; look up I say, forgive me,
he comes indeed! My master thought I was a witch, and I now
suspect myself for one. Oh, Master Samuel, how came you   8
hither? Here he is, mistress. What mean you to come now to
undo her and yourself too? Yet she had died and you had not
come as you did. Why do you not look upon him and be well?
Get you gone, we are all undone if my master come back and
find you: speak to her quickly, then kiss her and part; you will be
parted for ever else.   9

1 SAMUEL   How fares my love?

ANNABEL   Better than when I was in earthly being,
This bosom is a heaven to me; through death
I am arrived at bliss, most happily
To be so well revived thou mad'st me die.

2 FRISWOOD   I made you not die, as you will die, if you stand prat-
tling till my master return and take you: for Master Samuel, I
must tell you Master Samuel, he knows all Master Samuel.

SAMUEL   My father knows as much, and that's the cause
Of my adventuring hither to instruct you
3 In a strange practise; here it is in writing,

[*Giving* ANNABEL *a paper.*]

'T is such a secret that I durst not trust
My tongue with the conveyance of 't; nor have I
4 The confidence to hear it read: take it,
And, in my absence, join your best advices
To give it life and action; 't is rule
Which (though both hard and grievous to pursue)
Is all that can our hopes in love renew.

5 FRISWOOD   What horrible thing must we do, trow? Pray let me see
the paper, I hope there is no pistolling nor poisoning in it: though
my old Striker come short of the man he was to be with me, I
would be loath to shorten his days with the danger of my neck;
or making a bonfire in Smithfield. Pray let me see the paper.

6 SAMUEL   Not until my departure, gentle Friswood.

FRISWOOD   Is there such horror in it, that you dare not stand the
opening of the paper?

SAMUEL   Consider, sweet, our love is fever sick,
Even desperately to death;
7 And nothing but a desperate remedy
Is left us: for our bodily health, what sour
Unsavoury, loathsome medicines we will take
But to remove an ague?
What sharp incisions, searings and cruel corsives
Are daily suffered, and what limbs dissevered
8 To keep a gangrene from the vital parts,
That a dismembered body yet may live!
We in like case must, to preserve our love
(If we dare say we love), adventure life,
Fame, honour, which are all but love's attendants,
9 To maintain it.

ANNABEL   I understand you, sweet,   1
  And do, before I read your strong injunction,
  Resolve to give it faithful execution
  Whate'er it be. I ha' got courage now,
  And (with a constant boldness let me tell you)
  You dare not lay that on me I'll not bear:
  And love, predominant o'er all other passions,   2
  Shall bear me out in 't.

SAMUEL   Oh, you have made me happy.

FRISWOOD   As I live—my Master!—
  Kiss and away; whip quickly through the garden—
  Run you up to your chamber—I'll see you out myself.   3

SAMUEL   Thus let us breathe that till we meet again.

FRISWOOD   Whoop! What d' ye mean?

SAMUEL   We leave for truce at raising of the siege
  Our interchanged hearts, each other's pledge.   4

FRISWOOD   Go, fools, this sets you both but more on edge.

ANNABEL   Farewell.

SAMUEL   Farewell.

[*Exeunt*]   5

ACT TWO

Scene One

1   [*A room in Brittleware's china shop. Enter* BRITTLEWARE *and* RE-BECCA.]

BRITTLEWARE   Sweet wife, content thyself.

2   REBECCA   Yes, content myself! Shall I so! With what, you, John Bopeep? You must be my husband, and I must content myself, must I? No sir, 't is you that must content me, or 't is your heart must smart for 't.

3   BRITTLEWARE   If you could be content with all that I have, or all that I can do, and expect no further, I then might hope to pacify you.

REBECCA   All has not done it yet, you see, nor have you yet found out the way. Five years' practise one would think were sufficient, so long you have had me; and too long it is unless I had got a better name by 't, to be accounted barren—oh me.

4   BRITTLEWARE   Now 't is out. Zounds! What would you have me do? Where's the defect, think you? Is it not probable that you may be defective as well as I?

5   REBECCA   That I may be defective! I defy thee, lubber; I defy thee and all that say so, thou fribbling fumbler thou; I would some honest sufficient man might be judge betwixt us whether I be defective.

Scene Two

6   MONEYLACKS [*enters to them*]   How now, always wrangling?

REBECCA   Defective, quoth a'—

MONEYLACKS   What's the matter, landlord?

7   REBECCA   Do I look like a thing defective?

MONEYLACKS   Landlady!—

REBECCA   Oh, fearful!

MONEYLACKS   Mistress Brittleware, what's the matter?

8   REBECCA   You shall be judge, Sir Hugh, whether I be defective. You have lain here, Sir Hugh, these three years, have been our

constant lodger off and on, as we say; and can you think me de- 1
fective?

BRITTLEWARE   You will not be impudent?

MONEYLACKS   Good Master Brittleware, what's the matter?

BRITTLEWARE   The matter is, sir, she will be content with nothing!   2

MONEYLACKS   The best wife i' the world! And if you cannot afford
her that to content her, you are a most hardhearted husband.

REBECCA   What, nothing? Would you wish him to afford me nothing to content me? I must have something to content me; and
something he must find me, or I will make him look out for 't.   3

MONEYLACKS   Come, come, I know the quarrel; and I know you
will never get a child by falling out.

REBECCA   Nor any way else, so long as he is such a jealous beast as
he is.

MONEYLACKS   Oh, you must leave your jealousy, Master Brittle-   4
ware; that's a main hindrance.

BRITTLEWARE   I am not jealous, I.

REBECCA   Not, and stare like a mad ox upon every man that looks
upon me?

MONEYLACKS   Fie upon him, is he such a beast to be jealous of his   5
own wife? If every man were so, it would spoil the getting of
some children in a year.

REBECCA   And denies me all things that I have a mind to.

BRITTLEWARE   The best is the loss of your longings will not hurt   6
you; unless you were with child.

REBECCA   I must have my longings first; I am not every woman, I,
I must have my longings before I can be with child, I.

BRITTLEWARE   You must not long for every strange thing you see
or hear of, then.   7

REBECCA   As true as I live, he fribbles with me, Sir Hugh; I do but
now long for two or three idle things scarce worth the speaking
of, and do you think he will grant me one of 'em?

MONEYLACKS   What may they be he shall grant 'em?

REBECCA   One of my longings is to have a couple of lusty able-   8
bodied men, to take me up, one before and another behind, as
the new fashion is, and carry me in a man-litter into the great
bed at Ware.

man-litter: Sedan chair.
great bed at Ware: Mentioned also in Shakespeare's *Twelfth Night.*

1 MONEYLACKS There's one, and will you deny her this to hinder a child-getting?

REBECCA Then I do long to see the new ship, and to be on the top of Paul's steeple when it is new built. But that must not be yet. Nor am I so unreasonable but that I can stay the time: in the mean-
2 time I long to see a play, and, above all plays, *The Knight of the Burning*—what d' ye call 't?

MONEYLACKS *The Knight of the Burning Pestle.*

REBECCA *Pestle*, is it? I thought of another thing, but I would fain see it. They say there's a grocer's boy kills a giant in it, and an-
3 other little boy that does a citizen's wife thy daintiest—but I would fain see their best actor do me; I would so put him to 't, they should find another thing in handling of me, I warrant 'em.

BRITTLEWARE Heyday! So last frost she longed to ride on one of the dromedaries over the Thames, when great men were pleased
4 to go over it a foot.

MONEYLACKS Well, shall I make a convenient motion for you both?

REBECCA Quickly, sweet Sir Hugh, I long for that before you name it.

5 MONEYLACKS Have you this spring eaten any asparagus yet?

REBECCA Why, is that good for a woman that longs to be with child?

MONEYLACKS Of all the plants, herbs, roots or fruits that grow, it is the most provocative, operative and effective.
6 REBECCA Indeed, Sir Hugh?

MONEYLACKS All your best (especially your modern) herbalists conclude that your asparagus is the only sweet stirrer that the earth sends forth, beyond your wild carrots, corn flag (or glad-iol). Your roots of standergrass, (or of satyrion), boiled in
7 goat's milk are held good; your clary (or horminum) in divers

---

Paul's steeple: See Glossary.
The Knight of the Burning Pestle: This comedy by Beaumont and Fletcher (printed 1613) was one of the most popular of the period and a parody of an early play by Thomas Heywood: *The Four Prentices of London* (c. 1600).
corn flag: A kind of gladiolus, a yellow iris.
standergrass: The male orchid and allied plants.
satyrion: Any kind of orchid, so called for its supposed aphrodisiac qualities.
clary: (Clear-eye); any plant, such as fennel or celandine, considered good for the eyes.

ways good, and dill (especially boiled in oil) is also good: but, 1
none of these, nor saffron boiled in wine, your nuts of artichokes,
rocket, or seeds of ash tree (which we call kite keys) nor thousand such, though all are good, may yet stand up for perfection
with asparagus.

REBECCA Do you say so, Sir Hugh? 2

MONEYLACKS I have it from the opinion of most learned doctors,
rare physicians, and one that dares call himself so.

BRITTLEWARE What doctor is he, a fool on horseback?

MONEYLACKS Doctor Thou-Lord, you know him well enough.
3
REBECCA Yes, we know Doctor Thou-Lord, though he knows
none but Lords and Ladies, or their companions. And a fine conceited doctor he is, and as humorous, I warrant ye; and will
"thou" and "thee" the best Lords that dares be acquainted with
him: call Knights "Jack," "Will" and "Tom" familiarly; and great
Ladies, "Gills" and "sluts," too, and they cross him. And for his 4
opinion sake, and your good report, Sir Hugh, I will have sparagus every meal all the year long, or I'll make all fly for 't; and do
you look to 't, Fribble, for it will be for your commodity as well
as mine.

BRITTLEWARE And sure it is a rare commodity when a knight is 5
become a broker for to cry it up so.

REBECCA And let me have some presently for my next meal, or
you cannot imagine how sick I will be.

MONEYLACKS But mistake not me, nor the commodity we speak
of, Mistress Brittleware. Where would you have it? Here in our 6
house? Fie! the virtue of it is mortified if it pass the threshold
from the ground it grows on. No, you must thither, to the garden
of delight, where you may have it dressed and eaten in the due
kind; and there it is so provocative, and so quick in the hot oper-
ation, that none dare eat it, but those that carry their coolers with
'em, presently to delay, or take off the delightful fury it fills 'em 7
with.

REBECCA Is there conveniency for that, too?

MONEYLACKS Yes, yes; the house affords you as convenient
couches to retire to, as the garden has beds for the precious 8
plants to grow in: that makes the place a palace of pleasure, and
daily resorted and filled with lords and knights, and their ladies;
gentlemen and gallants with their mistresses—

---

rocket: Many plants are so called; perhaps here hedge mustard is
intended. Moneylacks' meaning is clear.

1   REBECCA   But do not honest men go thither with their wives, too?

MONEYLACKS   None other; some to their own costs, and some at other men's.

REBECCA   Why do we not go then? Or what stay we for, can you tell, fumbler?

2   MONEYLACKS   Nay, Mistress Brittleware, not so suddenly; towards the evening will be the fittest season of the day; meanwhile, go in and fit yourself for the walk; your husband and I are first for another business.

3   REBECCA   Noble Knight, I thank you, I hope my next longing shall be to bespeak you for a godfather.

MONEYLACKS   You shall not long long for that.

REBECCA   I take your noble word. [*Exits*]

4   BRITTLEWARE   She's gone, and now, Sir Hugh, let me tell you, you have not dealt well with me, to put this fagary into her foolish fancy.

MONEYLACKS   Wilt thou be an ass now? Do not I know how to fetch it out on her again, think'st thou? She shall not go, and yet be contented, too.

5   BRITTLEWARE   Ay, you tell me so.

MONEYLACKS   Why, thou wilt not be jealous of me now, that has lain in thy house these three years, wilt thou? Nor think me so foolish to provoke thee with an injury that know'st me and my ways so well?

6   BRITTLEWARE   I know something by your worship worth the price of a new pillory.

7   MONEYLACKS   Why, so then; and will I wrong thee, Jack, think'st thou, ha? No, nor mistrust thee neither: for, though thou art a jealous coxcomb over thy wife, and she a touchy thing under thee, yet thou and I, Jack, have been always confident of each other, and have wrought friendly and closely together, as ever Subtle and his lungs did; and shared the profit betwixt us, ha'n't we Jack, ha?

8   BRITTLEWARE   I think we have; and that you have some new device, some stratagem in hand now. Uds me, I now remember. Is the party come to town?

MONEYLACKS   Yes, and my Spring has seized him upon the way: and here I expect him instantly.

BRITTLEWARE   And will he be made a gentleman?

Subtle and his lungs: A reference to Ben Jonson's *The Alchemist.*

MONEYLACKS That's his ambition, Jack; and though you now keep 1
a china shop, and deal in brittle commodities (pots, glasses,
porc'lain dishes, and more trinkets than an antiquary's study is
furnished withal), you must not forget your old trade of barber
surgeon, 't is that must stead us now in our new project.

BRITTLEWARE I warrant you; is he a trim youth? 2

MONEYLACKS We must make him one, Jack. 'T is such a squab
as thou never sawest; such a lump, we may make what we will
of him. Spring has writ me here his full description. [*Takes out
paper*]

BRITTLEWARE Then sure we will make money of him. 3

MONEYLACKS Well said, Jack.

Scene Three

4

[*Enter* SPRING *with* HOYDEN *and* COULTER *to them.*]

MONEYLACKS 'S lid, he's come already. Now, Master Spring?

SPRING I come to present a gentleman to you, sir.

MONEYLACKS How, a gentleman? Will you abuse me? 5

SPRING [*to* HOYDEN] He finds your defect already; but be bold, sir.
[*To* MONEYLACKS] He desires to be a gentleman, sir; and (though
he be but coarse metal yet) he has that about him which, with
your help, may quickly make him a clear gentleman.

HOYDEN I have four hundred pounds, sir; and I brought it up to 6
town on purpose to make myself a clear gentleman of it.

MONEYLACKS It was well brought up; it appears also you have
some breeding, though but a yeoman's son.

HOYDEN 'T is true, I have a little learning, sir, and a little wit,
though last night I met with some upon the way at Hammersmith 7
that had more: yet I had enough to perceive I was cheated of a
matter of seven pound (almost all the odd money I had about
me) at "My Card afore thy Card"; a pox take the whole pack on
'em. 'S daggers if ever man that had but a mind to be a gentleman was so noddy pooped! Oh, how I could chafe to think on 't.

8

SPRING Oh, but you must not; it becomes not the temper of a gentleman.

HOYDEN So you told me; then I thank you, friend.

SPRING Your small acquaintance, sir.

HOYDEN I have had more acquaintance where I have found less

noddy pooped: Made a fool of.

1 love, and I thank you again, good small acquaintance: you told me indeed it became not a gentleman to cry for losing his money; and I told you then that I should, or would be a gentleman; whereupon, small acquaintance (because I was resolved to play no more), you advised me to give over; and you told me you would, upon our coming to the city, here bring me to a knight that was a

2 gentleman-maker, whom I conceive this to be. And here am I, and here's my four hundred pound, which my man has here drawn up to town, and here I mean to quarter it.

COULTER   But I will see what pennyworths you bargain for first, by your Mastership's leave.

3 MONEYLACKS   Drawn and quartered! You have a wit, sir, I find that already.

HOYDEN   Yes, sir, I have a downright country wit, and was counted a pretty spark at home. Did you never hear of little Tim of Taunton? But I now mean to have a finical city wit, and a su-

4 perfinical court wit too, before I see mine uncle.

MONEYLACKS   You may, sir.

HOYDEN   And be able to jest and jeer among men of judgment: I have a many small jests, petty Johns, as I call 'em: but I will have a clubbing wit, and a drinking wit; and be able to hold play with

5 the great poets, ay: and with dry jests to maul the malapert'st lesser ones (that hold themselves better than the biggest) out o' the pit of wit, ay, before I see mine uncle.

MONEYLACKS   You may have all, sir, if you quarter your four hundred pound discreetly. But, who is your uncle, I pray?

6 HOYDEN   For that, you shall pardon me, till I am a gentleman. But I assure you, he is a great gentleman in the city here; and I neither must nor dare see him till I am one, at least: and I will tell you presently how I mean to quarter my money.

7 COULTER   They'll quarter that and you, too, if I zee not the better to the matter.

MONEYLACKS   Dost thou know the uncle he speaks of?

SPRING   No, nor cannot learn who it is for my life.

BRITTLEWARE   Some great man sure, that's ashamed of his kin-
8 dred: perhaps some suburb Justice, that sits o' the skirts o' the city, and lives by 't.

MONEYLACKS   Well said, Jack.

HOYDEN   Look you, sir, thus had I cast it. Small acquaintance, pray do you note it, too. I love your advice, that at first sight of
9 me (which was but last night) could relieve me from cheaters.

BRITTLEWARE From some of his own companions, to cheat you 1
more himself. [*Aside*]

HOYDEN The first hundred pound to be for the making of me a
gentleman: the second hundred shall be for apparel.

SPRING He speaks half like a gentleman already.

BRITTLEWARE Right, there's half disposed of. 2

HOYDEN The third hundred I'll spend in pleasure: hark, small acquaintance, we'll have wenches.

[*Whispers to* SPRING.]

SPRING What wants he of a gentleman? And go no further, but 3
save the last hundred.

HOYDEN Oh, small acquaintance, that must walk, too: but all for
profit to support my gentility hereafter.

SPRING As how?

HOYDEN I will be cheated of it. 4

MONEYLACKS How?

HOYDEN Not in gross, but by retail, to try men's several wits, and
so learn to shift for myself in time and need be.

BRITTLEWARE Do you hear this? 5

COULTER There's a plot now!

MONEYLACKS I protest, I admire him: I never found like craft in
a yeoman's son before.

HOYDEN No words on 't, I beseech you, sir; nor name that foolish 6
word, yeoman's son, any more. I came to change my copy, and
write "Gentleman": and to go the nighest way to work, my small
acquaintance here tells me, to go by the Heralds is the farthest
way about.

MONEYLACKS Well, sir, we will take the speediest course for you 7
that may be possible.

BRITTLEWARE The season of the year serves most aptly, too,
Both for purging and bleeding:
Give your name into this book, sir.

HOYDEN Timothy Hoyden, sir. 8

BRITTLEWARE [*writing*] Timothy Hoyden.

HOYDEN But must I bleed, sir?

by the Heralds: That is, by applying officially for grant of letters
patent.

1   MONEYLACKS   Yes, you must bleed: your father's blood must out. He was but a yeoman, was he?

HOYDEN   As rank a clown, none dispraised, as any in Somersetshire.

MONEYLACKS   His foul, rank blood of bacon and pease porridge
2   must out of you to the last dram.

HOYDEN   You will leave me none in my body then, I shall bleed to death, and you go that way to work.

SPRING   Fear nothing, sir, your blood shall be taken out by degrees, and your veins replenished with pure blood still, as you
3   lose the puddle.

HOYDEN   How must that be done?

COULTER   Ay, that ich would hear.

MONEYLACKS   I commend you that you seek reason: it must be
4   done by meats and drinks of costly price; muscatel caudles, jellies, and cock-broths. You shall eat nothing but shrimp porridge for a fortnight; and now and then a pheasant's egg souped with a peacock's feather. Ay, that must be the diet.

HOYDEN   Delicate!

5   COULTER   This stands to reason indeed.

MONEYLACKS   Then, at your going abroad, the first air you take shall be of the Asparagus Garden, and you shall feed plentifully of that.

6   HOYDEN   Of the air, do you mean?

MONEYLACKS   No, of th' asparagus. And that, with a concoction of goat's milk, shall set you an end, and your blood as high as any gentleman's lineally descended from the loins of King Cadwallader.

7   HOYDEN   Excellent, I like all excellently well, but this bleeding. I could never endure the sight of blood.

MONEYLACKS   That shows the malignant baseness of your father's blood within you!

HOYDEN   I was bewitched, I think, before I was begot, to have a
8   clown to my father: yet, sir, my mother said she was a gentlewoman.

SPRING   Said? What will not women say?

Cadwallader: The last king of the Britons who, in the seventh century, defended Wales from attack by the Saxons. Merlin prophesied his future return to expel the invaders.

HOYDEN Nay, small acquaintance, she professed it upon her death- 1
bed to the curate and divers others, that she was sister to a gentleman here in this city; and commanded me in her will, and upon
her blessing, first to make myself a gentleman of good fashion,
and then to go to the gentleman my uncle.

SPRING What gentleman is that? 2

HOYDEN I must not, nor I wo' not tell you that, till I am a gentleman myself: would you ha' me wrong the will o' the dead, small
acquaintance? I will rather die a clown as I am first.

MONEYLACKS Be content, sir; here's half a labour saved; you shall
bleed but o' one side: the father's side only. 3

HOYDEN Say you so?

MONEYLACKS The mother vein shall not be pricked.

HOYDEN I thank you, sir; I would 't were done once.

MONEYLACKS But when this is done, and your new blood infused 4
into you, you shall most easily learn the manners and behaviour.

SPRING The look, the garb, the congee—

BRITTLEWARE And all the compliments of an absolute gentleman.

HOYDEN Oh brave! 5

MONEYLACKS For which you shall have best instructions;
You'll run a chargeable course in 't, that I'll tell you:
And may yet if you please retain your money;
Cross your mother's will and die a clown.

HOYDEN By no means, sir. 6

COULTER I begin to believe honestly of the knight.

MONEYLACKS Do you note this skin of his here?

BRITTLEWARE Skin? 'T is a hide, sir.

HOYDEN 'T is somewhat thick and foul indeed, sir. 7

MONEYLACKS He must have a bath, and that will be more charge.

SPRING 'T is pity he should be fleaed.

HOYDEN I thank you, small acquaintance; pray, let me have a bath,
whate'er it cost me, rather than flea me. 8

MONEYLACKS Well, sir, this house shall be your lodging, and this,
the master of it, an excellent chirurgeon, and expert in these affairs, shall be your attendant.

HOYDEN My man may attend me too, may he not?

SPRING Yes, by all means, and see the laying out of your money. 9

COULTER   I like that best: sure, they are honest men.

MONEYLACKS   Is that your man? What, does he wear a coulter by his side?

COULTER   No, sir, my name is Coulter; I myself am a Coulter, and this is but my hanger-on, as I am my master's.

MONEYLACKS   Thou may'st make a country gentleman in time, I see that by thy wit.

COULTER   All my friends will be glad on 't.

MONEYLACKS   Come, gentlemen, I'll lead you the way.

[*Exeunt*]

Scene Four

[*A street. Enter* TOUCHWOOD, GILBERT, *and* WALTER.]

TOUCHWOOD   But how can you assure me, gentlemen, that this is true?

GILBERT   We saw 't not acted, sir, nor had reported it,
But on those terms of honour you have sworn to;
In which you are engaged first to forgive
Your son: then never to reveal to friend,
Or foe, the knowledge of the fact.

WALTER   You cannot now but receive
Your son into your favour, that did urge him
To do some outrage, some villainous shame or mischief
Upon that family, as he would shun your curse.

TOUCHWOOD   This is a mischief with a witness to it;
He has done it home, it seems.

GILBERT   Sir, can a son
Do his father's will too fully?

TOUCHWOOD   You may be pleased to call him.

[*Exit* WALTER.]

I would now put on an anger, but I fear
My inward joy's too great to be dissembled:
Now for a rigid brow that might enable
A man to stand competitor for the seat
Of austere justice—

[*Enter* SAMUEL *and* WALTER.]   1

           Are you come to boast
The bravery of your fact, with a dissembled
Show of obedience; as if you had merited
Forgiveness and a blessing; when my shame
For thy lewd action makes me turn and hide   2
My face?—for fear my laughter be descried. [*Aside, laughing*]

GILBERT   Pray turn not from him, sir.

TOUCHWOOD   I have heard, sir, of your workmanship; but may
A man receive it on your word for truth?
                                                                   3
SAMUEL   It is too true, unless you please in mercy
To pardon, and preserve me from the rigour
Of justice, and the sharper censure
That I shall suffer in all good opinion.

TOUCHWOOD   I mean you shall out o' the noise on 't presently;   4
So—there's a hundred pieces, get you gone;
Provide you for a journey into France,
Bear yourself well, and look you come not home
A verier coxcomb than you went abroad:
Pray wear no falling bands and cuffs above   5
The price of suits and cloaks, lest you become
The better half undone in a bout at buffets.

SAMUEL   I hope you shall hear well of me.

TOUCHWOOD   Amen.

SAMUEL   Pray bless me, sir.   6

TOUCHWOOD   My blessings be upon thee,
Go, get thee gone, my tenderness will show
Itself too womanish else.

GILBERT   Goodness of nature.   7

WALTER   We'll help to set you forward.

[*Exeunt all except* TOUCHWOOD.]

TOUCHWOOD   Thank ye, gentlemen: 8
Be but my son, thou shalt not want a father,
Though somebody must seek one; ha, ha, ha—
I'd give another hundred pieces now,
With all my heart, that I might be untonguetied,
And triumph o'er my adversary now,
And dash this business in his angry teeth:

bout at buffets: Sparring match.

1   Strike Striker's teeth out with his own abuse:
    Perhaps he knows 't already, if he does,
    I may take notice, and make bold to jeer him:
    This is his usual walk.

Scene Five

2

STRIKER [*enters*]   I was to blame
    To give it so much credit at the first,
    As to be troubled at it.

TOUCHWOOD   'T is the rascal.

3

STRIKER   That he, the son of my despite and scorn,
    Should gain of Fate a lot to see my niece,
    Much less a face to ask her for his wife.

TOUCHWOOD   Perhaps he's casting of his will.

4   STRIKER   Yet, the vexation that I was but told so,
    Lies gnawing in my stomach, that, until
    I vomit it upon that dunghill wretch,
    I cannot eat nor sleep to do me good.
    And I thank Chance he's here.

5   TOUCHWOOD   He comes, and so have at him.

STRIKER   Hum, hum, hum, humh.

TOUCHWOOD   And ha, ha, ha to thee, old puppy.

STRIKER   Sirrah, sirrah, how dar'st thou keep a son that dares but
6   look upon my niece? There I am w' ye, sir.

TOUCHWOOD   Sirrah, and sirrah to thy withered jaws, and down
    that wrinkled throat of thine: how dar'st thou think a son of mine
    dares for displeasing me, look but with foul contempt upon thy
    loathed issue?

7

STRIKER   Impudent villain, I have heard he has seen her.

TOUCHWOOD   Has he but seen her? Ha, ha, ha, I fear I shall out
    with it. I would not be foresworn: I'll keep 't in if I can. [*Aside*]

8   STRIKER   Yes, malapert Jack, I have heard that he has seen her,
    but better had'st thou pissed him 'gainst the wall, than he presume
    to love her: and there I am w' ye, sir.

TOUCHWOOD   Hast thou but heard he has seen her; I tell thee, thou
    old booby thou, if he had seen, felt, heard and understood her:
    nay, had he got her with child, and then left her, he were my son,
9   and I would cherish him.

STRIKER Dar'st thou speak so, thou old reprobate? 1

TOUCHWOOD Thou dost not hear me say it is so, though I could wish it were with all my heart, because I think it would break thine.

STRIKER Hugh, hugh, hugh! [*Coughs*]

2

TOUCHWOOD I hope I shall keep it within the compass of mine oath; yet there was a touch for him. [*Aside*]

STRIKER Oh, thou hell-bred rascal, thou: hugh, hugh! [*Coughs and spits*]

TOUCHWOOD So, so, up with it, lungs, lights, liver, and all; choke up, in a churl's name. 3

STRIKER Hugh, hugh!

TOUCHWOOD I have put him into these fits forty times at least, and not without hope it will throttle him at last [*aside*].—If you do break a gut, or a rib or two with straining, a rope will be your only remedy. And so I leave you: by the way, you have not heard me say that I know anything by your niece: but what I know, I'll keep to myself. 4

STRIKER And hang thyself, I care not what thou know'st. Yet thus far take me w' ye, sir. 5

TOUCHWOOD Not a step, unless I were sure I were going to the devil, huh, huh: no, sir, you shall not trip me: you shall not fetch it out of me: tush, my son's my son, and keep your niece to yourself. Huh. And if she has anything of his, you may keep that too, huh; and so, choke up again with all my heart, and much good do it you. [*Exits*] 6

STRIKER Huh, huh—hem! So he's gone, the villain's gone, in hope that he has killed me, when my comfort is he has recovered me; I was heartsick with a conceit which lay so mingled with my phlegm that I had perished, if I had not broke it, and made me spit it out. Hem, 't is gone, and I'll home merrily. 7
I would not that he should know the good he has done me
For half my estate; nor would I be at peace with him
To save it all: his malice works upon me,
Past all the drugs and all the doctors' counsels, 8
That e'er I coped with. He has been my vexation
These thirty years; nor have I had another
E'er since my wife died. If the rascal knew't,
He would be friends, and I were instantly
But a dead man, I could not get another
To anger me so handsomely. [*Exits*] 9

Scene Six

1   [*A room in Striker's house. Enter* STRIKER *and* FRISWOOD.]

FRISWOOD   You are welcome home, sir.

STRIKER   And merrily too, Fid. Hem, light at heart.
    I met with my physician, dog-leech Touchwood;

2   And cleared my stomach, and now I am light at heart.
    And thou shalt hear on 't, Fid, anon perhaps.

FRISWOOD   You are the better able, then, to hear
    And bear what I must tell you.

STRIKER   Where's my niece?

3   How does she, ha?

FRISWOOD   As well as a young woman
    In her case may do, sir.

STRIKER   Ha! How's that?

4 FRISWOOD   'T will out, and I as fit to tell you as another.

STRIKER   Out with it then.

FRISWOOD   'T is true, I faced you down there was no league
    Between young Touchwood, and your niece, in hope
    To turn her heart from him before the knowledge

5   Of anything that passed should be a grief to you:
    But since, I have discovered 't is too late,
    And she can be fit bride for no man else.

STRIKER   He has not lain with her, has he?

6 FRISWOOD   You speak as just as Gorman's lips.

STRIKER   I hope he has not lipped her so:
    Prithee, what canst thou mean?

FRISWOOD   Sir, if you think
    The knowledge of a truth of this sad nature

7   May prejudice your health, by drawing a choleric fit into you,
    You were best to send for your physician your dog-leech
    Touchwood, as you called him, to break your bed of phlegm, by
      laughing at you.

STRIKER   What dost thou mean now, I have asked thee twice?

    Gorman's lips: Possibly gourmand's lips. A gourmand betrays himself
by greedily smacking his lips (*conjecture*).

FRISWOOD   I say young Touchwood has touched, and clapped your   1
        niece;
    And (which is worse) with scorn and foul disdain
    Has left and quite forsaken; and is gone:
    (They say) sent by his father to travel.

STRIKER   'T was this the villain hammered on today,   2
    When he spoke, mystically, doubtful words,
    Reflecting on this mischievous sense: hell, hell, hell.

FRISWOOD   'T were good you would forsake the thought of hell, sir,
    And think upon some timely course to save
    Her credit, and the honour of your house by marriage.   3

STRIKER   You counsel very well.
    But, were you privy in their love's affair?

FRISWOOD   Indeed I knew too much on 't. Think of a course, good
        sir.
                                                                    4
STRIKER   I know no course for her and you but one,
    Young whore and bawd, and that is instantly
    To pack you out of doors to seek your living,
    And there I will be w' ye.

FRISWOOD   Sir, that you must not.   5

STRIKER   'S precious! Dost thou "must" me in mine own house?

FRISWOOD   In your own house, sir, kill us if you please,
    And take the sin upon you; but out of it
    You must not dare to thrust us with your shame: 6
    Which I will so divulge, as you shall find
    Your house to be no sanctuary for yourself;
    And there I'll be with you.

STRIKER   This is lusty.
                                                                    7
FRISWOOD   Consider wisely that I know you, sir,
    And can make foul relation of some passages
    That you will shame to hear.

STRIKER   Hold your peace!
                                                                    8
FRISWOOD   Remember, sir, near thirty years ago,
    You had a sister, whose great marriage portion
    Was in your hands: good gentlewoman, she
    Unfortunately loving a false squire,
    Just as your niece hath now, did get a clap.
    You know, sir, what I mean?   9

1 STRIKER You'll hold your peace?

FRISWOOD I'll speak it though I die for 't; better here
Than in a worse place: so clapped, I say, she was,
I know not yet by whom—you do, and bear
An inward grudge against somebody to this hour for 't.

2 But to my story, good gentlewoman she,
Was, by your most unbrotherly cruel usage,
Thrust out-a-doors, as now you threaten us:
And miserably, big bellied as she was,
Leaving her, most unjustly detained her portion
In your false hands, forsook you and the town,

3 To fly the air, where her disgrace was spread.
Some jewels and some gold she had concealed:
But to what part o' th' world she took, we know not,
Nor did you ever care, but wished her out on 't,
By any desperate end, after her flight

4 From portion, blood and name; and so perhaps
Immediately she was: for which, this judgment
Is justly fall'n upon you.

STRIKER Yet hold thy peace!

FRISWOOD Neither by threats, nor bribes, nor all persuasion,
5 Until you take your niece into your care.
What will the world say when it hears this story
Of your own natural sister, and your cruelty,
When you shall second it with your niece's shame?

STRIKER I never was so mated, so astonished.

6 FRISWOOD Nay, more than this, old Striker, I'll impeach
You for foul incontinence; and shaking your
Old bullion trunks over my truckle bed.

STRIKER Thou art not desperate? Wilt thou shame thyself?

FRISWOOD I value neither shame, nor name, nor fame;
7 And wealth I have none to lose. You have enough
To pay for all, I take it.

STRIKER Oh, I am sick.

FRISWOOD Be of good cheer, I'll send for your physician.

8 STRIKER Sick, sick at heart; let me be laid to bed. [*Exits*]

FRISWOOD I hope I have laid the heat of his severity,
So sometimes great offences pass for none,
When severe judges dare not hear their own. [*Exits*]

ACT THREE

Scene One

[*The Asparagus Garden. Enter* GARDENER *and* MARTHA, *his wife.*] 1

GARDENER   Pray let's agree upon 't, good wife, you are my wife I take it, and I should have the command, yet I entreat and am content you see.

MARTHA   And so would any man, I think, that has such a help and comings in by his wife as you have; 't is not your dirty sparagus, your artichokes, your carps, your tulips, your strawberries can bring you in five hundred pound a year, if my helping hand and brain, too, were not in the business. 2

GARDENER   Let us agree upon 't: and two or three years' toil more, while our trade is in request and fashion, will make us purchasers. I had once a hope to have bought this Manor of Marshland for the resemblance it has to the Low Country soil you came from, to ha' made you a bankside lady. We may in time be somewhat. But what did you take yesterday, Mat, in all? What had you, ah? 3

MARTHA   Poor piddling doings; some four and twenty pound. 4

GARDENER   What did the rich old merchant spend upon the poor young gentleman's wife in the yellow bedchamber?

MARTHA   But eight and twenty shillings, and kept the room almost two hours. I had no more of him. 5

GARDENER   And what the knight with the broken citizen's wife (that goes for ladylike) in the blue bedchamber?

MARTHA   Almost four pound.

GARDENER   That was pretty well for two.

MARTHA   But her husband, and a couple of servingmen, had a dish of sparagus, and three bottles of wine, besides the broken meat into one o' th' arbours. 6

GARDENER   Everything would live, Mat: but here will be great courtiers and ladies today, you say.

MARTHA   Yes, they sent last night to bespeak a ten-pound dinner, but I half fear their coming will keep out some of our more constant, and more profitable customers. 7

GARDENER   'T will make them the more eager to come another time then, Mat. Ha' they paid their reckoning in the parlour?

MARTHA   Yes, but butchingly, and are now going away. 8

279

Scene Two

1 [*Enter* GENTLEMAN *and* GENTLEWOMAN *to them.*]

GARDENER   Oh, here they are going.

GENTLEMAN   I protest, Master Gardener, your wife is too dear: sixteen shillings for a dish of sparagus, two bottles of wine, and a little sugar; I wonder how you can reckon it.

2

MARTHA   That was your reckoning in all, sir. We make no account of particulars, but all to mall, as they do in the Netherlands.

GENTLEMAN   Your Dutch account, Mistress, is too high for us to trouble you any more.

3 MARTHA   That's as you please, sir; a fair day after you.

[*Exeunt* GENTLEMAN *and* GENTLEWOMAN.]

Who would be troubled with such pinching guests?

GARDENER   Ay, 't is good to misreckon such to be rid on 'em.

4 MARTHA   They are e'en as welcome as the knight that comes hither alone always, and walks about the garden here half a day together to feed upon ladies' looks as they pass to and fro; the peeping knight, what do you call him?

GARDENER   Oh, Sir Arnold Cautious.

5 MARTHA   You may call him Cautious, I never saw five shillings of his money yet.

GARDENER   No, he comes but to feed his eyes, as you say, with leering at good faces, and peeping at pretty insteps.

MARTHA   Sir Hugh Moneylacks, our gather-guest as we call him, sends us no such dull customers: Oh, that good gentleman! Never did any tavern, inn, or new ordinary give tribute to a more deserving gentleman—oh, here come gallants.

6

Scene Three

7

[*Enter* GILBERT, WALTER, *and* SAMUEL *(in disguise) to them.*]

Three, and ne'er a woman! Strange! These are not the courtiers we look for.

8 GILBERT   This is his daily haunt. I warrant thee we find him.

all to mall: All together.

WALTER And it shall take, ne'er fear it, Sam. 1

GILBERT By your leave, Master and Mistress, or rather Lord and Lady of the new plantation here.

WALTER Nay, Prince and Princess of the Province of Asparagus.

SAMUEL The Island of Two Acres here, more profitable than twice two thousand in the Fens, till the drainers have done there. 2

MARTHA You are pleasant, gentlemen. What is your pleasure?

GILBERT Saw you Sir Arnold Cautious here today?

MARTHA Not yet, sir.

GILBERT Ha' you a room i' your house for us? 3

MARTHA Have you any more company to come to you?

WALTER Yes, we expect some gentlemen.

MARTHA Gentlemen, did you say?

GILBERT Yes indeed, gentlemen. No gentlewomen, I assure you. 4

MARTHA In truth, sir, all the rooms within are gone.

GILBERT What, they are not gone abroad, are they?

MARTHA You are always pleasant sir, I mean they are all taken up.

GILBERT There are some taken up in 'em, is 't not so? 5

MARTHA Still you are pleasant sir. They are indeed bespoken for great courtiers and ladies, that are to dine here.

GARDENER If you will bestow yourselves in the garden, and make choice of your arbour, you shall have the best cheer the house can afford ye, and you are welcome. [*Exits*] 6

GILBERT Be it so then; let's walk about, gentlemen. Pray, send us some wine.

WALTER And a dish of your sparagus.

MARTHA You shall have it, gentlemen. [*Exits*] 7

GILBERT Did you note the wit o' the woman?

WALTER Ay. Because we had no wenches, we must have no chamber room, for fear she disappoint some that may bring 'em.

SAMUEL She spake of great courtiers and ladies that are to come. 8

WALTER Some good stuff, perhaps.

GILBERT Why, I assure you, right noble, and right virtuous persons, and of both sexes, do frequent the place.

SAMUEL And I assure you, as ignoble and vicious do pester it too 9

1 much: and these that respect profit merely have not the wit, and
less the virtue, to distinguish betwixt the best and the worst but
by their purses.

WALTER 'T is enough for them to weed their garden, not their
guests. Oh, here comes our collation.

2

Scene Four

[*Enter* TWO BOYS. *They cover a table and lay two bottles of wine,
dishes of sugar, and a dish of asparagus.*]

3
GILBERT And what's the price of this feast, boy?

BOY Plait-il, Monsieur?

GILBERT What, art thou a Frenchman?

BOY No, I took you for one, sir; to bargain for your meat before
4 you eat it, that is not the generous English fashion. You shall
know anon, sir.

GILBERT Go, get you gone with your wit, and tell your prodigal
fools so.

WALTER Go, we'll call when we want attendance.

5
[*Exeunt* BOYS.]

GILBERT Sam, you are too sad; let not your disguise alter you with
us. Come, here's a health to Hans in Kelder, and the mother of
the boy, if it prove so.

6 SAMUEL I'll pledge it.

WALTER We want Sir Hugh Moneylacks here to discourse the
virtues of this precious plant asparagus, and what wonders it hath
wrought in Burgundy, Almain, Italy and Languedoc before the
herborists had found the skill to plant it here.

7 SAMUEL What's he to whom we seek?

WALTER Who, mine uncle Sir Arnold Cautious? He'll come, ne'er
doubt him; he seldom misses a day to pry and peer upon the
beauties that come to walk here.

GILBERT 'T is such a knightling, I'll but give ye his character and
8 he comes, I warrant thee. He is an infinite admirer of beauty, and
dares not touch a woman: he is aged about fifty, and a bachelor:
he defies wedlock, because he thinks there is not a maidenhead in
any marriageable beauty to be found among women.

SAMUEL Yet you say he is an admirer and hunter after the sight of
9 beauty.

GILBERT   He gets a crick in his neck oft times with squinting up at   1
windows and balconies; and, as he walks the streets, he peeps on
both sides at fair breasts and faces, as he were seeking birds'
nests; and follows pretty feet and insteps like a hare tracker.

WALTER   This is still mine uncle.

GILBERT   And when he sees a coach of ladies about to alight, he   2
makes a stand, in hope to see a delicate leg slip through a laced
smock, which, if he chance to discover, he drivels.

SAMUEL   Well, how your plot may hold to my purpose, I cannot
see. He is the unlikeliest man to have a wench put upon that you
can mention.   3

GILBERT   I grant the attempt is hard, but the higher will be the
achievement. Trust my experience, Sam: for, as in every instrument are all tunes to him that has the skill to find out the stops,
so, in every man there are all humours to him that can find their
faucets, and draw 'em out to his purpose.   4

WALTER   Fear not the plot as we have cast it, nor the performance
in the comedy, though against mine own natural uncle.

GILBERT   The unnatural uncle, thou wouldst say: he ne'er did thee
good in 's life. Act but thine own part, and be not out, Sam, and
fear nothing.   5

WALTER   He's somewhat too young to act a roarer; but what lads
have we seen pass for soldiers?

                                                                   6
Scene Five

[*Enter* THREE COURTIERS *and* LADIES, SIR ARNOLD CAUTIOUS *following aloof.*]

SAMUEL   Oh, here come the great guests.   7

GILBERT   And these are noble ones indeed; these are courtiers clinquant, and no counterfeit stuff upon 'em. I know 'em all; every
lady with her own husband, too: what a virtuous, honest age this
is! And see, if thine uncle be not at his old game, bopeep i' the
tail of 'em. He shall follow 'em no further. Sir Arnold Cautious!   8
Noble Knight, you are well encountered.

[*Exeunt* COURTIERS *and* LADIES.]

CAUTIOUS   Good Master Goldwire, do you know these ladies—or,
be they ladies, ha?   9

1 GILBERT Yes, and noble ones, the three Graces of the court, the Lady Stately, the Lady Handsome and the Lady Peerless. Do you not know 'em?

CAUTIOUS No, not I.

2 GILBERT How the slave twitters [*aside*]. You look not up at greatness, you mind too much the worldly things that are beneath you. If you had such a lady under you (of your own I mean), you would mind her.

CAUTIOUS Oh fie, fie, fie.

3 GILBERT Look no more after 'em, they are gone: besides, they are virtuous, and too great for you. When will you get a convenient wife of your own, to work out the dry itch of a stale bachelor?

CAUTIOUS Go, go, you are a wag; I itch not that way.

4 GILBERT Will you go this way with me then, and hear what I will say to you?

CAUTIOUS With all my heart, I am free from business.

5 GILBERT You have a nephew, whose sister I married, a virtuous wife she is, and I love him the better for 't. He is a younger brother and born to no great fortune. Now, you are very rich, a bachelor, and therefore, I think, childless—

CAUTIOUS In troth, Master Goldwire, you must pardon me, I may not stay with you: I had almost forgot a most important business.

SAMUEL E'en now he had none.

6 GILBERT Nay, good Sir Arnold Cautious, you know not what I'll say.

CAUTIOUS I say he is an unthrift, a squanderer, and must not expect supplies from me.

7 GILBERT He does not, shall not, not to the value of a token. Pray stay, and hear me, sir. 'T is no ill air to stay in.

CAUTIOUS Ay, with all my heart, good Master Goldwire; I like the air well—and your motion hitherto.

8 GILBERT Will you be pleased to do your kinsman the favour to further him in a match—I mean an honest lawful wedding match —but with your countenance, and a good word at most?

CAUTIOUS The most unthankful office in the world. Pray, use some other friend in 't: indeed, I stay too long.

9 GILBERT Hear but who it is that he loves, how likely he is to obtain, what abundant profit the match may bring him, and the

desperate undoing danger he falls into if he be not matched, and 1
then do your pleasure.

CAUTIOUS   Why, what new danger is he towards, more than the old
ill company he was wont to keep?

GILBERT   Oh, sir, he is now in league with a companion more
dreadful than 'em all, a fellow that is in part poet, and in part 2
soldier.

CAUTIOUS   Bounce, bounce!

GILBERT   You have hit upon his name! His name is Bounce. Do
you know him, sir?   3

CAUTIOUS   Not I, nor desire acquaintance with either of his qualities.

GILBERT   He is a gentleman, sir, that has been upon some unfortunate late services that have not answered his merit.

CAUTIOUS   And now he is come home to right himself, by writing   4
his own meritorious acts, is he?

GILBERT   Good in troth, I wish you would see 'em, to come over
'em with a jeer or two; I know you are good at it. They are in an
arbour here close by, drinking to their Muses, and glorifying one
another for either's excellency in the art most poetically.   5

CAUTIOUS   Glorify, do you say? I have heard poets the most en-
vious detractors of one another of all creatures, next to the very
beggars.

GILBERT   Abroad perhaps, and asunder, but, together there's no 6
such enmity. You never saw 'em drink: pray see 'em, sir, it may
take your nephew off of his ningle, who hath infected him with
poetry already; and twenty to one, if he fail in the match which I
was about to mention, he will win him away to the wars, too, and
then he may be lost for ever.   7

CAUTIOUS   Good Master Goldwire, go to your company. I am
not a man of reckoning amongst such; besides, I seldom drink betwixt meals.

WALTER   At his own cost, he means.   8

GILBERT   I commend your temper; you shall not be in the reckoning; but I beseech you, let me prevail with you. See, we are upon
'em. Save you, gentlemen. I have brought you a noble friend,
your uncle: I know he is welcome to you, brother Wat; and you,
I am sure, will make him so, Master Bounce, when you shall hear
he is an admirer of poetry and war.   9

1   CAUTIOUS   Even afar off, I assure ye. I never durst approach near the fury of either of the fiery qualities.

SAMUEL   It is your modesty, not fear, that keeps you at distance, I imagine.

2   CAUTIOUS   Poets may imagine anything: imagination is their wealth; some of 'em would be poor else. Are you turned poet, nephew?

WALTER   For my private recreation, sir.

3   CAUTIOUS   What, by writing verses to win some mistresses to your private recreation? Mean you so?

SAMUEL   You dare not, sir, blaspheme the virtuous use
Of sacred poetry, nor the fame traduce
Of poets, who not alone immortal be,
But can give others immortality.
Poets that can men into stars translate,
4   And hurl men down under the feet of Fate.
'T was not Achilles' sword, but Homer's pen
That made brave Hector die the best of men:
And if that powerful Homer likewise would,
Helen had been a hag, and Troy had stood.

5   GILBERT   Well said, poet, thou tumblest out old ends as well as the best of 'em.

SAMUEL   Poets they are the life and death of things,
Queens give them honour, for the greatest Kings
Have been their subjects.—

6   CAUTIOUS   Enough, enough. You are the first good poet that I e'er saw wear so good a countenance. Leave it, I would not have a gentleman meddle with poetry for spoiling of his face: you seldom see a poet look out at a good visnomy.

SAMUEL   Think you so, sir?

7   CAUTIOUS   Yes, and that is a poetical policy: where the face is naturally good without spot or blemish, to deface it by drinking or wenching, to get a name by 't.

SAMUEL   A death-deserving scandal!

8   [*He attacks* SIR ARNOLD. WALTER *throws* SAMUEL *and offers to stab him.* GILBERT *holds* WALTER'S *dagger.*]

GILBERT   Hold, hold!

SAMUEL   Thy malice and thy ignorance have doomed thee!

GILBERT   Gentlemen, what mean ye?

9   WALTER   My blood must not endure it!

GILBERT   You have wronged us all, and me the most.   1

WALTER   The wrong is chiefly mine; yet you add to it
By hind'ring my just vengeance.

SAMUEL   I'll find a time to right you, or myself! [*Exits*]

WALTER   My next sight of thee is thy death!
I fear you are hurt, sir; are you, pray, sir, tell me?   2

CAUTIOUS   Let me first admire thy goodness and thy pity,
My own, true, natural nephew.

GILBERT [*aside*]   Now it works.

CAUTIOUS   I now consider, and will answer thee
In a full measure of true gratitude.   3

WALTER   But, good sir, are you not hurt? If you bleed, I bleed with
you.

CAUTIOUS   Oh, sincere nephew, good boy, I am not hurt,
Nor can I think of hurt, my thoughts are bent
Upon thy good. You were speaking of a choice, sir, [*to* GILBERT]   4
My nephew would be match to; let me know the party.

GILBERT   Will you, sir, stand his friend?

CAUTIOUS   Let me but know the party and her friend,
And instantly about it.

GILBERT   He is catched. [*Aside*]   5

WALTER [*to* CAUTIOUS]   How am I bound to you!

CAUTIOUS   Nephew, I am yet bound to thee, and shall not rest till I
am disengaged by doing this office for thee. What is she, let me
know?
6
GILBERT   Sir, as we walk you shall know all. I'll pay the reckoning
within as we pass.

CAUTIOUS   But by the way, nephew, I must bind you from poetry.

WALTER   For a wife you shall, sir.

GILBERT   Poetry, though it be of a quite contrary nature, is as   7
pretty a jewel as plain dealing, but they that use it forget the
proverb.

[*Exeunt*]

8

Scene Six

[*Enter* COURTIERS *and* LADIES.]

FIRST COURTIER   Come, madams, now if you please after your garden feast,   9

1 To exercise your numerous feet, and tread
A curious knot upon this grassy square;
You shall fresh vigour add unto the spring,
And double the increase, sweetness and beauty
Of every plant and flower throughout the garden.

2 FIRST LADY   If I thought so, my lord, we would not do
Such precious works for nothing; we would be
Much better housewives, and compound for shares
O' th' gardener's profit.

SECOND LADY   Or at least hedge in
Our sparagus dinner reckoning.

3 SECOND COURTIER   I commend your worldly providence:
Madam, such good ladies will never dance
Away their husbands' lands.

FIRST COURTIER   But, madams, will ye dance?

FIRST LADY   Not to improve the garden, good my lord;
4 A little for digestion, if you please.

FIRST COURTIER   Music, play.

[*They dance.*]

You have done nobly, ladies, and much honoured
5 This piece of earth here with your graceful footing.

FIRST LADY   By your fair imitation, good my lords.

FIRST COURTIER   May the example of our harmless mirth
And civil recreation purge the place
Of all foul purposes.

6 FIRST LADY   'T is an honest wish;
But wishes weed no gardens. Hither come
Some wicked ones, they say.

FIRST COURTIER   We seek not to abridge their privilege;
7 Nor can their ill hurt us; we are safe.

FIRST LADY   But let us walk; the time of day calls hence.

FIRST COURTIER   Agreed.

[*Exeunt*]

8 ## Scene Seven

[*Enter* MONEYLACKS, HOYDEN, SPRING, BRITTLEWARE, MISTRESS
BRITTLEWARE, *and* COULTER.]

MONEYLACKS   You are now welcome to th' Asparagus Garden,
9 landlady.

REBECCA I have been long acoming for all my longings: but now I 1
hope I shall have my belly full on 't.

MONEYLACKS That you shall, fear not.

REBECCA Would I were at it once.

MONEYLACKS Well, because she desires to be private, go in with
your wife, Master Brittleware, take a room, call for a feast and 2
satisfy your wife; and bid the mistress of the house to provide for
us.

BRITTLEWARE I will, sir.

[*Exeunt* BRITTLEWARE *and* WIFE.] 3

MONEYLACKS And how do you feel yourself, Master Hoyden,
after your bleeding, purging and bathing, the killing of your gross
humours by your spare diet, and your new infusion of pure
blood, by your quaint feeding on delicate meats and drinks? How
do you feel yourself? 4

HOYDEN Marry, I feel that I am hungry, and that my shrimp diet
and sippings have almost famished me, and my purse, too. 'S lid,
I dare be sworn, as I am almost a gentleman, that every bit and
every spoonful that I have swallowed these ten days, has cost me
ten shillings at least. 5

SPRING Is it possible you consider this, and be almost a gentleman?

HOYDEN Small acquaintance, I do not lie to you. Truth's truth, as
well in a gentleman as a beggar, for I am both almost, and perhaps not the first that can write so. 6

SPRING Do you note how his wit rises?

HOYDEN There's one of my hundred pounds gone that way, all but
twelve pieces.

COULTER You see now what a fine hand you have made of your 7
money, since you got it out of my clutches.

HOYDEN Then there's my apparel, a hundred pound went all in
three suits, of which this is the best.

SPRING But what do you think of your wit, hundred pound?

HOYDEN Marry, I think that was the best laid out, for, by it, I 8
have got wit enough to know that I was as clearly cosened out of
it as heart can wish. O' my soul and conscience, and as I am
almost a gentleman, and a man had come to London for nothing
else but to be cheated, he could not be more roundlier rid of his
money. 9

1 MONEYLACKS Well, sir, if you repine at your expenses now, that you want nothing but your bellyful of sparagus to finish my work of a gentleman in you, I will if you please, in lieu of that, stuff up your paunch with bacon and bag pudding and put you back again, as absolute a clown as ever you came from plough.

2 COULTER I would he 're come to that once.

SPRING Take heed how you cross him.

3 HOYDEN Nay, pray sir, be not angry (though to the shame of a gentleman I say it), my teeth do e'en water at the name of the sweet country dish you spoke of (bacon and bag pudding), yet I will forebear it. But you say I shall fill my belly with this new daintril that you spoke of; these sparrow bills, what do you call 'em?

MONEYLACKS You shall have your belly full.

HOYDEN Top full, I beseech you.

4 COULTER Hum.—

MONEYLACKS You shall. But I must tell you, I must ha' you turn away this grumbling clown that follows you. He is as dangerous about you as your father's blood was within you, to cross and hinder your gentility.

5 HOYDEN True; you said you would help me to a boy no bigger than a monkey.

SPRING And you shall have him, a pretty little knave, you may put him in your pocket.

6 COULTER Yes, wuss, to pick 's money out if he had it; shortly 't will come to that bevore 't be long.

HOYDEN Coulter, you must to the plough again; you are too heavy a clog at the heels of a gentleman.

COULTER Ay, with all my heart, and I con you thanks, too.

7 HOYDEN The clown, my father's heir, will be glad of you.

MONEYLACKS Have you an elder brother?

8 HOYDEN You do not hear me say he is my brother; but the clown my father had a former son by a former wife, that was no gentlewoman as my mother was, and he is a clown all over, and incurable. Even get you to him, like to like will agree well. Here's a crown for you, 't will carry you afoot to Taunton. And so, get you gone like a clown as you are.

9 COULTER 'T is well you allow me some money yet: we shall have you beg all the way home shortly, when your cheaters have done w' ye.

MONEYLACKS How, villain!   1

SPRING Why do you not correct him, sir?

COULTER Nay, why do not you? He dares not. Though he could
spare his clown's blood, he dares not venture his gentleman's
blood so, nor you yours; 't is all too vine, I doubt. Therefore,
keep it, make much on 't. I would be loth a jail should stay   2
my journey, or, by my cursen soul, I would see what colour
the best on 't were before I go. But if I don't your errand to
your brother, and tell 'n how you do vlout 'n behind 'is back,
then say cut's a cur. And so, a vart vor a varewell to the proudest
o' ye; and if you be en-angered tak' 't in your angry teeth! [*Exits*]
                                                                             3
SPRING *and* MONEYLACKS Ha, ha, ha!

SPRING What a rude rascal 't is! You are happy that he is gone.

MONEYLACKS And so am I; he hindered half my work. Seven
years' time is too little to make a gentleman of one that can suffer such a clown within seven mile of him.   4

HOYDEN Would he were beyond Brentford on his way then by this
time, for me. But you forget the way you were in; you said you
would fill my belly; and then fall to practise fine compliments and
congees to make me a perfect gentleman, and fit me to see my
unknown uncle.   5

MONEYLACKS All shall be done.

Scene Eight   6

[*Enter* BRITTLEWARE *and* REBECCA *to them.*]

HOYDEN See, if my surgeon and his wife have not filled themselves, and come wiping their lips already.

MONEYLACKS So shall you presently. Now, landlady, are you   7
pleased with your asparagus?

REBECCA With the asparagus I am; and yet, but half pleased neither, as my husband shall very well know.

MONEYLACKS Well, we will leave you to talk with him about it.
Come, sir, let us into the house.   8

[*Exeunt* MONEYLACKS, SPRING, *and* HOYDEN.]

cut's a cur: The dog of a common person had its tail cut short, or
curtailed, to mark it: used as a term of abuse. Compare with "Then call
me Cut" (*Twelfth Night*).

1   BRITTLEWARE   But half pleased, sweetheart?

2   REBECCA   No indeed, John Brittleware; the asparagus has done its part; but you have not done your part, John; and if you were an honest man, John, you would make Sir Hugh's words good of the asparagus, and be kinder to me. You are not kind to your own wife, John; in the asparagus way, you understand me; for ought I see, pompions are as good meat for such a hoggish thing as thou art.

   BRITTLEWARE   Well, when we come at home, Beck, I know what I know.

3   REBECCA   At home! Is 't come to that? And I know what I know; I know he cannot love his wife enough at home, that won't be kind to her abroad. But the best is, I know what my next longing shall be.

4   BRITTLEWARE   More longings yet! Now, out of the unsearchable depths of woman's imagination, what may it be?

   REBECCA   It begins to possess me already, still more and more: now 't is an absolute longing, and I shall be sick till I have it.

   BRITTLEWARE   May I know it, forsooth? Tell it, that you may have it.

5   REBECCA   I dare tell it you, but you must never know that I have it.

   BRITTLEWARE   If you dare, tell it.

6   REBECCA   Dare? Nay, be as jealous as you will, thus it is. I do long to steal out of mine own house unknown to you, as other women do, and their husbands ne'er the wiser, hither to this same Sparagus Garden and meet some friend that will be kind to me.

   BRITTLEWARE   How, how!

7   REBECCA   In private; unknown to you, as I told you. 'T is unpossible I shall ever have a child else, and you so jealous over me as you are.

   BRITTLEWARE   Art thou a woman and speak this?

8   REBECCA   Art thou a man; five years married to me, and ask me now if I be a woman?

   BRITTLEWARE   Art thou so full of the Devil to fly out in this manner?

   REBECCA   Why, his horns fly not out of me to fright thee, do they?

9   BRITTLEWARE   Oh, for a hell that has not a woman in 't!

Scene Nine

[*A* GENTLEMAN *and* CITY WIFE *pass by them.*]   1

REBECCA   Look you there, John Jealousy, there's an example before your eyes if nothing hang in your sight; there you may see
the difference between a sour husband and a sweet-natured gentleman! Good heart, how kindly he kisses her! And how featly
she holds up the neb to him! Little heart! When will you be so   2
kind to your own wife, John?

BRITTLEWARE   Is that his wife, think you?

REBECCA   No, no, I know her; 't is Mistress Hollyhock, the precise
draper's wife. Oh, how my longing grows stronger in me; I see
what shift soever a woman makes with her husband at home, a   3
friend does best abroad.

Scene Ten

                                                                 4
[*Enter a* SERVANT *to the* GENTLEMAN *and* CITY WIFE.]

SERVANT   Indeed, my Mistress will not take this money; there
wants two shillings.

CITY WIFE   Why, is my piece too light?   5

SERVANT   Too light for the reckoning, Mistress. It comes to two
and twenty shillings, and this is but twenty.

GENTLEMAN   Unreasonable, how can she reckon it?

SERVANT   I know what you had, sir, and we make no bills.

GENTLEMAN   Well fare the taverns yet, that though they cosened   6
never so much, would down with it one way or other, and their
Jacks go again. Now tell your mistress, and that will hinder her
somewhat.

SERVANT   Not a jot, sir.

GENTLEMAN   Then tell her the Countess of Copt Hall is coming   7
to be her neighbour again, and she may decline her trade very
dangerously.

SERVANT   My Mistress scorns your words, sir.

GENTLEMAN   You rogue!
                                                                 8
CITY WIFE   Nay, sweet cousin, make no uproar, for my reputation's sake. Here youth, there's two shilling more, commend
me to your Mistress.

1   [*Exeunt* GENTLEMAN *and* CITY WIFE. *Exit* SERVANT.]

BRITTLEWARE   She pays the reckoning, it seems.

REBECCA   It seems then he has been kind to her another way.

2

Scene Eleven

[*Enter* MONEYLACKS, HOYDEN, SPRING, *and* MARTHA *to them.*]

MONEYLACKS   How is 't? I hope you are not wrangling now, but
3   better pleased than so.

REBECCA   No, no, Sir Hugh; 't is not the sparagus can do 't, unless
the man were better.

HOYDEN [*to* SPRING]   But may I now be confident that I am almost
a gentleman?
4

SPRING   Without that confidence you are nothing.

MONEYLACKS   There wants nothing now, but that you may learn
the rules and rudiments, the principles and instructions for the
carriages, congees and compliments, which we'll quickly put into
5   you by practise.

HOYDEN   And then the spending the little rest of my money, and I
am a clear gentleman, and may see my uncle.

MONEYLACKS   Right, right.

HOYDEN   And I will write it, and crowd it into as many bonds as I
6   can, a' purpose to write "gentleman"; "Timothy Hoyden of Taunton"—no—"of London, Gentleman": London is a common place
for all gentlemen of my rank, is it not?

SPRING   Excellent. Do you not mark how finely he comes on?

HOYDEN   But as I hope to live and die a gentleman, Mistress What-
7   shi'call, your reckoning was devilish dear; 's daggers, three pound
for a few cuckoo pintles; they were no better, I think.

SPRING   Now you fall back again, and derogate from the conditions of a gentleman most grossly to think anything too dear you
eat or drink.

8   HOYDEN   Pox on't, I had forgot.

MONEYLACKS   When he has his rules and principles, which must be
his next study, he will remember.

HOYDEN   Pray, let's about it quickly.

MONEYLACKS   Now we'll go. But you forget me, Mistress. [*Aside*
9   *to* MARTHA]

MARTHA No indeed, Sir Hugh, here's two pieces for last week and 1
this.

MONEYLACKS 'T is well. Landlord and landlady, will you go?

BRITTLEWARE Would you would long to be at home once!

REBECCA So I do, perhaps, and to be here again, and there again; 2
and here, and there, and here again; and all at once.

BRITTLEWARE Hey, kicksy winsey.

REBECCA And I do long to go to Windsor, too, to know if the
prophecy be as true there as 't is reported here.

MARTHA How did you hear it goes, forsooth? 3

REBECCA That all old women shall die, and many young wives
shall have cuckolds to their husbands.

MARTHA I heard forsooth, that all young wives should die that
were pure maids when they were married.
4
REBECCA And none other?

MARTHA So report goes, forsooth.

REBECCA You speak very comfortably; it may be a long journey to
the world's end yet.

BRITTLEWARE It seems you are not proscribed by the prophecy 5
then?

REBECCA I thank my destiny.

HOYDEN My first work, when I am complete gentleman, shall be
to get them a child, and make 'em friends. 6

MONEYLACKS A most gentlemanly resolution.

REBECCA And truly, the city is much bound to such well-affected
gentlemen.

[*Exeunt*]

ACT FOUR

Scene One

1   [*The street before Striker's house. Enter* TOM HOYDEN *and* COULTER.]

TOM   Is it possible that half this can be true, that a half brother of mine can be made such an ass all over?

COULTER   'T is all true, as I am a cursen fellow, Master Thomas, every word on 't. I scorn to lie in a sillibub, I. What luck had I to
2   meet you! I never thought to zee you at London.

TOM   'S dagger's death, it has as good as veezed me out o' my wits to think on 't. Was my vather's blood so quaisome to him (with a mischief to 't) that he must let it out to be a geantleman, because his mother was one (by her own report)? For our own
3   parts we nother know nor care where hence she coame nor whither she's gone, (but dead she is). She brought my vather a good purse o' money, and kept another in store, it zeems, till she could keep 't no longer, and then bestowed it well and wisely upon Chitty vace her zon, to make him a geantleman, and told him what great house he coame on by her side. For she was a Striker, forzooth,
4   and ga'n directions to vind an old uncle of his here in Cuckoldshire, one Master Striker; but virst she bade him put himself into vashion, and be sure to bear 's zelf like a geantleman; and he has ta'en a wise course to compass it, it zeems. I warrant he ha' made a vool o' his vour hundred pound by this time.

5 COULTER   Ay, and o' his zelf, too, and his cony catchers ha' handled him. And you had zeen 't, you would ha bepissed yourzelf vor woe, how they blooded him.

TOM   Ah.

6 COULTER   And then how they zpurged his guts out.

TOM   Ah.

COULTER   A bots light on 'em, 't would ha' made a dog zick to zee 't, how like a zcalded pig he looked.

TOM   Ha, ha, ha.

7 COULTER   And then how they did veed 'en with a zort of zlip zlaps not all worth a mess o' milk porridge to make him vine, forzooth.

TOM   Ah.

8 COULTER   You'll zee zuch an altrication in him as never was zeen in a brother.

TOM But I won't zee 'n yet, as voul a clown as I am and as vine a   1
geantleman as he is. I have a trick i' my zconce to make a younger
brother on 'n.

COULTER Ay, that would be zeen now.

TOM I ha' 't, and 't is a vine one. I coame to London to zeek the
vool my brother, and ha' the same directions from our Curate (to   2
whom my mother told all) that Tim had to vind his uncle Striker's house, and I ha' 'quired it out. And this is it, and thou shalt
zee what I chill do now. Wh' are within! [*He knocks.*]

3

Scene Two

FRISWOOD [*enters to them*] Who would you speak with?

TOM By your leave, vorsooth, I would speak with the Master o'
the house; I understand his worship's name is Master Striker.   4

FRISWOOD He is so, sir, but he is not in case to buy any cattle at
this time.

TOM Nor do I come to zell 'n any; my coming is of a dead body's
errand vorsooth.

FRISWOOD What strange fellow is this, trow?   5

TOM I pray, vorsooth, and you be old enough (as it zeems you
be) to remember when my mother was a maid, did you know a
zuster of Master Striker's that was married into Zummerzetshire?

FRISWOOD What was her name, I pray?   6

TOM Her cursen name was Audrey, she zaid, and a Striker she
was bevore she was married; but my vather made a Hoyden.

FRISWOOD Hoyden!

TOM Yes, Hoyden, zo I zay. There be very good volks o' the   7
name, as you shall well know. I cham one myzelf, and she need
not be ashamed I wuss o' the kin she coame on, to huggermugger
it as she did to her dying day.

FRISWOOD Most wonderful! But, is she dead?

TOM Yes vaith, she's deed, and as zumptiously buried, though I   8
zay 't, as any yeoman's wife within ten mile of Taunton, any time
these ten and twenty year.

FRISWOOD Pray, what were you to her?

TOM I tell you my vather married her; and I should be her zon I
think.   9

1 FRISWOOD Good heaven, how things will come about!

TOM Coulter, keep thy countenance, Coulter. I'll make 'em believe I am her very natural zon, zee what will come on 't.

COULTER I'll keep my countenance, and zet a face on 't too, and need be.

2 FRISWOOD Your uncle Striker at this time is very sick, sir, but I will acquaint him with your desire. Pray, walk into the next room the while, sir.

TOM If he should die now, Coulter, and make me his heir?

3 COULTER Ay, marry Master, so you might make a better journey on 't than the gentleman your brother.

[*They go in.*]

4 FRISWOOD This, to me, is the greatest wonder of all; that I am presently possessed of my master's sullen sickness, which has e'er drawn him to death's door, and my mistress's unfortunate condition, are nothing to this country hoyden's relation.

5 ## Scene Three

[*Enter* TOUCHWOOD *to her.*]

FRISWOOD Oh, Master Touchwood, you are the welcom'st gentleman that ever could come into so heavy a house.

6 TOUCHWOOD A stinking one it is, I am sure; that nasty carrion thy master is i' my nose already. I think I were best go no further.

FRISWOOD Let not the sadness of this place dismay you.

TOUCHWOOD But is he dead already, ha?

7 FRISWOOD Not altogether dead, sir.

TOUCHWOOD The worse luck. And how does your mistress? Ha, ha, ha. Well, I say nothing.

FRISWOOD She is in bodily health, sir, but very sad and much disconsolate, poor damsel.

8 TOUCHWOOD Not for her grandsire, is she? If the worst dog he keeps howls for him, I'll worry sheep with mine own teeth, and truss for him. But why is she sad, prithee tell me? Ha, ha, ha.

FRISWOOD I marvel at your mirth, sir.

9 TOUCHWOOD I would now give her a new gown to tell me the true

cause, that I might save mine oath and roar out my rejoicings. 'T 1
was a devilish trick of the rascal's to bind me by oath never to
speak of it, but to those that should tell me of it first. I have such
a coil to keep it in now. Prithee tell me, what has the old traveller
that is now bound for the Low Countries gi'n thy mistress in his
will, canst tell?

FRISWOOD Alas, he is offended with her; she has displeased him
somewhat. That is the main cause of his mortal sickness.

TOUCHWOOD That's my boy, there boy, there, that was a home
blow. [*Aside*]

FRISWOOD She comes not at him, sir, nor dares not see him. Do 3
you know anything by her, sir?

TOUCHWOOD No, no, no, not I. 'S bores, I bit my tongue too hard!

FRISWOOD If you do, sir, would you speak a good word for her,
that he may die in charity with her. 4

TOUCHWOOD The jade jeers me; I'll stay no longer i' the house.

FRISWOOD Nay, good sir, say not so, after so many messages and
entreaties by all the best o' the parish, and an exhortation made
to you by the minister himself, did you vouchsafe to come? And
will you now come short to see my master now the doctors have 5
given him over, and he is dying?

TOUCHWOOD I confess 't was my desire to see that dying that
brought me hither. Where is he? I'll hold my nose and have at
him.

FRISWOOD I hope you will be friends with him now, sir, for he's 6
e'en agoing.

TOUCHWOOD Friends? I'll rather go with him, and fight it out by
the way.

7

Scene Four

[*Enter* STRIKER, *brought in a chair, with the* CURATE, *to them.*]

FRISWOOD Look you, sir, here he is. 8

TOUCHWOOD What? Up, and in a chair?

FRISWOOD Yes, sir; he will not yield by any persuasion to die in
his bed.

TOUCHWOOD Then he may live to be hanged yet, for ought I see. 9

1 CURATE See, sir, your neighbour Touchwood comes to be reconciled to you.

TOUCHWOOD You are quite besides the book, sir Domine. I have no friends in hell to send to by him. No, sir, I come to see him die as he lived, a hateful miscreant.

2 CURATE Let me pray and beseech you to speak more charitably, or else not to offend the dying man with your presence.

TOUCHWOOD Do I come to humour him, or you, or myself, think you? You, that take upon you and do rather go about to sooth him in his sickness than to fright him out of his pain, rather en-
3 courage to live than rid the world of him and his abominations.

CURATE Best look into yourself, sir. The world's a stage, on which you are both actors, and neither to be his own judge.

TOUCHWOOD But he has played many vile and beastly parts in it. Let him go, I would see his last exit and hiss him out of it. Hark,
4 the ravens cry "pawk" for him, and yet he dies not.

FRISWOOD Oh, you are a hardhearted man.

TOUCHWOOD My heart's not hard enough to break his. I would it were. Where's your kindhearted mistress? Fetch her, and try what she can do.

5 STRIKER Huh. Huh, huh. [Coughs]

CURATE What have you done, sir?

TOUCHWOOD So, so, so, so, it works, it works.

STRIKER Out, snarling hellhound, my curse upon thee and thy
6 cursed son that has undone my niece and me. Curse upon curse light on ye.

CURATE Oh, fearful.

TOUCHWOOD How heartily he prays; sure he is near his end.

7 CURATE Pray, sir, depart. You are too uncharitable.

TOUCHWOOD My son undone thy niece? Has he not done her, think'st thou? Ha, ha, ha.

STRIKER [coughs] Huh, huh, huh. Villain, thou know'st what he has done. Huh, huh.

8 TOUCHWOOD I know not whether I know or no; tell me, and I'll tell thee.

FRISWOOD I'll tell you then that which you know already,
Although you keep it for a joy within you.
Your wicked son has, by her own confession,
9 Done that unto her, that unless he play

The honest man's part and marry her, he will   1
Full dearly answer it in hell.

STRIKER   Huh, huh, huh.

TOUCHWOOD   Speak English. Has he lain with her?

FRISWOOD   'T is so;   2
She has confessed it to her grandfather,
To me, and Master Pankridge here is made
Acquainted with it.

TOUCHWOOD   Ha, ha, ha.

CURATE   The virgin says   3
She is depucelated by your son.

TOUCHWOOD   Depucelated—ha, ha, ha.

CURATE   It is no laughing matter, therefore send
Speedily for your son, before the rumour
Make it ridiculous. As yet none knows it   4
But we, a slender few.

TOUCHWOOD   Will you direct
Your divine rhetoric there to him, and win him
But to entreat me in this case, and try
What I will say to 't.   5

CURATE   Be persuaded, sir.

STRIKER   In this extremity I do entreat that they may marry.

TOUCHWOOD   I have my ends upon thee! Quickly die,
And take thine own; thy base submission   6
Has rendered thee more odious, more loathsome
To me than all thy former villainies.

STRIKER   Huh, huh, huh.

TOUCHWOOD   And hark thee ere thou diest, for now th' art going;
Before my son shall wed that whore thy niece,   7
She shall bring all the hands of all the whoremasters
In city, court and kingdom (black coats and all,
I will spare none) unto a fair certificate
That she is clear of all men but my son.

STRIKER   Huh, huh, huh.   8

TOUCHWOOD   Nay, more;
That she is clear of him, too, and that he
Has ne'er topped her in the way we treat of
Before he wed her. For my son shall not ride
In his old boots upon his wedding night.   9

1 So, now die and sink
   Into thy grave, to rid us of thy stink.

CURATE I have not known such want of charity.

FRISWOOD Unconscionable wretch, thou hast killed my master.

2 STRIKER Ugh, ugh, no Fid—ugh, hem! He has cured me,
   I am light at heart again; he has cured me.
   He has played the good physician 'gainst his will,
   And a halter be his fee for 't.

TOUCHWOOD The devil I have, and his dam it shall!

3 STRIKER Ah, hem! I am light at heart again.

TOUCHWOOD Oh, damned old counterfeit.

FRISWOOD Well fare your heart, old master.

STRIKER Though she prove bastard-bellied, I will own her,
   Cherish, maintain and keep her from thy son.

4 TOUCHWOOD Oh, I could tear that tongue out.

STRIKER   Keep her child, too.

TOUCHWOOD Do, and her next, and fill thy house with bastards.

STRIKER I'll hold 'em more legitimate than thy brood.

5 CURATE What mean you, gentlemen?

STRIKER For thou, thy son, thy house is all a bastard.

TOUCHWOOD Bear witness, he calls my house a bastard.

FRISWOOD Ha, ha, ha.

6 TOUCHWOOD I'll make thy house to smoke for 't.

STRIKER Bear witness here, he says he will fire my house.

CURATE For neighbourhood and charity, speak lower.

STRIKER 'T is petty treason. I'll be wi' ye there, sir.

7 TOUCHWOOD And hang thyself, old scarecrow!

FRISWOOD Will you eat a piece of gingerbread for your wind, sir.

TOUCHWOOD Out, witch!

8 [*He kicks her.*]

FRISWOOD Oh, murder, murder!

STRIKER I'll lay as many actions on thee as thou hast bones in that
   swine's foot of thine.

9 FRISWOOD My nails shall right me. I'll teach him to kick a woman.

CURATE Hold, Mistress Friswood! 1

FRISWOOD Oh, villain! Kick a woman!

TOUCHWOOD Thou laid'st this plot to murder me, thou man-killer.

STRIKER Bloodsucker, thou liest!

CURATE Help from above, within, or any whence, in the name of 2
sanctity, I conjure you. *Flectere si nequeo superos, Acheronta movebo.*

Scene Five 3

[*Enter* TOM *and* COULTER *to them.*]

TOM What's the matter? By your leave, which is my zick uncle?
Are you scuffling for 's money before he be dead?

COULTER We'll part you with a vengeance. 4

TOUCHWOOD Ha' you your tenants, your clowns here brought in to
butcher me?

STRIKER Slave, thy are thine, brought in to spoil and rob me. I
know 'em not. 5

CURATE I fear I've conjured up fiends indeed; how infernally they
look!

TOM No, sir, we come with no zick intendment on neither nother
zide; but an you be Master Striker, we are o' your zide, an 't be
to cut all the rest into potherbs. [*To* TOUCHWOOD] 6

FRISWOOD No, this is my master.

TOM Zay but the word then, and have at 'em!

TOUCHWOOD Had you your ambuscado for me?

CURATE They are a pair of the sedan mules, I take it. 7

COULTER Moyls sir, we be no moyls, would you should well know.

TOM We be cursenfolk as good as yourzelf. And get you out o'
the house by mine uncle's leave here.

TOUCHWOOD Your uncle! Oh, brave! 8

TOM Or, if I baste you not well a fine, and lambskin your jackets
till your bones rattle i' your hides, then zay 'cha bewrayed the
house I coame on.

Flectere si nequeo . . . : "If I fail to bend the gods above, I shall move
the gods below" (Virgil: *Aeneid*). 9

1   TOUCHWOOD   Well, sir, I'll go, and leave you to your uncle. Rejoice, sir, with your kindred. I hope you will have more shortly if your niece prove fruitful. Come, Master Pankridge, will you go?

  CURATE   With joy for your recovery and manners to your privacy, Right Worshipful, I leave you to talk with Clown your nephew.

2   TOUCHWOOD   Tarry, tarry. As sure as a club, this clown is sent for out of the country to solder up his cracked niece in matrimony, and therefore calls him uncle. I could spoil the match, but, by my oath, I dare not. And therefore, Clown, take thy course. Come, let us go, Master Pankridge.

3   [*Exeunt* TOUCHWOOD *and* CURATE.]

  STRIKER   And why you my nephew, sir?

  TOM   And why not I your nephew? Ha'n't she told you, and ha' not I told you as much as the matter's worth? And do ye mean to
4   vlee from the bargain?

  STRIKER   What new afflictions hourly find me out?

  FRISWOOD   And for your health, I hope, sir.

  STRIKER   Sir, I'll have better testimony than your own.
  'T is true I lost a sister, but till you
5   Bring stronger proof she was your mother, sir,
  Your clownship must not uncle me. Am I wi' you, sir?
  Kings' crowns have been pretended to by impostures,
  And knavery is as rife in russet wool
  As in the proudest purple. Get you gone.
6   There I am wi' you directly.

  TOM   Is 't come to this, now?

  COULTER   Your project will not hold, Master Thomas, best zeek your brother Tim, he has a zertification from the parish and the priest too, of all your mother's mind; and you could cozen him
7   on 't, and come again, and uncle this weese gentleman whether he woll or no. 'T would be vine, i' vaith.

  TOM   Agreed. Well, sir, vor this time I ha' no more to zay t' ye, since you be so budge. But he that made you, save you.

8   [*Exeunt* TOM *and* COULTER.]

  STRIKER   Farewell, sir, I do begin to think there's something in 't.

  FRISWOOD   He made me think he was your sister's son, I am sure.

  STRIKER   I will not think so; no, he was set on
  By some of my maligners to abuse me.
9   It had been good to ha' laid him by the heels;

But let him go. Call down my niece out of   1
The melancholy mist she's chambered in.

[*Exit* FRISWOOD.]

All makes for her; their vexing me restores
Her to my love again; and reason good;   2
She's mine own natural niece: and though
She's lost the husband and the name she sought,
Yet she appears a Striker, and I will cherish her.

     3

Scene Six

[*Enter* ANNABEL, *who kneels to her grandfather.*]

STRIKER   Come, you shall grieve no longer, I am friends wi' ye.   4
Stand up, stand up, I say, and look up, too;
Off with this mourning veil, and dry those tears.
I have considered that right noble parents
Have pardoned in their children as great faults;
But let it be your warning, not your license.
     5

ANNABEL   For your security, I am content,
And would entreat to live in that retirement
Which your fair justice and my foul offence
Of late confined me to, to weep and sigh
My loathèd life away.   6

STRIKER   No more. You shall
No longer live reclused in wilful darkness;
Enjoy your former liberty; see, and be seen:
And (as you weigh my pardon and my love)
Let not your blemish dwell upon your face;   7
Nor any argument of grief or shame
Be legible there to the most curious eye.
But let your cheek be cheerful, and your brow
Crowned with as great a confidence, as may
Comply with virgin modesty; and that
Add to your beauty with full strength of art   8
Beyond the eye, to take a lover's heart.

ANNABEL   In all I will obey you.

STRIKER   If I make
Choice of a husband for you then, you'll take him.   9

1 ANNABEL   'T will but become my duty.

STRIKER   A good girl.

FRISWOOD [*enters*]   Sir, here's the knight come again, that has been
here in the time of your sickness to have seen you and my mistress, but could not, and left a letter for you once—he that looks
2 women through so.

STRIKER   Oh, Sir Arnold Cautious. Did you tell him I was o' the
mending hand?

FRISWOOD   Yes, I told him you were so so.

3 STRIKER   Give me my gown and cap though, and set me charily in
my sickly chair. His letter is a treaty of a match betwixt his
nephew and my niece. Go fetch him up.

[*Exit* FRISWOOD.]

4 In, niece, and be not seen until I call you—until you hear me
call, do you hear?

[*Exit* ANNABEL.]

Could I but catch this Cautious coxcomb knight now—I'll put
fair for 't.
5

Scene Seven

6 [*Enter* FRISWOOD *with* CAUTIOUS.]

FRISWOOD   Here is the knight, sir.

STRIKER   Why reach you not a chair? I hope, Sir Arnold,
You'll pardon the necessity of my rudeness;
I cannot rise, nor stoop to you—uh, uh, uh.
7
CAUTIOUS   Rather excuse me, sir, that press upon you
Thus in your weakness. But you understand
My business by my letter if you have read it.

STRIKER   Yes sir.—Go forth, but be not far, I pray you [*to* FRIS-
8 WOOD].

[*Exit* FRISWOOD.]

I have heard your nephew is a wild young man.

CAUTIOUS   A very bashful boy, I assure you. That's the reason
9 That I am won to be a spokesman for him.

STRIKER Oh, no dissembling, sir, you know he is wild,   1
And suffers under your displeasure for 't—uh, uh, uh.

CAUTIOUS A witch could not guess righter, but they say
That dying men are prophets oftentimes.
Suppose he has been wild, let me assure you
He's now reclaimed, and has my good opinion,   2
And is as like in person and behaviour
To gain the maid's affection.

STRIKER Speak to the purpose; pray, what's his estate?

CAUTIOUS Ay, there's the point indeed; why, sir, he has
A hundred pound a year, and is withal   3
A hopeful and a handsome gentleman.

STRIKER Hopeful, and handsome! Uh, uh, uh.

CAUTIOUS You, sir, have wealth enough.

STRIKER And she has choice enough
Of greater matches, could I get her   4
In a marriage vein. But she'll not look
Upon a man, not she; but lives retired
Here in my house, and is a careful nurse.
She's fitter, sir, to be an old man's nurse
Than any young man's bride. Uh, uh, uh, uh.   5

CAUTIOUS Is she so grave in youth? I have often sought
A sight of her, but never could obtain it.

STRIKER Not without my consent, I warrant you.
She's nearer to a mother than a maid;
I tell you truth, sir, and you know deceit   6
Becomes not dying men—uh, uh, uh. For virtue and obedience
She's fitter for yourself than for your nephew.
But to the point: a hundred pound a year
You say he has, and hopes and handsomeness
Which may acquire, with your assurance of
So much for jointure—yes—a thousand pound   7
In portion with her: but, sir, let me tell you
I'd rather give six thousand unto one
Of mine own choice, which she will not refuse,
If I but say "this is the man, and take him."

CAUTIOUS Will not your niece be seen? I fain would see her.   8

STRIKER At hand. She will not out of my presence, sir,
Nor ever was by man, not since the clock
Of her virginity struck eleven, not she;
Except at door or window as men pass.
And so perhaps your nephew may have seen her.   9

1 CAUTIOUS   In troth, no other wise, and so he told me.
    May I not see her, sir?

STRIKER   I tell you true;
    Deceit, you know, becomes not dying men—uh, uh, uh.
    And therefore hark you, sir, I have a purpose
2   (That if she take the man whom I will choose)
    To make her my sole heir, provided that
    She match before I die—uh, uh. I cannot last.

CAUTIOUS   Pray let me see your niece.

STRIKER   Friswood—why, Friswood!

3 CAUTIOUS   Is that her name?

STRIKER   No, sir, I call my maid.

CAUTIOUS   A maid? I took her for an old woman.

STRIKER   A maid, upon my virtue; and I fear
4   That her frigidity has mortified my niece;
    Deceit becomes not dying men you know.
    Friswood, I say!—I bade her not be far.
    I dare not strain myself to call her louder.

CAUTIOUS   I'll call her for you sir, Fris—!

5 STRIKER   Hold, sir, hold, pray use this whistle for me,
    I dare not strain myself to wind it I,
    The doctors tell me it will spend my spirits.

[CAUTIOUS *whistles*.]

6   So, so, enough, sir.

[*Enter* FRISWOOD.]

                   Fie, fie upon you.
    Go call my niece, uh, uh.
7

[*Exit* FRISWOOD.]

CAUTIOUS   Be of good cheer, sir, and take courage, man.
    What, you have been a Striker in your days,
    And may be again. I would not have him die. [*Aside*]
8
STRIKER   Uh—alas, I cannot last.

[*Enter* FRISWOOD.]

                  Why comes she not?
9 FRISWOOD   I cannot get her from her work, nor to

Believe me that you sent for her, because 1
I told her that a gentleman was with you.

STRIKER   There was your fault; then I must call myself.
Why, Anna-bel, ah, ah, ah, Anna-bell!

[*Exit* FRISWOOD.] 2

CAUTIOUS   Take heed, strain not yourself too hard, but send again.
The rarest beauty that I e'er beheld,
Which with a maidenhead of that growth

[*Enter* ANNABEL.] 3

Would be an absolute wonder, her sweet modesty
And meek obedience justifies that too,

[ANNABEL *kneels at* STRIKER'S *feet.*]

And makes her up a miracle of nature. 4
My former misbelief I do renounce,
And at first sight (which is the birth of love)
A faith grows in me, strengthened by the word
Of this expiring man, that chastity
Has not forsaken beauty.
                                                                              5
STRIKER   You shall hear him [*to* ANNABEL].

ANNABEL   What? To propound a husband? Honoured sir,
Although I rather wish to die a virgin,
Yet my obedience to your grave behests
Shall sway my will; your choice shall be my liking. 6
But let me thus much favour beg, before
You make that choice, that you will not destroy
The building you have reared; your care and cost
Hath built me up by virtuous education
Unto that height that I consider heaven,
And wax so old in that high contemplation, 7
That to look down on youthful vanities
Were to be at a stand; and to delight in 'em
Were to fall back again; and to be linked
In marriage to a man whose wild affections
Are bent to worldly pleasures a main perdition. 8

CAUTIOUS   I dare not speak to her for my nephew now,
Nor (though I love her strangely) for myself. [*Aside*]

ANNABEL   Do you tell me of his nephew, sir? Even he,
The knight himself, I hold to be too young
For a well-governed man, as the world goes. 9

1 CAUTIOUS I ha' not the heart to wrong her, she's too good. [*Aside*]

FRISWOOD [*enters*] Sir, here's a gentleman presses at my heels
To speak with you.

2

Scene Eight

[*Enter* GILBERT *with his arm in a scarf.*]

CAUTIOUS   Master Goldwire, what's your haste?

3 GILBERT I come to cry you mercy, and this good gentleman,
And this sweet gentlewoman, who I take it
Is his fair niece of whom you are in treaty.
If it be not already gone too far,
Let me entreat you not to put your finger
4 Further i' the business in behalf of your nephew.

CAUTIOUS You first moved me to 't.

GILBERT   'T is that repents me:
Your base unworthy nephew has abused me.
I do not speak it for a slight hurt he has gi'en me,
5 But for his breach of faith to another virgin.

ANNABEL Oh me! And would you speak for such a man?

GILBERT And the false way, the plot he had upon you.
To put you on this enterprise, the quarrel
In which he rescued you to endear himself to you,
6 Was a mere counterfeit squabble, a very trick
Contrived betwixt him and his brother poet
T' abuse your goodness.
I leave it to your consideration, sir.
I am in haste, and so I wish you health, sir.
7 And you much happiness in a husband, lady.

[*He gives her a letter. Exits.*]

ANNABEL Has given me here a letter, I want but
Place fit to peruse it. [*Aside*]

8 CAUTIOUS Had he a plot upon me, I'll have my plot, too,
And now woo for myself, sir, if you please.

STRIKER Sir, let me tell you, I think well of you—uh, uh;
Deceit becomes not dying men, you know.
She would make e'en too good a wife for you;
9 For I have heard, sir, of your disposition

Never to marry without best assurance,   1
First, of virginity, and then of chastity
In her that you would choose; and let me tell you—uh, uh,
I know not where you can be so well fitted.
She's right—uh, uh, if you dare take a weak man's word;
Deceit would ill become me—uh, uh.
                                                                         2
CAUTIOUS   I take you at your word, and thank you, sir.

STRIKER   Uh, uh, uh, uh—Oh, lay me in my bed.
You need not leave me yet, sir.

CAUTIOUS   No, sir, no.
It shall be a match or no match ere I go.   3

[*Exeunt all,* STRIKER *led forth.*]

Scene Nine   4

[*Brittleware's Shop. Enter* MONEYLACKS, SPRING, BRITTLEWARE.
and HOYDEN.]

MONEYLACKS   Now, sir, have you your rules by heart?
                                                                         5
HOYDEN   Both rules and rudiments I have all *ad unguem.*

MONEYLACKS   Repeat your principles.

HOYDEN   Principles to be imprinted in the heart of every new-
made gentleman: to commend none but himself, to like no man's
wit but his own, to slight that which he understands not, to lend   6
money and never look for 't again, to take up upon obligation
and lend out upon affection, to owe much but pay little, to sell
land but buy none, to pawn but never to redeem again, to fight
for a whore, to cherish a bawd and defy a tradesman.

MONEYLACKS   And can you observe and keep these rules think   7
you?

HOYDEN   I hope I can, sir, and have begun pretty well already.
You see I have spent and lent all my money, and pawned all my
clothes but these a' my back, as I am a clear gentleman: and, for
the rest of the rudiments, and the several carriages and deport-   8
ments by garb, by congee, compliment et cetera, which are to be
attained by practise when I come abroad and amongst 'em, you
shall gain credit by me.

MONEYLACKS   I commend your confidence. Now, Master Spring

ad unguem: To a hair; perfectly polished.

1 and Master Brittleware, play you the complimentasters before him a little for his further instruction. Imagine, then, a couple of courtiers scarcely acquainted fall to—and look that you congee in the new French bum-trick. Here, landlord, take his cloak and hat to appear more generous.

2 [BRITTLEWARE *takes them from* HOYDEN.]

HOYDEN   Bum-trick?

MONEYLACKS   Come, meet and begin. Play but two or three bouts at most at single rapier compliment, and one or two at backsword
3 and you ha' done. Now, observe, sir [*to* HOYDEN].

HOYDEN   Single rapier and backsword compliment foil?

SPRING   Noble Master Finewit, the single example of court ceremony, if my apprehension deal fairly with me.

BRITTLEWARE   Sir, how auspiciously have I fall'n upon the knowl-
4 edge of you by virtue of the same apprehension.

MONEYLACKS   So, there's one!

Scene Ten
5

[*Enter* GILBERT, WALTER *and* SAMUEL *aside.*]

GILBERT   What's here?

SAMUEL   Peace. Let's see a little more.
6
HOYDEN   As I am a gentleman a neat bout, and fairly come off o' both sides.

SPRING   Sir, I shall ever bless the promptness of my memory in being so fortunate to collect the fallacious acquaintance of so
7 complete a goodness.

HOYDEN   "Sweet sir, I shall ever bless . . ." et cetera. [*He writes in his tables.*]

BRITTLEWARE   Oh, you are pleased out of that noble worth which can convert all things to the form and image of its own perfection
8 to make yourself glorious with that which is miserably impoverished in itself.

MONEYLACKS   Good, there's two!

HOYDEN [*writing*]   "Miserably impoverished in itself."—Oh sweet.

French bum-trick: Dishonest trick.

SPRING Sir, you have such a conquering way in humility that he shall be sure to come off vanquished that offers to contend with you. 1

BRITTLEWARE This is the noblest of all humanity, to piece up the defect of your friend with a glory of your own.

MONEYLACKS A plain hit, that. There were three bouts well played. 2

HOYDEN [*writing*] "Piece up the defect of your friend with a glory of your own." Most stately fine, as I am a gentleman.

MONEYLACKS So much for single rapier, now for your secret swipe at backsword.

HOYDEN Ay, that I would see, like the hackling of the miller's legs. Now for a delicate backblow. 3

SPRING See you yon fellow I held compliment with?

HOYDEN Yes, sir, a well-spoken gentleman and a lovely.

SPRING The arrantest trifle in a kingdom. 4

HOYDEN What? He is not, is he?

SPRING Made only to make physic work; a very lump of laughter.

HOYDEN Ha, ha, ha.

MONEYLACKS You have done well. Now you, sir [*to* BRITTLE-WARE]. 5

BRITTLEWARE Do you note him yonder that passed from you?

HOYDEN That gallant, sir?

BRITTLEWARE The very scorn at court; so empty, not one passable part about him. 6

MONEYLACKS Good.

BRITTLEWARE A very tilting stock for young practisers to break their jests on.

MONEYLACKS Enough. 7

HOYDEN Good and enough! Do you call this good enough, to abuse one another thus?

MONEYLACKS Yes, this is backsword compliment. This wipes off the false praise which the first thrust on. You must be seen in both, or you are no true garbist else. 8

HOYDEN I shall soonest hit o' this, for, from a whelp, I could give scurvy language.

GILBERT Now break in upon 'em. Save you, Sir Hugh!

HOYDEN Oh, coarse salutation: "Save you, Sir Hugh!" 9

1 MONEYLACKS   How got you hither, gentlemen?

WALTER   Here we are, sir, and have seen part of your practise—your courtly exercise.

MONEYLACKS   Peace. But how got you in, and a stranger with ye?

2 GILBERT   He shall betray nothing.

SAMUEL   We found fair entrance into the house.

[GILBERT *and* WALTER *whisper aside with* MONEYLACKS.]

BRITTLEWARE   'S foot, where's my wife then?

3 SAMUEL   If your wife be the gentlewoman o' the house, sir, she's now gone forth in one o' the new hand-litters—what call ye it—a Sedan.

BRITTLEWARE   Oh Sedana. [*Exits*]

4 SPRING   He's run mad with his horns.

HOYDEN   He's run with my hat and cloak, by your leave.

SPRING   He'll come again, ne'er doubt him.

5 HOYDEN   You say so, small acquaintance, but I could ne'er see anything of mine again since I came amongst you if it once got out of my sight. What money have I left, trow? [*Counts his money*]

BRITTLEWARE [*returning*]   I pray, gentlemen, which way took she?

SAMUEL   Down towards the Strand, I tell you, in a new litter, with the number one and twenty in the breech on 't.

6 BRITTLEWARE   A litter of one and twenty in the breech? High time to run! [*Exits*]

GILBERT   You see, we have our plot in action, too, Sir Hugh, and it runs fairly on.

7 MONEYLACKS   But what a rogue art thou to put such a slur upon thine own uncle; first to put him on for thyself, then you, with a counterfeit trick, to put him off o' that course, to run desperately headlong to break his own neck in a match. What a rogue art thou to use thine uncle thus!

8 WALTER   Nay, what a wretch were you, if you should cross your daughter in such a fortune.

MONEYLACKS   Which if I do, cut my windpipe. What, the young rascal Touchwood is gone into France they say.

WALTER   Ay, he's safe enough.

9 MONEYLACKS   Sir Cautious to be catched! If I do not love my

daughter the better for her lucky leg-stretching, I am a villain. I am taken with such kind of roguery.

GILBERT   Take heed you have not a cross-plot in that itching pate of yours to spoil all now.

MONEYLACKS   Then cut my weasand, I say.

GILBERT   And I swear I will, or cut these hands off. I thought good to tell you so because I know what tricks you have done, and what discoveries you have made for small parcels of ready money.

MONEYLACKS   Hoo, pox! I want no money. Now look, there comes Master Hoyden. Salute these gallants.

HOYDEN   What, without a hat or cloak?

MONEYLACKS   The better for a young beginner.

HOYDEN   Sweet sir—I shall ever bless my auspicious stars that shined me into the fallacious acquaintance of so singular goodness.

GILBERT   Sir—you forget yourself.

HOYDEN   Most singular sweet sir, most miserably impoverished in itself.

GILBERT   Good sir, forbear, make not an idol of me.

HOYDEN   You piece up the defect of your friend with a glory of your own.

SAMUEL   Can you say this gentleman was a clown within this fortnight?

HOYDEN   Within this fortnight I assure you, sir, as rank a clown o' one side as ever held cow to bull.

SAMUEL   Had it been o' both sides it had been miraculous.

HOYDEN   Now note me, sir. Do you see that fellow I left?

SAMUEL   Yes, 't is my friend.

HOYDEN   The arrantest coxcomb in a country.

SAMUEL   How, sir?

HOYDEN   Made only to make physic work.

SAMUEL   You do not know him, sure.

HOYDEN   A tilting stock for young practisers to break jests on. There's a wipe for you at backsword compliment!

SAMUEL   There's another for you, sir!

[*Kicks him*]

1 HOYDEN You knock at the wrong door, sir, and I pity your ignorance. Go to school as I have done and learn more wit. Kick a gentleman!

2 ## Scene Eleven

[*Enter* TOM HOYDEN *and* COULTER *to them.*]

COULTER Here he is, and here be all the crew on 'em, and more.

3 TOM Here? Thou mock'st, he is not here. Sure, these be all lords, I think.

WALTER How now, what's he?

SPRING 'S lid, 't is his clown brother he spake of!

4 TOM Is 't possible? Icha made a sweet jaunt after you, and have I vound a vine fool o' thee. Where's thy vour hundred pound? Is that made a vool on too, trow? Where's the zartificate my mother ga' thee to vind thine uncle? Gi' me that, chill zee what I can do wi' it.

HOYDEN Away, clown, I know thee not. Canst thou compliment?

5 TOM Compliment! Yes, I can compliment dagger out o' sheath, an I zet on 't.

COULTER I hope he'll veeze you and make your zilken jacket hum. Well said, Master Thomas, to 'em; and to 'em all I'll zide ye.

6 GILBERT, WALTER, *and* SAMUEL [*together*] Master Thomas does he call him?

7 TOM Yes, Master Thomas; and what zay you to that? As good a master as the best o' ye, and ye go to that, for, by uds shall jidge me, I think you are all but a company of cheaterlings, and if you do not give the vool my brother zartification for the wrongs you ha' done him—and me in him—I'll canvas it out o' the carcasses o' zome o' ye. By uds' dagger's death will I. Draw, Coulter, and among 'em.

MONEYLACKS Hold, sir, you shall have satisfaction.

TOM Oh, shall I zo. Put up again, Coulter.

8 GILBERT This is a stout roaring clown.

MONEYLACKS Where's the master o' the house?

SPRING He's run mad after his wife; now he should look to his house.

9 TOM Cha mich ado to vorbear beating o' thee yet, my vingers do zo itch at thee.

HOYDEN   I understand thee not, as I am a gentleman.   1

TOM   But now I think on 't, Coulter, we'll have all again, and by a quieter way; and teach 'em to lick honey, catch birds with chaff, or go to plow with dogs.

ALL   Ha, ha, ha.

HOYDEN   Ha, ha, ha. Who understands the barbarian, trow?   2

COULTER   Uds' vish, master, they do nothing but jeer to you all this while now.

TOM   Do they jeer? Let 'em jeer and gibe, too. I'll vetch one's warrant shall outjeer 'em all, an he be above ground.   3

MONEYLACKS   You shall not need, sir; go but in till the master of the house comes home, and you shall have your desire.

TOM   You zay very well, sir. Zay well is good, but do well is better. Let's zee what you will do now.

GILBERT   Remember, we have warned you, Sir Hugh. We must leave you.   4

TOM   Nay, I chill look to you. Sirrah, come in my hand.

MONEYLACKS   Now for a trick to rid us of this clown,
   Or our trade sinks, and up our house is blown.   5

[*Exeunt all.*]

ACT FIVE

Scene One

1 [*A room in Touchwood's house. Enter* TRAMPLER *and* TOUCH-
WOOD.]

TRAMPLER   'T is as I tell you, Master Touchwood; your son has
lost a fair fortune in the young gentlewoman, and, as I conceive,
by your wilfulness Sir Arnold Cautious licks his lips at her, I as-
2 sure you. And a sweet lick it is, six thousand pound in present
portion.

TOUCHWOOD   A sweet lick he has indeed, if he knew all.

TRAMPLER   He does know all, sir.

TOUCHWOOD   If he did, I know what I know—good oath, let me
3 not lose thy virtue. [*Aside*]

TRAMPLER   He knows moreover that Master Striker her grandfather has covenanted to give her two thousand pound more at the
birth of his first child lawfully begotten on her body.

TOUCHWOOD   Ha, ha, ha, but what if her first child prove illegiti-
4 mate?

TRAMPLER   That is not to be thought, sir.

TOUCHWOOD   Yes, and spoken, too, if I durst; but good oath let
me not lose thy virtue. [*Aside*]

5 TRAMPLER   And then he had entered into ten-thousand-pound
bond to leave her his heir if she survive him.

TOUCHWOOD   But he's well recovered, you say.

TRAMPLER   Very lusty, very lively, sir.

6 TOUCHWOOD   Then hang him, he'll never die! I am feared I must
be fain to give him over; I shall never vex him to death. No, no, I
shall never do 't.

TRAMPLER   No, sir, I heard himself say that your vexing him has
been his physic and the best means to keep him alive.

7 TOUCHWOOD   Did he say so? I'll tear this match in pieces presently,
and see how that will work on him. I'll do it. What's an oath to
me in respect of sending him to the devil. I'll do 't.

TRAMPLER   I would you could, sir, and recover her for your son
yet.

8 TOUCHWOOD   Umh.

318

TRAMPLER Because I love the young gentleman well. 1

TOUCHWOOD Umh.

TRAMPLER Though I assure you the writings are all passed, signed, sealed and delivered. But I have 'em in my hands yet, and can do you a pleasure.

TOUCHWOOD Humh. 2

TRAMPLER And came purposely to advise you because I love your son.

TOUCHWOOD Umh. What a world of villainy lies in the jobber nowl of a lawyer. 3

TRAMPLER Think of it, sir, and be speedy.

TOUCHWOOD Right learned in the law and my son's friend Master Trampler, Master Ambodexter Trampler, you are a most notorious knave, and you shall hear on 't o' both sides, as you take fees.

TRAMPLER Nay, an you be so hot, Master Touchwood, I am gone. 4
[*Exits*]

TOUCHWOOD I know my course; either I will crack the heartstrings of Striker in crossing this match with the cracked credit of his niece, or else I will be friends with him; and that will kill him outright. But my oath still troubles me.— 5

Scene Two

[*Enter* GILBERT *and* WALTER *to him.*] 6

TOUCHWOOD Oh, gentlemen, you are welcome.

WALTER Ha' you heard, sir, of your son yet?

TOUCHWOOD Not I, he lacks no money yet it seems. Young travellers make no other use of their fathers.

GILBERT But ha' you heard the news of his young mistress? 7

TOUCHWOOD What, of Sir Cautious being catched, the wise and wary gentleman, your uncle, that would not believe there could be a marriageable maid, though she were justified by a jury of midwives, and therefore purposed to have died a bachelor? That he should now be catched with a pipped nutshell, and a maggot in 't! 8

WALTER Sure, he was strangely wrought to 't.

GILBERT Ay, you must think there have been knavish heads used in the business.

TOUCHWOOD But I will cross it and their knaveries, whate'er they are. 9

1 WALTER I hope you will not cross mine uncle in such a fortune
though.

TOUCHWOOD What, to marry a wench?

WALTER No, so much wealth, sir.

2 TOUCHWOOD Pray let me use my Christian liberty, my conscience
pricks me to 't, it must be done. Now, what say you, sir?

[*Enter* SERVANT *who whispers aside with* TOUCHWOOD.]

GILBERT We might ha' spared this labour: he was resolved before
we came, it seems, to spoil the marriage.

3 WALTER We could not be too sure though. We are now sure
enough, that our dissuasions will spur him on the faster.

GILBERT And are we no less sure that Sir Hugh Moneylacks will
set his strength to lift Sir Cautious off o' the hooks, in hope of a
matter of five pound, though he forfeit the obligation of his

4 throat by 't?

WALTER All the danger is that Sir Hugh will be with mine uncle
too soon and prevent the match before he be too deep engaged
in 't.

GILBERT For that, my letter of instructions which I have given

5 Annabel shall prevent him; and Striker keeps Sir Cautious in his
house so warily that, until the intended wedding hour, Sir Hugh
shall not obtain admittance.

[*Exit* SERVANT.]

6 TOUCHWOOD Go fetch 'em in and make the warrant. Ha, ha, ha.
Gentlemen, will you hear a complaint my man tells me of certain
clowns that desire my warrant to apprehend for notorious cheaters—whom do you think?

GILBERT I cannot guess.

7 WALTER I know none, I hope.

TOUCHWOOD Even Sir Hugh Moneylacks, the mourning knight,
and some of his associates.

GILBERT O' my life, it is the roaring clown about the new-made
gentleman his brother.

8

Scene Three

[*Enter* TOM *and* COULTER *to them.*]

9 TOUCHWOOD What, is it you, sir? Master Striker's nephew, as I

take it. You called his great worship uncle lately, as I take it, and did your best to roar me out of his house. 1

TOM   'Z heart Coulter, we be vallen into the baker's ditch.

TOUCHWOOD   And do you bring your complaints to me, sir, ha?

COULTER   Zet a good vace on 't, and vear no cholers though. 2

TOM   I am a honest man, and a true man for all that, and I thought you the vittest to make my complaint to because you were the next Justice, to as pestilence a piece of villainy as ever you were master of in all your life. I come but vor justice, and to pay vor what I take. An' 't be avorehand, here it is. [*Offers money*] Whether it be vor your clerk or yourself who makes or meddles with it, your man has my complaint in writing. Pray let me have your warrant. 3

TOUCHWOOD   You shall, but first, tell me how came it that you called that Striker uncle.

TOM   Vor cause that he is uncle to a vool that I ha' to my brother, and I thought I might be zo bold wi' 'en, and he was not against it at virst till you were gone; and then he bade me go zeek better testimony, and zo I went and vound my brother Tim, his own zuster's zon, I assure you. 4

TOUCHWOOD   His sister's son? 5

TOM   Where he was made such a Tim, as ne'er was heard on in Taunton, amongst a many cheaters. By mass, here are a couple o' 'em!

COULTER   These were o' the crew.

TOUCHWOOD   How, now, my masters? Sure, fellow, thou art mistaken. 6

TOM   No, sir, I am not mistaken, I. But I take 'em, I, where I vind 'em, ay. And I charge your justiceship with 'em, ay, till they bring out my brother, ay.

TOUCHWOOD   Bring out your brother? Why, what has your brother done? 7

TOM   Done? Nay, they have done and undone him amongst 'em; and I think devoured him quick, too, vor he is lost and nowhere to be vound.

TOUCHWOOD   Do you know the meaning of any of this gentlemen? 8

GILBERT   If he were your brother, sir, that you found at Sir Hugh Moneylacks' lodging, you know we left him in your hands.

WALTER   We stepped in but by chance, and such a youth we found there, and we left him in your and their hands that had the managing of him. 9

1 TOM   Zo you did, but what then did me the rest but plied me, and my man Coulter here, with wine and zack; and something in it I dare be zwore that laid us azleep, when we miztrusted nothing but vair play. Oh speak, Coulter, oh!

COULTER   And then, when we were vast azleep, they all gave us
2 the zlip. The knight was gone, and the squire was gone, and Master Tim was gone. But he was made away with, without all peradventure; for all the 'parrel that he wore was left behind. And then —speak, Master.

TOM   And then the master o' the house came home and made a monstrous wonderment for the loss of his wife. He could not vind
3 her, he zaid, and so he vair and vlatly thrust us out o' doors and is gone ahunting after his wife again. Speak, Coulter.

GILBERT   Alas, poor Brittleware.

COULTER   And then we came for your warrant to vind all these
4 men again.

TOM   And to take 'em where we vind 'em, and these were zome on 'em, when time was. And pray look to 'em.

TOUCHWOOD   I know not what to make o' this, but sure there's something in 't. And for these gentlemen, I'll see them forthcom-
5 ing.

WALTER   We thank you, sir.

GILBERT   And I undertake Sir Hugh Moneylacks will be at the bride house.

TOUCHWOOD   And thither will I instantly.
6
GILBERT and WALTER [together]   We'll wait upon you, sir.

TOM   And I chill make bold to wait upon you till I be better zartified.

TOUCHWOOD   You shall, come on your way; come, gentlemen.

7 GILBERT   Well, here is such a knot now to untie,
As would turn Oedipus his brain awry.

[Exeunt all.]

8
Scene Four

[A Street. Enter CURATE and BRITTLEWARE.]

CURATE   Be appeased and comforted, good Master Brittleware.
9   Trouble not your head in running after your fate, nor break your

weighty brains in seeking ways after your wife's heels, which are 1
so light by your own report, they cannot crack an egg.

BRITTLEWARE Her credit yet they may, and mine.

CURATE Besides, your wife is your wife where e'er she is, abroad
as well as at home; yea, lost perhaps as well as found. I am now
going to yoke a heifer to a husband that perhaps will say so 2
shortly.

Scene Five

3

[*Enter* TRAMPLER *to them.*]

CURATE Whither away, Master Trampler?

TRAMPLER To the wedding house, where I think I saw your wife
last night, Master Brittleware. 4

BRITTLEWARE Did you say, sir, did you?

TRAMPLER I cannot say directly, but I think it was she. Does she
not call the gentlewoman aunt that keeps Master Striker's house?

BRITTLEWARE Yes, Mistress Friswood, she is her aunt, sir.

CURATE Come, go with us, and find her. 5

Scene Six

[*Enter the sedan chair with* HOYDEN *in it in woman's clothes.*] 6

BRITTLEWARE Pray, gentlemen, stay, for I suppose she's here.
Here's number one and twenty, and this is sure the litter.

LITTERMAN What peep you for? You ought not to do, sir.

BRITTLEWARE By what commission ought you to carry my wife in 7
a closestool under my nose?

LITTERMAN 'T is a close chair, by your leave. And I pray forbear,
you know not who we carry.

BRITTLEWARE I know the clothes she wears, and I will see the
party. 8

HOYDEN I know that voice, and let me see the man. [*Revealing
himself*] It is my surgeon!

TRAMPLER A surgeon! I took you for a china shopkeeper, Master
Brittleware. These by-trades are for some purposes, and I smell
knavery. 9

1 CURATE And lawyers commonly are the best upon that scent.

BRITTLEWARE Gentlemen, this is a man that lay in my house.

HOYDEN A gentleman you would say, or my cost was ill bestowed there.

2 BRITTLEWARE These are my goods he wears; that was my mother's gown and feloniously he wears it.

HOYDEN 'T is all I have to show for four hundred pound I laid out in your house; and Sir Hugh put it upon me, and hired these men to carry me—whither was it?

3 LITTERMAN Up to a lodging in St. Giles's, sir.

HOYDEN —Where he promised to finish his work of a gentleman in me, and send me to my uncle.

CURATE *O monstrum horrendum*—a man in woman's clothes.

TRAMPLER 'T is felony by the law.

4 BRITTLEWARE Has Sir Hugh gi'en me the slip to finish his work in private? It shall all out, I am resolved though I bewray myself in 't. Pray gentlemen, assist me with this party to Master Justice Striker's. You say my wife is there.

5 TRAMPLER Yes, you shall thither.

BRITTLEWARE And there I'll take a course you shall smell knavery enough.

HOYDEN I find I am abused enough o' conscience; and shall be carried to mine uncle now before my time, and not as a gentle-
6 man but as a gentlewoman, which grieves me worst of all.

CURATE *Hinc illae lachrimae.* The youth is sure abused indeed.

HOYDEN Oh!

TRAMPLER Come, leave your crying. And you beasts, up with your
7 luggage, and along with us! I'll fetch such drivers as shall set you on else.

LITTERMAN Let us be paid for our labour, and we'll carry him to Bridewell, if you please.

HOYDEN Oh, oh, that ever I was borne in this groaning chair.
8
[Exeunt all.]

O monstrum horrendum: "Oh, terrifying monster . . ." the description of the Cyclops in Virgil's *Aeneid.*
Hinc illae lachrimae: "Hence these tears . . ." The Curate now quotes a tag from Terence.

Scene Seven

[*A room in Striker's house. Enter* FRISWOOD *and* REBECCA.]   1

FRISWOOD   It was well I sent for thee, niece, to help me deck the
bride here; and that the jealous fool thy husband thinks thou art
gone astray the while. It will be a means for thee to take thy liberty
another night, and pay him home indeed, when he shall not have
the power to mistrust thee. It is the common condition of cuck-   2
olds to mistrust so much aforehand, that, when they are dubbed
indeed, they have not a glimpse of suspicion left.

REBECCA   Their horns hang i' their light then. But, truly Aunt, for
mine own part, I had rather my husband should be jealous still
than be cured in that right kind, though I confess the ends of all   3
my longings, and the vexations I have put him to
Were but to run jealousy out of breath,
And make him pant under the frivolous weight
He bears; that is, a cuckold in conceit;
Which without doubt he labours with by this time.
And when he finds me clear, 't will be as well   4
(I hope) and better than if it were done
By the broad way of foul pollution.

FRISWOOD   Nay, I do not persuade you take the downright way;
Nothing against your conscience, niece. I sent
For him to ha' come and found you here by chance,   5
But he has shut up house and is run mad
About the town I hear, to all your haunts.

REBECCA   He shall come hither and renounce his jealousy.
And then entreat me, too, before I go.   6

FRISWOOD   Yes, that's a wise wife's part.

                                                                         7

Scene Eight

[*Enter* STRIKER *and* CAUTIOUS *to them.*]

STRIKER   What, 's the bride ready?   8

FRISWOOD   Yes, sir, she's dressed.

1 REBECCA   And dressed, and dressed indeed.
Never was maid so dressed. Oh, sir, you are happy [*to* CAUTIOUS],
The happiest knight, and are now in election
Of the most sweet encounter in a bride
That e'er your chivalry could couch a lance at.

2 CAUTIOUS   I thank you, Mistress, and I'll bring her shortly
To bestow money wi' ye in china wares.

REBECCA   She is herself the purest piece of porc'lain
That e'er had liquid sweetmeats licked out of it.

CAUTIOUS   And purer, too, I hope.

3 STRIKER   Go call her down.

FRISWOOD   She's at her private prayers yet, sir, she.

STRIKER   When she has done, then hasten her away.

4 [*Exeunt* FRISWOOD *and* STRIKER.]

REBECCA   Such brides do seldom make their grooms their prey.
[*Exits*]

STRIKER   Do you now conclude, Sir Arnold, you are happy?

5 CAUTIOUS   As man can be, being so near a wife.

Scene Nine

6 MONEYLACKS [*enters to them*]   By your leave, gentlemen.

STRIKER [*aside*]   He come? I fear a mischief.

7 MONEYLACKS   How comes it father Striker and son Cautious in
election
That you huddle up a match here for my child,
And I not made acquainted, as unworthy,
Until the very intended marriage hour?

STRIKER   Who sent you hither? I sent not for you now, sir.
And there I am wi' ye, sir.

8 MONÉYLACKS   'T is true, I covenanted not to come at you
Until you sent for me, unless you found
Young Touchwood had the love of Annabel.
You have heard he has touched her, has he not?

9 STRIKER   Hold your peace!

MONEYLACKS   Has he not made her Touchwood, too?   1

STRIKER   Can you say so?

MONEYLACKS   Yes, and struck fire, too, in her tinderbox.

STRIKER   You will not speak thus.

MONEYLACKS   To you I need not, for you know 't already;   2
But to my friend Sir Cautious, whom I honour,
And would not see so shipwrecked, I may speak it.

STRIKER   Will you undo your daughter?

MONEYLACKS   My daughter?
No, you shall not put her upon me now,   3
She is your daughter, sir. If I but call her mine,
Or suffer her to ask me a bare blessing,
You'll thrust her out. No, you adopted her
In your own name, and made a Striker of her,
No more a Moneylacks.
                                                              4

STRIKER   The beggarly Knight is desperate,
And should he out with it, my shame were endless.
This is the way or none to stop his mouth;
'T is but a money matter [aside]. Stay a little.

MONEYLACKS   Go not away, Sir Arnold, I must speak wi' ye.   5

CAUTIOUS   I am not going, sir.

STRIKER   Be not a madman, here, here's forty pieces;
I know you used to strike for smaller sums,
But take it for your silence and, withal,
My constant love and my continual friendship.   6

MONEYLACKS   Give me your hand o' that. Enough, Sir Arnold.

CAUTIOUS   What say you to me, Sir Hugh?

STRIKER   What does he mean, trow?
                                                              7
MONEYLACKS   You must not have my daughter.

CAUTIOUS   No, Sir Hugh?

MONEYLACKS   Unless you mean to take another's leavings.

STRIKER   Oh, devilish reprobate.   8

CAUTIOUS   How mean you that?

MONEYLACKS   Till she had buried first another husband,
And he leave her a widow. I am her father
And claim a father's interest in her choice;   9
And I have promised her to one already

1   This very day, because I was not privy
    To your proceedings; and have taken here
    This fair assumpsit, forty pieces, sir.
    You might admire how I should have 'em otherwise.

STRIKER   Here's an impudent villain.

2   MONEYLACKS   For these I give a hundred, if you wed her.

CAUTIOUS   To show my love unto your daughter, sir, I'll pay 't.

MONEYLACKS   Security in hand were good.

CAUTIOUS [*to* STRIKER]   Pray lend me, sir, a hundred pieces.

STRIKER   I dare not cross this devil—I must fetch 'em. [*Exits*]

3

MONEYLACKS   'T will ne'ertheless be my disparagement.

CAUTIOUS   What, when they know her grandfather disposed her,
    That has the care of her and gives her portion?
    And then he can ha' but his money, can he?

4   MONEYLACKS   Oh, but the wench, the wench is such a wench;
    Scarce two such married in a diocese
    In twice two twelve months, for right and straight ones.

CAUTIOUS   There said you well: the straight ones I like well;
    But those that men call right, or good ones, suffer
    By a construction.

5

MONEYLACKS   Amongst the lewd.

Scene Ten

6

STRIKER [*enters with a purse to them*]   Here, sir.

MONEYLACKS   But is here weight
    and number sir?

STRIKER   Now the fiend stretch thee—you may take my word.

7   MONEYLACKS   Here I am wi' ye, sir.

Scene Eleven

8   [*Enter* GILBERT, WALTER, TOUCHWOOD, TOM, *and* SAMUEL.]

GILBERT   Though you are fully bent to cross the marriage,
    Yet let's entreat you not to be too sudden.

TOUCHWOOD   Till they come to the word, for better, for worse,
    I will not touch at it.

9

STRIKER   How now? What mates break in upon us here?

TOUCHWOOD I come not as a guest, sir, or spectator   1
To your great wedding, but o' the King's affairs,
In which I must crave your assistance, sir.
Deny 't me, or my entrance, if you dare.

STRIKER It is some weighty matter sure then.

TOUCHWOOD   So it is, sir,   2
But not to trouble your sconce with too much business,
At once pursue your own; we will attend a while.

CAUTIOUS In that he has said well. I would the bride
And priest were come once. I am content they stand
For witnesses. What, my kind nephew, are you here?   3
I thank you for this plot, you see what 't is come to.

WALTER 'T is not all finished yet, sir.

CAUTIOUS   But it may be
All in good time, the bride is coming now.
You and your brother poet are grown friends, I see.   4

TOUCHWOOD What's he? [*Looking at* SAMUEL]

GILBERT A friend of Wat's he brought for company.

TOM He was amongst 'em too, at the cheating exercise, and yond 's
The knight himself; I know 'em all, I trow.   5

TOUCHWOOD And you'll stand to this, that your lost brother
Was Striker's sister Audrey's son?

TOM I ha' told you twenty times, and yet, because you say you'll
stand my vriend, I'll tell you more. She was with child with Tim
bevore my vather married her (she brought him in her belly from   6
this town where they get children without vear or wit), but vor
her money and 's own credit's zake, my vather was well paid to
keep it vor his own. And nobody knew to the contrary, not Tim
himself, to this hour.

TOUCHWOOD Then how cam'st thou to know it?   7

TOM My vather told it me upon his deathbed, and charged me on
his blessing never to open my mouth to man, woman, nor child,
zo I told nobody but volks on 't.

TOUCHWOOD Well, hold thy peace, 't is an absolute wonder! Now
to the wedding.   8

Scene Twelve

[*Enter* CURATE, TRAMPLER, ANNABEL, FRISWOOD, REBECCA.]

CAUTIOUS How's this? My bride in mourning habit   9

1   And her head in willow!

STRIKER   What's the meaning of it?

REBECCA   I said she was dressed as never bride was dressed.

TOUCHWOOD   A solemn show, and suiting well the scene!
2   She seems round bellied, and you mark it, too.

ANNABEL   My habit and my dressing suits my fortune.

STRIKER [to CURATE]   Pray, sir, do your office, her conceit
We will know afterward.

CURATE   Hem, hem.
3

ANNABEL   Oh, oh. [*Sinks*]

FRISWOOD   Oh me! Why, mistress, look up, look up I say.

REBECCA   Clap her cheek, rub her nose.

4 FRISWOOD   Sprinkle cold water on her face.

REBECCA   Cut her lace, cut her lace, and bow her forward so, so,
so.

TOUCHWOOD   I'll lay my life she quickens now with child.

5 ANNABEL   Oh.

MONEYLACKS   What think you is the matter?

CAUTIOUS   Women, how is it with her?

FRISWOOD   Sir, as with other women in her case.

6 CAUTIOUS   How's that, I pray you?

REBECCA   'T will out, 't will out; you have been doing something
aforehand, sir.

CAUTIOUS   Have I?

7 REBECCA   It seems so by the story.

CAUTIOUS   Is she so dressed?

TOUCHWOOD   Ha, ha, ha.

FRISWOOD   You may leave laughing, it was your son that did it.
8

STRIKER   I am undone, my house disgraced forever.

TOUCHWOOD   He knew 't beforehand, now I may declare 't.
Speak o' thy conscience, didst not?

    willow: A willow garland was worn as a symbol of grief for unre-
quited love or the loss of a mate.

STRIKER   Oh, my heart.   1

TOUCHWOOD   Oh, the hangman.

CAUTIOUS   "Deceit becomes not dying men, you know."
Into a whirlpool of confusion
Sink thou and all thy family, accursed miser.

TOUCHWOOD   This was a sure way now, Sir Cautious,   2
To marry a maid, there's one i' the mother's belly.

STRIKER   Uh, uh, uh, uh.

CAUTIOUS   You knew not where I could be so well fitted.

STRIKER   Uh, uh, uh.   3

CAUTIOUS   A rot o' your dissembling entrails, spit 'em out.
You durst not strain yourself to wind your whistle,
Your doctor told you it would spend your spirits,
So made me whistle for her.

STRIKER   Uh, uh, uh.   4

TOUCHWOOD   Cheer up, cheer up, I may be friends wi' ye now.
Here's one has cause, and knows the way to vex ye,
To preserve life in you as well as I.

STRIKER   Ahem, ahem—I will outlive you both.   5
This day's vexation is enough for a lifetime.

CAUTIOUS   And may it last thee to thy life's last hour.

TOUCHWOOD   Now let me talk wi' ye. And come you hither, sir.

TRAMPLER   I tell you true; your writings are so passed that if you
go   6
Not off by composition, you'll shake your whole estate.

CAUTIOUS   Come hither, nephew.
I'll give thee a thousand pound, and take her off me.

WALTER   I cannot with my reputation now,
But I will do my best to work a friend to 't.   7

CAUTIOUS   Prithee do, try thy poetical soldier.

MONEYLACKS   That clown come hither, too? I fear I am trapped.

TOUCHWOOD   'T is all as I have told you, and without question
The man in question is your sister's son.   8

STRIKER   Would it might prove so that I had yet a nephew,
For now my niece is lost.

TOUCHWOOD   Here's one shall find him out, or stretch a neck
for 't.
Sir Hugh, you are charged for making of a gentleman.   9

1   MONEYLACKS   Now I am in.

TOUCHWOOD   And more than so, for making him away.

MONEYLACKS   What gentleman?

TOM   Marry, my brother Tim.

2   TOUCHWOOD   Your patience yet awhile. Now gentlemen all,
Sir Cautious and the rest, pray hear a story.
I have been often urged to yield the cause
Of the long quarrel 'twixt this man and me:
Thirty years' growth it has. He never durst
Reveal the reason; I, being sullen, would not.

3   STRIKER   You will not tell it now?

TOUCHWOOD   Indeed I will.
He had a sister (peace to her memory)
That in my youth I loved, she me so much
4   That we concluded we were man and wife,
And dreadless of all marriage lets we did
Anticipate the pleasures of the bed.
—Nay, it shall out. Briefly, she proved with child.
This covetous man, then, greedy of her portion
(Of which for the most part he was possessed)
5   Forces her with her shame to leave his house.
She makes her moan to me, I, then (which since
I have with tears a thousand times repented),
Against my heart, stood off in hope to win
Her dowry from him, when she, gentle soul
6   (Whom I must now bewail), when she I say,
Not knowing my reserved intent, from him and me,
From friends and all the world for ought we knew,
Suddenly slipped away. After five years
I took another wife, by whom I had
The son that has done that the woman says:
7   But where I left, if this man's tale be true,
She had a son, whom I demand of you.

TOM   I shall have a kind of an uncle of you anon,
And you prove Tim's vather.

TRAMPLER   The young gentleman that Sir Hugh had in handling is
8   in the house, and Master Brittleware with him.

CURATE   Only we kept 'em back, till our more serious office were
ended.

TOUCHWOOD   Pray 'em in. Let's see him.

9   [*Exit* TRAMPLER.]

GILBERT Sir, will it please you first to see a match quickly clapped 1
up? This gentleman whom I know every way deserving, were
your niece now in her prime of fortune and of virtue, desires to
have her, and she him as much.

TOUCHWOOD He shall not have her.

STRIKER How can you say so? 2

WALTER He knows his son I fear. [*Aside*]

TOUCHWOOD My son shall make his fault good and restore her
honour to her if he lives; in meed for your fair sister's wrong and
my misdeed my son shall marry her; provided he take her in his
conscience unstained by any other man. 3

STRIKER On that condition I'll give her all the worldly good I
have.

SAMUEL *and* ANNABEL [*together*] We take you at your word.

TOUCHWOOD My son! 4

SAMUEL I take her not with all faults, but without any least blemish.

ANNABEL My supposed stains thus I cast from me.

TOM 'Z nails, a cushion! How warm her belly has made it. 5

ANNABEL And that all was a plot 'twixt him and me and these
gentlemen. This paper may resolve you.

SAMUEL 'T is mine own hand by which I instructed her, by a dissembled way to wound her honour.

ANNABEL Which, to preserve my love, again I'd do, 6
Hoping that you forgive it in me, too.

CAUTIOUS Now am I cheated both ways.

WALTER The plot is finished. Now thanks for your thousand
pound, sir. 7

TOUCHWOOD You are mine own, welcome into my bosom [*to*
SAMUEL].

Scene Thirteen 8

[*Enter* HOYDEN, TRAMPLER, BRITTLEWARE *to them.*]

TOM Whoop, who comes here? My brother Tim dressed like Master Mayor's wife of Taunton Dene! 9

1   HOYDEN   'T is all I could get to 'scape with out of the cos'ning house, and all I have to show of four hundred pound, but this certificate and this small jewel which my dying mother ga' me, and I had much ado to hide it from the cheaters, to bring unto mine uncle: which is he?

2   STRIKER   Let's see your token, sir.

TOUCHWOOD   This is a jewel that I gave my Audrey.

HOYDEN   That was my mother.

TOM   And that's your vather he zays.

3   HOYDEN   And a gentleman? What a devilish deal of money might I have saved! For, gentlemen, let me tell you, I have been cosened black and blue, back-gulled and belly-gulled, and have nothing left me but a little bare compliment to live upon, as I am a clear gentleman.

STRIKER   Will you bestow some of it upon me?

4   HOYDEN   Uncle, you shall. First I'll give you a hit at single rapier compliment, and then a wipe or two with the backsword compliment and I ha' done.

STRIKER   Pray begin.

5   HOYDEN   Noble Master Striker, the grave magistrate (if my apprehension deal fairly with me), whose praises reach to heaven for the fair distribution of equal justice, the poor man's sanctuary, the righter of widows' and the orphans' wrongs.

STRIKER   Enough, enough; you have said very well.

6   HOYDEN   Note you yond Justice sits upon the bench?

TOUCHWOOD   Yes, I do note him.

7   HOYDEN   The stocks were fitter for him; the most corrupted fellow about the suburbs, his conscience is stewed in bribes, all his poor neighbours curse him. 'T is thought he keeps a whore now, at threescore.

TOUCHWOOD   A very western soothsayer, thou art my own.

HOYDEN   His niece is much suspected.

8   TOUCHWOOD   Nay, there you went too far. This is his niece, and my daughter now.

HOYDEN   I know no niece he has, I speak but backsword compliment.

STRIKER   You put me well in mind, though. Here's one that, ere

western soothsayer: Here silly, or perhaps merely modern, soothsayer.

the parson and we part, I'll make an honest woman. [*Takes* FRIS- 1
WOOD]

TOUCHWOOD   And for your part, Sir Hugh, you shall make satisfaction and bring in your confederates.

HOYDEN   Here's one that came to complain of me for my robes
here, but I ha' lost my small acquaintance.   2

MONEYLACKS   I'll answer for him, too, and give you all the satisfaction that I can.

TOUCHWOOD   What you cannot shall be remitted; we have all our
faults.

BRITTLEWARE   And have I found thee, Beck, in so good company?   3

REBECCA   Ay, Jack. Be you jealous no more, and I will long no
more to vex thee.

FRISWOOD   Live lovingly and honestly, I charge you,
Or come not at me when I am married.   4

TOUCHWOOD   This younker I'll take care for,
And make him a new gentleman by new breeding,
Without the diet, bathing, purge or bleeding.

HOYDEN   Sweet sir, I thank you.

TOM   I'll home again then and make Taunton ring on 't.   5

STRIKER   Our quarrel in this piece of folly ends.

TOUCHWOOD   He parted us, and he has made us friends.

CAUTIOUS   Nephew and gentlemen, I am friends with all.
You had your plot upon me; I had mine.   6

STRIKER   Let's in, and end all differences in wine.

EPILOGUE

At first we made no boast, and still we fear
We have not answered expectation here.
Yet give us leave to hope, as hope to live,
That you will grace as well as justice give.
We do not dare your judgments now, for we
Know lookers-on more than the gamesters see;
And whate'er poets write, we act, or say,
'T is only in your hands to crown a play.

THE END

The Lady
of Pleasure

(*1637*)

INTRODUCTION

James Shirley was born in 1596 and educated at both Oxford and Cambridge, where he published some verse. He was ordained, but resigned his living at St. Alban's in Hertfordshire when he became converted to the Church of Rome. After a few years as master of the Grammar School at St. Albans his first comedy *Love's Tricks* was acted in London in 1625. He then decided to move to the capital and set up as a "play-maker," becoming a popular figure among his fellow-playwrights and in Court circles. King Charles is said to have suggested, through the agency of his Master of the Revels Sir Henry Herbert, the plot of *The Gamester,* acted in 1633. The story is in fact taken from the *Heptameron* of Margaret of Navarre.

Shirley's romantic comedy is descended from the line of Shakespeare and John Fletcher, and his fluent verse still retains echoes of the grace and rich allusiveness of these poets. Like them, Shirley uses frequent allusions to Ovid and the name of George Chapman appears with Shirley's on the title page of *The Ball,* licenced in 1632, but, in comparison with that of any of the older names, Shirley's style is rarefied and attenuated. It encompasses a very narrow emotional range, but can rise on occasion to a considerable intensity of expression. Personal relationships are discussed in the language of accountancy, and analogies drawn from hunting and warfare surround the pursuit of love.

Just as the poetry is narrow in its effects, so the world portrayed in *The Lady of Pleasure*—Shirley's most comprehensive picture of London society—is confined to the manners of its upper class characters. We are introduced to an exclusive and essentially private clique, graceful, witty and often sparkling. If the major theme of the comedy is ostensibly a gentle satire on the folly of Lady Bornwell's conspicuous display and modish extravagance, this is not what really impresses us about the play. Rather we are struck by the way in which Shirley has anticipated the Comedy of Manners of a later theatrical age. The anxieties that underlie fashionable life, the irreligion, the

loss of moderation and that exemplary hospitality which char-
acterised the country life from which Lady Bornwell has fled
are scarcely more than hinted at. What breaks the glassy surface of this comedy of high life is not her husband's plot to cure
her extravagance so much as the threat to her honour and the
injury to her vanity into which her lack of prudence has led her.
At the moment of realisation Shirley has no language with
which to express Lady Bornwell's response. He must resort to
a visual device—the looking glass which tells her all and us
little. No Elizabethan dramatist could have passed up such an
occasion for self-revelation, but Shirley's language is, like his
society, a display, an artful and complimentary mirror to his
fashionable audience.

Shirley's death punctuates the destruction of the London
revealed in these plays. After several days' exposure to the
effects of the Great Fire of 1666 he suffered shock, from which
he died very shortly.

The Lady of Pleasure was licenced in October 1635 and first
printed in 1637.

CHARACTERS

SIR THOMAS BORNWELL

LORD A

SIR WILLIAM SCENTLOVE

MASTER ALEXANDER KICKSHAW } gallants

MASTER JOHN LITTLEWORTH

HAIRCUT, a barber

MASTER FREDERICK, nephew to Lady Bornwell

STEWARD to Sir Thomas Bornwell

STEWARD to Celestina

SECRETARY to Lord A

SERVANTS

LADY [ARETINA] BORNWELL, wife of Sir Thomas

CELESTINA [BELLAMOUR], a young widow

ISABELLA
friends of Celestina
MARIANA

DECOY, a procuress

GENTLEWOMEN

SCENE: The Strand, London

ACT ONE

Scene One

[*A room in Sir Thomas Bornwell's house. Enter* LADY BORNWELL *and* STEWARD.]

STEWARD   Be patient, madam; you may have your pleasure.

LADY BORNWELL   'T is that I came to town for. I would not
Endure again the country conversation,
To be the lady of six shires! The men,
So near the primitive making, they retain
A sense of nothing but the earth; their brains,
And barren heads standing as much in want
Of ploughing as their ground. To hear a fellow
Make himself merry and his horse, with whistling
Sellinger's Round! To observe with what solemnity
They keep their wakes, and throw for pewter candlesticks!
How they become the morris, with whose bells
They ring all in to Whitsun-ales; and sweat,
Through twenty scarfs and napkins, till the hobbyhorse
Tire, and the Maid Marian, dissolved to a jelly,
Be kept for spoon meat!

STEWARD   These, with your pardon, are no argument
To make the country life appear so hateful;
At least to your particular, who enjoyed
A blessing in that calm, would you be pleased
To think so, and the pleasure of a kingdom;
While your own will commanded what should move
Delights, your husband's love and power joined
To give your life more harmony. You lived there
Secure, and innocent, beloved of all;
Praised for your hospitality, and prayed for:
You might be envièd; but malice knew
Not where you dwelt. I would not prophesy,
But leave to your own apprehension,
What may succeed your change.

LADY BORNWELL   You do imagine,
No doubt, you have talked wisely, and confuted
London past all defence. Your master should

Sellinger's Round: A country dance tune.
wakes: Feasts, like the country Whitsun fairs where the Morris Men danced.

343

1   Do well to send you back into the country,
       With title of superintendent bailiff.

STEWARD   How, madam!

LADY BORNWELL   Even so, sir.

2   STEWARD   I am a gentleman,
       Though now your servant.

LADY BORNWELL   A country gentleman,
       By your affection to converse with stubble.
       His tenants will advance your wit, and plump it so
       With beef and bag pudding!

3   STEWARD   You may say your pleasure,
       It becomes not me dispute.

LADY BORNWELL   Complain to
       The lord of the soil, your master.

4   STEWARD   You're a woman
       Of an ungoverned passion, and I pity you.

SIR THOMAS BORNWELL [*enters*]   How now? What's the matter?

STEWARD   Nothing, sir. [*Exits*]

5   BORNWELL   Angry, sweetheart?

LADY BORNWELL   I am angry with myself,
       To be so miserably restrained in things,
       Wherein it doth concern your love and honour
       To see me satisfied.

6   BORNWELL   In what, Aretina,
       Dost thou accuse me? Have I not obeyed
       All thy desires? against mine own opinion
       Quitted the country, and removed the hope
       Of our return, by sale of that fair lordship
       We lived in? changed a calm and retired life
7   For this wild town, composed of noise and charge?

LADY BORNWELL   What charge, more than is necessary for
       A lady of my birth and education?

BORNWELL   I am not ignorant how much nobility
8   Flows in your blood; your kinsmen great and powerful
       I' the state; but with this, lose not you memory
       Of being my wife. I shall be studious,
       Madam, to give the dignity of your birth
       All the best ornaments which become my fortune;
       But would not flatter it, to ruin both,
9   And be the fable of the town, to teach

Other men loss of wit by mine, employed   1
To serve your vast expenses.

LADY BORNWELL   Am I then
Brought in the balance? So, sir!

BORNWELL   Though you weigh   2
Me in a partial scale, my heart is honest,
And must take liberty to think you have
Obeyed no modest counsel, to affect,
Nay, study ways of pride and costly ceremony:
Your change of gaudy furniture, and pictures
Of this Italian master, and that Dutchman;   3
Your mighty looking glasses, like artillery,
Brought home on engines; the superfluous plate,
Antique and novel; vanities of tires;
Fourscore-pound suppers for my lord, your kinsman,
Banquets for t' other lady aunt, and cousins,
And perfumes that exceed all: train of servants,   4
To stifle us at home, and show abroad
More motley than the French or the Venetian,
About your coach, whose rude postillion
Must pester every narrow lane, till passengers
And tradesmen curse your choking up their stalls;   5
And common cries pursue your ladyship,
For hindering of their market.

LADY BORNWELL   Have you done, sir?

BORNWELL   I could accuse the gaiety of your wardrobe,
And prodigal embroideries, under which   6
Rich satins, plushes, cloth of silver, dare
Not show their own complexions; your jewels,
Able to burn out the spectators' eyes,
And show like bonfires on you by the tapers:
Something might here be spared, with safety of
Your birth and honour, since the truest wealth   7
Shines from the soul, and draws up just admirers.—
I could urge something more.

LADY BORNWELL   Pray do, I like
Your homily of thrift.

BORNWELL   I could wish, madam,   8
You would not game so much.

LADY BORNWELL   A gamester too!

BORNWELL   But are not come to that acquaintance yet,
Should teach you skill enough to raise your profit.   9

1   You look not through the subtlety of cards,
And mysteries of dice; nor can you save
Charge with the box, buy petticoats and pearls,
And keep your family by the precious income;
Nor do I wish you should: my poorest servant
2   Shall not upbraid my tables, nor his hire,
Purchased beneath my honour. You make play
Not a pastime but a tyranny, and vex
Yourself and my estate by it.

LADY BORNWELL   Good! Proceed.

3 BORNWELL   Another game you have, which consumes more
Your fame than purse; your revels in the night,
Your meetings called the Ball, to which repair,
As to the court of pleasure, all your gallants,
And ladies, thither bound by a subpoena
Of Venus, and small Cupid's high displeasure;
4   'T is but the Family of Love translated
Into more costly sin! There was a play on 't,
And had the poet not been bribed to a modest
Expression of your antic gambols in 't,
Some darks had been discovered, and the deeds, too,
5   In time he may repent, and make some blush,
To see the second part danced on the stage.
My thoughts acquit you for dishonouring me
By any foul act; but the virtuous know,
'T is not enough to clear ourselves, but the
Suspicions of our shame.

6 LADY BORNWELL   Have you concluded
Your lecture?

BORNWELL   I have done; and howsoever
My language may appear to you, it carries
No other than my fair and just intent
7   To your delights, without curb to their modest,
And noble freedom.

LADY BORNWELL   I'll not be so tedious
In my reply; but, without art or elegance,

---

the box: Here, the dice box.
the Ball: A reference to Shirley's play of this name. The purity of the
entertainment at the Ball is symbolised in a Masque where Diana puts
Venus to flight, but will allow Cupid to remain only if he will throw
away his darts.
Family of Love: See note to *Eastward Ho,* Act V, Sc. ii.

Assure you, I keep still my first opinion: 1
And though you veil your avaricious meaning
With handsome names of modesty and thrift,
I find you would intrench and wound the liberty
I was born with. Were my desires unprivileged
By example, while my judgment thought 'em fit,
You ought not to oppose; but when the practise   2
And track of every honourable lady
Authorise me, I take it great injustice
To have my pleasures circumscribed, and taught me.
A narrow-minded husband is a thief
To his own fame, and his preferment, too;   3
He shuts his parts and fortunes from the world,
While, from the popular vote and knowledge, men
Rise to employment in the state.

BORNWELL   I have
No great ambition to buy preferment at
So dear a rate.   4

LADY BORNWELL   Nor I to sell my honour,
By living poor and sparingly; I was not
Bred in that ebb of fortune, and my fate
Shall not compel me to it.
                                                                              5
BORNWELL   I know not,
Madam; but you pursue these ways—

LADY BORNWELL   What ways?

BORNWELL   In the strict sense of honesty, I dare
Make oath they are innocent.   6

LADY BORNWELL   Do not divert,
By busy troubling of your brain, those thoughts
That should preserve 'em.

BORNWELL   How was that?
                                                                              7
LADY BORNWELL   'T is English.

BORNWELL   But carries some unkind sense.

DECOY [enters]   Good morrow, my sweet madam.

LADY BORNWELL   Decoy! welcome;
This visit is a favour.   8

DECOY   Alas, sweet madam,
I cannot stay; I came but to present
My service to your ladyship; I could not
Pass by your door, but I must take the boldness
To tender my respects.   9

1 LADY BORNWELL   You oblige me, madam;
But I must not dispense so with your absence.

DECOY   Alas, the coach, madam, stays for me at the door.

LADY BORNWELL   Thou shalt command mine; prithee, sweet
2   Decoy—

DECOY   I would wait on you, madam, but I have many
Visits to make this morning; I beseech—

LADY BORNWELL   So you will promise to dine with me.

DECOY   I shall
3   Present a guest.

LADY BORNWELL   Why, then good morrow, madam.

DECOY   A happy day shine on your ladyship! [Exits]

[Reenter STEWARD.]

4
LADY BORNWELL   What's your news, sir?

STEWARD   Madam, two gentlemen.

LADY BORNWELL   What gentlemen? Have they no names?

STEWARD   They are,
5   The gentleman with his own head of hair,
Whom you commended for his horsemanship
In Hyde Park, and becoming so the saddle,
The t' other day.

LADY BORNWELL   What circumstance is this
6   To know him by?

STEWARD   His name's at my tongue's end:—
He liked the fashion of your pearl chain, madam;
And borrowed it for his jeweller to take
A copy by it.

7 BORNWELL   What cheating gallant's this? [Aside]

STEWARD   That never walks without a lady's busk,
And plays with fans—Master Alexander Kickshaw,—
I thought I should remember him.

LADY BORNWELL   What's the other?

8
STEWARD   What an unlucky memory I have!
The gallant that still danceth in the street,
And wears a gross of ribbon in his hat;
That carries oringado in his pocket,
And sugarplums, to sweeten his discourse;
9   That studies compliment, defies all wit

In black, and censures plays that are not bawdy— 1
Master John Littleworth.

LADY BORNWELL   They are welcome; but
Pray entertain them a small time, lest I
Be unprovided.

BORNWELL   Did they ask for me? 2

STEWARD   No, sir.

BORNWELL   It matters not, they must be welcome.

LADY BORNWELL   Fie! how's this hair disordered? Here's a curl
Straddles most impiously. I must to my closet. [*Exits*] 3

BORNWELL   Wait on 'em; my lady will return again.

[*Exit* STEWARD.]

I have to such a height fulfilled her humour,
All application's dangerous; these gallants 4
Must be received, or she will fall into
A tempest, and the house be shook with names
Of all her kindred. 'T is a servitude
I may in time shake off.

KICKSHAW *and* LITTLEWORTH [*enter*]   Save you, Sir Thomas! 5

BORNWELL   Save you, gentlemen!

KICKSHAW   I kiss your hand.

BORNWELL   What day is it abroad?

LITTLEWORTH   The morning rises from your lady's eye: 6
If she look clear, we take the happy omen
Of a fair day.

BORNWELL   She'll instantly appear,
To the discredit of your compliment;
But you express your wit thus. 7

KICKSHAW   And you modesty,
Not to affect the praises of your own.

BORNWELL   Leaving this subject, what game's now on foot?
What exercise carries the general vote
O' the town, now? Nothing moves without your knowledge. 8

KICKSHAW   The cocking now has all the noise; I'll have
A hundred pieces on one battle.—Oh,
These birds of Mars!

LITTLEWORTH   Venus is Mars' bird, too.
9

1 KICKSHAW   Why, and the pretty doves are Venus's,
To show that kisses draw the chariot.

LITTLEWORTH   I am for that skirmish.

BORNWELL   When shall we have
More booths and bagpipes upon Banstead downs?
2 No mighty race is expected?—But my lady
Returns!

LADY BORNWELL [reenters]   Fair morning to you, gentlemen!
You went not late to bed by your early visit.
You do me honour.

3 KICKSHAW   It becomes our service.

LADY BORNWELL   What news abroad? You hold precious intelligence.

LITTLEWORTH   All tongues are so much busy with your praise,
They have not time to frame other discourse.
4 Will 't please you, madam, taste a sugarplum?

BORNWELL   What does the goldsmith think the pearl is worth
You borrowed of my lady?

KICKSHAW   'T is a rich one.

BORNWELL   She has many other toys, whose fashion you
5 Will like extremely: you have no intention
To buy any of her jewels?

KICKSHAW   Understand me—

BORNWELL   You had rather sell, perhaps. But leaving this.
I hope you'll dine with us.
6 KICKSHAW   I came o' purpose.

LADY BORNWELL   And where were you last night?

KICKSHAW   I, madam? Where
I slept not; it had been sin, where so much
Delight and beauty was to keep me waking.
7 There is a lady, madam, will be worth
Your free society; my conversation
Ne'er knew so elegant and brave a soul,
With most incomparable flesh and blood;
So spirited! so courtly! Speaks the languages,
Sings, dances, plays o' the lute to admiration!
8 Is fair, and paints not; games too, keeps a table,
And talks most witty satire; has a wit
Of a clean Mercury—

Mercury: The messenger and herald of the Gods, regarded as the patron of travellers, merchants and rogues.

LITTLEWORTH Is she married?　　　　　　　　　　　　　　1

KICKSHAW No.

LADY BORNWELL A virgin?

KICKSHAW Neither.

LITTLEWORTH What! a widow! Something　　　　　　　2
Of this wide commendation might have been
Excused. This such a prodigy!

KICKSHAW Repent,
Before I name her: she did never see
Yet full sixteen, an age, in the opinion　　　　　　　　3
Of wise men, not contemptible. She has
Mourned out her year, too, for the honest knight
That had compassion of her youth, and died
So timely. Such a widow is not common;
And now she shines more fresh and tempting
Than any natural virgin.　　　　　　　　　　　　　4

LADY BORNWELL What's her name?

KICKSHAW She was christened Celestina; by her husband,
The Lady Bellamour: this ring was hers.

BORNWELL You borrowed it to copy out the posy.　　　5

KICKSHAW Are they not pretty rubies? 'T was a grace
She was pleased to show me, that I might have one
Made of the self-same fashion; for I love
All pretty forms.

LADY BORNWELL And is she glorious?　　　　　　　6

KICKSHAW She is full of jewels, madam; but I am
Most taken with the bravery of her mind,
Although her garments have all grace and ornament.

LADY BORNWELL You have been high in praises.

KICKSHAW I come short;　　　　　　　　　　　　7
No flattery can reach her.

BORNWELL Now my lady
Is troubled, as she feared to be eclipsed:
This news will cost me somewhat. [Aside]

LADY BORNWELL You deserve　　　　　　　　　　8
Her favour, for this noble character.

KICKSHAW And I possess it, by my stars' benevolence.

LADY BORNWELL You must bring us acquainted.

BORNWELL I pray do, sir;
I long to see her, too.—Madam, I have　　　　　　9

1   Thought upon 't, and corrected my opinion.
Pursue what ways of pleasure your desires
Incline you to, not only with my state,
But with my person; I will follow you:
I see the folly of my thrift, and will
Repent in sack and prodigality,
2   To your own heart's content.

LADY BORNWELL   But do not mock.

BORNWELL   Take me to your embraces, gentlemen,
And tutor me.

3   LITTLEWORTH   And will you kiss the ladies?

BORNWELL   And sing and dance. I long to see this beauty;
I would fain lose a hundred pounds at dice now.—
Thou shalt have another gown and petticoat
Tomorrow;—will you sell me running horses?
4   We have no Greek wine in the house, I think;
Pray send one of our footmen to the merchant,
And throw the hogsheads of March beer into
The kennel, to make room for sack and claret.
What think you to be drunk yet before dinner?
We will have constant music, and maintain
5   Them and their fiddles in fantastic liveries:
I'll tune my voice to catches.—I must have
My dining room enlarged, to invite ambassadors;
We'll feast the parish in the fields, and teach
The military men new discipline,
Who shall charge all their great artillery
6   With oranges and lemons, boy, to play
All dinner upon our capons.

KICKSHAW   He's exalted!

BORNWELL   I will do anything to please my lady,
7   Let that suffice; and kiss o' the same condition.
I am converted; do not you dispute,
But patiently allow the miracle.

LADY BORNWELL   I am glad to hear you, sir, in so good tune.

SERVANT [*enters*]   Madam, the painter.

8   LADY BORNWELL   I am to sit this morning.

BORNWELL   Do,
While I give new directions to my steward.

KICKSHAW   With your favour, we'll wait on you.
Sitting's but a melancholy exercise without

March beer: A strong ale, brewed in March.

Some company to discourse.   1

LADY BORNWELL   It does conclude
A lady's morning work. We rise, make fine,
Sit for our picture, and 't is time to dine.

LITTLEWORTH   Praying's forgot.

KICKSHAW   'T is out of fashion.   2

[*Exeunt*]

                                                              3

Scene Two

[*A room in Celestina's house. Enter* CELESTINA *and her* STEWARD.]

CELESTINA   Fie! What an air this room has!   4

STEWARD   'T is perfumed.

CELESTINA   With some cheap stuff. Is it your wisdom's thrift
To infect my nostrils thus? Or is 't to favour
The gout in your worship's hand, you are afraid
To exercise your pen in your account book?   5
Or do you doubt my credit to discharge
Your bills?

STEWARD   Madam, I hope you have not found
My duty, with the guilt of sloth or jealousy,
Unapt to your command.   6

CELESTINA   You can extenuate
Your faults with language, sir, but I expect
To be obeyed. What hangings have we here!

STEWARD   They are arras, madam.
                                                              7
CELESTINA   Impudence! I know 't.
I will have fresher, and more rich; not wrought
With faces that may scandalise a Christian,
With Jewish stories stuffed with corn and camels.
You had best wrap all my chambers in wild Irish,
And make a nursery of monsters here,   8
To fright the ladies come to visit me.

Jewish stories: Clearly, an arras depicting the story of Joseph and his
brothers.
wild Irish: That is, coarse Irish linen.

1   STEWARD   Madam, I hope—

    CELESTINA   I say I will have other,
    Good Master Steward, of a finer loom;
    Some silk and silver, if your worship please
    To let me be at so much cost. I'll have
2   Stories to fit the seasons of the year,
    And change as often as I please.

    STEWARD   You shall, madam.

    CELESTINA   I am bound to your consent, forsooth! And is
    My coach brought home?

3   STEWARD   This morning I expect it.

    CELESTINA   The inside, as I gave directions,
    Of crimson plush?

    STEWARD   Of crimson camel plush.

    CELESTINA   Ten thousand moths consume 't! Shall I ride through
4   The streets in penance, wrapt up round in hair cloth?
    Sell 't to an alderman, 't will serve his wife
    To go a feasting to their country house;
    Or fetch a merchant's nurse-child, and come home
    Laden with fruit and cheesecakes. I despise it!

5   STEWARD   The nails adorn it, madam, set in method,
    And pretty forms.

    CELESTINA   But single gilt, I warrant.

    STEWARD   No, madam.

    CELESTINA   Another solecism! Oh fie!
6   This fellow will bring me to a consumption
    With fretting at his ignorance. Some lady
    Had rather never pray, than go to church in 't.
    The nails not double gilt! To market with 't;
    'T will hackney out to Mile End, or convey
7   Your city tumblers, to be drunk with cream
    And prunes at Islington.

    STEWARD   Good madam, hear me.

    CELESTINA   I'll rather be beholding to my aunt
    The countess, for her mourning coach, than be
8   Disparaged so. Shall any juggling tradesman
    Be at charge to shoe his running horse with gold,
    And shall my coach nails be but single gilt!
    How dare these knaves abuse me so?

shoe his running horse with gold: Such a horse "Toby with his golden
shoes" is mentioned in Shirley's *Hyde Park*, Act IV, Sc. iii.

STEWARD   Vouchsafe   1
To hear me speak.

CELESTINA   Is my sedan yet finished,
And liveries for my men-mules, according
As I gave charge?

STEWARD   Yes, madam, it is finished,   2
But without tilting plumes at the four corners;
The scarlet's pure, but not embroidered.

CELESTINA   What mischief were it to your conscience
Were my coach lined with tissue, and my harness
Covered with needlework? If my sedan   3
Had all the story of the prodigal
Embroidered with pearl?

STEWARD   Alas, good madam,
I know 't is your own cost; I am but your steward,
And would discharge my duty the best way.
You have been pleased to hear me; 't is not for   4
My profit that I manage your estate,
And save expense, but for your honour, madam.

CELESTINA   How, sir! My honour?

STEWARD   Though you hear it not,   5
Men's tongues are liberal in your character,
Since you began to live thus high. I know
Your fame is precious to you.

CELESTINA   I were best
Make you my governor: audacious varlet!   6
How dare you interpose your doting counsel!
Mind your affairs with more obedience,
Or I shall ease you of an offence, sir.
Must I be limited to please your honour,
Or, for the vulgar breath, confine my pleasures?
I will pursue 'em in what shapes I fancy,   7
Here, and abroad; my entertainments shall
Be oftener, and more rich. Who shall control me?
I live i' the Strand, whither few ladies come
To live, and purchase, more than fame. I will
Be hospitable then, and spare no cost
That may engage all generous report   8
To trumpet forth my bounty and my bravery,
Till the court envy, and remove. I'll have
My house the academy of wits, who shall
Exalt their genius with rich sack and sturgeon,
Write panegyrics of my feasts, and praise   9

1   The method of my witty superfluities.
The horses shall be taught, with frequent waiting
Upon my gates, to stop in their career
Toward Charing Cross, spite of the coachman's fury;
And not a tilter but shall strike his plume,
2   When he sails by my window; my balcony
Shall be the courtier's idol, and more gazed at
Than all the pageantry at Temple Bar,
By country clients.

STEWARD   Sure my lady's mad.

3   CELESTINA   Take that for your ill manners.

[*Strikes him.*]

STEWARD   Thank you, madam.—
I would there were less quicksilver in your fingers. [*Exits*]

4   CELESTINA   There's more than simple honesty in a servant
Required to his full duty; none should dare
But with a look, much less a saucy language,
Check at their mistress' pleasure. I'm resolved
To pay for some delight, my estate will bear it;
I'll rein it shorter when I please.

5   STEWARD [*reenters*]   A gentleman
Desires to speak with your ladyship.

CELESTINA   His name?

STEWARD   He says you know him not; he seems to be
Of quality.

6   CELESTINA   Admit him.

[*Exit* STEWARD. *Enter* HAIRCUT.]

Sir, with me?

7   HAIRCUT   Madam, I know not how you may receive
This boldness from me; but my fair intents
Known, will incline you to be charitable.

CELESTINA   No doubt, sir.

HAIRCUT   He must live obscurely, madam,
8   That hath not heard what virtues you possess;
And I, a poor admirer of your fame,
Am come to kiss your hand.

CELESTINA   That all your business?

HAIRCUT   Though it were worth much travel, I have more
9   In my ambition.

CELESTINA Speak it freely, sir.   1

HAIRCUT You are a widow.

CELESTINA So!

HAIRCUT And I a bachelor.

CELESTINA You come a-wooing, sir, and would perhaps   2
Show me a way to reconcile the two?

HAIRCUT And bless my stars for such a happiness.

CELESTINA I like you, sir, the better, that you do not
Wander about, but shoot home to the meaning;
It is a confidence will make a man   3
Know sooner what to trust to: but I never
Saw you before, and I believe you come not
With hope to find me desperate upon marriage.
If maids, out of their ignorance of what
Men are, refuse these offers, widows may,
Out of their knowledge, be allowed some coyness: 4
And yet I know not how much happiness
A peremptory answer may deprive me of;—
You may be some young lord, and though I see not
Your footmen and your groom, they may not be
Far off, in conference with your horse. Please you   5
To instruct me with your title, against which
I would not willingly offend.

HAIRCUT I am
A gentleman; my name is Haircut, madam.

CELESTINA Sweet Master Haircut! Are you a courtier?   6

HAIRCUT Yes.

CELESTINA I did think so, by your confidence.
Not to detain you, sir, with circumstance,
I was not so unhappy in my husband,
But that 't is possible I may be a wife   7
Again; but I must tell you, he that wins
My affection, shall deserve me.

HAIRCUT I will hope,
If you can love, I shall not present, madam,
An object to displease you in my person: 8
And when time, and your patience, shall possess you
With further knowledge of me, and the truth
Of my devotion, you will not repent
The offer of my service.

CELESTINA You say well.   9

1   How long do you imagine you can love, sir?
     Is it a quotidian, or will it hold
     But every other day?

HAIRCUT   You are pleasant, madam.

CELESTINA   Does it take you with a burning at the first,
2   Or with a cold fit? for you gentlemen
     Have both your summer and your winter service.

HAIRCUT   I am ignorant what you mean, but I shall never
     Be cold in my affection to such beauty.

CELESTINA   And 't will be somewhat long ere I be warm in 't.
3

HAIRCUT   If you vouchsafe me so much honour, madam,
     That I may wait on you sometimes, I shall not
     Despair to see a change.

CELESTINA   But, now I know
4   Your mind, you shall not need to tell it when
     You come again; I shall remember it.

HAIRCUT   You make me fortunate.

STEWARD [reenters]   Madam, your kinswomen,
     The Lady Novice, and her sister, are
5   New lighted from their coach.

CELESTINA   I did expect 'em.
     They partly are my pupils. I'll attend them.

[Exit STEWARD.]

6   HAIRCUT   Madam, I have been too great a trespasser
     Upon your patience; I will take my leave:
     You have affairs, and I have some employment
     Calls me to court; I shall present again
     A servant to you. [Exits]

7   CELESTINA   Sir, you may present,
     But not give fire, I hope.—Now to the ladies.
     This recreation's past, the next must be
     To read to them some court philosophy. [Exits]

ACT TWO

Scene One

[*A room in Sir Thomas Bornwell's house. Enter* SIR THOMAS BORN- 1
WELL.]

BORNWELL 'T is a strange humour I have undertaken,
   To dance, and play, and spend as fast as she does;
   But I am resolved: it may do good upon her
   And fright her into thrift. Nay, I'll endeavour 2
   To make her jealous, too; if this do not
   Allay her gamboling, she's past a woman,
   And only a miracle must tame her.

STEWARD [*enters*] 'T is master Frederick, my lady's nephew.

BORNWELL What of him? 3

STEWARD Is come from the university.

BORNWELL By whose directions?

STEWARD It seems, my lady's.

BORNWELL Let me speak with him 4
   Before he sees his aunt.

[*Exit* STEWARD.]

   I do not like it.

   5

[*Reenter* STEWARD, *with* FREDERICK, *in his college dress.*]

   Master Frederick, welcome! I expected not
   So soon your presence; what's the hasty cause?

FREDERICK These letters, from my tutor, will acquaint you. 6

[*Gives* BORNWELL *letters.*]

STEWARD Welcome home, sweet Master Frederick!

FREDERICK Where's my aunt?

STEWARD She's busy about her painting, in her closet; 7
   The outlandish man of art is copying out
   Her countenance.

FREDERICK She is sitting for her picture?

   outlandish: Here, meaning both foreign and bizarre.

359

1   STEWARD   Yes, sir; and when 't is drawn she will be hanged
      Next the French cardinal, in the dining room.
      But when she hears you are come, she will dismiss
      The Belgic gentleman, to entertain
      Your worship.

2   FREDERICK   Change of air has made you witty.

      BORNWELL   Your tutor gives you a handsome character,
      Frederick, and is sorry your aunt's pleasure
      Commands you from your studies; but I hope
      You have no quarrel to the liberal arts:
3   Learning is an addition beyond
      Nobility of birth. Honour of blood,
      Without the ornament of knowledge, is
      A glorious ignorance.

      FREDERICK   I never knew
      More sweet and happy hours than I employed
4   Upon my books. I heard
      A part of my philosophy, and was so
      Delighted with the harmony of nature,
      I could have wasted my whole life upon it.

      BORNWELL   'T is pity a rash indulgence should corrupt
5   So fair a genius! She's here; I'll observe. [Aside]

      [Enter LADY BORNWELL, KICKSHAW, and LITTLEWORTH.]

      FREDERICK   My most loved aunt!

6   LADY BORNWELL   Support me, I shall faint.

      LITTLEWORTH   What ails your ladyship?

      LADY BORNWELL   Is that Frederick,
      In black?

      KICKSHAW   Yes, madam; but the doublet's satin.
7
      LADY BORNWELL   The boy's undone!

      FREDERICK   Madam, you appear troubled.

      LADY BORNWELL   Have I not cause? Was not I trusted with
      Thy education, boy, and have they sent thee
8   Home like a very scholar!

      KICKSHAW   'T was ill done,
      Howe'er they used him in the university,
      To send him to his friends thus.

      FREDERICK   Why, sir? Black
9   (For 't is the colour that offends your eyesight),

Is not, within my reading, any blemish;   1
Sables are no disgrace in heraldry.

KICKSHAW 'T is coming from the college thus, that makes it
Dishonourable. While you wore it for
Your father, it was commendable; or were
Your aunt dead, you might mourn, and justify.   2

LADY BORNWELL What luck I did not send him into France!
They would have given him generous education,
Taught him another garb, to wear his lock,
And shape, as gaudy as the summer; how
To dance, and wag his feather à la mode,   3
To compliment, and cringe; to talk not modestly,
Like, "ay forsooth," and "no forsooth"; to blush,
And look so like a chaplain!—There he might
Have learned a brazen confidence, and observed
So well the custom of the country, that
He might, by this time, have invented fashions   4
For us, and been a benefit to the kingdom;
Preserved our tailors in their wits, and saved
The charge of sending into foreign courts
For pride and antic fashions.—Observe
In what a posture he does hold his hat now!   5

FREDERICK Madam, with your pardon you have practised
Another dialect than was taught me when
I was commended to your care and breeding.
I understand not this; Latin or Greek
Are more familiar to my apprehension: 6
Logic was not so hard in my first lectures
As your strange language.

LADY BORNWELL Some strong waters; oh!

LITTLEWORTH Comfits will be as comfortable to your stomach,
madam.   7

[*Offers his box*]

LADY BORNWELL I fear he's spoiled for ever! He did name
Logic, and may, for aught I know, be gone
So far to understand it. I did always   8
Suspect they would corrupt him in the college.—
Will your Greek saws and sentences discharge
The mercer? Or is Latin a fit language

I fear he's spoiled forever: The situation of the nephew almost spoiled
by the university occurs in Shirley's *The Gamester*.

1 To court a mistress in?—Master Alexander,
   If you have any charity, let me
   Commend him to your breeding.—I suspect
   I must employ my doctor first, to purge
   The university that lies in's head;
2 It alters his complexion.

KICKSHAW   If you dare
   Trust me to serve him—

LADY BORNWELL   Master Littleworth,
   Be you joined in commission.

3 LITTLEWORTH   I will teach him
   Postures and rudiments.

LADY BORNWELL   I have no patience
   To see him in this shape; it turns my stomach.
   When he has cast his academic skin
4 He shall be yours. I am bound in conscience
   To see him bred; his own state shall maintain
   The charge, while he's my ward.—Come hither, sir.

FREDERICK   What does my aunt mean to do with me?

STEWARD   To make you a fine gentleman, and translate you
5 Out of your learned language, sir, into
   The present Goth and Vandal, which is French.

BORNWELL   Into what mischief will this humour ebb?
   She will undo the boy; I see him ruined,
   My patience is not manly; but I must
6 Use stratagem to reduce her; open ways
   Give me no hope. [*Aside*]

STEWARD   You shall be obeyed, madam.

[*Exeunt all but* FREDERICK *and* STEWARD.]

7
FREDERICK   Master Steward, are you sure we do not dream?
   Was 't not my aunt you talked to?

STEWARD   One that loves you
   Dear as her life. These clothes do not become you,
   You must have better, sir—
8
FREDERICK   These are not old.

STEWARD   More suitable to the town and time; we keep
   No Lent here, nor is 't my lady's pleasure you
   Should fast from anything you have a mind to;
9 Unless it be your learning, which she would have you

Forget with all convenient speed that may be,   1
For the credit of your noble family.
The case is altered since we lived i' the country;
We do not now invite the poor o' the parish
To dinner, keep a table for the tenants;
Our kitchen does not smell of beef; the cellar
Defies the price of malt and hops; the footmen   2
And coach drivers may be drunk like gentlemen,
With wine; nor will three fiddlers upon holidays,
With aid of bagpipes, that called in the country
To dance, and plough the hall up with their hobnails,
Now make my lady merry. We do feed   3
Like princes, and feast nothing else but princes;
And are these robes fit to be seen amongst 'em?

FREDERICK   My lady keeps a court then! Is Sir Thomas
Affected with this state and cost?

STEWARD   He was not;   4
But is converted: and I hope you will not
Persist in heresy, but take a course
Of riot, to content your friends; you shall
Want nothing, if you can be proud, and spend it
For my lady's honour. Here are a hundred   5
Pieces, will serve you till you have new clothes;
I will present you with a nag of mine,
Poor tender of my service, please you accept;
My lady's smile more than rewards me for it.
I must provide fit servants to attend you,
Monsieurs, for horse and foot.   6

FREDERICK   I shall submit,
If this be my aunt's pleasure, and be ruled;
My eyes are opened with this purse already,
And sack will help to inspire me. I must spend it?

STEWARD   What else, sir?   7

FREDERICK   I'll begin with you: to encourage
You to have still a special care of me,
There is five pieces,—not for your nag.

STEWARD   No, sir; I hope it is not.

FREDERICK   Buy a beaver   8
For thy own block; I shall be ruled. Who does
Command the wine cellar?

STEWARD   Who commands but you, sir?

FREDERICK   I'll try to drink a health or two, my aunt's,   9

1   Or anybody's; and if that foundation
     Stagger me not too much, I will commence
     In all the arts of London.

STEWARD   If you find, sir,
     The operation of the wine exalt
2   Your blood to the desire of any female
     Delight, I know your aunt will not deny
     Any of her chambermaids to practise on;
     She loves you but too well.

FREDERICK   I know not how
3   I may be for that exercise—Farewell, Aristotle!
     Prithee commend me to the library
     At Westminster; my bones I bequeath thither,
     And to the learned worms that mean to visit 'em.
     I will compose myself; I begin to think
     I have lost time indeed.—Come to the wine cellar.

4
     [*Exeunt*]

Scene Two

5

[*A room in Celestina's house. Enter* CELESTINA, MARIANA, *and* ISA-
     BELLA.]

MARIANA   But shall we not, madam, expose ourselves
6   To censure for this freedom?

CELESTINA   Let them answer,
     That dare mistake us. Shall we be so much
     Cowards, to be frighted from our pleasure
     Because men have malicious tongues, and show
     What miserable souls they have? No, cousin,
7   We hold our life and fortunes upon no
     Man's charity; if they dare show so little
     Discretion to traduce our fames, we will
     Be guilty of so much wit to laugh at them.

ISABELLA   'T is a becoming fortitude.

8
CELESTINA   My stars
     Are yet kind to me; for, in a happy minute
     Be it spoke, I'm not in love, and men shall never
     Make my heart lean with sighing, nor with tears
     Draw on my eyes the infamy of spectacles.
9   'T is the chief principle to keep your heart

Under your own obedience; jest, but love not.   1
I say my prayers, yet can wear good clothes,
And only satisfy my tailor for them.
I will not lose my privilege.

MARIANA   And yet they say your entertainments are,
Give me your pardon, madam, to proclaim   2
Yourself a widow, and to get a husband.

CELESTINA   As if a lady of my years, some beauty,
Left by her husband rich, that had mourned for him
A twelvemonth too, could live so obscure i' the town,
That gallants would not know her, and invite   3
Themselves, without her chargeable proclamations!
Then we are worse than citizens: no widow
Left wealthy can be thoroughly warm in mourning,
But some one noble blood, or lusty kindred,
Claps in, with his gilt coach, and Flandrian trotters,
And hurries her away to be a countess.   4
Courtiers have spies, and great ones with large titles,
Cold in their own estates, would warm themselves
At a rich city bonfire.

ISABELLA   Most true, madam.

CELESTINA   No matter for corruption of the blood: 5
Some undone courtier made her husband rich,
And this new lord receives it back again.
Admit it were my policy, and that
My entertainments pointed to acquaint me
With many suitors, that I might be safe,   6
And make the best election, could you blame me?

MARIANA   Madam, 't is wisdom.

CELESTINA   But I should be
In my thoughts miserable, to be fond
Of leaving the sweet freedom I possess,   7
And court myself into new marriage fetters.
I now observe men's several wits, and windings,
And can laugh at their follies.

MARIANA   You have given
A most ingenious satisfaction.   8

CELESTINA   One thing I'll tell you more, and this I give you
Worthy your imitation, from my practise:
You see me merry, full of song and dancing,
Pleasant in language, apt to all delights

Flandrian trotters: Flanders trotting mares.

1   That crown a public meeting; but you cannot
Accuse me of being prodigal of my favours
To any of my guests. I do not summon,
By any wink, a gentleman to follow me,
To my withdrawing chamber; I hear all
Their pleas in court, nor can they boast abroad,
2   And do me justice, after a salute,
They have much conversation with my lip.
I hold the kissing of my hand a courtesy,
And he that loves me, must, upon the strength
Of that, expect till I renew his favour.
3   Some ladies are so expensive in their graces,
To those that honour them, and so prodigal,
That in a little time they have nothing but
The naked sin left to reward their servants;
Whereas, a thrift in our rewards will keep
Men long in their devotion, and preserve
4   Ourselves in stock, to encourage those that honour us.

ISABELLA   This is an art worthy a lady's practise.

CELESTINA   It takes not from the freedom of our mirth,
But seems to advance it, when we can possess
Our pleasures with security of our honour;
5   And, that preserved, I welcome all the joys
My fancy can let in. In this I have given
The copy of my mind, nor do I blush
You understand it.

ISABELLA   You have honoured us.

6   CELESTINA'S GENTLEWOMAN [*enters*]   Madam, Sir William Scentlove's come, to wait on you.

CELESTINA   There's one would be a client.—Make excuse
For a few minutes.

7   [*Exit* GENTLEWOMAN.]

MARIANA   One that comes awooing?

CELESTINA   Such a thing he would seem, but in his guiltiness
Of little land, his expectation is not
So valiant as it might be. He wears rich clothes,
8   And feeds with noblemen; to some, I hear,
No better than a wanton emissary,
Or scout for Venus' wild fowl; which made tame,
He thinks no shame to stand court sentinel,
In hope of the reversion.

9   MARIANA   I have heard

That some of them are often my lord's tasters,   1
The first fruits they condition for, and will
Exact as fees, for the promotion.

CELESTINA   Let them agree, there's no account shall lie
For me among their traffic.

GENTLEWOMAN [*reenters*]   Master Haircut, madam,   2
Is new come in, to tender you his service.

CELESTINA   Let him discourse a little with Sir William.

MARIANA   What is this gentleman, Master Haircut, madam?
I note him very gallant, and much courted
By gentlemen of quality.   3

CELESTINA   I know not,
More than a trim gay man; he has some great office,
Sure, by his confident behaviour:
He would be entertained under the title
Of servant to me, and I must confess,   4
He is the sweetest of all men that visit me.

ISABELLA   How mean you, madam?

CELESTINA   He is full of powder;
He will save much in perfume for my chamber,
Were he but constant here. Give them access.   5

[*Exit* GENTLEWOMAN. *Enter* SIR WILLIAM SCENTLOVE *and* HAIRCUT.]

SCENTLOVE   Madam, the humblest of your servants is
Exalted to a happiness, if you smile
Upon my visit.   6

HAIRCUT   I must beg your charity
Upon my rudeness, madam; I shall give
That day up lost to any happiness,
When I forget to tender you my service.   7

CELESTINA   You practise courtship, gentlemen.

SCENTLOVE   But cannot
Find wherewith more desert to exercise it.
What lady's this, I pray?

CELESTINA   A kinswoman   8
Of mine, Sir William.

SCENTLOVE   I am more her servant.

CELESTINA   You came from court, now, I presume?

HAIRCUT   'T is, madam,   9

1 The sphere I move in, and my destiny
Was kind to place me there, where I enjoy
All blessings that a mortal can possess,
That lives not in your presence; and I should
Fix my ambition, when you would vouchsafe
Me so much honour, to accept from me
2 An humble entertainment there.

CELESTINA   But by
What name shall I be known? in what degree
Shall I be of kindred to you?

3 HAIRCUT   How mean you, madam?

CELESTINA   Perhaps you'll call me sister, I shall take it
A special preferment; or it may be
I may pass under title of your mistress,
If I seem rich, and fair enough, to engage
Your confidence to own me.

4 HAIRCUT   I would hope—

CELESTINA   But 't is not come to that yet: you will sir,
Excuse my mirth.

HAIRCUT   Sweet madam!

5 CELESTINA   Shall I take
Boldness to ask what place you hold in court?
'T is an uncivil curiosity;
But you'll have mercy to a woman's question.

HAIRCUT   My present condition, madam, carries
6 Honour and profit, though not to be named
With that employment I expect i' the state,
Which shall discharge the first maturity
Upon your knowledge; until then, I beg
You allow a modest silence.

7 CELESTINA   I am charmed, sir;
And if you 'scape ambassador, you cannot
Reach a preferment wherein I'm against you.
But where is Sir William Scentlove?

HAIRCUT   Give him leave
8 To follow his nose, madam, while he hunts
In view,—he'll soon be at a fault.

CELESTINA   You know him?

HAIRCUT   Know Scentlove? not a page but can decipher him;
The waiting women know him to a scruple;
9 He's called the blister-maker of the town.

CELESTINA   What's that?   1

HAIRCUT   The laundry ladies can resolve you,
And you may guess: an arrant epicure,
As this day lives, born to a pretty wit,
A knight, too; but no gentleman. I must
Be plain to you;—your ladyship may have   2
Use of this knowledge, but conceal the author.

SCENTLOVE   I kiss your fairest hand.

MARIANA   You make a difference;
Pray reconcile them to an equal whiteness.
                                                                            3
SCENTLOVE   You wound my meaning, lady.

CELESTINA   Nay, Sir William
Has the art of compliment.

SCENTLOVE   Madam, you honour me
'Bove my desert of language.   4

CELESTINA   Will you please
To enrich me with your knowledge of that gentleman?

SCENTLOVE   Do you not know him, madam?

CELESTINA   What is he?
                                                                            5
SCENTLOVE   A camphire ball; you shall know more hereafter;
He shall tell you himself, and save my character;
Till then,—you see he's proud.

CELESTINA   One thing, gentlemen,
I observe in your behaviour, which is rare
In two that court one mistress: you preserve   6
A noble friendship; there's no gum within
Your hearts; you cannot fret, or show an envy
Of one another's hope; some would not govern
Their passions with that temper!

SCENTLOVE   The whole world   7
Shall ne'er divorce our friendship.—Master Hiarcut!
Would I had lives to serve him! He is lost
To goodness does not honour him.

HAIRCUT   My knight!
                                                                            8
CELESTINA   This is right playing at court shuttlecock. [Aside]

GENTLEWOMAN [reenters]   Madam, there is a gentleman desires
To speak with you, one Sir Thomas Bornwell.

gum . . . fret: Imitation velvet was gummed and easily fretted or
frayed out.

1 CELESTINA Bornwell?

GENTLEWOMAN He says he is a stranger to your ladyship.

SCENTLOVE I know him.

HAIRCUT Your neighbour, madam.

2 SCENTLOVE Husband to
The lady that so revels in the Strand.

HAIRCUT He has good parts, they say, but cannot help
His lady's bias.

CELESTINA They have both much fame
3   I' the town, for several merits. Pray admit him.

[*Exit* GENTLEWOMAN.]

HAIRCUT What comes he for? [*Aside*]

4 BORNWELL [*enters*] Your pardon, noble lady, that I have
Presumed, a stranger to your knowledge—

[*Salutes* CELESTINA]

CELESTINA Sir,
5   Your worth was here before you, and your person
Cannot be here ungrateful.

BORNWELL 'T is the bounty
Of your sweet disposition, madam.—Make me
Your servant, lady, by her fair example,
To favour me.
6
[*Offers to salute* ISABELLA, *who turns from him.*]

—I never knew one turn
Her cheek to a gentleman that came to kiss her,
But she'd a stinking breath [*aside*].—Your servant, gentlemen.
7   Will Scentlove, how is 't?

CELESTINA [*to* MARIANA] I am sorry, coz,
To accuse you; we in nothing more betray
Ourselves to censure of ridiculous pride,
Than answering a fair salute too rudely.
8   Oh, it shows ill upon a gentlewoman
Not to return the modest lip, if she
Would have the world believe her breath is not
Offensive.

BORNWELL Madam, I have business
9   With you.

SCENTLOVE   His looks are pleasant.   1

CELESTINA   With me, sir?

BORNWELL   I hear you have an excellent wit, madam;
  I see you are fair.

CELESTINA   The first is but report;   2
  And do not trust your eyesight for the last,
  'Cause I presume you're mortal, and may err.

HAIRCUT   He is very gamesome.

BORNWELL   You have an excellent voice,
  (They say you catched it from a dying swan),   3
  With which, joined to the harmony of your lute,
  You ravish all mankind.

CELESTINA   Ravish mankind?

BORNWELL   With their consent.

CELESTINA   It were the stranger rape;   4
  But there's the less indictment lies against it:
  And there is hope your little honesties
  Cannot be much the worse, for men do rather
  Believe they had a maidenhead, than put
  Themselves to the rack of memory how long   5
  'T is since they left the burden of their innocence.

BORNWELL   Why, you are bitter, madam!

CELESTINA   So is physic;
  I do not know your constitution.
                                                                                        6
BORNWELL   You shall, if 't please you, madam.

CELESTINA   You're too hasty,
  I must examine what certificate
  You have first, to prefer you.

BORNWELL   Fine! certificate?   7

CELESTINA   Under your lady's hand and seal.

BORNWELL   Go to;
  I see you are a wag.

CELESTINA   But take heed how   8
  You trust to 't.

BORNWELL   I can love you in my wedlock,
  As well as that young gallant o' the first hair,
  Or the knight-bachelor; and can return
  As amorous delight to your soft bosom.   9

1 CELESTINA   Your person and your language are both strangers.

BORNWELL   But may be more familiar; I have those
That dare make affidavit for my body.

CELESTINA   Do you mean your surgeon?

2 BORNWELL   My surgeon, madam?
I know not how you value my abilities,
But I dare undertake as much, to express
My service to your ladyship, and with
As fierce ambition fly to your commands,
As the most valiant of these lay siege to you.

3

CELESTINA   You dare not, sir.

BORNWELL   How, madam?

CELESTINA   I will justify it.
You dare not marry me; and I imagine
4 Some here, should I consent, would fetch a priest
Out of the fire.

BORNWELL   I have a wife indeed.

CELESTINA   And there's a statute not repealed, I take it.

5 BORNWELL   You're in the right; I must confess you've hit
And bled me in a master vein.

CELESTINA   You think
I took you on the advantage; use your best
Skill at defence, I'll come up to your valour,
6 And show another work you dare not do:
You dare not, sir, be virtuous.

BORNWELL   I dare,
By this fair hand I dare; and ask a pardon,
If my rude words offend your innocence,
Which, in a form so beautiful, would shine
7 To force a blush in them suspected it,
And from the rest draw wonder.

HAIRCUT   I like not
Their secret parley; shall I interrupt them?

8 ISABELLA   By no means, sir.

SCENTLOVE   Sir Thomas was not wont
To show so much a courtier.

MARIANA   He cannot
Be prejudicial to you; suspect not
9 Your own deserts so much; he's married.

BORNWELL   I have other business, madam: you keep music: 1
I came to try how you can dance.

CELESTINA   You did?—I'll try his humour out of breath [*aside*].
Although I boast no cunning, sir, in revels,
If you desire to show your art that way,
I can wait on you.   2

BORNWELL   You much honour me;
Nay, all must join to make a harmony.

[*They dance.*]

I have nothing now, madam, but to beseech,   3
After a pardon for my boldness, you
Would give occasion to pay my gratitude:
I have a house will be much honoured,
If you vouchsafe your presence; and a wife
Desires to present herself your servant.
I came with the ambition to invite you,   4
Deny me not; your person you shall trust
On fair security.

CELESTINA   Sir, although I use not
This freedom with a stranger, you shall have
No cause to hold me obstinate.   5

BORNWELL   You grace me.
Sir William Scentlove—

HAIRCUT   I must take my leave.
You will excuse me, madam, court attendances—   6

CELESTINA   By any means.

BORNWELL   Ladies, you will vouchsafe
Your company?

ISABELLA   We wait upon you, sir.
                                                                7
[*Exeunt*]

                                                                8

                                                                9

ACT THREE

Scene One

1   [*Lord A's house. A dressing room, with table and looking glass;* HAIRCUT *preparing a peruke.*]

LORD A [*within*]   What hour is 't?

HAIRCUT   'Bout three o'clock, my lord.

2   LORD A   'T is time to rise. [*Enters, in his dressing gown.*]

HAIRCUT   Your lordship went but late
To bed last night.

LORD A   'T was early in the morning.

SECRETARY [*within*]   Expect awhile; my lord is busy. [*Enters*]

3

LORD A   What's the matter?

SECRETARY   Here is a lady
Desires access to you upon some affairs,
She says, may specially concern your lordship.

4   LORD A   A lady? What's her name?

SECRETARY   Madam Decoy.

LORD A   Decoy? Prithee admit her.

[*Exit* SECRETARY; *reenters with* DECOY.]

5

Have you business, madam,
With me?

DECOY   And such, I hope, as will not be
Offensive to your lordship.

6   LORD A   I pray speak it.

DECOY   I would desire your lordship's ear more private.

LORD A   Wait i' the next chamber till I call.

[*Exeunt* HAIRCUT *and* SECRETARY.]

7

                                                  Now, madam.

DECOY   Although I am a stranger to your lordship,
I would not lose a fair occasion offered,
To show how much I honour, and would serve you.

8   LORD A   Please you to give me the particular,

374

That I may know the extent of my engagement.
I am ignorant by what desert you should
Be encouraged to have care of me.

DECOY My lord,
I will take boldness to be plain; beside
Your other excellent parts, you have much fame
For your sweet inclination to our sex.

LORD A   How do you mean, madam?

DECOY   I' that way your lordship
Hath honourably practised upon some
Not to be named. Your noble constancy
To a mistress, hath deserved our general vote;
And I, a part of womankind, have thought
How to express my duty.

LORD A   In what, madam?

DECOY   Be not so strange, my lord; I knew the beauty
And pleasures of your eyes; that handsome creature
With whose fair life all your delight took leave,
And to whose memory you have paid too much
Sad tribute.

LORD A   What's all this?

DECOY   This: if your lordship
Accept my service, in pure zeal to cure
Your melancholy, I could point where you might
Repair your loss.

LORD A   Your ladyship, I conceive,
Doth traffic in flesh merchandize.

DECOY   To men
Of honour, like yourself. I am well known
To some in court, and come not with ambition
Now to supplant your officer.

LORD A   What is
The Lady of Pleasure you prefer?

DECOY   A lady
Of birth and fortune, one upon whose virtue
I may presume, the Lady Aretina.

LORD A   Wife to Sir Thomas Bornwell?

DECOY   The same, sir.

prefer: Here, propose.

1 LORD A   Have you prepared her?

DECOY   Not for your lordship, till I have found your pulse.
I am acquainted with her disposition,
She has a very appliable nature.

LORD A   And, madam, when expect you to be whipped
2   For doing these fine favours?

DECOY   How, my lord?
Your lordship does but jest, I hope; you make
A difference between a lady that
Does honourable offices, and one
3   They call a bawd. Your lordship was not wont
To have such coarse opinion of our practise.

LORD A   The Lady Aretina is my kinswoman.

DECOY   What if she be, my lord? The nearer blood,
The dearer sympathy.

4 LORD A   I'll have thee carted.

DECOY   Your lordship will not so much stain your honour
And education, to use a woman
Of my quality—

LORD A   'T is possible you may
5   Be sent off with an honourable convoy
Of halberdiers.

DECOY   Oh, my good lord!

LORD A   Your ladyship shall be no protection,
If you but stay three minutes.

6 DECOY   I am gone.—
When next you find rebellion in your blood,
May all within ten mile o' the court turn honest! [*Exits*]

LORD A   I do not find that proneness, since the fair
Bella Maria died; my blood is cold,
7   Nor is there beauty enough surviving
To heighten me to wantonness.—Who waits?

[*Reenter* HAIRCUT *and* SECRETARY.]

And what said my lady?

8 HAIRCUT   The silent language of her face, my lord,
Was not so pleasant, as it showed upon
Her entrance.

carted: Exposed to public view by being driven through the streets on
a cart; the punishment of bawds.

LORD A   Would any man that meets   1
This lady take her for a bawd?

HAIRCUT   She does
The trade an honour, credit to the profession.
We may, in time, see baldness, quarter noses,
And rotten legs to take the wall of footcloths.   2

LORD A   I have thought better; call the lady back—
I will not lose this opportunity.—
Bid her not fear.

[*Exit* SECRETARY.]
                                                             3

                    The favour is not common,
And I'll reward it. I do wonder much
Will Scentlove was not here today.

HAIRCUT   I heard him say this morning he would wait
Upon your lordship.—   4
She is returned, sir.

[*Reenter* SECRETARY *and* DECOY.]

SECRETARY   Madam, be confident, my lord's not angry.
                                                             5
LORD A   You return welcome, madam; you are better
Read in your art, I hope, than to be frighted
With any shape of anger, when you bring
Such news to gentlemen. Madam, you shall
Soon understand how I accept the office.

DECOY   You are the first lord, since I studied carriage,   6
That showed such infidelity and fury
Upon so kind a message. Every gentleman
Will show some breeding; but if one right honourable
Should not have noble blood—

LORD A   You shall return   7
My compliment, in a letter, to my lady
Aretina. Favour me with a little patience.—
Show her that chamber.

DECOY   I'll attend your lordship.
                                                             8
[*Exeunt* DECOY *and* HAIRCUT. SECRETARY *seats himself at a table.*]

---

   take the wall: Claim the privilege of walking next to the wall, the
cleaner and safer side of the pavement. "Footcloths" here, carpets.
   carriage: Here, conduct.

1   LORD A   Write,—"Madam, where your honour is in danger, my love must not be silent."

[*Enter* SIR WILLIAM SCENTLOVE *and* KICKSHAW.]

2

Scentlove and Kickshaw!

KICKSHAW   Your lordship's busy.

LORD A   Writing a letter;—nay, it shall not bar
Any discourse.

3

[*Walks alternately to the* SECRETARY *and to* SCENTLOVE *and* KICK-SHAW.]

SECRETARY   "Silent."

4

LORD A   "Though I be no physician, I may prevent a fever in your blood."—
And where have you spent the morning's conversation?

SCENTLOVE   Where you would have given the best barbary
In your stable, to have met on honourable terms.

5

LORD A   What new beauty? You acquaint yourselves
With none but wonders.

SCENTLOVE   'T is too low,—a miracle.

LORD A   It will require a strong faith.

SECRETARY   "Your blood."

6

LORD A   "If you be innocent, preserve your fame, lest this Decoy-madam betray it, to your repentance."—
By what name is she known?

SCENTLOVE   Ask Alexander.
He knows her.

7   KICKSHAW   Whom?

SCENTLOVE   The lady Celestina.

LORD A   He has a vast knowledge of ladies. 'Las, poor Alexander!
When dost thou mean thy body shall lie fallow?

8

KICKSHAW   When there is mercy in a petticoat:
I must turn pilgrim for some breath.

LORD A   I think
'T were cooler travel, if you examine it,
Upon the hoof through Spain.

9   SCENTLOVE   Through Ethiopia.

LORD A Nay, less labourious to serve a prenticeship   1
In Peru, and dig gold out of the mine,
Though all the year were dog days.

SECRETARY "To repentance."

LORD A "In brief, this lady, could you fall from virtue, within my   2
knowledge, will not blush to be a bawd."

SCENTLOVE But hang 't, 't is honourable journey-work;
Thou art famous by it, and thy name's up.

KICKSHAW So, sir!
Let me ask you a question, my dear knight: 3
Which is less servile, to bring up the pheasant,
And wait, or sit at table uncontrolled,
And carve to my own appetite?

SCENTLOVE No more;
Thou 'rt witty, as I am.   4

SECRETARY "A bawd."

SCENTLOVE How's that?

KICKSHAW Oh,
You are famous by 't, and your name's up, sir.   5

LORD A "Be wise, and reward my caution with timely care of
yourself, so I shall not repent to be known your loving kinsman
and servant."
Gentlemen, the lady Celestina,
Is she so rare a thing?   6

KICKSHAW If you'll have my
Opinion, my lord, I never saw
So sweet, so fair, so rich a piece of nature.

LORD A I'll show thee a fairer presently, to shame
Thy eyes and judgment; look on that.   7

[*Gives him a miniature.*]

So; I'll subscribe.

[*Signs his name to the letter.*]
                                                                         8
Seal it; I'll excuse your pen for the direction.

KICKSHAW Bella Maria's picture! She was handsome.

SCENTLOVE But not to be compared—

LORD A Your patience, gentlemen; I'll return instantly. [*Exits*]   9

1 KICKSHAW   Whither is my lord gone?

SECRETARY   To a lady i' the next chamber.

SCENTLOVE   What is she?

SECRETARY   You shall pardon me, I am his secretary.

2 SCENTLOVE   I was wont to be of his counsel. A new officer,
   And I not know 't? I am resolved to batter
   All other with the praise of Celestina:
   I must retain him.

LORD A [*reenters*]   Has not that object
3   Convinced your erring judgments?

KICKSHAW   What! this picture?

LORD A   Were but your thoughts as capable as mine
   Of her idea, you would wish no thought
   That were not active in her praise, above
4   All worth and memory of her sex.

SCENTLOVE   She was fair,
   I must confess; but had your lordship looked
   With eyes more narrow, and some less affection,
   Upon her face,—
5
KICKSHAW   I do not love the copies
   Of any dead, they make me dream of goblins;
   Give me a living mistress, with but half
   The beauty of Celestina.

6 [*Returns the miniature*]

   Come, my lord,
   'T is pity that a lord of so much flesh
   Should waste upon a ghost, when they are living
   Can give you a more honourable consumption.
7
SCENTLOVE   Why, do you mean, my lord, to live an infidel?
   Do, and see what will come on 't; observe still,
   And dote upon your vigils; build a chamber
   Within a rock, a tomb among the worms,
   Not far off, where you may, in proof apocryphal,
8   Court 'em not to devour the pretty pile
   Of flesh your mistress carried to the grave.
   There are no women in the world; all eyes,
   And tongues, and lips, are buried in her coffin!

LORD A   Why, do you think yourselves competent judges
9   Of beauty, gentlemen?

BOTH What should hinder us?   1

KICKSHAW I have seen and tried as many as another,
With a mortal back.

LORD A Your eyes are bribed,
And your hearts chained to some desires; you cannot
Enjoy the freedom of a sense.   2

KICKSHAW Your lordship
Has a clear eyesight, and can judge and penetrate.

LORD A I can, and give a perfect censure of
Each line and point; distinguish beauty from
A thousand forms, which your corrupted optics   3
Would pass for natural.

SCENTLOVE I desire no other
Judge should determine us, and if your lordship
Dare venture but your eyes upon this lady,
I'll stand their justice, and be confident   4
You shall give Celestina victory,
And triumph, o'er all beauties past and living.

KICKSHAW I dare, my lord, venture a suit of clothes,
You'll be o'ercome.

LORD A You do not know my fortitude.   5

SCENTLOVE Nor failty; you dare not trust yourself to see her.

LORD A Think you so, gentlemen? I dare see this creature
To make you know your errors, and the difference
Of her, whose memory is my saint. Not trust   6
My senses! I dare see, and speak with her.
Which holds the best acquaintance to prepare
My visit to her?

SCENTLOVE I will do 't, my lord.

KICKSHAW She is a lady free in entertainments.   7

LORD A I would give this advantage to your cause,
Bid her appear in all the ornaments
Did ever wait on beauty, all the riches
Pride can put on, and teach her face more charms
Than ever poet dressed up Venus in;   8
Bid her be all the Graces, and the queen
Of love in one, I'll see her, Scentlove, and
Bring off my heart, armed but with a single thought
Of one that's dead, without a wound; and when
I have made your folly prisoner, I'll laugh at you.   9

SCENTLOVE She shall expect you; trust to me for knowledge.

LORD A I'm for the present somewhere else engaged;
Let me hear from you. [*Exits*]

SCENTLOVE So! I am glad he's yet
So near conversion.

KICKSHAW I am for Aretina.

SCENTLOVE No mention of my lord.

KICKSHAW Prepare his lady,
'T is time he were reduced to the old sport;
One lord like him more would undo the court.

[*Exeunt*]

Scene Two

[*A room in Sir Thomas Bornwell's house. Enter* LADY BORNWELL
with a letter and DECOY.]

DECOY He is the ornament of your blood, madam;
I am much bound to his lordship.

LADY BORNWELL He gives you
A noble character.

DECOY 'T is his goodness, madam.

LADY BORNWELL I wanted such an engine. My lord has
Done me a courtesy, to disclose her nature;
I now know one to trust, and will employ her [*aside*].
Touching my lord, for reasons which I shall
Offer to your ladyship hereafter, I
Desire you would be silent; but, to show
How much I dare be confident in your secrecy,
I pour my bosom forth; I love a gentleman,
One whom there would not need much conjuration
To meet.—Your ear.

[*Whispers to her*]

DECOY I apprehend you, and I shall
Be happy to be serviceable. I am sorry
Your ladyship did not know me before now:
I have done offices: and not a few
Of the nobility but have done feats

Within my house, which is convenient   1
For situation, and artful chambers,
And pretty pictures to provoke the fancy.

LITTLEWORTH [*enters*]   Madam, all pleasures languish in your absence.

LADY BORNWELL   Your pardon a few minutes, sir.—You must   2
Contrive it thus.

[*Walks aside with* DECOY.]

LITTLEWORTH   I attend, and shall account it   3
Honour to wait on your return.

LADY BORNWELL   He must not
Have the least knowledge of my name or person.

DECOY   I have practised that already for some great ones,
And dare again, to satisfy you, madam;   4
I have a thousand ways to do sweet offices.

LITTLEWORTH   If this Lady Aretina should be honest,
I have lost time: she's free as air; I must
Have closer conference, and if I have art,
Make her affect me in revenge.   5

DECOY   This evening?
Leave me to manage things.

LADY BORNWELL   You will oblige me.

DECOY   You shall command my art, and thank me after. [*Exits*]
                                                                        6
LADY BORNWELL   I hope the revels are maintained within?

LITTLEWORTH   By Sir Thomas and his mistress.

LADY BORNWELL   How? his mistress?

LITTLEWORTH   The Lady Celestina; I never saw
Eyes shoot more amorous interchange.   7

LADY BORNWELL   Is 't so?

LITTLEWORTH   He wears her favour with more pride—

LADY BORNWELL   Her favour?

LITTLEWORTH   A feather that he ravished from her fan;   8
And is so full of courtship! which she smiles on.

LADY BORNWELL   'T is well.

LITTLEWORTH   And praises her beyond all poetry.

LADY BORNWELL   I am glad he has so much wit.   9

1 LITTLEWORTH   Not jealous! [*Aside*]

LADY BORNWELL   This secures me. What would make other ladies
    pale
With jealousy, gives but licence to my wanderings.
Let him now tax me, if he dare; and yet
2 Her beauty's worth my envy, and I wish
Revenge upon it, not because he loves,
But that it shines above my own. [*Aside*]

KICKSHAW [*enters*]   Dear madam!

LADY BORNWELL   I have it.—You two gentlemen profess
3 Much service to me; if I have a way
To employ your wit and secrecy?—

BOTH   You'll honour us.

LADY BORNWELL   You gave a high and worthy character
    Of Celestina.
4
KICKSHAW   I remember, madam.

LADY BORNWELL   Do either of you love her?

KICKSHAW   Not I, madam.

LITTLEWORTH   I would not, if I might.

5 LADY BORNWELL   She's now my guest,
And, by a trick, invited by my husband,
To disgrace me.—You, gentlemen, are held
Wits of the town, the consuls that do govern
The senate here, whose jeers are all authentic.
6 The taverns and the ordinaries are
Made academies, where you come, and all
Your sins and surfeits made the time's example.
Your very nods can quell a theatre,
No speech or poem good without your seal;
You can protect scurrility, and publish,
7 By your authority believed, no rapture
Ought to have honest meaning.

KICKSHAW   Leave our characters.

LITTLEWORTH   And name the employment.

8 LADY BORNWELL   You must exercise
The strength of both your wits upon this lady,
And talk her into humbleness or anger,
Both which are equal, to my thought. If you
Dare undertake this slight thing for my sake,
My favour shall reward it; but be faithful,
9 And seem to let all spring from your own freedom.

KICKSHAW This all! We can defame her; if you please, 1
My friend shall call her whore, or any thing,
And never be endangered to a duel.

LADY BORNWELL How's that?

KICKSHAW He can endure a cudgelling, and no man 2
Will fight after so fair a satisfaction:
But leave us to our art, and do not limit us.

LADY BORNWELL They are here; begin not till I whisper you.

[*Enter* SIR THOMAS BORNWELL, CELESTINA, MARIANA, *and* ISA-
BELLA.] 3

LADY BORNWELL Je vous prie, madame, d'excuser l'importunité
de mes affaires, qui m'ont fait offenser, par mon absence, une
dame de laquelle j'ai reçu tant d'obligations.

CELESTINA Pardonnez moi, madame; vous me faites trop d'hon- 4
neur.

LADY BORNWELL C'est bien de la douceur de votre naturel, que
vous tenez cette langage; mais j'espère que mon mari n'a pas
manqué de vous entretenir en mon absence.

CELESTINA En vérité, monsieur nous a fort obligé. 5

LADY BORNWELL Il eut trop failli, s'il n'eut taché de tout son
pouvoir à vous rendre toutes sortes de services.

CELESTINA C'est de sa bonté qu'il nous a tant favorisé.

LADY BORNWELL De la vôtre plutôt, madame, que vous fait 6
donner d'interprétation si bénigne à ses efforts.

CELESTINA Je vois bien que la victoire sera toujours à madame,
et de langage et de la courtesie.

LADY BORNWELL Vraiment, madame, que jamais personne a plus
désiré l'honneur de votre compagnie que moi. 7

CELESTINA Laissons-en, je vous supplie, des compliments, et
permettez à votre servante de vous baiser les mains.

LADY BORNWELL Vous m'obligez trop.

BORNWELL I have no more patience; let's be merry again 8
In our own language: madam, our mirth cools.
Our nephew!

[*Enter* FREDERICK, *intoxicated, and* STEWARD.]

LADY BORNWELL Passion of my brain! 9

1 FREDERICK   Save you, gentlemen! save you, ladies!

LADY BORNWELL   I am undone.

FREDERICK   I must salute; no matter at which end I begin.

[*Salutes* CELESTINA]

2

LADY BORNWELL   There's a compliment!

CELESTINA   Is this your nephew, madam?

LADY BORNWELL   Je vous prie, madame, d'exuser les habits et le
rude comportement de mon cousin. Il est tout fraîchement venu
3 de l'université, où on l'a tout gâté.

CELESTINA   Excusez moi, madame, il est bien accompli.

FREDERICK   This language should be French by the motions of
your heads, and the mirth of your faces.

4 LADY BORNWELL   I am dishonoured.

FREDERICK   'T is one of the finest tongues for ladies to show their
teeth in: if you'll Latin it, I am for you, or Greek it; my tailor
has not put me into French yet. Mille basia, basia mille.

CELESTINA   Je ne vous entends pas, monsieur;
5   I understand you not, sir.

FREDERICK   Why, so!
    You and I then shall be in charity;
    For though we should be abusive, we have the benefit
    Not to understand one another. Where's my aunt?
6   I did hear music somewhere; and my brains,
    Tuned with a bottle of your capering claret,
    Made haste to show their dancing.

LITTLEWORTH   Please you, madam,

[*Offering his box of sweetmeats to* CELESTINA.]

7

They are very comfortable.

STEWARD   Alas, madam,
    How would you have me help it? I did use
    All means I could, after he heard the music,
8   To make him drunk, in hope so to contain him;
    But the wine made him lighter, and his head
    Flew hither, ere I missed his heels.

KICKSHAW   Nay, he
    Spoke Latin to the lady.

9 LADY BORNWELL   Oh, most unpardonable!

Get him off quickly, and discreetly, too.   1
Or, if I live—

STEWARD   It is not in my power; he swears I am
An absurd sober fellow; and if you keep
A servant in his house to cross his humour,
When the rich sword and belt come home, he'll kill him.   2

LADY BORNWELL   What shall I do? Try your skill, Master Littleworth.

LITTLEWORTH   He has ne'er a sword.—Sweet Master Frederick—

BORNWELL   'T is pity, madam, such a scion should
Be lost; but you are clouded.   3

CELESTINA   Not I, sir,
I never found myself more clear at heart.

BORNWELL   I could play with a feather; your fan, lady.—
Gentlemen, Aretina, ta, ra, ra, ra! Come, madam.   4

FREDERICK   Why, my good tutor in election,
You might have been a scholar.

LITTLEWORTH   But I thank
My friends, they brought me up a little better.
Give me the town wits, that deliver jests   5
Clean from the bow, that whistle in the air,
And cleave the pin at twelvescore! Ladies do
But laugh at a gentleman that has any learning;
'T is sin enough to have your clothes suspected.
Leave us, and I will find a time to instruct you.
Come, here are sugarplums; 't is a good Frederick.   6

FREDERICK   Why, is not this my aunt's house in the Strand?
The noble rendezvous? Who laughs at me?
Go, I will root here if I list, and talk
Of rhetoric, logic, Latin, Greek, or any thing,
And understand 'em too; who says the contrary?   7
Yet, in a fair way, I contemn all learning,
And will be as ignorant as he, or he,
Or any taffeta, satin, scarlet, plush,
Tissue, or cloth o' bodkin gentleman,
Whose manners are most gloriously infected.—
Did you laugh at me, lady?   8

CELESTINA   Not I, sir;
But if I did show mirth upon your question,

cleave the pin at twelvescore: Littleworth completes his metaphor
from archery: "Strike the peg in the centre of the target at 240 yards."

1   I hope you would not beat me, little gentleman?

FREDERICK   How! "little gentleman?" You dare not say
These words to my new clothes, and fighting sword.

LADY BORNWELL   Nephew Frederick!

2   FREDERICK   "Little gentleman!"
'T is an affront both to my blood and person,
I am a gentleman of as tall a birth
As any boast nobility; though my clothes
Smell o' the lamp, my coat is honourable,
Right honourable, full of or and argent.—

3   A "little gentleman!"

BORNWELL   Coz, you must be patient;
My lady meant you no dishonour, and
You must remember she's a woman.

FREDERICK   Is she a woman? That's another matter.—
4   Do you hear? My uncle tells me what you are.

CELESTINA   So, sir.

FREDERICK   You called me "little gentleman."

CELESTINA   I did, sir.

5   FREDERICK   A little pink has made a lusty ship
Strike her topsail; the crow may beard the elephant,
A whelp may tame the tiger, spite of all
False decks and murderers; and a "little gentleman"
Be hard enough to grapple with your ladyship,
6   Top and top-gallant.—Will you go drink, uncle,
T' other enchanted bottle? You and I
Will tipple, and talk philosophy.

BORNWELL   Come, nephew.—
You will excuse a minute's absence, madam.—
7   Wait you on us.

STEWARD   My duty, sir.

[*Exeunt* Sir Thomas BORNWELL, FREDERICK, *and* STEWARD.]

LADY BORNWELL   Now, gentlemen.
8
KICKSHAW   Madam, I had rather you excuse my language
For speaking truth, than virtue suffer in
My further silence; and it is my wonder

murderers: Here, cannon charged with grapeshot. Frederick pursues
his metaphor dawn from naval battles.

That you, whose noble carriage hath deserved 1
All honour and opinion, should now
Be guilty of ill manners.

CELESTINA   What was that
You told me, sir?

LITTLEWORTH   Do you not blush, madam, 2
To ask that question?

CELESTINA   You amaze rather
My cheek to paleness. What mean you by this?
I am not troubled with the hiccup, gentlemen,
You should bestow this fright upon me. 3

LITTLEWORTH   Then
Pride and ill memory go together.

CELESTINA   How, sir?

KICKSHAW   The gentleman on whom you exercised 4
Your thin wit, was a nephew to the lady
Whose guest you are; and though her modesty
Look calm on the abuse of one so near
Her blood, the affront was impious.

LITTLEWORTH   I am ashamed on 't.
You an ingenious lady, and well mannered! 5
I'll teach a bear as much civility.

CELESTINA   You may be master of the college, sir,
For aught I know.

LITTLEWORTH   What college? 6

CELESTINA   Of the bears.
Have you a plot upon me? Do you possess
Your wits, or know me, gentlemen?

BORNWELL [reenters behind]   How's this?

KICKSHAW   Know you? Yes; we do know you to an atom. 7

LITTLEWORTH   Madam, we know what stuff your soul is made on.

CELESTINA   But do not bark so like a mastiff, pray.—
Sure they are mad.—Let your brains stand awhile,
And settle, gentlemen; you know not me;
What am I? 8

LITTLEWORTH   Thou 'rt a puppet, a thing made
Of clothes and painting, and not half so handsome
As that which played Susanna in the fair.

CELESTINA   I heard you visited those canvas tragedies, 9

1   One of their constant audience, and so taken
With Susan, that you wished yourself a rival
With the two wicked elders.

KICKSHAW   You think this
Is wit now. Come, you are—

2   CELESTINA   What, I beseech you?
Your character will be full of salt and satire,
No doubt. What am I?

KICKSHAW   Why, you are a woman—

3   CELESTINA   And that's at least a bow wide of your knowledge.

KICKSHAW   Would be thought handsome, and might pass i' the
    country
Upon a market day; but so miserably
Forfeit to pride and fashions, that if Heaven
Were a new gown, you'd not stay in 't a fortnight.

4   CELESTINA   It must be miserably out of fashion then.
Have I no sin but pride?

KICKSHAW   Hast any virtue,
Or but a good face to excuse that want?

5   CELESTINA   You praised it yesterday.

KICKSHAW   That made you proud.

CELESTINA   More pride!

KICKSHAW   You need not:—to close up the praise,
I have seen a better countenance in a sybil.

6   CELESTINA   When you wore spectacles of sack, mistook
The painted cloth, and kissed it for your mistress.

KICKSHAW   Let me ask you a question: how much
Have you consumed in expectation

7   That I would love you?

CELESTINA   Why I think as much
As you have paid away in honest debts
This seven year. 'T is a pretty impudence,
But cannot make me angry.

8   LITTLEWORTH   Is there any
Man that will cast away his limbs upon her?

KICKSHAW   You do not sing so well as I imagined,
Nor dance; you reel in your coranto, and pinch

coranto: a lively dance.

Your petticoat too hard: you've no good ear   1
 To the music, and incline too much one shoulder,
 As you were dancing on the rope, and falling.
You speak abominable French, and make
A curtsey like a dairymaid.—Not mad! [*Aside*]

LITTLEWORTH   Do we not sting her handsomely?   2

BORNWELL   A conspiracy!

KICKSHAW   Your state is not so much as 't is reported,
When you confer notes, all your husband's debts,
And your own reconciled; but that's not it
Will so much spoil your marriage.   3

CELESTINA   As what, sir?
Let me know all my faults.

KICKSHAW   Some men do whisper
You are not over honest.   4

CELESTINA   All this shall not
Move me to more than laughter, and some pity,
Because you have the shapes of gentlemen;
And though you have been insolent upon me,
I will engage no friend to kick or cudgel you,
To spoil your living and your limbs together: 5
I leave that to diseases that attend you,
And spare my curse, poor silken vermin! and
Hereafter shall distinguish men from monkeys.

BORNWELL   Brave soul!—You brace of horseleeches!
[*Coming forward*]—I have heard   6
Their barbarous language, madam; you are too merciful:
They shall be silent to your tongue; pray punish them.

CELESTINA   They are things not worth my character, nor mention
Of any clean breath; so lost in honesty,
They cannot satisfy for wrongs enough,   7
Though they should steal out of the world at Tyburn.

LITTLEWORTH   We are hanged already.

CELESTINA   Yet I will talk a little to the pilchards.—
You two, that have not 'twixt you both the hundred
Part of a soul, coarse woolen-witted fellows,   8
Without a nap, with bodies made for burdens!
You, that are only stuffings for apparel,
As you were made but engines for your tailors
To frame their clothes upon, and get them custom,
Until men see you move; yet, then you dare not,
Out of your guilt of being the ignobler beast,   9

1 But give a horse the wall, whom you excel
Only in dancing of the brawls, because
The horse was not taught the French way. Your two faces,
One fat, like Christmas, t' other lean, like Candlemas,
And prologue to a Lent, both bound together,
2 Would figure Janus, and do many cures
On agues, and the green disease, by frighting.
But neither can, with all the characters
And conjuring circles, charm a woman, though
She'd fourscore years upon her, and but one
Tooth in her head, to love, or think well of you:
3 And I were miserable, to be at cost
To court such a complexion, as your malice
Did impudently insinuate. But I waste time,
And stain my breath in talking to such tadpoles.
Go home, and wash your tongues in barley water,
Drink clean tobacco, be not hot i' the mouth,
4 And you may 'scape the beadle; so I leave you
To shame, and your own garters!—Sir, I must
Entreat you, for my honour, do not penance them,
They are not worth your anger. How shall I
Acquit your lady's silence?

5 BORNWELL Madam, I
Am sorry to suspect, and dare revenge.

CELESTINA No cause of mine.

BORNWELL It must become me to attend you home.

6 CELESTINA You are noble.—Farewell, mushrooms.

[*Exits with* SIR THOMAS BORNWELL.]

LADY BORNWELL Is she gone?

7 LITTLEWORTH I think we peppered her.

KICKSHAW I'm glad 't is over;
But I repent no service for you, madam.—

[*Enter* SERVANT, *with a letter and a jewel, which he delivers to*
KICKSHAW.]
8

To me? from whence?—a jewel! a good preface.
Be happy the conclusion! [*Reads and smiles*]

LADY BORNWELL Some love letter.

drink tobacco: That is, to smoke.

LITTLEWORTH He has a hundred mistresses: you may 1
    Be charitable, madam, I have none;
    He surfeits, and I fall away i' the kidneys.

KICKSHAW I'll meet.—

[*Exit* SERVANT.] 2

    'T is some great lady, questionless, that has
    Taken notice, and would satisfy her appetite. [*Aside*]

LADY BORNWELL Now, Master Alexander, you look bright o' the
    sudden;
    Another spirit's in your eye. 3

KICKSHAW Not mine, madam;
    Only a summons to meet a friend.

LADY BORNWELL What friend?

LITTLEWORTH By this jewel, I know her not. 4

LADY BORNWELL 'T is a she-friend. I'll follow, gentlemen;
    We may have a game at cent before you go.

KICKSHAW I shall attend you, madam.

LITTLEWORTH 'T is our duty. 5

[*Exeunt* KICKSHAW *and* LITTLEWORTH.]

LADY BORNWELL I blush while I converse with my own thoughts.
    Some strange fate governs me, but I must on;
    The ways are cast already, and we thrive 6
    When our sin fears no eye nor perspective. [*Exits*]

ACT FOUR

Scene One

[*A room in Decoy's house. Enter* TWO MEN *leading* KICKSHAW
1   *blinded, and go off suddenly.*]

KICKSHAW   I am not hurt; my patience to obey them,
Not without fear to have my throat cut else,
Did me a courtesy. Whither have they brought me?
[*Pulls off a bandage*] 'T is devilish dark; the bottom of a well
2   At midnight, with but two stars on the top,
Were broad day to this darkness. I but think
How like a whirlwind the rogues caught me up,
And smothered my eyesight. Let me see,
These may be spirits, and, for aught I know,
3   Have brought me hither over twenty steeples.
Pray Heaven they were not bailiffs! that's more worth
My fear, and this a prison. All my debts
Reek in my nostril, and my bones begin
To ache with fear to be made dice; and yet
This is too calm and quiet for a prison.—
4   What if the riddle prove I am robbed? and yet
I did not feel 'em search me. How now! music!

[*Music within. Enter* DECOY, *disguised like an old woman, with a
light.*]

5   And a light! What beldam's this? I cannot pray.—
What art?

DECOY   A friend. Fear not, young man, I am
No spirit.

KICKSHAW   Off!

6
DECOY   Despise me not for age,
Or this coarse outside, which I wear not out
Of poverty; thy eyes be witness; 't is
No cave, or beggar's cell, thou 'rt brought to; let
That gold speak here's no want, which thou mayst spend,
7   And find a spring to tire even prodigality,
If thou be'st wise.

[*Gives him a purse.*]

    leading Kickshaw blinded: Shirley uses the same stratagem to less
plausible effect in *The Witty Fair One* Act IV, Sc. iv.

KICKSHAW The devil was a coiner   1
　　From the beginning; yet the gold looks current.

DECOY Thou 'rt still in wonder: know, I am mistress of
　　This house, and of a fortune that shall serve
　　And feed thee with delights; 't was I sent for thee;
　　The jewel and the letter came from me.   2
　　It was my art thus to contrive our meeting,
　　Because I would not trust thee with my fame,
　　Until I found thee worth a woman's honour.

KICKSHAW Honour and fame! The devil means to have
　　A care on 's credit. Though she sent for me,   3
　　I hope she has another customer
　　To do the trick withal; I would not turn
　　Familiar to a witch. [Aside]

DECOY What say'st? Canst thou
　　Dwell in my arms tonight? Shall we change kisses,
　　And entertain the silent hours with pleasure,   4
　　Such as old Time shall be delighted with,
　　And blame the too swift motion of his wings,
　　While we embrace?

KICKSHAW Embrace! She has had no teeth   5
　　This twenty years, and the next violent cough
　　Brings up her tongue; it cannot possibly
　　Be sound at root. I do not think but one
　　Strong sneeze upon her, and well meant, would make
　　Her quarters fall away; one kick would blow
　　Her up like gunpowder, and loose all her limbs.   6
　　She is so cold, an incubus would not heat her;
　　Her phlegm would quench a furnace, and her breath
　　Would damp a musket bullet. [Aside]

DECOY Have you, sir,
　　Considered?   7

KICKSHAW What?

DECOY My proposition.
　　Canst love?

KICKSHAW I could have done; whom do you mean?
　　I know you are pleased but to make sport.   8

DECOY Thou art not
　　So dull of soul as thou appear'st.

KICKSHAW This is
　　But some device; my grannam has some trick in 't.—
　　Yes, I can love.   9

1 DECOY But canst thou affect me?

KICKSHAW Although to reverence so grave a matron
Were an ambitious word in me, yet since
You give me boldness, I do love you.

DECOY Then
2   Thou art my own.

KICKSHAW Has she no cloven foot? [*Aside*]

DECOY And I am thine, and all that I command,
Thy servants; from this minute thou art happy,
3   And fate in thee will crown all my desires.
I grieved a proper man should be compelled
To bring his body to the common market.
My wealth shall make thee glorious; and, the more
To encourage thee, howe'er this form may fright
Thy youthful eyes, yet thou wilt find, by light
4   Of thy own sense, for other light is banished
My chamber, when our arms tie lovers' knots,
And kisses seal the welcome of our lips,
I shall not there affright thee, nor seem old,
With rivelled veins; my skin is smooth and soft
As ermines, with a spirit to meet thine,
5   Active, and equal to the queen of love's,
When she did court Adonis.

KICKSHAW This doth more
Confirm she is a devil, and I am
Within his own dominions. I must on,
6   Or else be torn o' pieces. I have heard
These succubae must not be crossed. [*Aside*]

DECOY We trifle
Too precious time away; I'll show you a prospect
Of the next chamber, and then out the candle.
7
KICKSHAW Have you no sack i' the house? I would go armed
Upon this breach.

DECOY It shall not need.

KICKSHAW One word,
8   Mother, have not you been a cat in your days?

DECOY I am glad you are so merry, sir. You observe
That bed? [*Opens a door*]

succuba: A demon in female form believed to have carnal intercourse
with men during sleep.

KICKSHAW   A very brave one.   1

DECOY   When you are
Disrobed, you can come thither in the dark.
You shall not stay for me? Come, as you wish
For happiness. [*Exits*]

KICKSHAW   I am preferred, if I   2
Be modest and obey: she cannot have
The heart to do me harm, an she were Hecate,
Herself. I will have a strong faith, and think
I march upon a mistress, the less evil.
If I 'scape fire now, I defy the devil. [*Exits*]   3

Scene Two

[*A room in Sir Thomas Bornwell's house. Enter* FREDERICK *gaily*   4
dressed, LITTLEWORTH, *and* STEWARD.]

FREDERICK   And how do you like me now?

STEWARD   Most excellent.

FREDERICK   Your opinion, Master Littleworth.   5

LITTLEWORTH   Your French tailor
Has made you a perfect gentleman; I may
Converse now with you, and preserve my credit.
Do you find no alteration in your body
With these new clothes?   6

FREDERICK   My body altered? No.

LITTLEWORTH   You are not yet in fashion then? That must
Have a new motion, garb, and posture, too,
Or all your pride is cast away; it is not
The cut of your apparel makes a gallant,   7
But the geometrical wearing of your clothes.

STEWARD   Master Littleworth tells you right; you wear your hat
Too like a citizen.

LITTLEWORTH   'T is like a midwife;   8
Place it with best advantage of your hair.
Is half your feather moulted? This does make
No show; it should spread over, like a canopy;
Your hot-reined monsieur wears it for a shade,
And cooler to his back. Your doublet must
Be more unbuttoned hereabouts; you'll not   9

1 Be a sloven else, a foul shirt is no blemish;
   You must be confident, and outface clean linen.
   Your doublet and your breeches must be allowed
   No private meeting here; your cloak's too long,
   It reaches to your buttock, and doth smell
2 Too much of Spanish gravity; the fashion
   Is to wear nothing but a cape; a coat
   May be allowed a covering for one elbow,
   And some, to avoid the trouble choose to walk
   In querpo, thus.

3 STEWARD Your coat and cloak's a brushing
   In Long Lane, Lombard. [Aside]

FREDERICK But what if it rain?

LITTLEWORTH Your belt about your shoulder is sufficient
   To keep off any storm; beside, a reed
4 But waved discreetly, has so many pores,
   It sucks up all the rain that falls about one.
   With this defence, when other men have been
   Wet to the skin through all their cloaks, I have
   Defied a tempest, and walked by the taverns
   Dry as a bone.
5
STEWARD Because he had no money
   To call for wine. [Aside]

FREDERICK Why, do you walk enchanted?
   Have you such pretty charms in town? But stay;
6 Who must I have to attend me?

LITTLEWORTH Is not that
   Yet thought upon?

STEWARD I have laid out for servants.

LITTLEWORTH They are everywhere.
7
STEWARD I cannot yet be furnished
   With such as I would put into his hands.

FREDERICK Of what condition must they be, and how
   Many in number, sir?

8 LITTLEWORTH Beside your fencing,
   Your singing, dancing, riding, and French master,

   in querpo: Without a cloak.
   in Long Lane, Lombard: Simply, too long.
   a reed: Here, a walking stick.

Two may serve domestic, to be constant waiters   1
Upon a gentleman; a fool, a pimp.

STEWARD   For these two officers I have enquired,
   And I am promised a convenient whiskin:
   I could save charges, and employ the pie-wench,
   That carries her intelligence in whitepots;   2
   Or 't is but taking order with the woman
   That trolls the ballads, she could fit him with
   A concubine to any tune; but I
   Have a design to place a fellow with him
   That has read all Sir Pandarus' works; a Trojan
   That lies concealed, and is acquainted with   3
   Both city and suburban fripperies,
   Can fetch 'em with a spell at midnight to him,
   And warrant which are for his turn; can, for
   A need, supply the surgeon, too.

FREDERICK   I like thy providence; such a one deserves   4
   A livery twice a year.

STEWARD   It shall not need; a cast suit of your worship's
   Will serve; he'll find a cloak to cover it,
   Out of his share with those he brings to bed to you.
                                                      5
FREDERICK   But must I call this fellow pimp?

LITTLEWORTH   It is
   Not necessary; Tom, or Jack, or Harry.
   Or what he's known abroad by, will sound better,
   That men may think he is a Christian.
                                                      6
FREDERICK   But hear you, Master Littleworth: is there not
   A method, and degrees of title in
   Men of this art?

LITTLEWORTH   According to the honour
   Of men that do employ 'em. An emperor   7
   May give this office to a duke; a king
   May have his viceroy to negociate for him;
   A duke may use a lord; the lord a knight,
   A knight may trust a gentleman; and when
   They are abroad, and merry, gentlemen
   May pimp to one another.   8

FREDERICK   Good, good fellowship!
   But for the fool now, that should wait on me,
   And break me jests?

trolls: Here, to pass round.

1 LITTLEWORTH   A fool is necessary.

STEWARD   By any means.

FREDERICK   But which of these two servants
Must now take place?

2 LITTLEWORTH   That question, Master Frederick,
The school of heraldry should conclude upon:
But if my judgment may be heard, the fool
Is your first man; and it is known a point
Of state to have a fool.

3 STEWARD   But, sir, the other
Is held the finer servant; his employments
Are full of trust, his person clean and nimble,
And none so soon can leap into preferment,
Where fools are poor.

4 LITTLEWORTH   Not all; there's story for 't;
Princes have been no wiser than they should be.
Would any nobleman, that were no fool,
Spend all in hope of the philosopher's stone,
To buy new lordships in another country?
Would knights build colleges, or gentlemen
5 Of good estates challenge the field, and fight,
Because a whore will not be honest? Come,
Fools are a family over all the world;
We do affect one naturally; indeed
The fool is leiger with us.

6 STEWARD   Then the pimp
Is extraordinary.

FREDERICK   Do not you fall out
About their places.—Here's my noble aunt!

7 [*Enter* LADY BORNWELL.]

LITTLEWORTH   How do you like your nephew, madam, now?

LADY BORNWELL   Well! turn about, Frederick. Very well!

FREDERICK   Am I not now a proper gentlemen?
8 The virtue of rich clothes! Now could I take
The wall of Julius Caesar, or affront
Great Pompey's upper lip, and defy the senate.
Nay, I can be as proud as your own heart, madam,

leiger, extraordinary: Diplomatic language for *resident* and *specially
employed.*

You may take that for your comfort; I put on 1
That virtue with my clothes, and I doubt not
But in a little time I shall be impudent
As any page, or player's boy. I am
Beholding to this gentleman's good discipline;
But I shall do him credit in my practise. 2
Your steward has some pretty notions, too,
In moral mischief.

LADY BORNWELL   Your desert in this
Exceeds all other service, and shall bind me
Both to acknowledge and reward. 3

LITTLEWORTH   Sweet madam,
Think me but worth your favour; I would creep
Upon my knees to honour you, and for every
Minute you lend to my reward, I'll pay
A year of serviceable tribute. 4

LADY BORNWELL   You
Can compliment.

LITTLEWORTH   Thus still she puts me off; unless I speak
The downright word, she'll never understand me.
A man would think that creeping on one's knees
Were English to a lady. [*Aside*] 5

KICKSHAW [*enters splendidly dressed*]   How is 't, Jack?—Pleasures
attend you, madam!
How does my plant of honour?

LADY BORNWELL   Who is this? 6

KICKSHAW   'T is Alexander.

LADY BORNWELL   Rich and glorious!

LITTLEWORTH   'T is Alexander the Great.

KICKSHAW   And my Bucephalus 7
Waits at the door.

LADY BORNWELL   Your case is altered, sir.

KICKSHAW   I cannot help these things, the Fates will have it;
'T is not my land does this.

LITTLEWORTH   But thou hast a plough 8
That brings it in.

LADY BORNWELL   Now he looks brave and lovely.

FREDERICK   Welcome, my gallant Macedonian.

KICKSHAW   Madam, you gave your nephew for my pupil. 9

1 I read but in a tavern; if you'll honour us,
   The Bear at the Bridge foot shall entertain you.
   A drawer is my Ganymede, he shall skink
   Brisk nectar to us; we will only have
   A dozen partridge in a dish; as many pheasants,
2 Quails, cocks, and godwits shall come marching up
   Like the trained-band; a fort of sturgeon
   Shall give most bold defiance to an army,
   And triumph o'er the table.—

   LADY BORNWELL   Sir, it will
   But dull the appetite to hear more, and mine
3 Must be excused. Another time I may be
   Your guest.

   KICKSHAW   'T is grown in fashion now with ladies;
   When you please, I'll attend you, Littleworth.—
   Come, Frederick.
4
   FREDERICK   We'll have music; I love noise.
   We will outroar the Thames, and shake the bridge, boy.

   [*Exit with* KICKSHAW.]

5 LITTLEWORTH   Madam, I kiss your hand; would you would think
   Of your poor servant; flesh and blood is frail,
   And troublesome to carry, without help.

   LADY BORNWELL   A coach will easily convey it, or
   You may take water at Strand bridge.

6 LITTLEWORTH   But I
   Have taken fire.

   LADY BORNWELL   The Thames will cool it, sir.

   LITTLEWORTH   But never quench my heart; your charity
   Can only do that.

7 LADY BORNWELL   I will keep it cold
   Of purpose.

   LITTLEWORTH   Now you bless me, and I dare
   Be drunk in expectation. [*Exits*]

   LADY BORNWELL   I am confident
8 He knows me not, and I were worse than mad
   To be my own betrayer.—Here's my husband.

   BORNWELL [*enters*]   Why, how now, Aretina? What! Alone?
   The mystery of this solitude? My house
   Turn desert o' the sudden! All the gamesters
9 Blown up! Why is the music put to silence?

Or have their instruments caught a cold, since we
Gave them the last heat? I must know thy ground
Of melancholy.

LADY BORNWELL   You are merry, as
You came from kissing Celestina.

BORNWELL   I
Feel her yet warm upon my lip; she is
Most excellent company; I did not think
There was that sweetness in her sex. I must
Acknowledge, 't was thy care to disenchant me
From a dull husband to an active lover.
With such a lady I could spend more years
Than since my birth my glass hath run soft minutes,
And yet be young; her presence has a spell
To keep off age; she has an eye would strike
Fire through an adamant.

LADY BORNWELL   I have heard as much
Bestowed upon a dull-faced chambermaid,
Whom love and wit would thus commend. True beauty
Is mocked when we compare thus, itself being
Above what can be fetched to make it lovely;
Or, could our thoughts reach something to declare
The glories of a face, or body's elegance,
That touches but our sense; when beauty spreads
Over the soul, and calls up understanding
To look what thence is offered, and admire
In both I must acknowledge Celestina
Most excellently fair, fair above all
The beauties I have seen, and one most worthy
Man's love and wonder.

BORNWELL   Do you speak, Aretina,
This with a pure sense to commend? Or is 't
The mockery of my praise?

LADY BORNWELL   Although it shame
Myself, I must be just, and give her all
The excellency of women; and were I
A man—

BORNWELL   What then?

LADY BORNWELL   I know not with what loss
I should attempt her love. She is a piece
So angelically moving, I should think
Frailty excused to dote upon her form,
And almost virtue to be wicked with her. [*Exits*]

1

2

3

4

5

6

7

8

9

1 BORNWELL   What should this mean? This is no jealousy,
Or she believes I counterfeit. I feel
Something within me, like a heat, to give
Her cause, would Celestina but consent.
What a frail thing is man! It is not worth
2 Our glory to be chaste, while we deny
Mirth and converse with women. He is good
That dares the tempter, yet corrects his blood. [*Exits*]

3 ## Scene Three

[*A room in Celestina's house. Enter* CELESTINA, MARIANA, *and* ISA-
BELLA.]

4 CELESTINA   I have told you all my knowledge: since he is pleased
To invite himself, he shall be entertained,
And you shall be my witnesses.

MARIANA   Who comes with him?

CELESTINA   Sir William Scentlove, that prepared me for
The honourable encounter. I expect
5 His lordship every minute.

SCENTLOVE [*enters*]   My lord is come.

CELESTINA   He has honoured me.

6 [*Enter* LORD A *and* HAIRCUT.]

SCENTLOVE   My lord, your periwig is awry.

LORD A   You, sir—

[*While* HAIRCUT *is busy about his hair,* SIR WILLIAM SCENTLOVE
7 *goes to* CELESTINA.]

SCENTLOVE   You may guess at the gentleman that's with him;
It is his barber, madam, do you observe?
An your ladyship wants a shaver.

8 HAIRCUT   She is here, sir.
I am betrayed.—Scentlove, your plot. I may
Have opportunity to be revenged. [*Exits*]

SCENTLOVE   She is in the midst.

LORD A   She's fair, I must confess;
9 But does she keep this distance out of state?

CELESTINA Though I am poor in language to express
  How much your lordship honours me, my heart
  Is rich and proud in such a guest. I shall
  Be out of love with every air abroad,
  And for this grace done my unworthy house,
  Be a fond prisoner, become anchorite,
  And spend my hours in prayer, to reward
  The blessing and the bounty of this presence.

LORD A Though you could turn each place you move in to
  A temple, rather than a wall should hide
  So rich a beauty from the world, it were
  Less want to lose our piety and your prayer.
  A throne were fitter to present you to
  Our wonder, whence your eyes, more worth than all
  They look on, should chain every heart a prisoner.

SCENTLOVE 'T was pretty well come off.

LORD A By your example
  I shall know how to compliment; in this,
  You more confirm my welcome.

CELESTINA I shall love
  My lips the better, if their silent language
  Persuade your lordship but to think so truly.

LORD A You make me smile, madam.

CELESTINA I hope you came not
  With fear that any sadness here should shake
  One blossom from your eye. I should be miserable
  To present any object should displease you.—

LORD A You do not, madam.

CELESTINA As I should account
  It no less sorrow, if your lordship should
  Lay too severe a censure on my freedom.
  I will not court a prince against his justice,
  Nor bribe him with a smile to think me honest.
  Pardon, my lord, this boldness, and the mirth
  That may flow from me. I believe my father
  Thought of no winding sheet when he begot me.

LORD A She has a merry soul.—It will become
  Me ask your pardon, madam, for my rude
  Approach, so much a stranger to your knowledge.

CELESTINA Not, my lord, so much stranger to my knowledge;
  Though I have but seen your person afar off,

1   I am acquainted with your character,
     Which I have heard so often, I can speak it.

LORD A   You shall do me an honour.

CELESTINA   If your lordship will
     Be patient.

2   LORD A   And glad to hear my faults.

CELESTINA   That as your conscience can agree upon them:
     However, if your lordship give me privilege,
     I'll tell you what's the opinion of the world.

3   LORD A   You cannot please me better.

CELESTINA   You're a lord,
     Born with as much nobility as would,
     Divided, serve to make ten noblemen,
     Without a herald; but with so much spirit
     And height of soul, as well might furnish twenty.
4   You are learnèd, a thing not compatible now
     With native honour; and are master of
     A language that doth chain all ears, and charm
     All hearts, where you persuade; a wit so flowing,
     And prudence to correct it, that all men
5   Believe they only meet in you, which, with
     A spacious memory, make up the full wonders:
     To these you have joined valour, and upon
     A noble cause, know how to use a sword
     To honour's best advantage, though you wear none.
     You are as bountiful as the showers that fall
6   Into the spring's green bosom; as you were
     Created lord of Fortune, not her steward;
     So constant to the cause in which you make
     Yourself an advocate, you dare all dangers;
     And men had rather you should be their friend,
7   Than justice or the bench bound up together.

LORD A   But did you hear all this?

CELESTINA   And more, my lord.

LORD A   Pray let me have it, madam.

8   CELESTINA   To all these virtues there is added one,—
     (Your lordship will remember, when I name it,
     I speak but what I gather from the voice
     Of others)—it is grown to a full fame
     That you have loved a woman.

9   LORD A   But one, madam?

CELESTINA Yes, many; give me leave to smile, my lord,
  I shall not need to interpret in what sense;   1
  But you have showed yourself right honourable,
  And, for your love to ladies, have deserved,
  If their vote might prevail, a marble statue.
  I make no comment on the people's text,—
  My lord, I should be sorry to offend.   2

LORD A You cannot, madam; these are things we owe
  To nature for.

CELESTINA And honest men will pay
  Their debts.   3

LORD A If they be able, or compound.

CELESTINA She had a hard heart would be unmerciful,
  And not give day to men so promising;
  But you owed women nothing.   4

LORD A Yes, I am
  Still in their debt, and I must owe them love,
  It was part of my character.

CELESTINA With your lordship's
  Pardon, I only said you had a fame   5
  For loving women; but of late, men say
  You have, against the imperial laws of love,
  Restrained the active flowings of your blood,
  And with a mistress buried all that is
  Hoped for in love's succession, as all beauty
  Had died with her, and left the world benighted!   6
  In this you more dishonour all our sex
  Than you did grace a part; when everywhere
  Love tempts your eye to admire a glorious harvest,
  And everywhere as full blown ears submit
  Their golden heads, the laden trees bow down   7
  Their willing fruit, and court your amorous tasting.

LORD A I see men would dissect me to a fibre;
  But do you believe this?

CELESTINA It is my wonder,
  I must confess, a man of nobler earth   8
  Than goes to vulgar composition,
  (Born and bred high, so unconfined, so rich
  In fortunes, and so read in all that sum
  Up human knowledge, to feed gloriously,
  And live at court, the only sphere wherein
  True beauty moves; nature's most wealthy garden,   9

₁ Where every blossom is more worth than all
The Hesperian fruit by jealous dragon watched,
Where all delights do circle appetite,
And pleasures multiply by being tasted,)
Should be so lost with thought of one turned ashes.
₂ There's nothing left, my lord, that can excuse you,
Unless you plead, what I am ashamed to prompt
Your wisdom to?

LORD A   What's that?

CELESTINA   That you have played
₃ The surgeon with yourself.

LORD A   And am made eunuch?

CELESTINA   It were much pity.

LORD A   Trouble not yourself,
I could convince your fears with demonstration
₄ That I am man enough, but knew not where,
Until this meeting, beauty dwelt. The court
You talk of must be where the queen of love is,
Which moves but with your person; in your eye
Her glory shines, and only at that flame
₅ Her wanton boy doth light his quickening torch.

CELESTINA   Nay, now you compliment; I would it did,
My lord, for your own sake.

LORD A   You would be kind,
And love me then?
₆
CELESTINA   My lord, I should be loving,
Where I found worth to invite it, and should cherish
A constant man.

LORD A   Then you should me, madam.

₇ CELESTINA   But is the ice about your heart fallen off?
Can you return to do what love commands?—
Cupid, thou shalt have instant sacrifice,
And I dare be the priest.

LORD A   Your hand, your lip;

₈ [*Kisses her*]

Now I am proof 'gainst all temptation.

CELESTINA   Your meaning, my good lord?

LORD A   I, that have strength
₉ Against thy voice and beauty, after this

May dare the charms of womankind.—Thou art
Bella Maria, unprofanèd yet;
This magic has no power upon my blood.—
Farewell, madam! if you durst be the example
Of chaste as well as fair, you were a brave one.

CELESTINA   I hope your lordship means not this for earnest:
Be pleased to grace a banquet.

LORD A   Pardon, madam.—
Will Scentlove, follow; I must laugh at you.

CELESTINA   My lord, I must beseech you stay, for honour,
For her whose memory you love best.

LORD A   Your pleasure.

CELESTINA   And by that virtue you have now professed.
I charge you to believe me too; I can
Now glory that you have been worth my trial,
Which, I beseech you, pardon. Had not you
So valiantly recovered in this conflict,
You had been my triumph, without hope of more
Than my just scorn upon your wanton flame;
Nor will I think these noble thoughts grew first
From melancholy, for some female loss,
As the fantastic world believes, but from
Truth, and your love of innocence, which shine
So bright in the two royal luminaries
At court, you cannot lose your way to chastity.
Proceed, and speak of me as honour guides you.

[*Exit* LORD A.]

I am almost tired.—Come, ladies, we'll beguile
Dull time, and take the air another while.

[*Exeunt*]

ACT FIVE

Scene One

1 [*A room in Sir Thomas Bornwell's house. Enter* LADY BORNWELL, *and a* SERVANT *with a purse.*]

LADY BORNWELL   But hath Sir Thomas lost five hundred pounds
Already?

2 SERVANT   And five hundred more he borrowed.
The dice are notable devourers, madam;
They make no more of pieces than of pebbles,
But thrust their heaps together, to engender.
"Two hundred more the caster!" cries this gentleman.
"I am with you—I have that to nothing, sir."

3 Again; " 'T is covered!" and the table, too,
With sums that frightened me. Here one sneaks out,
And with a martyr's patience smiles upon
His money's executioner, the dice;
Commands a pipe of good tobacco, and
I' the smoke on 't vanishes. Another makes

4 The bones vault o'er his head, swears that ill throwing
Has put his shoulder out of joint, calls for
A bonesetter. That looks to the box, to bid
His master send him some more hundred pounds
Which lost, he takes tobacco, and is quiet.

5 Here a strong arm throws in and in, with which
He brushes all the table, pays the rooks
That went their smelts a piece upon his hand,
Yet swears he has not drawn a stake this seven year.
But I was bid make haste; my master may
Lose this five hundred pounds ere I come hither. [*Exits*]

6 LADY BORNWELL   If we both waste so fast, we shall soon find
Our state is not immortal. Something in
His other ways appear not well already.

[*Enter* SIR THOMAS BORNWELL, *and* SERVANTS, *one with a purse.*]

7 BORNWELL   Ye tortoises, why make ye no more haste?
Go pay to the master of the house that money,
And tell the noble gamesters I have another
Superfluous thousand; at night I'll visit 'em.
Do you hear?

8 SERVANT   Yes, an please you.

410

BORNWELL   Do 't ye drudges.   1

[*Exeunt* SERVANTS.]

  Ta, ra, ra!—Aretina!

LADY BORNWELL   You have a pleasant humour, sir.   2

BORNWELL   What! should a gentleman be sad?

LADY BORNWELL   You have lost—

BORNWELL   A transitory sum; as good that way
  As another.   3

LADY BORNWELL   Do you not vex within for 't?

BORNWELL   I had rather lose a thousand more, than one
  Sad thought come near my heart for 't. Vex for trash!
  Although it go from other men like drops
  Of their life blood, we lose with the alacrity
  We drink a cup of sack, or kiss a mistress.   4
  No money is considerable with a gamester;
  They have souls more spacious than kings. Did two
  Gamesters divide the empire of the world,
  They'd make one throw for 't all, and he that lost
  Be no more melancholy than to have played for   5
  A morning's draught. Vex a rich soul for dirt!
  The quiet of whose every thought is worth
  A province.

LADY BORNWELL   But when dice have consumed all,
  Your patience will not pawn for as much more.   6

BORNWELL   Hang pawning! sell outright, and the fear's over.

LADY BORNWELL   Say you so? I'll have another coach tomorrow
  If there be rich above ground.

BORNWELL   I forgot
  To bid the fellow ask my jeweller   7
  Whether the chain of diamonds be made up;
  I will present it to my Lady Bellamour,
  Fair Celestina.

LADY BORNWELL   This gown I have worn
  Six days already; it looks dull, I'll give it   8
  My waiting woman, and have one of cloth
  Of gold embroidered; shoes and pantables
  Will show well of the same.

BORNWELL   I have invited
  A covey of ladies, and as many gentlemen   9

1   Tomorrow, to the Italian ordinary;
     I shall have rarities and regalias
     To pay for, madam; music, wanton songs,
     And tunes of silken petticoats to dance to.

     LADY BORNWELL   And tomorrow have I invited half the court
2   To dine here. What misfortune 't is your company
     And ours should be divided. After dinner
     I entertain them with a play.

     BORNWELL   By that time
     Your play inclines to the epilogue, shall we
3   Quit our Italian host; and whirl in coaches
     To the Dutch magazine of sauce, the Stillyard,
     Where deal, and backrag, and what strange wine else
     They dare but give a name to in the reckoning,
     Shall flow into our room, and drown Westphalias,
     Tongues, and anchovies, like some little town
4   Endangered by a sluice, through whose fierce ebb
     We wade, and wash ourselves, into a boat,
     And bid our coachmen drive their leather tenements
     By land, while we sail home, with a fresh tide,
     To some new rendezvous.

5   LADY BORNWELL   If you have not
     Pointed the place, pray bring your ladies hither;
     I mean to have a ball tomorrow night,
     And a rich banquet for 'em, where we'll dance
     Till morning rise, and blush to interrupt us.

6   BORNWELL   Have you no ladies i' the next room, to advance
     A present mirth? What a dull house you govern!
     Farewell! A wife's no company.—Aretina,
     I've summed up my estate, and find we may have
     A month good yet.

7   LADY BORNWELL   What mean you?

     BORNWELL   And I'd rather
     Be lord one month of pleasures, to the height
     And rapture of our senses, than be years
     Consuming what we have in foolish temperance.
     Live in the dark, and no fame wait upon us!
8   I will live so, posterity shall stand
     At gaze when I am mentioned.

     backrag: Baccarach, a Rhenish wine sold by a Rhenish wine house
     in the Steelyard.
     Westphalias: That is, Westphalian hams or gammon.

LADY BORNWELL A month good!   1
  And what shall be done then?

BORNWELL I'll over sea,
  And trail a pike. With watching, marching, lying
  In trenches, with enduring cold and hunger,
  And taking here and there a musket shot,   2
  I can earn every week four shillings, madam;
  And if the bullets favour me to snatch
  Any superfluous limb, when I return,
  With good friends, I despair not to be enrolled
  Poor knight of Windsor. For your course, madam,
  No doubt you may do well; your friends are great;   3
  Or if your poverty, and their pride, cannot
  Agree, you need not trouble much invention,
  To find a trade to live by; there are customers.
  Farewell, be frolic, madam! If I live,
  I will feast all my senses, and not fall   4
  Less than a Phaeton from my throne of pleasure,
  Though my estate flame like the world about me. [*Exits*]

LADY BORNWELL 'T is very pretty!—

[*Enter* DECOY.]   5

  Madam Decoy!

DECOY What! melancholy,
  After so sweet a night's work? Have not I
  Showed myself mistress of my art?
                                                                      6
LADY BORNWELL A lady.

DECOY That title makes the credit of the act
  A story higher. You've not seen him yet?
  I wonder what he'll say.

LADY BORNWELL He's here.   7

[*Enter* KICKSHAW *and* FREDERICK.]

KICKSHAW Bear up,
  My little myrmidon; does not Jack Littleworth
  Follow?   8

FREDERICK Follow? He fell into the Thames
  At landing.

KICKSHAW The devil shall dive for him,

  Poor knight of Windsor: See note to *Eastward Ho,* Act IV, Sc. i.

1   Ere I endanger my silk stockings for him:
    Let the watermen alone, they have drags and engines.
    When he has drunk his julep, I shall laugh
    To see him come in pickled the next tide.

FREDERICK   He'll never sink, he has such a cork brain.

2   KICKSHAW   Let him be hanged or drowned, all's one to me;
    Yet he deserves to die by water, cannot
    Bear his wine credibly.

FREDERICK   Is not this my aunt?

3   KICKSHAW   And another handsome lady; I must know her. [*Goes
    up to* DECOY]

FREDERICK   My blood is rampant, too, I must court somebody;
    As good my aunt as any other body.

LADY BORNWELL   Where have you been, cousin?

4   FREDERICK   At the Bear
    At the Bridge foot, where our first health began
    To the fair Aretina, whose sweet company
    Was wished by all. We could not get a lay,
    A tumbler, a device, a bona roba,
5   For any money; drawers were grown dull:
    We wanted our true firks, and our vagaries.—
    When were you in drink, aunt?

LADY BORNWELL   How?

FREDERICK   Do not ladies
6   Play the good fellows too? There's no true mirth
    Without 'em. I have now such tickling fancies!
    That doctor of the chair of wit has read
    A precious lecture, how I should behave
    Myself to ladies; as now, for example. [*Goes up to* LADY BORN-
    WELL]
7
LADY BORNWELL   Would you practise upon me?

FREDERICK   I first salute you,
    You have a soft hand, madam; are you so
    All over?

8   LADY BORNWELL   Nephew!

FREDERICK   Nay, you should but smile.
    And then again I kiss you; and thus draw
    Off your white glove, and start, to see your hand

    julep: Rose water, or sweetened drink; here, of course, Thames water.

More excellently white: I grace my own
Lip with this touch, and turning gently thus,
Prepare you for my skill in palmistry,
Which, out of curiosity, no lady
But easily applies to: the first line
I look with most ambition to find out,
Is Venus' girdle, a fair semicircle,
Enclosing both the mount of Sol and Saturn;
If that appear, she's for my turn; a lady
Whom nature has prepared for the career;
And, Cupid at my elbow, I put forward:
You have this very line, aunt.

LADY BORNWELL   The boy's frantic!

FREDERICK   You have a couch or pallet; I can shut
The chamber door. Enrich a stranger, when
Your nephew's coming into play!

LADY BORNWELL   No more.

FREDERICK   Are you so coy to your own flesh and blood?

KICKSHAW   Here, take your playfellow; I talk of sport,
And she would have me marry her.

FREDERICK   Here's Littleworth.

[*Enter* LITTLEWORTH, *wet*.]

Why, how now, tutor?

LITTLEWORTH   I have been fishing.

FREDERICK   And what have you caught?

LITTLEWORTH   My belly full of water.

KICKSHAW   Ha, ha! Where's thy rapier?

LITTLEWORTH   My rapier is drowned,
And I am little better; I was held up by the heels,
And out came a ton of water, beside wine.

KICKSHAW   It has made thee sober.

LITTLEWORTH   Would you have me drunk
With water?

LADY BORNWELL   I hope your fire is quenched by this time.

FREDERICK   It is not now, as when "your worship walked
By all the taverns, Jack, dry as a bone."

KICKSHAW   You had store of fish under water, Jack.

1 LITTLEWORTH   It has made a poor John of me.

FREDERICK   I do not think but if we cast an angle
Into his belly, we might find some pilchards.

LITTLEWORTH   And boiled, by this time.—Dear Madam, a bed.

2 KICKSHAW   Carry but the water spaniel to a grassplot,
Where he may roll himself; let him but shake
His ears twice in the sun, and you may grind him
Into a posset.

FREDERICK   Come, thou shalt to my bed,
3 Poor pickerel.

DECOY   Alas, sweet gentleman!

LITTLEWORTH   I have ill luck an I should smell by this time;
I am but new ta'en, I am sure.—Sweet gentlewoman!

DECOY   Your servant.

4 LITTLEWORTH   Pray do not pluck off my skin;
It is so wet, unless you have good eyes,
You'll hardly know it from a shirt.

DECOY   Fear nothing.

5 [*Exeunt all but* KICKSHAW *and* LADY BORNWELL.]

LADY BORNWELL   He has sack enough, and I may find his humour.
[*Aside*]

KICKSHAW   And how is 't with your ladyship? You look
6 Without a sunshine in your face.

LADY BORNWELL   You are glorious
In mind and habit.

KICKSHAW   Ends of gold and silver!

LADY BORNWELL   Your other clothes were not so rich. Who was
7 Your tailor, sir?

KICKSHAW   They were made for me long since;
They have known but two bright days upon my back.
I had a humour, madam, to lay things by;
They will serve two days more: I think I have gold enough
8 To go to the mercer. I'll now allow myself
A suit a week, as this, with necessary
Dependances, beaver, silk stockings, garters,
And roses, in their due conformity;
Boots are forbid a clean leg, but to ride in.

poor John: Dried, salted hake.

My linen every morning comes in new, 1
The old goes to great bellies.

LADY BORNWELL   You are charitable.

KICKSHAW   I may dine with you sometime, or at the court,
To meet good company, not for the table.
My clerk o' the kitchen's here, a witty epicure, 2
A spirit, that, to please me with what's rare,
Can fly a hundred mile a day to market,
And make me lord of fish and fowl. I shall
Forget there is a butcher; and to make
My footman nimble, he shall feed on nothing
But wings of wild fowl. 3

LADY BORNWELL   These ways are costly.

KICKSHAW   Therefore I'll have it so; I have sprung a mine.

LADY BORNWELL   You make me wonder, sir, to see this change
Of fortune: your revenue was not late 4
So plentiful.

KICKSHAW   Hang dirty land, and lordships!
I would not change one lodging I have got,
For the Chamber of London.

LADY BORNWELL   Strange, of such a sudden, 5
To rise to this estate! No fortunate hand
At dice could lift you up so, for 't is since
Last night: yesterday, you were no such monarch.

KICKSHAW   There be more games than dice.

LADY BORNWELL   It cannot be 6
A mistress, though your person is worth love;
None possibly are rich enough to feed
As you have cast the method of your riots.
A princess, after all her jewels, must
Be forced to sell her provinces. 7

KICKSHAW   Now you talk
Of jewels, what do you think of this?

LADY BORNWELL   A rich one.

KICKSHAW   You'll honour me to wear 't; this other toy
I had from you; this chain I borrowed of you, 8
A friend had it in keeping.

[*Gives her the jewel and chain.*]

                    If your ladyship
Want any sum, you know your friend, and Alexander. 9

1   LADY BORNWELL   Dare you trust my security?

KICKSHAW   There's gold,
I shall have more tomorrow.

LADY BORNWELL   You astonish me;
Who can supply these?

2   KICKSHAW   A dear friend I have;
She promised we should meet again i' the morning.

LADY BORNWELL   Not that I wish to know
More of your happiness than I have already
Heart to congratulate,—be pleased to lay

3   My wonder.

KICKSHAW   'T is a secret—

LADY BORNWELL   Which I'll die
Ere I'll betray.

4   KICKSHAW   You have always wished me well;
But you shall swear not to reveal the party.

LADY BORNWELL   I'll lose the benefit of my tongue.

KICKSHAW   Nor be
Afraid at what I say. What think you first

5   Of an old witch, a strange ill-favoured hag,
That, for my company last night, has wrought
This cure upon my fortune? I do sweat
To think upon her name.

LADY BORNWELL   How, sir! A witch?

6   KICKSHAW   I would not fright your ladyship too much
At first, but witches are akin to spirits.
The truth is—Nay, if you look pale already,
I have done.

LADY BORNWELL   Sir, I beseech you.

7   KICKSHAW   If you have
But courage then to know the truth, I'll tell you
In one word; my chief friend is—the devil!

LADY BORNWELL   What devil? How I tremble!

8   KICKSHAW   Have a heart;
'T was a she-devil, too, a most insatiate,
Abominable devil, with a tail
Thus long.

LADY BORNWELL   Goodness defend me! Did you see her?

9   KICKSHAW   No, 't was i' the dark; but she appeared first to me

I' the likeness of a beldam, and was brought,   1
I know not how, nor whither, by two goblins,
More hooded than a hawk.

LADY BORNWELL   But would you venture
Upon a devil!

KICKSHAW   Ay, for means.   2

LADY BORNWELL   How black
An impudence is this! [*Aside*] But are you sure
It was the devil you enjoyed?

KICKSHAW   Say nothing;   3
I did the best to please her, but as sure
As you live, 't was a hellcat.

LADY BORNWELL   Do you not quake?

KICKSHAW   I found myself in the very room i' the morning,
Where two of her familiars had left me.   4

SERVANT [*enters*]   My lord is come to visit you.

KICKSHAW   No words,
As you respect my safety. I have told tales
Out of the devil's school; if it be known,
I lose a friend. 'T is now about the time   5
I promised her to meet again; at my
Return I'll tell you wonders. Not a word. [*Exits*]

LADY BORNWELL   'T is a false glass; sure I am more deformed:
[*Looks in her pocket mirror*] What have I done?—my soul is
miserable.   6

LORD A [*enters*]   I sent you a letter, madam.

LADY BORNWELL   You expressed
Your noble care of me, my lord.

[*Reenter* SIR THOMAS BORNWELL, *with* CELESTINA.]   7

BORNWELL   Your lordship
Does me an honour.

LORD A   Madam, I am glad
To see you here; I meant to have kissed your hand,
Ere my return to court.   8

CELESTINA   Sir Thomas has
Prevailed to bring me, to his trouble, hither.

LORD A   You do him grace.

BORNWELL   Why, what's the matter, madam?   9

1   Your eyes are tuning Lachrimae.

LADY BORNWELL As you
Do hope for Heaven, withdraw, and give me but
The patience of ten minutes.

2 BORNWELL Wonderful!
I will not hear you above that proportion.
She talks of Heaven:—Come, where must we to counsel?

LADY BORNWELL You shall conclude me when you please. [*Exits*]

BORNWELL I follow.

3 LORD A What alteration is this? I, that so late
Stood the temptation of her eye and voice,
Boasted a heart 'bove all licentious flame,
At second view turn renegade, and think
I was too superstitious, and full
Of phlegm, not to reward her amorous courtship
4 With manly freedom.

CELESTINA I obey you, sir.

BORNWELL I'll wait upon your lordship presently. [*Exits*]

LORD A She could not want a cunning to seem honest
5 When I neglected her. I am resolved.—
You still look pleasant, madam.

CELESTINA I have cause,
My lord, the rather for your presence, which
Hath power to charm all trouble in my thoughts.

6 LORD A I must translate that compliment, and owe
All that is cheerful in myself to these
All-quick'ning smiles: and rather than such bright
Eyes should repent their influence upon me,
I would release the aspects, and quit the bounty
Of all the other stars. Did you not think me
7 A strange and melancholy gentleman,
To use you so unkindly?

CELESTINA Me, my lord?

LORD A I hope you made no loud complaint; I would not
8 Be tried by a jury of ladies.

CELESTINA For what, my lord?

LORD A I did not meet that noble entertainment

Lachrimae: "Tears," a popular work for the lute by John Dowland.
meet: Here, match.

You were late pleased to show me.   1

CELESTINA   I observed
No such defect in your lordship, but a brave
And noble fortitude.

LORD A   A noble folly;
I bring repentance for 't. I know you have,   2
Madam, a gentle faith, and will not ruin
What you have built to honour you.

CELESTINA   What's that?

LORD A   If you can love, I'll tell your ladyship.   3

CELESTINA   I have a stubborn soul else.

LORD A   You are all
Composed of harmony.

CELESTINA   What love do you mean?

LORD A   That which doth perfect both; madam, you have heard   4
I can be constant, and if you consent
To grace it so, there is a spacious dwelling
Prepared within my heart for such a mistress.

CELESTINA   Your mistress, my good lord?

LORD A   Why, my good lady,   5
Your sex doth hold it no dishonour
To become mistress to a noble servant
In the new court Platonic way. Consider
Who 't is that pleads to you; my birth, and present
Value, can be no stain to your embrace;   6
But these are shadows when my love appears,
Which shall, in his first miracle, return
Me in my bloom of youth, and thee a virgin;
When I, within some new Elysium,
Of purpose made and meant for us, shall be   7
In every thing Adonis, but in his
Contempt of love; and court thee from a Daphne
Hid in the cold rind of a bashful tree,
With such warm language and delight, till thou
Leap from that bays into the queen of love,
And pay my conquest with composing garlands   8
Of thy own myrtle for me.

CELESTINA   What's all this?

LORD A   Consent to be my mistress, Celestina,
And we will have it springtime all the year;
Upon whose invitations, when we walk,   9

1   The winds shall play soft descant to our feet,
    And breathe rich odours to re-pure the air:
    Green bowers on every side shall tempt our stay,
    And violets stoop to have us tread upon 'em.
    The red rose shall grow pale, being near thy cheek,
2   And the white blush, o'ercome with such a forehead.
    Here laid, and measuring with ourselves some bank,
    A thousand birds shall from the woods repair,
    And place themselves so cunningly behind
    The leaves of every tree, that while they pay
    Us tribute of their songs, thou shalt imagine
3   The very trees bear music, and sweet voices
    Do grow in every arbour. Here can we
    Embrace and kiss, tell tales, and kiss again,
    And none but Heaven our rival.

CELESTINA   When we are
4   Weary of these, what if we shift our paradise,
    And through a grove of tall and even pine,
    Descend into a valley, that shall shame
    All the delights of Tempe; upon whose
    Green plush the Graces shall be called to dance,
5   To please us, and maintain their fairy revels,
    To the harmonious murmurs of a stream
    That gently falls upon a rock of pearl.
    Here doth the nymph, forsaken Echo, dwell,
    To whom we'll tell the story of our love,
    Till at our surfeit and her want of joy,
6   We break her heart with envy. Not far off,
    A grove shall call us to a wanton river,
    To see a dying swan give up the ghost,
    The fishes shooting up their tears in bubbles,
    That they must lose the genius of their waves—
    And such love linsey-woolsey, to no purpose.
7

LORD A   You chide me handsomely; pray tell me how
You like this language.

CELESTINA   Good my lord, forbear.

LORD A   You need not fly out of this circle, madam;
8   These widows are so full of circumstance!
    I'll undertake, in this time I have courted
    Your ladyship for the toy, to have broken ten,
    Nay, twenty colts, virgins I mean, and taught 'em
    The amble, or what pace I most affected.

9 CELESTINA   You're not, my lord, again, the lord I thought you;

And I must tell you now, you do forget 1
Yourself and me.

LORD A You'll not be angry, madam?

CELESTINA Nor rude (though gay men have a privilege),
It shall appear:—there is a man, my lord,
Within my acquaintance, rich in worldly fortunes, 2
But cannot boast any descent of blood,
Would buy a coat of arms.

LORD A He may, and legs
Booted and spurred, to ride into the country.

CELESTINA But these will want antiquity, my lord, 3
The seal of honour. What's a coat cut out
But yesterday, to make a man a gentleman?
Your family, as old as the first virtue
That merited an escutcheon, doth owe
A glorious coat of arms; if you will sell now 4
All that your name doth challenge, in that ensign,
I'll help you to a chapman, that shall pay,
And pour down wealth enough for 't.

LORD A Sell my arms!
I cannot, madam. 5

CELESTINA Give but your consent,
You know not how the state may be inclined
To dispensation; we may prevail
Upon the Heralds' office afterward.

LORD A I'll sooner give these arms to the hangman's axe, 6
My head, my heart, to twenty executions,
Than sell one atom from my name.

CELESTINA Change that,
And answer him would buy my honour from me;
Honour, that is not worn upon a flag,
Or pennon, that, without the owner's dangers, 7
An enemy may ravish, and bear from me;
But that which grows and withers with my soul,
Beside the body's stain: think, think, my lord,
To what you would unworthily betray me,
If you would not, for price of gold, or pleasure 8
(If that be more your idol), lose the glory
And painted honour of your house.—I have done.

LORD A Enough to rectify a satyr's blood.
Obscure my blushes here.

[*Enter* SCENTLOVE *and* HAIRCUT *behind.*] 9

1 HAIRCUT   Or this, or fight with me;
It shall be no exception that I wait
Upon my lord; I am a gentleman,
You may be less, and be a knight: the office
I do my lord is honest, sir. How many
2   Such you have been guilty of Heaven knows.

SCENTLOVE   'T is no fear of your sword, but that I would not
Break the good laws established against duels.

HAIRCUT   Off with your periwig, and stand bare.

3 [SCENTLOVE *takes off his periwig.*]

LORD A   From this
Minute I'll be a servant to your goodness;
A mistress in the wanton sense is common,
I'll honour you with chaste thoughts, and call you so.
4 CELESTINA   I'll study to be worth your fair opinion.

LORD A   Scentlove, your head was used to a covering,
Beside a hat; when went the hair away?

SCENTLOVE   I laid a wager, my lord, with Haircut,
5 Who thinks I shall catch cold, that I'll stand bare
This half hour.

HAIRCUT   Pardon my ambition,
Madam, I told you truth; I am a gentleman,
And cannot fear that name is drowned in my
6 Relation to my lord.

CELESTINA   I dare not think so.

HAIRCUT   From henceforth call my service duty, madam:
That pig's head, that betrayed me to your mirth,
Is doing penance for 't.

7 SCENTLOVE   Why may not I,
My lord, begin a fashion of no hair?

CELESTINA   Do you sweat, Sir William?

SCENTLOVE   Not with store of nightcaps.

8 [*Reenter* SIR THOMAS *and* LADY BORNWELL, *in conversation.*]

LADY BORNWELL   Heaven has dissolved the clouds that hung upon
My eyes, and if you can with mercy meet
A penitent, I throw my own will off,
9 And now in all things obey yours. My nephew

Send back again to the college, and myself   1
To what place you'll confine me.

BORNWELL   Dearer now
Than ever to my bosom, thou shalt please
Me best to live at thy own choice. I did
But fright thee with a noise of my expenses;   2
The sums are safe, and we have wealth enough,
If yet we use it nobly. My lord—madam,
Pray honour us tonight,

LADY BORNWELL   I beg your presence,
And pardon.   3

BORNWELL   I know not how my Aretina
May be disposed tomorrow for the country.

CELESTINA   You must not go before you have done
Me honour to accept an entertainment
Where I have power; on those terms I'm your guest.   4

BORNWELL   You grace us, madam.

LADY BORNWELL   Already
I feel a cure upon my soul, and promise
My after life to virtue. Pardon, Heaven,
My shame, yet hid from the world's eye. [*Aside*]   5

DECOY [*reenters behind*]   Sweet madam!

LADY BORNWELL   Not for the world be seen here! We are lost.
I'll visit you at home.

[*Exit* DECOY.]   6

                    But not to practise
What she expects: my counsel may recover her. [*Aside*]

KICKSHAW [*reenters*]   Where's madam?—Pray lend me a little
     money,   7
My spirit has deceived me; Proserpine
Has broke her word.

LADY BORNWELL   Do you expect to find
The devil true to you?

KICKSHAW   Not too loud.   8

LADY BORNWELL   I'll voice it
Louder, to all the world, your horrid sin,
Unless you promise me religiously,
To purge your foul blood by repentance, sir.

KICKSHAW   Then I'm undone.   9

1 LADY BORNWELL   Not while I have power
To encourage you to virtue; I'll endeavour
To find you out some nobler way at court,
To thrive in.

KICKSHAW   Do 't, and I'll forsake the devil,
2 And bring my flesh to obedience. You shall steer me.—
My lord, your servant.

LORD A   You are brave again.

KICKSHAW   Madam, your pardon.

BORNWELL   Your offence requires
3 Humility.

KICKSHAW   Low as my heart.—Sir Thomas,
I'll sup with you, a part of satisfaction.

BORNWELL   Our pleasures cool. Music: and when our ladies
4 Are tired with active motion, to give
Them rest, in some new rapture to advance
Full mirth, our souls shall leap into a dance.

[*Exeunt*]

5

THE END

BIBLIOGRAPHY

Editions

Eastward Ho
Edited by Felix Schelling, Belles Lettres Series, 1906.
Edited by T. M. Parrott, in *George Chapman's Plays*, Vol. 2, *Comedies*, 1914.

A Trick to Catch the Old One
Works, edited by A. Dyce, 1840.
Works, edited by A. H. Bullen, 1885-1886.
Edited by A. C. Swinburne, Mermaid Series, 1887.

The City Madam
The Plays, Edited by W. Gifford, 1805.
Edited by Cyrus Hoy, Regent Renaissance Series, 1961.
Edited by T. W. Craik, New Mermaids, 1964.

The Sparagus Garden
Printed 1640.
Reprinted in Pearson Reprints, 1873.

The Lady of Pleasure
Dramatic Works and Poems, Edited by W. Gifford and A. Dyce, 1833.
Edited by Sir E. Gosse, Mermaid Series, 1885.

References

Bentley, G. E., *The Jacobean and Caroline Stage,* 1940.
Boas, F. S., *An Introduction to Stuart Drama,* 1945.
Cambridge Bibliography of English Literature, edited by F. W. Bateson, 1940.
Cambridge History of English Literature, 1932.
Dodsley's Old English Plays, edited by W. C. Hazlitt, 1876.
Knights, L. C., *Drama and Society in the Age of Jonson,* 1937.
Nicoll, Allardyce, *British Drama,* 1925.

Jamieson, John, *A Dictionary of the Scottish Language,* abridged edition, 1846.
Nares, Robert, *Glossary,* 1822.
Onions, C. T., *A Shakespeare Dictionary.*
Oxford English Dictionary (shorter), 1933.

Brett-James, L., *The Growth of Stuart London.*
Jenkinson, Wilberforce, *London Churches before the Great Fire.*
Mitchell, R. J., and M. D. R. Leys, *A History of London Life.*

GLOSSARY OF LONDON PLACE NAMES

BANSTEAD DOWNS Near Epsom in Surrey, traditionally a centre for horse racing.

BARBICAN A City street so called because it ran over the site of an old watchtower, part of the fortifications of the old walled City.

BARNARD'S INN One of the old Inns of Chancery, like the Inns of Court, a place of residence and association of law students. Barnard was the occupier when the owner bequeathed the building to Lincoln Cathedral in the fifteenth century.

BARNET At the time these plays were written, a village of resort in Hertfordshire, north of London.

BEAR A well-known tavern in the Strand by Strand Bridge where the waters from the north of London were discharged into the Thames.

BILLINGSGATE The fishmarket.

BLACKFRIARS A locality a short distance from St. Paul's "noted in this period for three things: its theatre, a number of Puritans and the sale of feathers; the two latter professions being often united" (Nares). (See *Bartholomew Fair* Act V, Sc. v., and *The Alchemist,* both by Jonson.)

BLACKWALL Blackwall stairs on the north bank, a part of the London docks.

BLUE ANCHOR A tavern in Billingsgate.

BOW BELLS The bells of St. Mary-le-Bow, in Cheapside. The definition of a Cockney today is still a person born within the sound of Bow bells.

BRENTFORD A resort in Essex for City dwellers.

BRIDEWELL A house of correction for vagabonds and prostitutes, situated near the mouth of the River Fleet by the Thames. Beating hemp, the correction mentioned in *The City Madam* Act IV, Sc. ii, is the making up of bundles of hemp ready for steeping.

BURSE The New Exchange, built 1609, included a number of fashionable shops for fabrics and clothes in its arcades.

429

CHARING CROSS A district at the west end of the Strand, so called since Edward I set up a cross in the hamlet of Charing to mark the place where the remains of his wife Eleanor rested on the way to burial at Westminster.

CHEAPSIDE The old marketplace of London running east from a point near St. Paul's Cathedral.

COLD HARBOUR A building near the Isle of Dogs on the north bank of the Thames where beggars and debtors took sanctuary.

COUNTER There were two counters, or debtors' prisons, attached to the Mayor's court of justice at this period. One was in St. Margaret's Hill, Southwark, and served the borough of the City of London. The other was in Wood Street off Cheapside. Those prisoners who could afford it lodged on the Master's side, next in price came the Knights' ward, then the twopenny ward. The hole was a dungeon for those prisoners who could not afford better; the hell was an even worse accommodation. In 1641 Thomas Jordan wrote a play called *The Walks of Islington and Hogsdon, with the Humours of the Wood Street Counter*.

COVENT GARDEN The earliest London square development on the north side of the Strand at its east end. The piazza on two sides was designed by Inigo Jones in 1632. It rapidly became a centre of dissipation, and also in 1632 Brome wrote a play *Covent Garden Weeded* on this theme.

CUCKHOLD'S HAVEN On the south bank, a little east of Rother-hythe Church. *Eastward Ho* was revived in 1685 under this title.

EXCHANGE The Royal Exchange, built 1567 at the instigation of Sir Thomas Gresham (1519-1579), a celebrated financial agent and Lord Mayor. Often in Elizabethan plays he is referred to as a model of civic virtue and success. A second Exchange (see BURSE) was built in 1609. Thomas Heywood's (1574?-1641) play *If You Know Not Me, You Know Nobody* deals with Gresham and the building of the Exchange.

FLEET LANE, PIE CORNER Streets off Fleet Street noted for their cooks' shops.

FLEET STREET Runs east to Ludgate from the Strand over the old Fleet river. In it was a debtors' prison.

GOLDSMITHS' ROW The area around the Strand, Holborn and Fleet Street. Efforts were made in the reign of James I and again in 1630 to drive the smiths back into the City where they had complained of high rents. They also wanted to be nearer the fashionable private houses in the Strand.

GRAVESEND   A Thames-side port below London.

HOLBORN   A district and street to the north of Fleet Street which in this period was already becoming a centre for the trade in precious stones and metals, particularly the area on the site of the garden of Sir Christopher Hatton who came into its possession by royal favour in 1581.

ISLE OF DOGS   A marshy peninsula on the London bank of the Thames bounded by Wapping and Limehouse.

ISLINGTON   At the time these plays were written, a village north of London frequented by Sunday trippers.

KING'S BENCH   The prison at Westminster for debtors sent by the King's Bench, which was the supreme court of common law.

LAMBETH MARSH   A swampy tract on the south bank near Lambeth Church, a haunt of rogues and prostitutes.

LUDGATE   A prison for the better sort of debtor or bankrupt, set in the gatehouse of the old City gate. (See the COUNTER.)

MILE END   At this time a suburb to the east of the City.

MOORFIELDS   An area outside Moorgate on the north side of the old city walls; a duelling ground and haunt of beggars.

NEATHOUSE   A nursery garden, and place of entertainment near Chelsea; probably the original Asparagus Garden.

PARTRIDGE ALLEY   A haunt of prostitutes near Lincoln's Inn Fields.

PIE CORNER, FLEET LANE   Streets off Fleet Street noted for their cooks' shops.

PIMLICO   Then a summer resort for Londoners.

POOL   The Pool of London referred to that part of the Thames below the Tower between Wapping and Rotherhythe that served for anchorage in the stream.

ROMFORD   A small town in Essex.

RUFFIANS' HALL   In West Smithfield, where duels were commonly fought.

Sᴛ. Gɪʟᴇs-ɪɴ-ᴛʜᴇ-Fɪᴇʟᴅ   After 1600 the area round this church to the north of the Strand was developed as town houses for courtiers.

Sᴛ. Kᴀᴛʜᴀʀɪɴᴇ's   An old Royal hospital near the Tower used as a reformatory for prostitutes.

Sᴛ. Mᴀʀᴛɪɴ's   St. Martin's-le-Grand. Although the church itself was destroyed at the dissolution of the monasteries by Henry VIII in the 1530's, the tavern which replaced it claimed the ancient right of sanctuary successfully until 1697, thus attracting debtors, criminals and their hangers-on to the site. The parish, to the north of Cheapside, was known as the resort of dealers in fake jewelery and for its foreign handworkers.

Sᴛ. Pᴀᴜʟ's Sᴛᴇᴇᴘʟᴇ   In 1561, for the second time, St. Paul's steeple was destroyed by lightning. "Divers persons in time of the said tempest being in the River Thames . . . affirmed that they saw a long and spear-pointed flame of fire run through the top of the broach or shaft of Paul's steeple . . . did feel a marvellous strong air or whirlwind with a smell like brimstone coming from Paul's church and withal heard the rush of ye stones which fell from their steeple into the church." J. Pilkington, *The Burning of Paul's Church,* 1563. Although funds were collected in the reign of Charles I to repair the fabric of the cathedral, this was never achieved. "The head of this church hath been twice troubled with a burning fever, and so the City to keep it from a third danger let it stand without a head; then the world was all Church, and now the Church is all world." D. Lupton, *London and the Country Carbonadoed,* 1632.

Sᴍɪᴛʜғɪᴇʟᴅ   See Wᴇsᴛ Sᴍɪᴛʜғɪᴇʟᴅ.

Sᴛʀᴀɴᴅ   At this time a street lined with the houses of the fashionably rich: hence goldsmiths were attracted to this area from the City. (See Gᴏʟᴅsᴍɪᴛʜ's Rᴏᴡ.)

Tᴇᴍᴘʟᴇ Bᴀʀ   One of a number of "bars," or barrier gates, on the chief roads out of London which marked the limits of the common lands, or "liberties," and a vantage point from which to watch the Lord Mayor's Show. The Temple, lying between Fleet Street and the river, originally belonged to the Knights Templar and was converted to Inns of Court in the fourteenth century.

Tʏʙᴜʀɴ   From the sixteenth century until 1783, Tyburn was the principal place of public hangings near what is now Marble Arch.

The name was originally taken from that of a nearby stream which flowed into the Thams.

WAPPING A Thames dock on the London side where gallows stood to hang pirates.

WEST SMITHFIELD Until 1855 served as the London cattle market. (See *Oliver Twist,* chap. 21.) In the sixteenth century it was the scene of burnings for heresy, hence the reference in *The Sparagus Garden* Act I, Sc. v.

WHITEFRIARS Originally a Carmelite monastery on Fleet Street that became a debtors' sanctuary. (See the description in Sir Walter Scott's *The Fortunes of Nigel.*)

VOCABULARY

Accent   An utterance.

Accompt   Account.

Ancome   A boil or whitlow.

Angel   A gold coin worth one third of a pound.

Annuity   An annual rent charge.

Articulate   To enter into articles of agreement.

Assumpsit   A promise or contract, written or verbal.

At all   The cry of the dicecaster when he wishes to bet against all comers.

Attach   To seize for payment of debt.

Bag pudding   Suet or plum pudding is the accepted meaning, but just as likely it is a kind of haggis; a pudding made of "bags" or entrails.

Balloon   A field sport consisting of driving about a large inflated leather ball with a stick.

Band   A collar or ruff.

Bandog   Fierce dog, usually kept bound or tied up.

Basket, sheriff's   The basket containing remains of food sent to prisoners from the sheriff's table.

Bate   Abate.

Beadsman   A pensioner who prays for his benefactor's soul.

Black coats   The clergy.

Blue coat   The livery worn by a servant.

Bodkin, cloth of   Silk, with a warp of gold thread.

Bounce   An onomatopoeic sound for the noise of a discharging gun.

Braveries   Gallants.

Breech   Generally the underside of anything.

Brokage   A commission on a transaction.

Budge   Formal.

Buffin   A coarse cloth.

Bull-beggar   A hobgoblin.

434

Bullion trunks   Trunk hose, puffed out at the upper part.

Bumb blade   A broadsword.

Busk   A corset.

Butchingly   Protestingly.

Cap-a-pie   From head to toe.

Carcanet   A necklace.

Carriage   Deportment, management, conduct.

Cart   To carry publicly in a cart as a punishment (see *ride*).

Cast   An estimate, a conjecture.

Cate   A delicacy or sweetmeat.

Cater   A caterer.

Caudle   A hot sweetened wine or beer with spice.

Cautelous   Crafty.

Cazimi   An astrological term, denoting the centre of the sun.

Cent   A card game.

Ceruses   Cosmetics.

Chapman   A merchant, trader.

Character   A brief literary sketch of the qualities of a social type.

Charge   An expense.

Chargeable   Expensive.

Cheat-bread   Wheat bread.

Chirurgeon   A surgeon.

Clarissimi   Grandees.

Clinquant   Shining.

Closestool   A stool holding a chamber pot.

Cloth of bodkin   Silk, with a warp of gold thread.

Clown   A man of low birth (compare *lown*).

Cockatrice   A prostitute.

Cocking   Cockfighting.

Coil   A tumult.

Commodity   The old practise of repayment of part of a debt in kind.

Competence   A sufficient supply.

Composition   A legal settlement.

Compound   To pay a percentage to creditors.

Conceit   A thought, fanciful idea.

Congee   Leave-taking.

Con thanks   To give thanks.

Cony catching   Cheating or confidence trickery (see "A Notable Discovery of Cosenage" by Robert Greene, 1591).

Copy   A copyhold, or tenure of land belonging to a manor.

Corsive   Corrosive, or purgative medicine.

Coulter   A colter; plowshare, knife.

Counterbuff   A return blow.

Crank   Lively.

Crash   To fling.

Cry "at al"   So the dicecaster cries when he wishes to bet against all comers.

Curious   Difficult to please, unduly fastidious, precisely accurate.

Cursen   Christian.

Dauber   A cheater.

Direction   The address.

Discover   To display, reveal.

Drab   A slattern, harlot, prostitute.

Durance   A coarse, strong cloth, now obsolete. A strong felted cloth of woollen, usually made in imitation of buff leather.

Dutch widow   A cant term for a prostitute.

Earn   To yearn, grieve.

Engines   Something used to effect a purpose.

Execution   A writ of seizure.

Exordium   An introduction.

Extent   A writ of seizure.

Factor   One who transacts business for another.

Fadge   To succeed, or suit.

Fagary   A vagary.

Featly   Neatly.

Fetch over   To gull.

Figent   Fidgety.

Finical   Finicky, fastidious, refined.

Firk   To trick or cheat.

Flatcap   The flat hat of the citizen, in contrast to the pointed hat of the courtier.

Flibber de jib   A flibbertigibbet; gossiping woman, or fiend.

Foisting   Ill-smelling.

Foreright   Straight ahead.

Frame   A plot.

French fall   A fashionable kind of veil or collar.

Fribble   To trifle (verb); coxcomb (noun).

Frippery   An old clothes shop.

Froat   To rub oil into a garment to sweeten it.

Fur   A piece of undressed skin used as a shoehorn.

Galleas   A large galley.

Gallipots   Earthenware pots.

Garb   Style.

Garbist   A stylist, or follower of fashion.

Gear   Matter.

Geniture   Nativity.

Gernative   Addicted to grumbling.

Glyster   A clyster, or enema.

Godwit   A species of curlew (a bird related to the woodcock), considered a delicacy.

Goll   A cant term for fist.

Gossip   A godparent, close friend.

Gresco   Or cresco, a card game.

Gum-fret   Imitation velvet, gummed and therefore easily "fretted" or frayed out.

Hansel   To try out, or prove.

Hans in Kelder   A corruption of a Dutch phrase meaning an unborn child.

Hungerland Hungary, or Hungarian.

Hoy A small coasting ship, usually sloop rigged; a heavy barge for bulky cargo.

Hoyden A country lout.

Huggermugger To deal secretly.

Humour In medical theory still current in the seventeenth century, one of the four fluids—blood, phlegm, choler (yellow bile), and melancholy (black bile)—considered to be part of the constitution of the body. Their relative proportions were held to determine a person's health and temperament.

Hundred A subdivision of a county with its own court of law.

Infortunity Misfortune.

Ingle A close friend (compare *ningle*).

Inquest A nominating committee.

Intelligencer An informer.

Iwis Certainly.

Julep Rose water, or sweetened, cooling drink.

Ka me, ka thee Proverbial: "help me and I'll help you."

Kennel The gutter.

Kind Nature.

Lavolta A lively dance.

Lib To castrate.

Liberties A district of some British cities within which the execution of legal process was the exclusive right of one or more persons by royal grant. These persons were thus exempt from the jurisdiction of the sheriff.

Licket A rag or shred.

Linsey-woolsey Originally a coarse cloth of wool and flax, or cotton; fig. a medley of sense and nonsense.

Livery punk A prostitute for hire.

Longer day More time to meet a debt.

Lown, loon A man of low birth (compare *clown*).

Madam-punk A high class prostitute.

Make unready To undress.

Malkin   A country maid.

Malleation   Hammering.

Mandragora   Mandrake, the root of forgetfulness and conception. A forked root credited with human qualities.

Mankind   Ferocious.

Marle   To marvel.

Mercer   The act of buying and selling; also an agent in fabrics.

Millenary   A Millenarian; one who believes that the prophecy in the book of Revelation will be fulfilled with an earthly millennium of universal peace and the triumph of righteousness.

Miniver   Ermine.

Misproud   Arrogant.

Monmouth cap   A sailor's cap.

Motion   An offer, proposition; puppet show.

Muckinder   A handkerchief.

Mullipood   A multiple.

Mutton   A cant term for prostitute.

Neb   The mouth.

Night rail   A night gown.

Ningle   A close friend or favourite.

Noble   A coin worth one third of a pound.

Nowl   The nape of the neck, head.

Object   A goal, motive.

Ordinary   An eating or gaming house. The statutary charge for a meal at an ordinary was two shillings.

Oringado   Orangeado, candied orange peel.

Outcry   A public auction.

Outlander   A foreigner.

Outrecuidance   Arrogance.

Packing   Trickery.

Pagan   A prostitute.

Panadas   A dish of boiled bread, sweetened with sugar and currants.

Pantables   Slippers.

Peat   A pampered favourite, or spoiled girl.

Peevish   Trifling.

Peterman   A fisherman, commonly applied to Thames fishermen.

Pheeze   To beat.

Pilchard   A fish of the herring family, any of several sardines.

Pink   A pinnace, or light vessel.

Pinnace   A light sailing ship generally used as a tender for a large ship or warship.

Pintle   A pin.

Point-device   An appropriate trick.

Pompion   A pumpkin.

Precise   Strictly conventional.

Press   Press-ganging for naval service.

Prest   Ready.

Primero   A card game.

Protest   To make a formal written declaration of nonpayment of a bill.

Purchase   To gain, acquire.

Quaisome   Quarrelsome.

Quean   A disreputable woman, prostitute.

Quellio   A collar.

Quiblin   A trick.

Quillet   A subtle distinction, quirk.

Quirk   A clever or cunning evasion.

Reins   The kidneys, loins: considered the seat of passions.

Remora   The sucking-fish, said by Pliny in his *Natural History* to impede a ship's progress by fastening itself to the bottom.

Respect   To consider, heed.

Restore   To recover, revive.

Reversion   An inheritance.

Ride   To be drawn in a cart as a whore.

Ronlet   A small wine skin (*conjecture*).

Roses Knots of ribbon worn on the shoe.

Royal A gold coin.

's blood God's blood. (See *'s lid*.)

Schemes In astrology, diagrams of planets used for horoscopes.

Scrape shoe A toady.

Scrivener A clerk.

Seal for To subscribe as.

Secondings Support.

's foot God's foot. (See *'s lid*.)

Sheriff's basket The basket containing remains of food sent to prisoners from the sheriff's table.

Shift A means to an end.

Shift yourself To change clothes.

Shot-clog A gull or dupe who pays the "shot," or bill, for the whole company

Skink To pour.

's lid God's lid. Used as an oath. Similarly formed interjections include 's life, 's blood, and 's foot.

Stammel A cheap red woollen cloth.

Statute A bond incurring forfeiture on nonpayment of debt.

Stone A unit of varying weight; now 14 pounds.

Striker A sexually capable man.

Tierce A cask holding 42 gallons.

Tilter A swordsman.

Tire Attire or clothes.

Toledo A finely tempered sword made in Toledo, Spain.

Tool A victim.

Train A device to lure another; trick.

Trampler A lawyer.

Trine The aspect of two heavenly bodies which are a part of the zodiac, considered to be favourable.

Trull A whore.

Trunks Loose trousers.

Tuft-taffety A silk fabric having a pattern formed by tufts, or pile.

Uncase   To disrobe.

Unready   To be undressed.

Vagary   An excursion.

Vail   A gratuity, or profit.

Veeze   To beat (compare *pheeze*).

Verier   the comparative of very

Visnomy   the physiognomy, misused as face or countenance.

Wagtail   A loose woman.

Waistcoat   A camisole.

Waistcoateer   A prostitute.

Wall, take the   The right to walk next to the wall when meeting someone was formerly considered a privilege because narrow streets and lack of sidewalks made this position safer and cleaner.

Ward   The guard.

Watchet   A light blue.

Weasand   The windpipe.

Welkin   The element or sky.

Whiskin   A pander.

Windings   Crooked dealings.

Wind   To entangle, involve.